Also by Himilce Novas

Mangos, Bananas and Coconuts: A Cuban Love Story

Remembering Selena

The Hispanic 100

Everything You Need to Know About Latino History

Also by Rosemary Silva

Remembering Selena

LATIN AMERICAN
COOKING
ACROSS THE U.S.A.

LATIN AMERICAN

COOKING

ACROSS THE U.S.A.

by *Himilce Novas* and *Rosemary Silva*

ALFRED A. KNOPF NEW YORK 1997

To our editor, Judith Jones,
for brilliant, steadfast direction and inspiration—
gracias for leading the charge!

THIS IS A BORZOI BOOK
PUBLISHED BY ALFRED A. KNOPF, INC.

ISBN 0-679-44408-4
LC 97-74754

Manufactured in the United States of America
First Edition

CONTENTS

ACKNOWLEDGMENTS

Many hearts and hands helped us bring this project to fruition. First we wish to thank the Latino home cooks across America who opened their kitchens, recipe files, and family albums for us, and who generously shared their most treasured ancestral traditions. We also say *saludos!* to all the Latin restaurateurs, chefs, waiters, shopkeepers, mail-order companies, food lovers, farmers, and gardeners, too numerous to name, who happily passed on their knowledge of dishes, cooking methods, and ingredients—from *nopalitos* to malagueta chiles. We are indebted to the staff and the librarians of the New York Public Library, The Library of Congress, the University Research Library at U.C.L.A., and the Davidson Library at the University of California at Santa Barbara for their generosity during our many months of culinary research. For her unflagging enthusiasm and dedication, we wish to express our gratitude to our image researcher, Gillian Speeth, of Picture This.

Muchísimas gracias to friends Rebecca Woolston, Michael Luckett, Harry H. Derderian, and T. Bassing Mantenfel, who persevered at our dining table through countless tastings. Special thanks also go to family, friends, and heroes Ruth Elizabeth Jenks, Gail and Steve Humphreys, Guillermo Cabrera Infante, Bill Campbell, Eli and Bill Krach, Cristina Saralegui, Julia Child, M.F.K. Fisher, Susan Herner, Deb Brody, Wendy Carlton, Nicolás Kanellos, Shirley Daigler, Fran and Ted Halpern, Marilyn Gilbert, Nathan Rundlett, Carol Storke, Michael Smith, Marlyn Bernstein, Dorothy Allison, Hope and Marcus Thrane, Penny and Terry Davies of the Earthling Bookstore in Santa Barbara, S. Jill Levine, Andre and Pat Piot, Gil and Marti Garcia, David Perry and Jim Watkins of KQSB in Santa Barbara, Susan Gulbransen, Julie Barton, Henry Blumstein and Jackie Green, Steve Gilbar, everyone at the American Program Bureau, Edwina Cruise, Jeanne O'Shaughnessy, Jim and Dorothy Tate, and Maggie Lewis. Finally, our endless homage to M.B.E. for inspiration and revelation, in and out of the kitchen.

INTRODUCTION

When we lived in New York City, a favorite Saturday pastime was to devise an ethnic culinary itinerary for the day. Since Himilce is Cuban American, many Saturdays were designated Cuban, and we would spend the afternoon savoring *plátanos maduros fritos,* or fried sweet plantains, at Victor's Café 52, a Cuban fixture in the theater district, or comparing the crusty Cuban sandwiches crammed with layers of ham, roast pork, Swiss cheese, and pickles at the Cubano luncheonettes on the Upper West Side. Puerto Rican Saturday always fell in autumn, when the afternoons were cool enough for us to cycle to Spanish Harlem, known as El Barrio, and survey the tropical tubers and fruits at the now defunct La Marqueta, or visit one of the many *botánicas,* where practitioners of the Afro-Caribbean Santería religion dispense extracts, candles, and beads meant to heal and bring good luck. Brazilian Saturday always fell in bitter-cold January, since Little Brazil is nestled in midtown Manhattan, many steps closer to our warm apartment than, say, Little Colombia in Jackson Heights, Queens. Many bone-chilling wintry winds dissolved into tropical breezes over *moqueca de camarão,* shrimp stewed in a sublime coconut-tomato sauce, at Via Brasil on West 46th Street.

Wherever we traveled, we took up this game of culinary pursuit, exploring the dominant ethnic cuisines at each destination. On trips in the early 1990s to Los Angeles, aptly christened Ellis Island West for the approximately three dozen ethnic groups and sixty languages spoken there, we "discovered" Mexican, Salvadoran, Guatemalan, Nicaraguan, Belizean, Costa Rican, Chilean, and Argentinean enclaves, all of which dwarf those in the Big Apple. At that moment, we realized that it was possible, thanks to recent tides of immigration, to sample the cuisines of all twenty-six sovereign nations in Latin America—namely, Mexico, El Salvador, Nicaragua, Costa Rica, Guatemala, Honduras, Panama, Venezuela, Colombia, Ecuador, Peru, Bolivia, Chile, Argentina, Uruguay, Paraguay, Cuba, Puerto Rico, the Dominican Republic, Jamaica, Haiti, Belize, Suriname, Guyana, French Guiana, and Brazil—without ever leaving the country. The idea for a book exploring Latin American cooking in the continental United States was born. (We have omitted the cooking of Americans with roots in the smaller islands of the Caribbean situated in the arc known as the Lesser Antilles—which are mostly U.S., British, French, or Dutch colonies—as they have not had a dramatic impact on American culinary life.)

In many ways it seemed a daunting task to bring together so many culinary traditions and make sense of them all. But Americans of Latin American descent are bound together in the American psyche and census. Those with roots in Spanish-speaking Latin America, the first nineteen nations listed above, are known collectively as Latinos or Hispanics (a term created by the U.S. Bureau of the Census). In the minds of many (but not according to the U.S. Bureau of the Census), the term "Latino" not only connotes persons of Spanish-speaking Latin American ancestry, but also embraces those with roots in Latin American nations where Portuguese, English, or French is the official language—the last seven countries named above. Americans of Latin American descent, recognizing that there is greater visibility and political and economic clout in numbers, have embraced this Pan-Latinism and are apt to identify themselves not only as Mexican Americans, Puerto Ricans, Cuban Americans, or Jamaican Americans, etc., but also as Latinos or Latins or Hispanics. As a result, the various Latin flavors began to blend in many homes and professional kitchens. The result of this has been extraordinary, for Latinos are shaping a new American cooking style. And so we decided to keep all the culinary traditions in Latino America under one title.

As we began to take a closer look at the Latin American home cooking at our doorstep, we realized that this rich facet of American gastronomic life has received so little commentary that most Americans know only fragments of the story. For instance, we found that Texans, Californians, New Mexicans, and Arizonans can identify many of the chiles in Mexican American cooking, but most New Yorkers cannot tell a serrano chile from a poblano. Miamians can differentiate between fried green plantains and *yuca* fries, but most other Americans haven't a clue. New Mexicans know their *sopaipillas* and *biscochitos* but are not schooled in Puerto Rican *pollo* and Jamaican beef patties, as New Yorkers are.

We began our research with what we knew best. Himilce, who was raised on classic Cuban cuisine in Havana and New York City, also knew a lot about the Dominican,

Jamaican, and Mexican kitchens. Rosemary is well versed in Puerto Rican cuisine, since she learned to cook under the tutelage of her Irish American mother, who was a professional cook, ran a restaurant and catering business, and adored island cooking. Her mother learned her way around the Puerto Rican kitchen while growing up in New York City in the shadow of Spanish Harlem. In fact, she was so fond of *pasteles* (Puerto Rican–style tamales), *arroz con pollo,* flan, and the like that after she

Salvadoran food being sold at a San Francisco market. Many Salvadoran restaurants and cafés sprouted up in California following a large wave of Salvadoran immigration to the United States in the 1980s.

moved to Texas, she would send Rosemary's grandmother on vacation to San Juan once a year so that she could bring back ingredients like guava paste and pigeon peas.

After taking stock, we embarked on a culinary journey across Latino America, crisscrossing the country by airplane, car, and the Internet, sometimes taking along our two poodles—a black standard named Jellybean and an apricot teacup named Bunny. We wanted to see firsthand what some of the 13,496,000 Mexican Americans, 1,044,000 Cuban Americans, 652,000 Puerto Rican mainlanders, 565,000 Salvadoran Americans, 520,000 Dominican Americans, 379,000 Colombian Americans, 281,000 Haitian Americans, 269,000 Guatemalan Americans, 203,000 Nicaraguan Americans, 191,000 Ecuadoran Americans, 175,000 Peruvian Americans, 131,000 Honduran Americans, 100,000 Costa Rican Americans, 101,000 Argentinean Americans, 92,000 Panamanian Americans, 70,000 Belizean Americans, 69,000 Chilean Americans, 48,000 Venezuelan Americans, 38,000 Bolivian Americans, 22,000 Uruguayan Americans, 7,000 Paraguayan Americans, and Americans with roots in Jamaica, Brazil, Suriname, Guyana, and French Guiana were up to in the kitchen. We wanted to talk to as many of these home cooks as we could to learn about the origins of some of their dishes and to see if the recipes have changed in a multicultural American environment or if they have remained intact.

At first we were struck by all the differences we found in Latin kitchens. We discovered a multitude of dishes unique to particular cultures. For example, most Americans with Latin American roots are not familiar with *chilate,* the Salvadoran drink of ground corn simmered with allspice berries, or with the malagueta chile, the favorite pepper of Brazilian Americans. We discovered that a quesadilla is a tortilla filled with melted cheese (and sometimes stewed meat) to Mexican Americans, while to Salvadoran Americans it is pound cake. And what Guatemalan Americans call an enchilada, Mexican Americans refer to as a tostada. *Chicharrones* are deep-fried pork skins to Mexican Americans, but to Americans with roots in Central America they are deep-fried chunks of pork (which Mexican Americans know as *carnitas*). Yet the more we sifted through recipes and tasted new dishes in restaurants and private homes, the more apparent it became that Latin American cuisines may all have unique features, but they also have a lot in common. Their menus all stress flavorful salsas (sauces) and marinades for roasted or stewed pork, beef, poultry, fish, and shellfish. They use various root vegetables, beans, and rice, and include desserts based chiefly on milk products, like flan.

Another common theme that runs through all Latin American cooking in the United States is loyalty to tradition despite such obstacles as the unavailability of some authentic ingredients. Historically speaking, most Americans of Latin American descent—except, of course, those Mexican Americans whose families have lived within the boundaries of the present-day United States for centuries—are new immigrants, and that makes the majority particularly partial to hanging on to the old traditions. Large numbers of Puerto Ricans migrated to the U.S. mainland only after World War II. Cuban, Dominican, Costa Rican, and Colombian Americans began to reach American shores in significant numbers in the 1960s, and the rest of the Latin groups began immigrating to the United States in or after the 1970s. As "new" Americans, they depend heavily on ethnic markets, known as bodegas, and many tend to alter a recipe only by necessity. Mexican American home cooks of northern New Mexico, many of whose ancestors inhabited the state before the West was won, also prize authenticity to an extraordinary degree and replicate with pride the dishes handed down through generations. It is not by accident that the Albuquerque–Santa Fe area is leading the way in the preservation of heirloom (native nonhybrid) beans and chile peppers.

Another unifying theme in Latin American cooking in the United States is transformation. Change in the kitchen is inevitable when first- and second-generation Americans, who live with one foot in the old country, give way to a third and fourth generation with both feet planted firmly on American soil. These later generations add innovative ingredients to traditional family dishes to conform to popular taste and to take advantage of the enormous array of foods available in American markets. They also tend to do away with dishes that replay the same tired ingredients or are considered exotic by their fellow Americans (like roasted guinea pig). They also mix and match dishes from a whole variety of cuisines. We have dined at Nuyorican (Puerto Rican New York) tables where spaghetti is served with traditional *pernil asado* (marinated roast pork). In Los Angeles we have watched Peruvian American children wash down burgers and fries with imported Inka Cola. We have been to a Mexican American vegetarian birthday party in Chicago, where sweet corn tamales were served alongside tabbouleh and hummus.

Yet no matter how much they have assimilated, Americans of Latin American descent seem always to have a place in their hearts for an authentic meal. In Seattle we once met a Cuban American graphic artist who confessed that she flies to Miami once a year for the roast pork and *yuca con mojo* at the legendary Cuban restaurant Versailles. We know a doctor in Santa Barbara, California, who drives over one hundred miles to his mother's house in Los Angeles on weekends for traditional Colombian *ajiaco bogotano,* a marvelous chicken and potato stew. We also met a Mexican American on Wall Street who lunches regularly at the Hudson River Club, but for dinner makes his favorite enchiladas with the flour tortillas he gets by FedEx from Léona's de Chimayó in Chimayó, New Mexico.

Food suppliers have been capitalizing on Latin culinary allegiances for some time. For several decades Goya Foods, Inc., has been catering to Cuban Americans, Puerto Ricans, and other Caribbean Americans on the East Coast, who, no matter how long their families have been in the continental United States, have still not weaned themselves from island cooking. Recently Goya expanded its operations to the western states, where it hopes to win over Americans with roots in Mexico and Central and South America. Supermarkets in regions of the country that boast sizable Latin populations have also been paying keener attention to their customers' habits and have been

One of the countless Puerto Rican *botánicas* in New York City's Spanish Harlem, where practitioners of the Afro-Caribbean Santería religion dispense extracts, soaps, candles, and other items believed to heal, bring good luck, and bless the home

turning over more and more shelf space to Latin American products. Some are geared almost entirely to a Latin audience, such as the Mexican American Fiesta Mart chain in Houston and the Tianguis chain in Los Angeles.

The greater preponderance of Latin American products on supermarket shelves has also been fueled by the non–Latin American public, which since the 1980s has been leaning away from the muted flavors of the Old World and toward the explosive tastes of Asia and the Pacific Rim, Mexico, the Caribbean, and Central and South America. In this age of multiculturalism and global awareness, Americans are as eager to navigate uncharted gastronomic territory as they are cyberspace. Consider how many are apt to ask not whether it will be steak or spaghetti for dinner tonight, but whether it will be Chinese, Japanese, Thai, Mexican, or Indian. In big cities like New York, Los Angeles, Chicago, and Miami, they have the luxury of asking whether it will be Cuban, Jamaican, Puerto Rican, Nicaraguan, Brazilian, Argentinean, or Peruvian tonight. Americans everywhere now crave Mexican flavors to such a degree that sales of salsa have surpassed ketchup, and jalapeño bagels and scones and matzo quesadillas come as no surprise. Cooks are putting their own spin on Mexican classics, serving up goat cheese enchiladas, and there are tofu burritos, pesto tamales, and whatever else imaginable. Our experience zigzagging across America for this book tells us that as with Mexican food, Caribbean, Central American, and South American dishes will eventually make the leap from the "exotic" to the everyday. *Pupusas, patacones,* and *pasteles* may soon cross over to mainstream America in the way of salsa, enchiladas, and burritos.

Another theme that unites Latin American cuisines in the United States is the *nuevo* phenomenon. In the late 1980s and 1990s, chefs of Latin American descent and Latinophiles were part of the movement to elevate regional American cooking, a trend that gave rise to Nouvelle cuisine, California cuisine, and Louisiana Cajun cuisine, among others. Professional cooks created New Florida cuisine by refining the recipes of Caribbean Americans in Florida and Southwestern cuisine by updating Mexican American cooking of the southwestern United States. When American chefs in the 1990s cast their nets afar and invented Fusion cuisine by combining ingredients and methods from gastronomic traditions around the globe—particularly those of Europe, Asia, and the Pacific Rim—Latin and Latinophile chefs and restaurateurs followed suit.

For example, New Mexican chef John Sedlar of Abiquiu, in Los Angeles and San Francisco, was instrumental in creating Modern Southwest cuisine (also known as New Southwestern cuisine and Nouvelle New Mexican cuisine) by applying ingredients from the world's larder to a Mexican American canvas. His Flying Lobster Dude Ranch Sushi (New Mexican sushi of lobster with habanero vinaigrette and Japanese cucumber salad) is at once Mexican American, Japanese, and French. Many chefs followed suit. In New York City, the Arizona Cafe introduced New Yorkers to New Southwestern, with dishes like Curried Chicken Tortilla with Coconut Rice, Cucumber Raita and Spicy Peanut Sauce. Meanwhile, in Miami, Cuban-born chef Douglas Rodriguez of Yuca (a tropical tuber not to be confused with yucca, an evergreen plant with white flowers, and an acronym for Young Upwardly Mobile Cuban American) gave the world Nuevo Cubano by jazzing up Cuban classics. Later Claude Troisgros broke new ground by mingling Brazilian and French cooking at C.T. Restaurant in Manhattan.

Latin chefs took the next logical step by developing fusion repertoires incorporating all of Latin American cooking, a style that has been christened Nuevo Americano, Pan-Latin, and Nuevo Latino Cuisine. Douglas Rodriguez, who by this time was working in New York, unveiled Nuevo Latino in 1994 with the opening of Patria, on Park Avenue South. Patria's menu ranges across Latin America, but most dishes spring from a single cuisine, be it Ecuadoran, Cuban, Peruvian, Venezuelan, or Colombian. For instance, Rodriguez's Cuban Tamal, with its unorthodox combination of shredded pork, hearts of palm, and garlic broth, may be rooted in Cuban cuisine, but it is a dazzling original. And his *Caramiñola,* Colombian-style *yuca* stuffed with cheese in mushroom broth and spinach, is as much a surprise to a Colombian immigrant as it is to an Irish American.

⚜

Douglas Rodriguez and Patria started a Nuevo Latino craze that has spread across Manhattan and America. At Inca Grill in SoHo, where South American Eggs Benedict with Chorizo and Arepa is a popular brunch specialty, the menu epitomizes Nuevo Latino. In Houston, Nicaraguan-born chef Michael Cordua of the restaurant Americas weaves Italian elements into his Nuevo Latino menu with such dishes as Chilean Salmon with Portobello Risotto and Champagne Sauce. Cuban-born restaurateur Xiomara Ardolina and chef Patrick Healy of Oye! in Pasadena, California, have been pivotal in introducing Nuevo Latino to southern California with dishes like Cuban Black Bean Soup with Okra Croutons and Plantain Dumplings. Mark Miller of the Coyote Cafe in Santa Fe has added an interesting dimension to Nuevo Latino by cross-pollinating Latin flavors in a single dish, as in his Cuban Sandwich—a Cuban-Mex collaboration of roast pork, ham, Swiss cheese, black bean spread, and guacamole.

⚜

In creating and refining Nuevo Latino, these chefs (and others) have played a critical role in initiating non–Latins into the vast world of Latin American cooking in the United States. Armed with a new vocabulary and awakened tastebuds, Americans have been exploring the roots of Nuevo Latino. They may venture just to the corner supermarket, with its special Latin section, or perhaps even visit the many ethnic enclaves. In so doing, they are partaking with their neighbors of Latin American descent in the Nuevo Latino adventure that is but the latest chapter in the rich gastronomic history of America.

⚜

When we traveled back to the roots of Nuevo Latino on our odyssey across the U.S.A., we uncovered a world of home cooking rich with flavors, colors, textures, and intoxicating aromas. We could never have imagined some of the foods we would find, like *chuños* (freeze-dried Andean potatoes that can be stored forever on the shelf), Nicaraguan chocolate milk thickened with white rice, Peruvian Chinese fried rice, Argentine *ñoquis* (*gnocchi*), and Brazilian *dendê* oil (bright orange palm oil). Some we fell in love with, like Bolivian *pukas* (feta cheese and olive pastries), Chilean

A Goya Foods, Inc., float in one of the many Puerto Rican parades held annually in the Northeast

pastel de choclo con pollo (chicken pot pie with corn crust), and Salvadoran *salpicón* (marinated beef with mint and radish). The incredible richness of all these dishes is the result of the convergence of diverse civilizations in the Americas over the course of many centuries—Mayan, Incan, Taino, West African, Spanish, Portuguese, British, Dutch, German, Italian, Chinese, Japanese, East Indian, and many others. But that is a long story.

We also could never have imagined the delight that families experienced when they shared a recipe and memories with us or prepared their favorite dish right before our eyes. So here is the result of that journey, and we hope we have done justice to the recipes given to us, as well as to the invaluable cooking tips, personal stories, and shared memories. It is only fair to warn you that when you try a recipe from this book, you may be powerfully seduced—and driven to refuse all other foods as bland or hopelessly ordinary. Eventually you may begin experimenting and even adding your own ethnic twist to these dishes in an act of fusion cooking. Have fun! This is America, after all.

GOOD SOUP MEANS HEARTY

SOUP. PLAIN BROTHS ARE ONLY

FOR THE FAINTHEARTED.

SOUPS

CHICKEN SOUP WITH *YUCA*, PLANTAINS, AND POTATOES

Sancocho de gallina

Sancocho de gallina (Chicken Soup with *Yuca,* Plantains, and Potatoes) is one of the most delicious chicken soups ever conceived. It starts out as an ordinary chicken soup, with chunks of chicken, onions, and garlic, but halfway through the cooking in goes a wonderful medley of vegetables—nutty *yuca* (also known as cassava), mellow red-skinned potatoes, and slightly tart yellow plantains (actually a fruit)—that lends character and texture to the soup in just the right balance. The broth is very subtly spiced with cumin (it is barely discernible) to deepen all the flavors, and it is invigorated with lemon juice to create a perky backdrop for the vegetables. This soup is a marvelous introduction to *yuca* and plantains, since nothing more is required of the cook than peeling them, cutting them into chunks, and cooking them just like the potatoes in the soup. Versions of *sancocho* abound among the various Latin groups. Some are made with beef, veal, or pork in place of chicken, and some are so thick they are classified as stews rather than soups (see Dominican American Stew with Taro, *Calabaza,* and Yellow Plantains, page 155). This version happens to be Colombian American, and it follows tradition rather closely.

Do not cook the soup longer than directed, as the vegetables will begin to disintegrate and lose their integrity. As soon as the soup is cooked, be sure to remove the pot from the burner. If you are serving it later, warm it just before ladling it into bowls. The first step in the preparation of this soup—making the broth—can be done ahead of time. Then all there is to do is cook the vegetables in the broth, starting about an hour before the meal will be served.

1 chicken (3½ pounds)	⅛ teaspoon freshly ground black pepper,
3 quarts water	or to taste
2 small yellow onions, peeled and minced	¾ pound fresh or frozen (defrosted) *yuca*
4 medium cloves garlic, peeled	(cassava), peeled (see page 198 for
and minced	information on *yuca* and page 189 for
¼ teaspoon salt, or to taste	directions on peeling *yuca*)

2 medium red-skinned (new) potatoes, cut into ½-inch chunks

⅛ teaspoon ground cumin

2 yellow plantains, cut into ½-inch rounds and peeled (see page 183 for information on plantains and page 184 for instructions on peeling and cutting plantains)

⅓ cup freshly squeezed lemon juice

2 medium scallions, root ends removed and minced

2 tablespoons finely minced fresh cilantro

Rinse the chicken under cold running water. Put the chicken, water, half of the minced onions, 2 cloves garlic, and the salt and pepper in a large stockpot. Bring to a boil, covered, over medium-high heat, then reduce the heat and simmer the chicken, covered, for 1½ hours.

Remove the chicken from the stock to a large plate. Bone the chicken breasts and cut into bite-size chunks. Return the chunks of chicken breast to the pot. Reserve the rest of the chicken meat for another use.

Cut the pieces of *yuca* in half lengthwise, cut away the fibrous core in the center of each piece with a paring knife, then cut the *yuca* into ½-inch chunks. Add the *yuca,* potatoes, the remaining onions and 2 cloves garlic, and the cumin to the stock. Bring to a boil, covered, then reduce the heat and simmer, covered, for 20 minutes.

Add the plantains and lemon juice to the soup, and continue simmering until the plantains are tender, about 20 minutes. Remove the soup from the heat, and stir in the scallions and cilantro. Taste and adjust the seasoning, and serve at once.

Serves 8 to 10 as a first course and 4 to 5 as a main entrée

"LATIN FROM MANHATTAN" CHICKEN NOODLE SOUP

Sopa de pollo con fideos "Latin from Manhattan"

When winter takes up residence in New York City, the Big Apple seems to run on chicken soup, as millions seek out its steaming golden broth to fend off the cold and find comfort. Certainly more chicken soup (brimming with wontons, or egg drops, egg noodles, vermicelli, *capelli d'angelo, semi di melone,* tortellini, dumplings, matzo balls, kreplach, or rice, etc.) is ladled into bowls on a frosty day in New York City than in any other metropolis. The Puerto Ricans of New York City, known as Nuyoricans, have contributed to making the city a mecca of chicken soup with their *Sopa de pollo con fideos* (chicken soup with *fideos*)—the *fideos* being Caribbean-style *capelli d'angelo* sold as long, brittle threads wound into neat little bundles that resemble bird's nests. (*Fideos* originated in Catalonia, Spain, where they are shaped into one-inch curved strands as fine as angel's hair or as thick as tagliolini. Mexican *fideos* resemble the Spanish, while Caribbean ones are always long and fine.)

"Latin from Manhattan" Chicken Noodle Soup starts out as a fragrant broth that combines a good New York Jewish penicillin (some Nuyoricans buy it at Jewish delis or shops, like the famous David's Chicken on the Upper East Side, that specialize in roast chicken and matzo ball soup) and a few tablespoons of Puerto Rican *sofrito,* a spirited blend of sautéed onions, garlic, tomatoes, and bell peppers. All of these flavors are artfully woven together as the broth slowly simmers. Then chunks of potatoes and chicken are added to lend the soup body and texture. (Some cooks fortify the soup with garbanzo beans or pepperoni or Spanish-style chorizo, but these are strictly optional.) In the final minutes, in go the *fideos.* (Puerto Ricans are passionate about *fideos,* which are available in supermarkets all around the town, and they will rarely use another noodle.) Don't bother to prepare a second course when "Latin from Manhattan" Chicken Noodle Soup is on the menu, as everyone will want to line up for seconds and fill up on the soothing elixir.

**FOR THE BASIC SOUP
(MADE THE DAY BEFORE, IF POSSIBLE):**

- 1 chicken (about 3½ pounds)
- 1 turkey wing, or substitute 2 additional chicken wings
- 1 chicken bouillon cube
- 3 quarts cold water
- 3 medium ribs celery, quartered
- 1 medium carrot, peeled and quartered
- 1 small yellow onion, peeled and quartered

1 medium clove garlic, peeled
    and mashed
1 bay leaf

⅛ teaspoon black peppercorns
Salt, to taste

FOR THE *SOFRITO:*

½ small yellow onion, peeled and minced
1 small clove garlic, peeled and minced
1 teaspoon olive oil
1 small ripe tomato, chopped

¼ cup minced green bell pepper
1 tablespoon freshly squeezed
    lemon juice
⅛ teaspoon dried powdered oregano
    (not crumbled)

FOR THE SOUP:

1 pound red-skinned (new) potatoes,
    peeled and cut into ½-inch dice
2 tablespoons tomato sauce
6 ounces *fideos,* or substitute vermicelli
    or *capelli d'angelo**

Salt and freshly ground black pepper,
    to taste
2 tablespoons finely minced fresh
    Italian parsley

* Fideos *are available in Latin markets and some supermarkets, especially in cities and towns with a large Latin population.*

Prepare the basic soup: Put the chicken, turkey wing or 2 additional chicken wings, bouillon cube, and water in a stockpot or kettle. Bring to a boil, covered, over medium-high heat, then reduce the heat and simmer, covered, for 30 minutes, skimming as necessary. Add the celery, carrot, onion, garlic, bay leaf, peppercorns, and salt to taste, and continue to cook, covered, for 2 hours.

Strain the stock. Discard the turkey wing or chicken wings, vegetables, bay leaf, and peppercorns. Remove and discard the skin and bones from the chicken and reserve the meat for the soup. Refrigerate the stock until the fat congeals on the surface, about 8 hours or overnight. Just before using, skim the fat off the stock and reheat. (The stock will keep for about 5 days in the refrigerator, or it can be frozen indefinitely.)

Make the *sofrito:* Sauté the minced onions and garlic in the olive oil in a large pot over medium heat, stirring occasionally, until the onions are soft, about 4 minutes. Add the tomato, bell pepper, lemon juice, and oregano, and cook until the tomato is quite soft, about 6 minutes. Remove all but 4 tablespoons *sofrito.* Save the extra for another use.

Add the chicken stock to the *sofrito.* Bring to a boil, then reduce the heat and simmer, covered, for 20 minutes. Dice the reserved chicken and stir in the pieces, along with the potatoes and tomato sauce. Simmer, covered, for 20 minutes, or until the potatoes are tender when pierced with a fork. Gently break up the *fideos,* stir them into the soup, and simmer, covered, for another 8 minutes, or until the *fideos* are al dente. Taste and season with salt and black pepper to taste. Remove the soup from the heat and stir in the minced parsley. Ladle the soup into bowls and serve at once.

Serves 8 to 10 as a first course and 6 as a main entrée

TORTILLA SOUP

Sopa de tortilla

When winter winds blow, there is something wonderful about dipping into a steaming bowl of Tortilla Soup with its citrus-and-tomato-laced broth. The broth is only the beginning. Each spoonful reveals tender morsels of chicken, earthy tortilla strips, creamy avocado, and lively cilantro. In the America of yesteryear, Tortilla Soup was relished primarily by Mexican Americans who inherited family recipes that had been passed down from generation to generation. Slowly Tortilla Soup has found a place in the pantheon of American soups, and nowadays there are recipes for it, both classic and adventurous, from Latinos and non-Latinos alike in many of the current magazines and cookbooks.

This soup is hearty enough to be the centerpiece of a casual supper for a small gathering of friends or family. Start with a salad of mixed greens with Gorgonzola cheese and pecans, and finish with warm New Mexican *Sopaipillas* rolled in cinnamon sugar or dribbled with honey for dessert (see page 243).

FOR THE TORTILLA STRIPS:

4 yellow or blue corn tortillas

Vegetable oil, for frying

FOR THE BROTH:

1 tablespoon olive oil
½ cup finely minced yellow onion
2 large cloves garlic, peeled and
    finely minced
1 teaspoon finely minced jalapeño chile
½ teaspoon ground cumin

2 cups canned crushed tomatoes
5 cups homemade or canned
    chicken broth
1 corn tortilla, cut into ¼-inch-wide
    strips
2 tablespoons freshly squeezed
    lime juice

FOR THE SOUP:

1 cup chicken breast, grilled or poached,
    and cut on the bias into ½-inch dice
⅓ cup grated Monterey Jack cheese

1½ medium ripe Hass avocados,
    halved, peeled, pitted, and cut
    into ½-inch dice
2 tablespoons finely minced
    fresh cilantro

Cut the tortillas into strips ⅛-inch wide with a sharp knife or a pair of scissors. Pour enough vegetable oil into a large skillet to coat the bottom generously. Heat the oil over medium heat and fry half of the tortilla strips, turning once, until they are crisp and

Mexican American tortilla soup

golden, about 2 minutes per side. Transfer the tortilla strips with a slotted spatula to a large plate lined with paper towels and drain. Fry the second batch, adding more oil, if necessary.

Make the broth: Heat the tablespoon of olive oil in a large pot over medium heat. Sauté the minced onions, garlic, jalapeño, and cumin until the onions are lightly browned, about 4 minutes. Add the crushed tomatoes, chicken broth, and the 1 tortilla cut into strips, and bring the broth to a boil. Cover, reduce the heat, and simmer for 20 minutes.

Transfer the broth to a food processor, add the lime juice, and process until smooth. Return the broth to the pot and reheat it over medium heat. Pour the broth into 4 bowls. Place one fourth of the chicken, cheese, and avocado, in that order, in the center of each bowl. Garnish with the tortilla strips and cilantro, and serve at once.

Serves 4

MEXICAN TORTILLAS | While Léona Medina-Tiede, founder of the market Léona's de Chimayó in Chimayó, New Mexico (see Sources, page 304), revolutionized flour tortillas by creating flavors such as chocolate, blueberry, and pesto, it seems that the recipe for Mexican corn tortillas has remained untouched. However, the age-old method of hand-patting corn tortillas (and hand-rolling flour ones) is slowly dying out as more and more cooks across America turn to store-bought, machine-made tortillas, which unfortunately are not always so fresh. Luckily for tortilla aficionados, a number of *tortillerías* and family-run restaurants still make corn tortillas by hand that you can purchase hot off the grid-

A tortilla maker at a celebration known as Fiesta Days in southern California, June 1993

dle. For instance, La Azteca Tortillería in Los Angeles, known far and wide for its delicious handmade corn tortillas, employs a whole crew to pat out the tortillas starting in the wee hours of the morning to meet the demand. La Super-Rica Taquería, a tiny Mexican restaurant in Santa Barbara, California, is also well known in southern California for its corn tortillas that are handmade and grilled to perfection right before your eyes, then served while the steam still rises off of them. If you cannot find handmade corn tortillas in your area, you can have them shipped to you from a number of *tortillerías* across the country (see Sources, page 304). Or make them yourself at home. The process is simple. All you need is commercial instant *masa harina* (corn flour), water, and, most important, a tortilla press.

CREAM OF POTATO SOUP WITH CHICKEN, SOUR CREAM, AND CAPERS

Ajiaco con pollo

On weekends Robert M. Nagy, a much respected doctor of psychiatry in Santa Barbara, California, often heads to his mother's house in Rancho Palos Verdes for her *Ajiaco con pollo* (also known as *Ajiaco bogotano*), a heavenly one-pot Colombian dish that is best described as a hearty cream of potato soup studded with chunks of chicken and enlivened with capers and sour cream. Says his mother, María Victoria Montaña, who was born in Bogotá, Colombia: "When I was a child, I spent many hours in the kitchen listening to the maids gossip and watching our maid, Anita, prepare our meals. Once in a while I was allowed to 'help.' On Sundays, Anita often made a very rich and creamy *Ajiaco con pollo*. She would let me taste it as she went along, and those moments were sheer pleasure. I have tried to re-create Anita's dish faithfully from memory, along with treasured moments of my childhood and our family get-togethers on Sundays. This recipe comes closest to the *Ajiaco con pollo* that I remember."

Ajiaco con pollo is a luxurious dish for lunch or for a casual supper that always gets rave reviews. It is even more delicious the next day, after the flavors have completely worked their magic overnight in the refrigerator.

I small white onion, peeled and minced
3 medium cloves garlic, peeled
   and minced
2 tablespoons olive oil
I small whole chicken breast, skinned,
   boned, and cut into 4 pieces
4 medium leeks (1¾ to 2 pounds),
   white part only, rinsed thoroughly,
   drained, and thinly sliced
2 tablespoons butter
I quart homemade or canned
   chicken broth

4 large russet (Idaho) potatoes, peeled
   and thinly sliced
I cup milk
I cup half-and-half
¾ cup grated sharp Cheddar cheese
Salt and freshly ground white pepper,
   to taste
¼ teaspoon cayenne pepper (optional)
½ cup sour cream, for garnish
2 to 3 teaspoons capers (drained),
   for garnish

Sauté the minced onions and garlic in the olive oil in a large nonstick skillet over medium heat until the onions are soft, about 5 minutes. Reduce the heat to medium-low, add the 4 pieces of chicken breast, cover, and sauté until the chicken is browned on one side, about 3 minutes. Stir the onions, which by now will be brown, and turn the chicken pieces over and sauté the other side, covered, for another 3 minutes. Stir the onions again and continue to cook the chicken, covered, for 3 minutes more.

Sauté the leeks in the butter over medium heat in a large pot, stirring frequently, until they are limp but not browned, about 7 minutes. Add the chicken broth and potatoes. Bring the broth, covered, to a boil over medium-high heat. Reduce the heat and simmer, covered, until the potatoes are tender, about 15 to 20 minutes.

Purée half of the soup in a blender or food processor until smooth. Return the purée to the pot and stir in the milk and half-and-half. Cut the sautéed chicken into ½-inch slices and add them to the soup, along with the sautéed onions and garlic, Cheddar cheese, salt and white pepper, and cayenne. Heat the soup over medium heat, stirring occasionally, until it is hot. Ladle the *Ajiaco con pollo* into large bowls and garnish each with a dollop of sour cream and ½ teaspoon capers.

Serves 4 to 6

✳

TRIPE AND HOMINY SOUP

Menudo

Ecuadoran Americans insist on milk, German Americans on herring, Filipinos on bananas, but for millions of Mexican Americans *Menudo,* a hearty Tripe and Hominy Soup, is the only cure for *la cruda*—a hangover. On New Year's Day the soup, with its faintly sweet, chewy hominy and tender tripe in a robust chile-and-garlic-flavored broth, is dished up in Mexican restaurants and homes to combat the effects of the previous night's revelry. But *menudo* is not just an antidote for *la cruda.* It is a beloved soup that is welcomed at table anytime, but especially for breakfast on Sundays. In fact, many churches with congregations of Mexican immigrants cook up enormous batches of *menudo* to serve along with tacos and tamales after early morning Mass. (Second-generation Mexican Americans tend to opt for coffee and doughnuts instead.)

Tripe is the muscular lining of any ruminant's stomach, though more beef tripe is sold in this country than pig or sheep tripe. The most tender and prized is honeycomb tripe, which comes from the second stomach. Tripe can be found in most supermarkets, as well as in Latin, Chinese, and Vietnamese markets. (When purchasing tripe in Asian markets, make sure it is beef, since pork tripe is commonly sold as well.) The tripe sold in supermarkets has been cleaned, soaked, and partially cooked, and thus one need only rinse it in cold water and pat it dry with paper towels before cooking. Fresh tripe should have a pleasant odor and should be stored for no longer than a day in the refrigerator. If you are not recovering from *la cruda, menudo* is nice with a good Mexican brew, such as the reddish amber Dos Equis (XX). (Steer clear of the bland Mexican beers like Dos Equis (XX) Special Lager and Corona.)

Tripe is rather insipid on its own, but it readily absorbs other flavors during long simmering. For that reason, *menudo* is conventionally cooked with a calf's foot or pig's foot; the marrow and meat give a flavor boost to the soup, and the gelatinous skin lends body. Calves' and pigs' feet are available in most supermarkets and in Latin, Chinese, and Southeast Asian markets. If you cannot find calves' or pigs' feet, substitute spareribs in this recipe.

FOR THE SOUP:

2 pounds fresh beef tripe, rinsed, patted dry, and cut into 1-inch squares

1 calf's or pig's foot, cut into pieces, or substitute ½ pound spareribs

3 quarts water

¼ teaspoon salt

1 small yellow onion, peeled and minced

3 large cloves garlic, peeled and minced

1 tablespoon mild ground dried red chile, or to taste (see the note on ground dried red chile on page 167)

1 teaspoon dried powdered oregano (not crumbled)

Freshly ground black pepper, to taste

1½ cups canned or cooked white or yellow hominy (also called *posole*), drained*

FOR THE GARNISH:

3 medium scallions, root ends removed and finely minced

2 limes, cut into wedges

½ cup finely minced fresh cilantro

2 tablespoons dried powdered oregano (not crumbled)

8 corn tortillas (optional)

Mexican hot sauce, your favorite brand

Hominy is large white, yellow, or blue corn kernels from which the germ and hull have been removed. Canned and dried hominy are sold in some supermarkets and in Mexican markets. Dried hominy is also available by mail order (see Sources, page 302). If you use dried hominy, first reconstitute it. (Follow the instructions for cooking hominy in the recipe for Posole on page 146, but use ½ cup dried hominy instead of 1 cup.) Do not use hominy grits (ground dried hominy) in this recipe.

Put the tripe, the calf's or pig's foot, and the water in a large stockpot. Add the salt. Bring to a boil over medium-high heat, then reduce the heat and simmer, uncovered, skimming off any foam that rises to the surface, for 2 hours.

Transfer the calf's or pig's foot to a cutting board and remove all the meat from the bones and cartilage. Discard the bones and cartilage. Cut the meat into small pieces and return to the stockpot.

Stir in the minced onions, garlic, ground red chile, oregano, and black pepper to taste, and continue to simmer for 1½ hours. Add the hominy and bring the *menudo* to a boil, then reduce the heat and simmer for another hour. Taste and adjust the seasoning.

Place the scallions, lime wedges, minced cilantro, and oregano in little individual bowls so that each person can garnish to taste. Remove the soup from the heat. Ladle the *menudo* into 4 bowls and serve with corn tortillas that have been warmed in a dry skillet, the bowls of garnishes, and hot sauce for those who like heat.

Serves 4

WHITE BEAN SOUP

Sopa de habicas

" **S**opa de habicas, or White Bean Soup, is one of the treasured recipes that the Spanish Jews carried with them when they were expelled from Spain in 1492," says Lorraine Roses, Professor of Spanish and Director of Latin American Studies at Wellesley College, and her daughter, Aviva Ben-Ur, a doctoral candidate in Jewish history. "The soup was comfort food that could be re-created everywhere the Jews wandered—including from Spain to the Caribbean and then on to America—to remind them of the home they had lost. As the proverb goes, *En todas partes se cuecen habas* (Beans are cooked everywhere)."

Lorraine and Aviva's White Bean Soup, adapted from the recipe files of dozens of American Jews with Caribbean roots, has warmed many a heart and soul on snowy nights in Boston. "Though thousands of years of history simmer in this fragrant soup, with its soothing golden broth and tender ivory-colored beans, it is timeless and will enrich the souls of generations to come," says Lorraine. "Like most bean soups, this one requires little tending and is even more flavorful the next day," adds Aviva. They both agree that White Bean Soup makes a won-

Lorraine Roses and Aviva Ben-Ur making the rounds of Latin markets in Boston

derful supper when served with crusty garlic bread and a warm, homey dessert, like walnut-filled baked apples or apple crisp.

1 cup dried white beans, such as Great Northern, navy, or cannellini (white kidney) beans, rinsed	1 pound meaty beef short ribs, trimmed of as much fat as possible
2 quarts water	½ cup tomato sauce
2 tablespoons olive oil	2 medium ripe tomatoes, diced
2 medium Spanish onions, peeled and minced	1 teaspoon dried tarragon
1 large clove garlic, peeled and finely minced	Salt and freshly ground black pepper, to taste

Put the beans and water in a large soup pot and bring to a boil. Lower the heat, cover, and simmer for 1 hour.

Heat the olive oil in a large skillet over medium heat. Sauté the onions and garlic in the oil until the onions are limp, about 8 minutes. Push the onions aside and add the short ribs. Brown the ribs on both sides, about 4 minutes per side, stirring the onions so that they do not burn.

Add the onions and ribs, the tomato sauce, tomatoes, tarragon, and salt and black pepper to the beans. Bring to a boil over medium-high heat, then lower the heat and simmer, covered, for 1 hour.

With a slotted spoon, scoop up about 1 cup of the beans and purée them in a food processor or electric blender. Stir the purée into the soup. Now remove the short ribs and trim the beef from the bones. Discard the bones and cut the meat into 1-inch pieces and return to the soup. Correct the seasoning and serve the soup at once.

Serves 6 as a first course

SHRIMP CHOWDER

Chupe de camarones

This beautiful coral-pink soup, with rosy shrimp and red-skinned potatoes, is marvelously complemented by the aromatic flavor of cilantro to create a classic of the Peruvian table. Peruvian American Dolores Carver, who lives and works as a receptionist in Chicago, relies on her recipe for *Chupe de camarones* whenever she entertains. "This soup is so elegant and delicious. It's also fast and easy to make, so I don't have to stand in front of the stove when I have guests. I just simmer the *chupe* a few hours ahead and hold off on adding the shrimp until I reheat it before serving. *Chupe de camarones* is really a cross between a soup and a stew. If I'm serving it as a first course, I add less corn and potatoes to make a bona fide soup, as in this recipe. If it is the main dish, I double up on the corn and potatoes for a stew."

While some people make *Chupe de camarones* with both rice and potatoes, Dolores Carver always chooses just one or the other. (For *Chupe de camarones* with rice, simply add ½ cup long-grain rice along with—or in place of—the potatoes.) In mid- to late summer, Dolores cooks with fresh ears of corn, cut into rounds, Peruvian-style, in place of whole kernel corn. In Peru, the fruity ají, a bright yellow, very hot Andean chile (see page 162), or the rocoto, an extremely hot red or yellow chile (see page 165), most often gives *Chupe de camarones* its heat. The plump rocoto has such a bite that it is known affectionately as *levanta muertos,* or "raising the dead," and *gringo huanuchi,* or "gringo killer." Since the availability of ají chiles is rather limited and rocotos are not sold at all in the United States, some Peruvian Americans and other chile lovers grow their own from seeds available by mail order (see Sources, page 302). We like a little citrus flavor in *Chupe de camarones,* so we serve it with a plate of lemon or lime wedges on the side.

2 tablespoons olive oil

I medium yellow onion, peeled and finely chopped

2 medium cloves garlic, peeled and minced

I large ripe tomato, diced

¼ ají chile, seeded, deribbed, and finely minced, or substitute ½ serrano or jalapeño chile, or to taste

I teaspoon sweet paprika

¼ teaspoon dried powdered oregano (not crumbled)

1½ quarts homemade or canned chicken broth

2 medium (¾ pound) red-skinned (new) potatoes, peeled and cut into ½-inch cubes

½ cup frozen whole kernel corn, or I medium ear fresh corn, cut into I-inch rounds

I pound shrimp, peeled, deveined, and rinsed under cold running water

¾ cup half-and-half

Salt and freshly ground black pepper, to taste

3 tablespoons minced fresh cilantro or dill

2 limes or I lemon, cut into wedges (optional)

Heat the olive oil in a 3- to 4-quart saucepan over medium heat and sauté the chopped onions and garlic, stirring occasionally, until the onions are golden brown, about 10 minutes. Stir in the diced tomatoes, chile, paprika, and oregano, and sauté for 3 minutes more.

Add the chicken broth and potatoes, bring to a boil, and then reduce the heat, cover, and simmer until the potatoes are very tender, about 25 minutes. (If you are using rounds of fresh corn, add them along with the potatoes.) Next add the shrimp and the corn (if frozen), and cook until the shrimp turn bright pink, about 5 minutes.

Stir in the half-and-half, and taste and season with salt and pepper, as needed. Heat the soup, stirring frequently, until it is hot. Ladle the *Chupe de camarones* into large soup bowls, garnish with minced fresh cilantro or dill, and serve at once with lime or lemon wedges.

Serves 4 as a main dish and 6 as an appetizer

CRAB SOUP

Sopa de jaiba

This splendid soup from the Honduran American table is filled with delicate, sweet crabmeat, chunks of nutty *yuca,* and faintly tart plantains in a broth enhanced with tomatoes, red pepper, coconut milk, and lemon juice. Crab Soup makes a special first course or a veritable feast when ladled into large deep bowls. This soup may sound fancy, but it is not fussy. The trickiest part is getting the crustaceans to take a steam bath, but as long as you are not extremely squeamish about it—the way Woody Allen is in the live lobster skirmish in *Annie Hall*—and as long as you remember to hold the lid on the pot, it should really be a breeze. Many of the Honduran crab soups that we have sampled in the United States are served with the crabmeat still in the shell. So that the soup is less messy to eat, we have taken the liberty of extracting the crabmeat from the shells and adding it to the soup in the final stage of cooking.

Crab Soup is not suited to long simmering on the back of the stove; cook it for the requisite time only, so that the vegetables and the crabmeat remain in whole pieces. Hard-shell blue crabs from the Atlantic and Gulf coasts, available year-round, are the pivotal ingredient in this soup, and they should be as fresh as possible. In fact, we recommend buying the crabs close to cooking time or, at the very least, on the same day you prepare the soup. Live blue crabs should be active and kicking; do not take home any sluggish or still ones, as they are near death and their meat will be inferior. Some folks just cannot face steaming the crabs while they are still alive. If it is any consolation, crabs have a rather simple nervous system, and they perish within seconds. This soup may be made by substituting 2 quarts chicken stock for the crab cooking liquid and 1 pound fresh lump crabmeat for the crabs.

1½ quarts water

6 medium hard-shell blue crabs, live

1 pound fresh or frozen (defrosted) *yuca*, peeled (see page 198 for information on *yuca* and page 189 for directions on peeling *yuca*)

2 tablespoons olive oil

½ cup finely minced yellow onion

2 medium cloves garlic, peeled and finely minced

1 medium ripe tomato, minced

½ cup finely minced red bell pepper

2 yellow plantains, cut into ½-inch rounds and peeled (see page 183 for information on plantains and page 184 for instructions on peeling and cutting plantains)

5 tablespoons freshly squeezed lemon juice

1 cup canned unsweetened coconut milk

1 tablespoon finely minced fresh cilantro

Salt and freshly ground black pepper, to taste

1 lemon or 2 limes, cut into wedges (optional)

Pour the water into a crab pot or any large pot with a steamer basket. Bring the water to a boil over medium-high heat. Holding a crab firmly with metal tongs, rinse under cold running water and then put it in the steamer basket, cover, and press down on the lid so that the crab cannot escape. Repeat until all the crabs are in the basket. Steam the crabs for 10 minutes, or until they turn bright red, then remove to a large plate and allow them to cool enough to be handled. Strain the crab steaming liquid, add enough water to make 2 quarts, and reserve.

Remove the crabmeat from the crabs: Fold back and then pull off the pointed apron on the underside of a crab. Hold the bottom of the crab with one hand and pull up on the top shell at the spot where the apron was detached. Discard the top shell. With your fingers, scoop out any loose material and then remove the gills (the pointed sponge sacs) from each side of the crab. Break the crab in half, down the middle. Pick out the meat from the body of the crab and put it in a medium bowl. Twist off the legs and the claws where they meet the body. Crack the claws with a nutcracker and remove the meat. Reserve the claw shells along with the legs. Repeat this process with the remaining crabs. Cover the crabmeat and refrigerate.

Put the reserved claw shells and legs and the crab steaming liquid into a large stockpot. Cover, bring to a boil, then reduce the heat and simmer 25 minutes. Strain the crab cooking liquid and reserve.

Cut the *yuca* pieces in half lengthwise. Cut away the fibrous core in the center of each piece with a paring knife, then cut the *yuca* into ½-inch chunks.

Heat the olive oil over medium heat in the stockpot, and sauté the minced onions and garlic until the onions are limp, about 3 minutes. Stir in the minced tomatoes and bell pepper, and sauté until the tomatoes break down, about 6 minutes. Add the reserved crab cooking liquid and the *yuca*, cover, and bring to a boil. Reduce the heat and simmer, covered, for 20 minutes.

Add the plantains and lemon juice to the soup and continue simmering, covered, until the plantains are tender, about 20 minutes. Stir in the coconut milk, reserved crabmeat, and cilantro, and heat to serving temperature. Stir gently so that the crabmeat does not break up. Taste and adjust the seasoning, adding salt and freshly ground black pepper, as needed. Serve at once with lemon or lime wedges, if desired, for those who like more citrus flavor.

Serves 6 as a first course and 4 as a main dish

CHILLED ROASTED SWEET RED PEPPER AND COCONUT SOUP

Soupe froide au poivron rouge et coco

Creamy and delicate Chilled Roasted Sweet Red Pepper and Coconut Soup is a superb beginning to a late summer or early autumn meal when bell peppers in vivid splashes of color overflow their baskets at farmers' markets and vegetable stands. This version has all the ingredients of classic Haitian sweet red pepper soup, but the red bell peppers are roasted, not boiled the traditional way, to concentrate their natural sweetness. Coconut milk, which betrays the recipe's tropical roots, adds a subtle yet surprising note, and a dusting of ground dried red chile, like a burst of crimson, intensifies the soup's visual appeal. If you love spicy food, try garnishing with hot ground red chile rather than mild to serve as a counterpoint to the mellowness of the sweet bell peppers.

This soup is quick and easy to assemble, once you have charred the red bell peppers and peeled and seeded them. (The job will go all the more swiftly if you make certain that the peppers are blistered and charred all over, and then you steam them in a paper or plastic bag that is tightly sealed for the allotted amount of time.) Since the soup has to chill in the refrigerator, you can prepare it hours or even a day in advance.

2½ pounds red bell peppers (about 5
   large), roasted (see the directions for
   roasting peppers on page 167)

1 tablespoon butter

1 small yellow onion, peeled and minced

2 cups homemade or canned
   chicken broth

2 tablespoons tomato paste

½ cup plus 4 teaspoons canned
   unsweetened coconut milk

½ cup half-and-half

Salt and freshly ground white pepper,
   to taste

2 teaspoons ground dried red chile or
   paprika—mild, medium, or hot—for
   garnish (see the note on ground
   dried red chile on page 167)

Cut the roasted red peppers into 2-inch pieces. Melt the butter in a 3- to 4-quart saucepan over medium heat, and sauté the minced onions, stirring occasionally, until they are lightly browned, about 8 minutes. Stir in the red peppers, chicken broth, and tomato paste. Bring to a boil over medium-high heat, then reduce the heat, cover, and simmer, stirring occasionally, for 20 minutes.

Purée the peppers with their cooking liquid in a food processor or electric blender until smooth. Return the pepper purée to the saucepan, and stir in ½ cup of the coconut milk and the half-and-half. Taste and season with salt and white pepper, as needed.

Allow the soup to cool to room temperature, then chill it thoroughly, covered, in the refrigerator. Ladle the soup into 4 serving bowls, dribble 1 teaspoon coconut milk in a pattern in each bowl, dust each with about ½ teaspoon ground chile or paprika, and serve at once.

Serves 4

ORANGE-SCENTED ROASTED PUMPKIN SOUP

Sopa de calabaza con aroma de naranja

As the theory goes, pumpkins and winter squashes originated in Mexico and Guatemala and were domesticated, along with corn and chiles, by the pre-Inca many thousands of years ago. Long before the Pilgrims sat down at the table for that first Thanksgiving, these gourds had spread throughout Central and South America and the Caribbean. It's no wonder that recipes for pumpkin soup abound among

Americans of Latin American descent. While we have never tasted two Latin pumpkin soups that were exactly alike, each Latin American group gravitates toward the same core ingredients. For instance, we have savored few Jamaican American pumpkin soups that were not spiced with thyme and Scotch bonnet chiles, and a rare Cuban American one that did not call for chicken stock (most South American pumpkin soups are made with beef stock). After many years of sampling traditional and Nuevo Latino pumpkin soups (the most innovative one had corn and Chinese wontons in it!), we have determined that our all-time favorites are Dominican American Oscar de la Renta's Pumpkin and Crab Soup, which is featured in the *New York Cookbook,* and this silky Dominican roasted pumpkin soup with a subtle orange note, which we first tasted at a Dominican lunch counter in New York City's Washington Heights section, the heart of Dominican America.

This recipe calls for *calabaza* (also known as West Indian pumpkin, green pumpkin, and Cuban squash), which may be found in Latin markets. If you cannot obtain *calabaza,* substitute a winter squash that is not too sweet and has a creamy texture, such as butternut or banana squash. Avoid the supersweet Tahitian and kabocha, and the common American pumpkin variety (used for carving jack-o'-lanterns), as it tends to be watery and bland, as well as any of the winter squashes with grainy or stringy flesh, like spaghetti squash. Most *calabazas* and butternut and banana squashes weigh in at more than the 2 pounds called for in this recipe. We always roast the extra squash along with the 2 pounds and then snack on the surplus wedges, which we sprinkle with extra-virgin olive oil or tamari sauce.

2 pounds fresh *calabaza* or butternut or
    banana squash, seeds removed and cut
    into 3-inch-wide wedges (rind intact)
Approximately 1½ tablespoons olive oil
1 tablespoon butter
1 medium yellow onion, peeled
    and chopped
½ teaspoon ground ginger
½ teaspoon ground nutmeg

2½ cups chicken stock, preferably
    homemade
1¼ cups orange juice
1 to 1¼ cups half-and-half
Salt and freshly ground white pepper,
    to taste
1 seedless orange, cut into paper-thin
    slices, for garnish

Brush the *calabaza* or squash wedges lightly with the olive oil and place them, skin side down, on a nonstick baking sheet. Roast the wedges on the upper rack of a preheated 450°F oven until they are very brown (and even have a few charred spots) and tender when pierced with a fork, about 35 minutes. Remove the pumpkin from the oven to a large plate and allow it to cool enough to be handled. Peel what will now be a very thin skin off the bottom of the pumpkin wedges; it should come off easily in sheets. (Peel off only the skins, not the brown outer layer on the rest of the pumpkin.) Discard the skins and slice the pumpkin wedges into 1-inch pieces.

Melt the butter in a 3- to 4-quart saucepan over medium heat and sauté the chopped onions, stirring occasionally, until they are lightly browned, about 8 minutes. Stir in the ginger and nutmeg. Add the reserved pumpkin, the chicken stock, and the orange juice, bring to a slow boil, and then reduce the heat, cover, and simmer, stirring occasionally to break down the pumpkin, for 25 minutes.

Purée the mixture in an electric blender or food processor until smooth. Return the purée to the saucepan, heat it over low heat, and slowly stir in the half-and-half until the soup reaches a desired consistency. (Depending on the density of the pumpkin or squash used, you may need to add up to 1¼ cups half-and-half.) Taste and season with salt and white pepper, as needed. Cook the soup until it is heated through, stirring constantly, about 3 minutes. Do not allow it to boil.

Remove the pumpkin soup from the heat and serve at once, or allow it to cool to room temperature, refrigerate it for at least 3 hours, and then serve the soup chilled. In either case, garnish each bowl with an orange slice.

Serves 4

GRINGO POTATO-CHEDDAR SOUP

El locro gringo

If you have never had *locro,* an Andean potato soup, you're in for a treat. It's an utterly comforting potato-cheese soup—rich, colorful, and velvet-smooth—that makes a sophisticated beginning to a meal, particularly of rabbit, duck, or venison. Many Ecuadoran Americans so love *locro* that they serve it not as a starter, but as an entrée with a side dish of avocado slices, perhaps garnished with sautéed red onions and roasted walnuts in a mango vinaigrette, to balance the thick texture of the soup.

Ecuadoran American David Chiriboga, chair of the Department of Health Promotion and Gerontology at the University of Texas Medical Branch at Galveston, as a child savored a Yankee version of *locro,* which he treasures to this day. As David explains: "My father emigrated from Ecuador to the United States in the 1920s, and he and my mother settled in New England. I grew up in Newton, Massachusetts, and as far as I know, we were the only Hispanic family in the town. As a result, we assimilated quickly and so did our Ecuadoran recipes. For instance, for countless generations the branch of my family in Quito, Ecuador, has used a mild fresh cheese akin to American farmer cheese in *locro.* But here in America we came to substitute the sharper semifirm cheeses prized in New England, like Vermont Cheddar. For that reason I call this soup *El locro gringo*."

Despite assimilation, says David, the family's *locro* did not lose all of its uniquely Ecuadoran qualities: "We have always prepared the soup with ground *achiote* seeds (also known as annatto), which lend *locro* its pleasing blush. *Achiote* seeds have a slight musky flavor, which is an acquired taste for some Americans, but the seeds are valued above all as a food coloring. In fact, many American foods, such as butter, margarine, and orange Cheddar, are colored with annatto, though the flavor of it does not come through. In some regions of Ecuador, paprika takes the place of ground *achiote* seeds in *locro*."

David Chiriboga still enjoys making *El locro gringo* the way his mother taught him back in Massachusetts, not only because it's delectable and a cinch to prepare at the end of a long day, but also because it's a soup that goes straight to his heart. These days David serves his *locro* to yet another generation of Ecuadoran Americans. His sons, Carlos and David, adore the creamy soup but favor buttery popcorn on the side instead of their father's avocado slices.

2 medium yellow onions, peeled
    and minced
1 large clove garlic, peeled and minced
1½ tablespoons olive oil
1 teaspoon ground *achiote* seeds (also
    called annatto), or substitute an
    equal amount mild paprika*
3 pounds russet (Idaho) potatoes, peeled
    and cut into 1-inch cubes

1 quart chicken stock or water
1 cup milk
1 cup (4 ounces) grated white Cheddar,
    mild, medium, or sharp
Salt and freshly ground white pepper,
    to taste
½ cup finely minced fresh cilantro,
    for garnish

*Achiote *seeds are available ground or whole in Latin American and East Indian markets. They should be brick red in color; a brownish hue indicates that they are old and have lost their flavor. If you can find only whole* achiote *seeds, grind them by first bringing them to a boil in enough water to cover and then simmering for 5 minutes. Cool the seeds in the water to room temperature. Drain and grind in an electric mini-chopper or a clean coffee grinder, or with a mortar and pestle.*

Sauté the onions and garlic in the olive oil in a 3- to 4-quart saucepan over medium heat, stirring frequently, until the onions are quite limp, about 10 minutes. Stir in the ground *achiote* seeds or paprika.

Add the potatoes and chicken stock or water, and bring to a boil over medium-high heat. Reduce the heat, cover, and gently boil the potatoes until they are very tender when pierced with a fork, about 25 to 30 minutes.

With a slotted spoon, transfer about half of the cooked potatoes to a medium mixing bowl. Mash them with a potato masher, add ½ cup of the cooking liquid, and then beat with an electric mixer or by hand until smooth. (Do not use a blender or food processor or else the potatoes will turn into a sticky, starchy glue.) Return the potato

Gringo Potato–Cheddar Soup (continued)

purée to the saucepan, stir in the milk, and cook the soup over medium heat until it is hot, but do not allow it to boil.

Stir in the Cheddar cheese, and then remove the soup from the heat. Season to taste with salt and white pepper. Ladle the *locro* into bowls, garnish with minced cilantro, and serve at once.

Serves 6

CHILLED AVOCADO SOUP WITH MANGO-CILANTRO SALSA

Sopa fría de paltas con salsa de mango y culantro

This traditional Chilean recipe for velvety chilled avocado soup has been given a *nuevo* twist of mango-cilantro salsa to produce a blast of tropical flavor and color. Chilled Avocado Soup with Mango-Cilantro Salsa is best from June to late August, when the weather is balmy and both mangos and the summer varieties of avocados are at their peak, although decent avocados and imported mangos are available sporadically in some regions of the country during the rest of the year. The Mango-Cilantro Salsa can be prepared a day in advance, but the avocado soup must be made on the day it is served.

4 cups chicken stock, preferably
  homemade
4 medium ripe Hass avocados
I cup half-and-half
2 tablespoons freshly squeezed
  lemon juice

½ teaspoon Worcestershire sauce
Salt and freshly ground white pepper,
  to taste
Mango-Cilantro Salsa, chilled
  (see page 29)

Warm the chicken stock in a large saucepan over medium-low heat. Cut the avocados in half, remove the pits, peel off the skin, and cut the flesh into 2-inch pieces. Process the avocado pieces and the half-and-half in an electric blender or food processor until smooth.

Remove the chicken stock from the heat and stir in the avocado purée, lemon juice, and Worcestershire sauce. Season to taste with salt and white pepper, and then refrigerate for at least 3 hours. Ladle the avocado soup into chilled bowls, and garnish each with Mango-Cilantro Salsa.

Serves 6

THE AVOCADO

A tropical and subtropical fruit, the avocado was grown in Mexico as early as 7000 B.C. In fact, the word "avocado" is derived from the Nahuatl (pre–Columbian Mexican) word for testicle, *ahuacatl*. Before Columbus reached the New World, the avocado had found its way to South America and the Caribbean. Upon discovering the curious fruit, Spanish explorers named it *aguacate* (and the Portuguese *abacate*), an approximation of *ahuacatl*. This name has stuck throughout Latin America, except in several South American countries like Chile and Argentina, where it is known by the Incan term *palta,* and Colombia, where it is called *cura*. To speakers of English in the United States, the fruit was known first as alligator pear and then avocado.

The most widely cultivated avocado varieties in the United States are the flavorful rough-skinned black-green Hass (named after postman Rudolph Hass who first planted this variety in the United States in 1926) and the less popular, smooth-skinned dark green Fuerte. Hass avocados are cultivated primarily in California (many southern Californians have them growing in their backyard), while Fuerte avocados are grown mainly in Florida. Hass avocados are generally nutty-tasting and contain as much as fifty percent more oil than the faintly sweet, mild, and sometimes watery Fuerte avocados. Some avocado varieties, such as the Fuerte, also grow in minuscule sizes and are known as mini avocados, cocktail avocados, or cukes.

Avocados ripen best when picked while they are still hard and left to sit at room temperature for a week or so. They will ripen much faster if placed in a paper bag. An avocado is ripe if it gives when gently pressed with the thumb. Ripe avocados will keep for a few days in a cool place and up to 1 week stored in the refrigerator. Since the flesh of the avocado quickly darkens once it is cut, add avocado to a dish at the last minute. A spritz of lemon or lime juice will slow down the discoloration process. Store an "opened" avocado in the refrigerator with the skin attached and the pit in place. Be sure to sprinkle it with lemon or lime juice before wrapping it tightly in plastic.

Avocados assume many guises in Latin American cooking in the United States. They make their way into hors d'oeuvres, salads, soups, sauces, main dishes, and even drinks and desserts. Throughout Latino America, cooks stuff the avocado with a variety of fillings. Colombian Americans love diced avocado in soups and stews, as well as in milk shakes, while Brazilian Americans relish avocado ice cream. Cuban Americans might serve avocados diced or sliced with vinaigrette or, like Guatemalan Americans and Chilean Americans, as the main ingredient in a chilled soup. Venezuelan Americans, Puerto Ricans, and other Latinos often add diced or sliced avocados to salads. Mexican and Venezuelan Americans commonly mash them for guacamole and its Venezuelan cousin *guasacaca,* and garnish meat dishes and soups with diced avocado. Mexican Americans also cook with the leaves of scented varieties of avocado trees that are reminiscent of basil or anise. Avocado leaves can be purchased in some Latin markets or plucked from avocado trees that have not been sprayed with insecticides.

AN *ANTOJITO* IS AN APPETIZER,

BUT IT MEANS LITERALLY "A

LITTLE WHIM." AS EVERYONE

KNOWS, A LITTLE WHIM CAN

STRIKE SUDDENLY, AT ANY

TIME OF DAY. . . .

APPETIZERS

AND SALADS

SALSAS

The word *salsa* actually means "sauce"—any sauce, but in America it has come to connote uncooked dips or table condiments featuring chiles. Some salsas call for chiles as the main ingredient, but most are replete with chopped fresh tomatoes. *Salsa verde,* or "green salsa," traditionally made with tomatillos and green chiles, has been catching on, and *nuevo* brands have appeared, featuring other green ingredients like cactus and green olives. Nuevo Latino chefs have been hard at work creating fruit salsas made with mango, papaya, peach, pineapple, and other fruits, and vegetable salsas with such things as corn, black beans, and pinto beans, which are used to garnish soups, and meat, poultry, fish, and shellfish dishes. Chef Douglas Rodriguez of Patria in New York City has taken salsas into the next realm with such creations as smoked queso blanco salsa, anchovy salsa, dried shrimp salsa, and cucumber-dill salsa. Others have done likewise, and nowadays you can find just about anything in salsas.

A wide variety of traditional and *nuevo* salsas, with varying degrees of heat, are sold in supermarkets, and they enjoy such popularity that annual sales of salsa have surpassed that of ketchup for several years in a row now. While salsas, as they have been newly defined, are ubiquitous in Mexican American and Southwestern cooking, they are also prevalent in the kitchens of other Americans of Latin American descent who worship the chile, especially Peruvian, Ecuadoran, and Chilean Americans, and, to a lesser extent, Brazilian and Argentine Americans. (Of course, hot sauces, which in the American definition are liquid chile seasonings that are used sparingly, can be found in other corners of Latino America as well.)

CHILE SALSAS

Many salsas rooted in Latin America are based almost entirely on chiles—and contain no tomatoes at all. These salsas can be quite *picante,* so exercise caution.

PERUVIAN AMERICAN HOT SALSA

Salsa picante

3 ají chiles, seeded, deribbed, and finely minced, or substitute 3 large jalapeño chiles (see page 162 for information on ajís)

1 small yellow onion, peeled and finely minced

2 medium scallions, green and white parts finely minced

3 large cloves garlic, peeled and finely minced

2 tablespoons extra-virgin olive oil

2 tablespoons red wine vinegar

Combine all the ingredients in a medium mixing bowl and refrigerate for 1 hour.

For Ecuadoran American Ají Salsa *(Salsa de ají picante)*: Put the chiles in a medium mixing bowl. Omit the rest of the above ingredients. Stir in ½ cup finely minced red onion, add enough freshly squeezed lemon juice to cover, and salt to taste. Cover and refrigerate for at least 3 hours. Add a little water to cut the lemon juice, if desired, and serve.

For Brazilian American Malagueta Chile and Lime Salsa *(Môlho de pimenta e limão)*: (See page 164, and Sources, page 305, for information on malagueta chiles.) Purée 3 bottled malaguetas or 3 seeded fresh Scotch bonnet or Jamaican Hot chiles with 1 small yellow onion, 1 medium clove garlic, and ½ cup freshly squeezed lime or lemon juice in a food processor or electric blender. Add salt to taste and serve.

TOMATO SALSAS

Tomato salsas are best when made with luscious vine-ripened tomatoes; those anemic, waxy hothouse varieties impersonating tomatoes at supermarkets just won't do.

CHILEAN AMERICAN FRESH TOMATO SALSA

Pebre

3 medium ripe tomatoes, finely chopped
1 small yellow onion, peeled and minced
1 large clove garlic, peeled and minced
1 serrano or jalapeño chile, seeded and
    minced, or to taste
1 tablespoon extra-virgin olive oil
1½ tablespoons freshly squeezed lemon
    or lime juice, or red wine vinegar

2 tablespoons finely minced
    fresh cilantro
1 tablespoon finely minced fresh parsley
Salt and freshly ground black pepper,
    to taste

Combine all the ingredients in a medium mixing bowl. Taste and add salt and pepper to taste. Cover and refrigerate for 1½ hours. Serve with stews like *Porotos granados* (Stewed Beans with Corn, Pumpkin, and Sweet Basil, see page 180, as well as grilled and roasted meats, and tortilla chips. Note that some versions of *Pebre* omit the tomatoes entirely and call for more chiles and olive oil.)

For Mexican American Salsa (called *Salsa mexicana, Salsa cruda, Salsa fresca,* and in Texas, *Pico de gallo,* which is orange-jicama salad elsewhere): Omit the olive oil, lemon or lime juice, parsley, and black pepper. Add a pinch of sugar. Serve at room temperature with virtually any savory Mexican dish that is not cooked in a sauce.

For Ecuadoran American Tomato Ají Salsa *(Salsa de ají):* Omit the garlic, olive oil, lemon or lime juice, parsley, and black pepper. Mix together all the remaining ingredients except the chiles in a medium mixing bowl. Seed 2 ají chiles (see page 162), or substitute 2 serranos or jalapeños and purée in an electric blender or food processor with ¼ cup water until smooth. Stir the chile purée into the salsa a little at a time, tasting it with each addition until it reaches the hotness you like. Serve at room temperature with grilled meats or stews, and tortilla chips.

For Argentine American Creole Salsa *(Salsa criolla):* Mix together 2 tablespoons ground dried red chile (see the note on page 167) and 2 teaspoons dry mustard in a large bowl. Beat in ⅓ cup red wine vinegar and ½ cup extra-virgin olive oil with a whisk. Add 3 diced medium tomatoes, 1 finely minced medium onion, 2 finely minced cloves garlic, and 2 tablespoons finely minced fresh parsley. Cover and refrigerate for 3 hours. Serve with roasted, grilled, or barbecued meats.

MEXICAN AMERICAN TOMATILLO SALSA

Salsa verde

8 large fresh tomatillos, or
    substitute one 13-ounce can whole
    tomatillos, drained*
2 jalapeño or serrano chiles, roasted,
    peeled, and seeded (see page 167 for
    directions on roasting chiles),
    or to taste

1½ tablespoons chopped fresh cilantro
1 tablespoon chopped onion (optional)
1 small clove garlic (optional)
¼ teaspoon granulated sugar, or to taste
Salt to taste

* Tomatillos, also called tomates verdes, fresadillas, *and* tomatitos, *belong to the same nightshade family as the tomato and look like small green tomatoes with papery brown husks attached. They are used when firm and green, and taste like a combination of apples, lemons, and herbs. Fresh tomatillos can be found sporadically year-round in Latin markets, some supermarkets, and gourmet shops.*

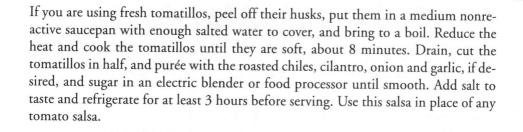

If you are using fresh tomatillos, peel off their husks, put them in a medium nonreactive saucepan with enough salted water to cover, and bring to a boil. Reduce the heat and cook the tomatillos until they are soft, about 8 minutes. Drain, cut the tomatillos in half, and purée with the roasted chiles, cilantro, onion and garlic, if desired, and sugar in an electric blender or food processor until smooth. Add salt to taste and refrigerate for at least 3 hours before serving. Use this salsa in place of any tomato salsa.

NUEVO FRUIT AND VEGETABLE SALSAS

Use only fruits and vegetables at their peak. Fruit and vegetable salsas are rather delicate, so plan on serving them the same day that you prepare them.

MANGO-CILANTRO SALSA

Salsa de mango y culantro

I medium ripe mango, peeled, flesh cut
  away from the pit, and diced
½ cup finely minced red onion
¼ cup finely minced fresh cilantro

I tablespoon freshly squeezed lime juice
½ red jalapeño chile or serrano chile,
  seeded and finely minced, or to taste

Mix together all of the ingredients in a small bowl. Cover and chill the salsa in the refrigerator for at least 3 hours. Try this salsa with Chilled Avocado Soup (see page 22), broiled or grilled fish, or shellfish.

PEACH-HABANERO SALSA

Salsa de durazno y chile habanero

3 large ripe peaches, peeled, pitted, skins removed, and minced

½ habanero chile, seeded and finely minced, or to taste

2 tablespoons finely minced red onion

Juice of 1 lime

1 tablespoon light brown sugar

¼ teaspoon ground cinnamon

¼ teaspoon ground cloves

Salt, to taste

Gently mix together all the ingredients in a medium mixing bowl. Cover and refrigerate for 2 hours. This is a nice accompaniment to pork.

BERRY SALSA

Salsa de baya

1 cup fresh blackberries, olallieberries, loganberries, boysenberries, or red, black, or golden raspberries

1½ tablespoons finely minced fresh cilantro

1½ tablespoons finely minced fresh mint

½ red serrano or jalapeño chile, finely minced, or to taste

1 tablespoon freshly squeezed lime juice

Salt, to taste

Mash ½ cup of the berries in a small mixing bowl. Stir in the remaining ½ cup whole berries and the rest of the ingredients, and serve at once. This goes well with roast pork, lamb chops, grilled chicken, and duck.

BLACK BEAN AND CORN SALSA

Salsa con frijoles negros y maíz

2 medium fresh ears of corn, roasted
   or steamed, and cooled
I cup black beans, cooked and drained
¼ cup finely minced red onion
¼ cup finely minced red bell pepper
3 tablespoons freshly squeezed lime or
   lemon juice
2 tablespoons finely minced
   fresh cilantro

I tablespoon extra-virgin olive oil
I red jalapeño chile, seeded and finely
   minced, or to taste
I large clove garlic, peeled and finely
   minced
½ teaspoon ground cumin
Salt, to taste

Cut the corn kernels from the cob with a sharp knife. Stir together the kernels and all of the remaining ingredients except the salt in a medium mixing bowl. Taste and add salt, as needed. Cover and refrigerate until ready to serve. Serve with grilled meat and chicken.

MARINATED BEEF
WITH MINT
AND MIXED GREENS

Ensalada de salpicón salvadoreño-americana

Salvadoran *salpicón* is a minced roast beef salad bathed in a dressing of citrus fruit flavors. The beef is tossed with just the right amount of finely minced onion and radish to perk it up but not overpower it and to achieve a balance in textures. Fresh mint adds a refreshing, cool note. In our *salpicón,* medium-rare beef, either roast beef or charcoal-grilled or broiled steak, cut into ¼-inch dice, takes the place of the usual finely minced well-done beef. We also like to substitute scallions for onions for more green to contrast with the red radishes, and

Marinated Beef with Mint and Mixed Greens (continued)

Texis, a Salvadoran restaurant chain in L.A., serves typical Salvadoran fare, such as *pupusas, salpicón,* and *tamales de elote.*

we add two flavors not found in traditional *salpicón*—namely, Worcestershire sauce and olive oil.

Salpicón is a popular item on the menu in America's *pupuserías* (Salvadoran restaurants that specialize in the *pupusa,* or stuffed corn patty). There it is traditionally served chilled or at room temperature with yellow rice, puréed beans, and a garnish of lettuce, tomato, and cucumber. One of the nicest ways to sample *salpicón* is to serve it atop a simple bed of mixed greens as an appetizer or as a light lunch or supper with a basket of warm, crusty bread. (We occasionally spoon it on Kaiser rolls for *salpicón* sandwiches.)

¼ cup olive oil, preferably extra-virgin
3 tablespoons freshly squeezed
    orange juice
2 tablespoons freshly squeezed lime or
    lemon juice
½ tablespoon red wine vinegar
¼ teaspoon Worcestershire sauce
Freshly ground black pepper, to taste

1 pound (about 2 cups) medium-rare
    roast beef or steak, cut into
    ¼-inch dice
2 medium scallions, root ends trimmed
    and finely minced
½ cup finely minced radishes
¼ cup finely minced fresh mint
6 ounces mixed greens

Mix the olive oil, orange juice, lime or lemon juice, vinegar, Worcestershire sauce, and black pepper thoroughly in a large bowl to make a dressing. Gently toss the beef, scallions, radishes, and mint in the dressing.

Arrange the mixed greens on each of 4 large dinner plates. Spoon the marinated beef in the center of each bed of greens. Spoon any dressing left in the bowl over the mixed greens and serve the *salpicón* at once with crusty bread, if desired.

Serves 4 as a first course and 2 or 3 as a main course

CHORIZO

Chorizo is coarsely ground pork sausage. Most Latin groups have their own recipes for preparing chorizo. For instance, Guatemalan Americans are known for their chorizo flavored with garlic, oregano, cumin, and tomatillos. However, only two types of chorizo are available in supermarkets in the United States, especially in California, the Southwest, and other regions of the country with sizable Latin communities. One type is Spanish-style chorizo, which is made from pork cured with smoke and stuffed into natural casings. The firm-textured links may be panfried or grilled in their casings, or sliced for soups and other dishes.

The other is Mexican-style chorizo, which is made with fresh pork highly seasoned with red chile, garlic, cumin, oregano, and vinegar. It is spicier than the Spanish-style chorizo and is stuffed into plastic rather than natural casings. It is also sold in patty or bulk form. Most commercial brands of Mexican-style chorizo have a high moisture content and are soft enough to mash with a spoon, while homemade chorizo has a firmer, more crumbly texture. Mexican-style chorizo is customarily mashed or crumbled (if the chorizo is in link form, it is removed from the casings just before cooking), and then panfried slowly so that the spices do not burn. Some Mexican markets in the United States make their own Mexican-style chorizo, and most carry commercial brands. Mexican-style chorizo is also available in some supermarkets, especially in the Southwest, California, and Texas, and areas with a significant Mexican American population.

Americans of Latin American descent recognize that homemade chorizo is far superior to commercial brands, which are laden with fat, cereal fillers, and preservatives. Here is the basic recipe for Mexican-style chorizo in bulk form.

1 pound lean ground pork
1½ tablespoons ground dried red chile, mild, medium, or hot (see the note on ground dried red chile on page 167)
1 tablespoon white vinegar
1 medium clove garlic, peeled

1 teaspoon sweet paprika
¼ teaspoon ground cumin
¼ teaspoon salt
⅛ teaspoon freshly ground black pepper
⅛ teaspoon dried powdered oregano (not crumbled)

Process all the ingredients in a food processor for a few seconds, or until well blended. Use at once, refrigerate for up to 3 days, or store in an airtight container in the freezer for up to 1 month.

Makes 1 pound

BAYAMO'S FRIED WONTONS WITH CHORIZO, CHILES, AND MONTEREY JACK

*Wontons fritos con chorizo,
chile y queso Monterey Jack a la Bayamo*

Bayamo, a trendy eatery in Greenwich Village, bills itself as the Home of Chino-Latino Cuisine. Its name makes reference to Bayamo, Cuba, where Chinese indentured laborers first set up camp on the island in the eighteenth century. Over time the Chinese left an indelible stamp on the local cuisine. In the decade after Fidel Castro seized power in Cuba, in 1959, many of the island's 25,000 Cuban Chinese fled to American shores. Some made their way to New York City, where a few opened Cuban-Chinese restaurants in Chelsea and on the Upper West Side, such as the landmark Asia de Cuba. Before the '60s were over, Cuban-Chinese food was big in New York City. However, the trend did not last, and most Cuban-Chinese establishments closed their doors. In an effort to keep the Cuban-Chinese tradition alive in lower Manhattan, restaurateur Stewart Rosen opened Bayamo in 1984, with the support of his wife, Christine, who is a steel sculptor, and son Matthew. By hiring as chef Antelmo Rodriguez, a Mexican American, Rosen has taken the tradition one step further by creating a truly Chino-Latino menu.

Rodriguez, who hails from Estado de Puebla, Santa Inés, Mexico, learned as a youngster how to prepare regional Mexican dishes from his mother, Rosa Mendoza. Now at Bayamo, he turns out a sumptuous Classic Cuban Sandwich with roast pork, ham, Swiss cheese, and pickles one moment and Ribbons of Duckling Stir-Fried the next, as well as an occasional Chino-Latino fusion dish like tantalizing Fried Wontons with Chorizo, Chiles, and Monterey Jack.

The beauty of Fried Wontons with Chorizo, Chiles, and Monterey Jack is that the wontons can be prepared days or even weeks ahead, stored in the freezer in whatever size batches suit your fancy, and then cooked while still frozen.

1 pound Mexican-style chorizo,
  preferably homemade (see page 33),
  in sausage, patty, or bulk form*
1 fresh jalapeño chile, seeded and finely
  minced (optional)
1 large clove garlic, peeled and
  finely minced
8 ounces Monterey Jack cheese, grated
1 large egg, beaten

One 12-ounce package wonton skins,
  freshly made brands from an Asian
  grocery store or supermarket
  varieties
Vegetable oil, for deep-frying
Hoisin sauce for dipping, available in
  most large supermarkets and in
  Chinese markets

*Chorizo is available in Mexican markets and in some supermarkets, but the best chorizo is homemade.

Prepare the filling: Crumble the chorizo with a fork in a large skillet (if it is in casings, remove them first). Add the jalapeño, if desired, and garlic, and panfry over medium heat, stirring occasionally, for 15 minutes. Gently pat the cooked chorizo with paper towels to absorb any excess oil. (This may be necessary if you are using store-bought chorizo.) Remove the chorizo to a medium mixing bowl and stir in the Monterey Jack.

Beat the egg in a small bowl. Peel off a few wonton skins from the stack and place them flat on a work surface. Cover the rest of the stack of wonton skins with a damp towel to prevent drying. Hold a wonton skin in the palm of one hand so that it looks diamond-shaped. Spoon a teaspoon of the chorizo filling in the center of the wonton skin. Moisten the top 2 edges with the beaten egg, then fold the bottom half up over the filling so that the edges meet, forming a triangle. Press the edges to seal, then pull the lower corners of the triangle straight down. Bring the corners together and pinch them so that they seal, forming a "hat." Place the filled wonton on a baking sheet that will fit in your freezer and cover with damp paper towels. Repeat this process, using a second baking sheet, if necessary, until you run out of wonton skins or filling. Once all the wontons are filled, remove the paper towels, cover them with plastic wrap, and place in the freezer for 30 minutes.

Heat the vegetable oil to 375°F in a deep-fat fryer, a kettle with a wire basket insert (use about 5 cups oil), or a deep frying pan. Remove the wontons from the freezer and deep-fry them, a dozen at a time, for 1 to 2 minutes, or until golden. (At this stage, you may also leave the wontons in the freezer until they are completely frozen, then transfer them to airtight plastic bags and store them in the freezer for later use.) Transfer the fried wontons to a platter or tray lined with paper towels to drain. Serve them with hoisin sauce in a bowl for dipping.

Makes about 5 to 6 dozen wontons

BLACK BEAN AND BACON DIP

Frijoles molidos

Frijoles molidos, a dip of warm, earthy black beans, puréed until creamy, is topped with sour cream, crisp crumbled bacon, and pungent cilantro, and scooped up with blue and white corn tortilla chips or warm tortillas. It serves as a memorable Costa Rican American nosh for casual get-togethers before a crackling fireplace on crisp autumn and winter nights, or, in the heat of summer, *Frijoles molidos* can be chilled and then garnished just before serving to create a cooling dip. Don't worry about having too many leftovers. In a flash this dip metamorphoses into black bean soup, black bean enchiladas with tomato sauce, black bean burritos with shredded Cheddar and salsa, or a nice accompaniment to meat, poultry, and vegetarian main dishes. You can even slather the dip on toast with bacon, lettuce, and tomato for a B.B.B.L.T.—black bean,

A Mexican American woman makes tacos on Olvera Street in the heart of the old Mexican quarter near City Hall in Los Angeles.

bacon, lettuce, and tomato. This is all possible, of course, if the leftovers do not vanish from the refrigerator first.

Traditional recipes for *Frijoles molidos* do not call for lemon juice, but we find that a few tablespoons add just the right zip. If you are preparing this dip for a large group, the recipe can be easily doubled.

10 ounces dried black beans, any
    pebbles and debris removed, rinsed
    under cold running water, and
    soaked overnight
3 tablespoons olive oil
½ cup finely minced yellow onion
3 large cloves garlic, peeled and minced
3 tablespoons freshly squeezed
    lemon juice

½ teaspoon Tabasco sauce, or to taste
½ teaspoon salt, or to taste
3 tablespoons finely minced
    fresh cilantro
⅓ cup sour cream
5 bacon strips, fried and crumbled

Pour the soaked black beans into a colander and rinse them under cold running water. Put the beans in a medium pot with enough water to cover, then bring to a boil over medium heat. Reduce the heat and simmer the black beans for 1½ hours, or until they are tender, adding more water, if necessary, to keep them covered. Drain the beans, then purée them with 1 cup fresh water in a food processor fitted with a metal blade or an electric blender until smooth.

Heat the olive oil in a large skillet over medium heat and sauté the minced onions and garlic until the onions are limp, about 4 minutes. Reduce the heat to medium-low and add the puréed black beans, lemon juice, Tabasco sauce, and salt. Cook for 10 minutes, stirring occasionally so that the beans do not stick to the skillet. If the beans bubble too vigorously, reduce the heat to low. Remove the beans from the heat and allow them to rest for 15 minutes so that they set. (At this point you can also cool the beans and store them in the refrigerator for up to 2 days.)

Stir in 2 tablespoons of the cilantro, then spoon the black beans into a medium serving bowl. Top with dollops of sour cream, and then the crumbled bacon and the remaining tablespoon of cilantro.

Serves 6 to 8 as an hors d'oeuvre or side dish

GRILLED BEEF-HEART KEBABS

Anticuchos

The smoky, pungent aroma of *Anticuchos,* spice-laden beef-heart tidbits threaded on skewers, sizzling on a grill, is enough to make Peruvian Americans wax nostalgic about the old days. *Anticuchos,* a Quechua word meaning "a dish from the Andes cooked on a stick," are perhaps Peru's most celebrated street food, the equivalent of the American hot dog. They actually make ideal cocktail fare, for they can be plucked from the skewers after grilling and pierced with toothpicks. Or serve *anticuchos* for lunch or a light dinner with a loaf of crusty garlic bread and a salad of robust greens like arugula, escarole, purslane, radicchio, or watercress that can stand up to the intense flavors of the beef hearts.

Peruvian Americans like their *anticuchos* hot—fiery hot. The marinade for authentic *anticuchos* calls for extra potent *ajíes mirasol,* but these dried chiles are not widely available in the United States (see page 162 for more information on the *ají mirasol*). Substitute a hot fresh chile, such as the jalapeño or serrano, in the amount that you can tolerate.

Grilled Beef–Heart Kebabs (continued)

I beef heart (about 4 pounds), trimmed
   of all visible fat and fibrous tissue

I cup red wine vinegar

2 tablespoons finely minced
   fresh cilantro

I tablespoon finely minced fresh hot
   chile, such as jalapeño or serrano, or
   to taste

I large clove garlic, peeled and
   finely minced

2 tablespoons finely minced yellow onion

2 tablespoons olive oil

I ½ teaspoons ground cumin

I teaspoon dried powdered oregano
   (not crumbled)

Salt and freshly ground black pepper,
   to taste

6 to 8 bamboo or metal skewers

Rinse the beef heart and pat it dry with paper towels. Cut the heart into 24 cubes with a sharp knife.

Mix together the vinegar, cilantro, chile, and garlic in a large, shallow dish to make an *adobo* (marinade). Marinate the beef-heart cubes in the *adobo,* covered in plastic wrap, in the refrigerator overnight.

If you plan to grill the beef-heart cubes, prepare the fire, using charcoal, about 30 minutes before starting the next step. Also, if you are using bamboo skewers, begin soaking them in water so that they will not burn when exposed to high heat.

Sauté the minced onions in the olive oil in a small skillet over medium heat until they are limp, about 4 minutes. Remove the skillet from the heat, and stir in the cumin, oregano, and salt and black pepper.

Thread 3 beef-heart cubes on each of 8 skewers for appetizers, or 4 cubes on 6 skewers for main entrées. Baste the beef-heart cubes with the *adobo* and the onion-spice mix. When the coals are ready, place the skewers on an oiled grill. Grill the beef-heart cubes, basting two more times and turning once, until they are reddish gold, about 1½ to 2 minutes per side. If you broil the beef-heart cubes, place them about 3 inches from the broiler for approximately 4 minutes. Serve the *anticuchos* on the skewers as an appetizer or main entrée, or remove them from the skewers and insert a toothpick in each piece for hors d'oeuvres. Serve at once.

Serves 8 as an appetizer, 6 as a main entrée,
and 10 to 12 as hors d'oeuvres

CUBAN SANDWICH

Sandwich cubano

Thin slices of succulent ham, garlicky roast pork, mild-mannered Swiss cheese, sharp pickles, crisp, airy Cuban bread, and a dab of mustard and mayo are all the necessary ingredients for a Cuban Sandwich. But the key to a great versus a good "Cuban" lies in the grilling. Five-star Cuban sandwiches are grilled in a sandwich press until the ham, pork, and pickles have warmed in their own steam, the Swiss cheese oozes out the sides, and the outer crust of the bread has metamorphosed into a crisp and buttery wafer-thin layer. (Cuban restaurants use a sandwich press, but you can substitute a waffle iron.) Of course, what makes a Cuban sandwich great is a matter of debate. Some loyalists argue that the pork and ham should be grilled before assembly; others strictly outlaw the use of mustard. Some devotees insist on mile-high sandwiches à la Dagwood Bumstead with upward of twenty layers of ham, pork, and cheese, while many contend that far fewer taste better—and are easier to manage. No matter the outcome of this never-ending debate, when you are looking for a great nosh, nothing surpasses a Cuban sandwich washed down with a mango milk shake, a *materva* or *malta* (Cuban soft drinks), or a Coca-Cola.

1 loaf Cuban Bread (see page 233)	½ pound roast pork, thinly sliced
Mayonnaise	8 thin dill pickle slices
Yellow mustard	½ pound Swiss cheese, thinly sliced
½ pound deli ham, thinly sliced	

Note: When Cuban Americans raid the refrigerator in the middle of the night, they may reach for a medianoche, literally a "midnight sandwich," a smaller version of the Cuban Sandwich with all the same fixings, but on a soft, round egg bun rather than on crusty Cuban bread. For the medianoche, substitute 8 store-bought or homemade egg buns for the Cuban bread, prepare according to the same directions, but use half the meats and cheese on each sandwich, and serve 2 per person.

Cut the bread into 3 x 6-inch pieces with a serrated knife. Slice the bread horizontally to open. Spread a thin layer of mayonnaise on the 4 top halves and a thin layer of mustard on the 4 bottom halves. Arrange one fourth of the ham evenly on each of the bottom halves, then stack a fourth of the pork, 2 pickle slices, and a fourth of the cheese on each. Cover the sandwiches with the top halves of the bread.

Grill the sandwiches in a buttered sandwich press until they are flat, the bread is browned, and the cheese has melted. If you do not have a sandwich press, substitute a waffle iron. (A less desirable alternative is to lay the sandwiches on a cutting board, put a dish over them, and press on the dish to flatten. In a skillet, sauté each sandwich in 1 tablespoon butter over medium heat, turning once, until browned on each side. Press on the sandwiches with the plate several times throughout the cooking process to flatten more.) Cut each sandwich in half and serve at once.

Serves 4

OUR FAVORITE PLACES
FOR CUBAN SANDWICHES

Victor's Café 52, 236 West 52nd Street, New York, NY (212-586-7714)

Versailles, 3555 SW 8th Street, Miami, FL (305-445-7614)

Lario's on the Beach, 820 Ocean Drive, Miami, FL (305-532-9577)

La Carreta, 3632 SW 8th Street, Miami, FL (305-444-7501)

El Colmao, 2328 West Pico Boulevard, Los Angeles, CA (213-386-6131)

Café Tropical, 2900 Sunset Boulevard, Los Angeles, CA (213-661-8391)

La Cubana, 720 East Colorado Street, Glendale, CA (818-243-4398)

Manny's Pastries, 633 Hyde Park Avenue, Roslindale, MA (617-325-2718)

FRIED *ADOBO* CHICKEN

Chicharrones de pollo

Not to be confused with *chicharrones,* the pork cracklings popular in many Latin American cuisines, *Chicharrones de pollo* are pieces of fried chicken that have first been cut with bones and all—a technique that betrays the Chinese presence in the Caribbean—and then marinated for many hours. *Chicharrones de pollo* are an old standby in Puerto Rican, Cuban American, and Dominican American households, perhaps because the fried chicken is the most flavorful and tender on the planet. The secret to its succulence lies in the *adobo*—a Spanish-Caribbean marinade of vinegar, lime, lemon, or sour orange juice; garlic; and herbs and spices, with slight variations from culture to culture.

Classic Dominican *adobo* for *Chicharrones de pollo* is composed of lime or lemon juice, soy sauce (another sign of the Chinese presence in the Caribbean), and garlic. Some traditional recipes also call for adding rum to the *adobo.* (If you wish to try this version, simply add ⅓ cup to the *adobo* recipe below.) The chicken pieces are marinated in the *adobo* for at least 4 hours so that they become tender and absorb all the flavors. According to tradition, *Chicharrones de pollo* are served as an appetizer, but Dominican American friends in New York City tell us that in America the dish is sometimes served for dinner, alongside Dominican-style stewed red beans (*habichuelas rojas*) and coconut rice, or garlic mashed potatoes, with a salad or coleslaw for starters.

FOR THE ADOBO:

⅓ cup freshly squeezed lime or
   lemon juice

3 tablespoons soy sauce
3 large cloves garlic, peeled and minced

FOR THE CHICKEN:

I frying chicken (about 3 pounds),
   drumsticks and wings intact, each
   breast cut into 4 pieces and each
   thigh cut into 2, rinsed and
   patted dry

I cup unbleached all-purpose flour
½ teaspoon sweet paprika
Freshly ground black pepper, to taste
Vegetable oil, for frying

Prepare the *adobo* by combining the lime or lemon juice, soy sauce, and garlic in a large bowl. Toss the chicken pieces in the *adobo* so that they are thoroughly coated. Marinate the chicken, covered, in the refrigerator for at least 4 hours, turning the pieces after 2 hours have elapsed.

Mix together the flour, paprika, and black pepper in a medium shallow dish. Shake the *adobo* off the chicken pieces and roll them, one by one, in the flour so that they are evenly coated.

Heat 2 inches vegetable oil in a deep fryer, kettle, or large deep skillet to 325°F. Fry the chicken in batches of 4 pieces until golden, approximately 6 minutes per side. Note that the drumsticks will take a little longer to cook. (Do not fry more than 4 pieces at once or else the oil will cool down during cooking.) Remove the chicken pieces with tongs to a plate lined with paper towels and drain. Arrange the chicken on a baking sheet and keep warm in a low oven. Cook the remaining 3 batches of chicken and serve at once.

Serves 6 to 8 as an appetizer and 4 as a main dish

CHICKEN-JICAMA SALAD WITH CILANTRO MAYONNAISE

Ensalada de pollo y jícama con mayonesa de culantro

This refreshing salad is a symphony of crisp, subtly sweet jicama, gentle poached chicken, and mildly sweet and nutty Jarlsberg cheese in a cilantro mayonnaise, highlighted by minced red bell pepper and green onions. Remembering the traditional Waldorf Salad, we figured that jicama, which has the crunchy texture of an apple but is not so sweet, would work beautifully as a Latino variation. (See page 196 for information about jicama.) Since jicama does not turn brown when exposed to air like apples, this salad can be made way in advance and chilled in the refrigerator.

FOR THE SALAD:

1½ pounds skinless, boneless chicken breasts, poached, cooled to room temperature, and cut into ½-inch dice

1 pound jicama, peeled and cut into ½-inch dice (see page 196 for information on jicama)

1 cup (about 4 ounces) grated Jarlsberg cheese, or another mild semisoft cheese

½ cup minced red or orange bell pepper

2 medium scallions, root ends removed and finely minced

FOR THE CILANTRO MAYONNAISE:

2 egg yolks, at room temperature
3 tablespoons chopped fresh cilantro
2 tablespoons fresh lemon juice
1 teaspoon Dijon mustard

Pinch each of salt and freshly ground
 black pepper
1 ½ cups vegetable oil
1 head Bibb lettuce or Boston lettuce,
 leaves separated

Toss together the chicken, jicama, Jarlsberg, bell pepper, and scallions in a large mixing bowl.

Prepare the mayonnaise: Process the egg yolks, cilantro, lemon juice, mustard, and salt and pepper in an electric blender or food processor for 30 seconds. With the machine still running, pour in the vegetable oil in a fine stream to make a thick mayonnaise. (To make the mayonnaise by hand, whisk the egg yolks, cilantro, lemon juice, mustard, and salt and pepper in a large bowl. Whisk in the oil a drop at a time until 2 tablespoons have been added, and then pour the oil in a thin stream.)

Fold about ¾ cup of the mayonnaise into the salad and coat thoroughly. Chill in the refrigerator, about 2 hours. To serve, place 1 or 2 lettuce leaves on each of 6 large plates. Spoon about 1 cup salad in the center of the leaves and serve at once.

Serves 6

XIOMARA'S CRISPY *BACALAO* CAKES WITH *CRIOLLO* GAZPACHO

Frituras de bacalao con gazpacho criollo a la Xiomara

This appetizer, which represents a fusion of California, Japanese, French, and Latin American cooking, is the inspiration of Cuban American Xiomara Ardolina, the owner and manager of two restaurants in Pasadena, California, both under the direction of distinguished executive chef and restaurant consultant Patrick Healy: Xiomara, featuring California-French cuisine, and Oye!, where the cooking is Nuevo Americano. All the dishes on Oye!'s Latin-inspired menu, such as Maine Lobster Tamal with Fresh Oregon Morels and Caramelized Chocolate Plantain Cream Cake with Mango and Raspberry Sauces, are sublime, but our absolute favorite is Crispy *Bacalao* Cakes with *Criollo* Gazpacho.

Xiomara has based the dish on childhood memories of her mother's specialty, *Bacalao a la vizcaína,* a delicious codfish stew, which she prepared every Friday for the family's dinner in their home in the Havana suburb of San Francisco de Paula: "My mother salted the cod one day ahead and cooked it with tomatoes, peppers, onions, garlic, and white wine, letting it simmer slowly on the corner of the stove. Our home was filled with the fragrant smell of this hearty dish. Those Friday dinners were my favorite meal of the week," recalls Xiomara. "I decided to re-create my mother's *Bacalao a la vizcaína* in a lighter, more contemporary way, forming cakes with the *bacalao* and serving them fried atop a bed of greens, bathed in a refreshingly spicy gazpacho made with the same vegetables that went into *Bacalao a la vizcaína.*"

Xiomara Ardolina at one of her restaurants

FOR THE *BACALAO* CAKES:

1½ pounds *bacalao* (boneless salt
 cod fillets)*

2¾ cups milk

1½ cups extra-virgin olive oil

3 large egg yolks

Salt and freshly ground black pepper,
 to taste

4 large egg whites

2 cups Panko flakes (Japanese
 bread crumbs) or unseasoned
 dry bread crumbs†

½ cup vegetable oil, for panfrying

FOR THE *CRIOLLO* GAZPACHO:

2 medium red bell peppers, seeded,
 deribbed, and coarsely chopped

5 very ripe Roma (plum) tomatoes,
 seeded and coarsely chopped

¼ hothouse (English) cucumber, peeled,
 seeded if necessary, and coarsely
 chopped, or substitute 1 small
 seeded cucumber

¼ small yellow onion, peeled and
 coarsely chopped

½ shallot, peeled and coarsely chopped

½ jalapeño chile, seeded

1 large clove garlic, peeled

2 tablespoons red wine vinegar

3 tablespoons extra-virgin olive oil

Salt and freshly ground black pepper,
 to taste

FOR THE BED OF MIXED GREENS:

½ pound field greens

2 tablespoons extra-virgin olive oil

1 tablespoon freshly squeezed
 lemon juice

Salt and freshly ground black pepper,
 to taste

*Bacalao is available in Latin markets and some general supermarkets.
†Panko flakes are available in Japanese markets and some markets catering to other Asians.

Rinse the cod under cold running water, and then soak it in enough cold water to cover for at least 8 hours or overnight, changing the water once.

Prepare the gazpacho: Purée all the vegetables in an electric blender with the vinegar and olive oil until smooth. Strain the gazpacho through a fine chinois into a ceramic or glass bowl, and season to taste with salt and pepper. Chill the gazpacho, covered with plastic wrap, in the refrigerator for at least 3 hours.

Prepare the *bacalao* cakes: Put the cod fillets and 2 cups of the milk in a large saucepan, bring to a boil over medium heat, and cook the cod for 2 minutes more. Drain the cod on paper towels, discarding the milk.

Scald the remaining ¾ cup milk in a small saucepan. Heat ½ cup of the olive oil in a large skillet over medium heat until hot but not smoking. Add the cod fillets and sauté gently, until the cod is dry but not brown, about 5 minutes. Remove the cod

Xiomara's Crispy Bacalao *Cakes with* Criollo *Gazpacho (continued)*

from the heat and transfer it with a spatula to a bowl or a mixer. Beat with a fork or with the mixer paddle. Alternately add the scalded milk, the remaining cup of olive oil, and then slowly add the egg yolks. Season the cod with salt and pepper to taste.

Shape the cod into small cakes about 2 inches in diameter. Lightly beat the egg whites in a shallow bowl. Arrange the Panko flakes or bread crumbs on a plate or in a shallow bowl. Dip the *bacalao* cakes, one by one, into the egg whites, and then dredge them in the bread crumbs until completely coated.

Before cooking the *bacalao* cakes, toss the mixed greens in olive oil and lemon juice and season with salt and pepper. Heat the vegetable oil in a large skillet. Panfry the *bacalao* cakes until golden brown on both sides, turning once, about 4 minutes per side.

Assemble the dish by ladling ¼ cup chilled gazpacho into each of 8 pasta plates. Arrange a bed of field greens in the center of each plate atop the gazpacho. Place 2 *bacalao* cakes on top of each bed of greens and serve immediately.

Serves 8

CORN PANCAKES WITH SMOKED SALMON, CAVIAR, AND WASABI CREAM SAUCE

*Cachapas de jojoto con salmón ahumado,
caviar y salsa de crema y de wasabi*

Venezuelan Americans serve *Cachapas de jojoto,* corn pancakes, as a bread or wrapper with any number of dishes, just as Mexican Americans (and some of the rest of us) do tortillas. One evening we were enjoying Wipeout Rolls—sushi rolls with smoked salmon, cream cheese, avocado, and cucumber—at Arigato, a nouvelle Japanese restaurant in Santa Barbara, California, when the inspiration hit for our own fusion dish: smoked salmon and caviar atop *Cachapas de jojoto.* Back in the kitchen, we found that the combination tasted marvelous, but that the dish needed a finishing touch. And so we added a Japanese-inspired wasabi cream sauce. The wasabi utterly loses its bite in this sauce, so do not worry about that burning sensation in your nostrils you get from eating wasabi paste on sushi rolls. Since fine imported and domestic sturgeon caviars are dreadfully expensive, we rely on American salmon caviar and American golden caviar. Inexpensive Masago caviar, the crisp, tiny-grained orange roe California sushi chefs favor, is also pleasing in this dish to both the palate and the pocketbook.

Corn Pancakes with Smoked Salmon, Caviar, and Wasabi Cream Sauce make a fabulous appetizer or a light lunch on a special occasion. The pancakes can be made in just about 15 minutes, so if you prepare the sauce ahead, this dish can be assembled in under 30 minutes.

FOR THE WASABI CREAM SAUCE:
1 cup dry white wine
2 tablespoons finely minced yellow onion
2 cups heavy cream

2 teaspoons wasabi powder, available at Japanese markets and select supermarkets

FOR THE CORN PANCAKES:
1/2 cup yellow cornmeal
2 tablespoons unbleached all-purpose flour
1/2 teaspoon baking soda
1/2 teaspoon salt
1/2 cup half-and-half

1/2 cup buttermilk
1 large egg
1/2 cup fresh, canned, or frozen (defrosted) corn kernels
Olive oil, for frying

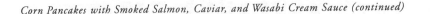

Corn Pancakes with Smoked Salmon, Caviar, and Wasabi Cream Sauce (continued)

FOR THE GARNISH:

**3 ounces smoked salmon, sliced into
eighteen 2-inch squares**

**2 ounces caviar, such as American
salmon caviar, American golden
caviar, Masago caviar, or your favorite**

2 tablespoons finely minced fresh chives

Prepare the wasabi cream sauce: Bring the wine and onion to a boil in a medium saucepan over medium heat. Boil until the wine has reduced to about ½ cup, approximately 10 minutes. Whisk in the heavy cream and the wasabi powder. Lower the heat slightly and allow the sauce to simmer until it reduces to 1½ cups, approximately 30 minutes. Immediately strain the sauce through a bowl-strainer, return it to the saucepan, cover, and keep warm.

Prepare the corn pancakes: Mix together the cornmeal, flour, baking soda, and salt in a medium mixing bowl. Blend the half-and-half, buttermilk, and egg in a separate mixing bowl. Stir the liquid into the dry ingredients, and then fold in the corn kernels.

Heat approximately 1 tablespoon olive oil in a large skillet over medium-high heat. Stir the batter so that the corn kernels and cornmeal rise to the top, and then spoon about 1 tablespoon batter into the skillet. Repeat until you have 4 or 5 pancakes in the skillet. As soon as bubbles form on the pancakes and their edges brown, flip them over and fry until golden on the other side, about 30 to 45 seconds. Continue with the remaining batter, frying only 4 or 5 pancakes at a time and adding olive oil when necessary. You should have 18 to 20 pancakes.

Assemble the dish: Put 3 corn pancakes in the center of each of 6 plates. Spoon the wasabi cream sauce around the pancakes. Put 1 slice of smoked salmon atop each pancake. Garnish each salmon slice with a dollop of caviar, dust the plates with chives, and serve at once.

Serves 6

SHRIMP-AND-
POTATO CROQUETTES

Bombas de camarones y papas

Dominican *Bombas de camarones y papas*—croquettes of creamy mashed potatoes perked up with Muenster cheese and minced parsley, stuffed with sautéed shrimp and onions and deep-fried to a delicious golden brown—are irresistible. Shrimp-and-Potato Croquettes can also be rolled into bite-size balls, fried, and served as finger food. For a lighter version, shape the croquettes into thick patties and sauté them in a skillet rather than deep-frying them. A squeeze of lemon or lime juice is the traditional accent to these croquettes, but they're also good dabbed in tartar sauce or sprinkled with some hot sauce. For a subtle shift in flavor, try replacing the parsley with an equal amount finely minced fresh dill or cilantro.

2 pounds russet (Idaho) potatoes, peeled
   and cut into 1-inch chunks*
1 tablespoon butter
2 large egg yolks
1 cup grated Muenster cheese (about
   6 ounces), firmly packed
2 tablespoons finely minced fresh
   parsley
Salt and freshly ground white pepper,
   to taste

1 tablespoon olive oil
1 small yellow onion, peeled and finely
   minced
½ pound medium shrimp, peeled,
   deveined, and cut into ½-inch pieces
¾ cup unbleached all-purpose flour
3 large eggs, lightly beaten
1 cup seasoned dry bread crumbs
Canola oil, for frying
Lemon or lime wedges, for garnish

* Avoid waxy potatoes such as the red-skinned or White Rose, since they do not have the fluffy texture of starchy potatoes like the russet that makes for excellent mashed potatoes.

Peel the potatoes and cut them into 1-inch chunks, dropping them into a large pot of salted water as they are cut. Bring the potatoes to a boil and cook them until tender when pierced with a fork, about 20 minutes.

Drain the potatoes thoroughly and transfer them to a medium mixing bowl. Add the butter and coarsely mash the potatoes with a fork or potato masher. Stir in the egg yolks, Muenster cheese, parsley, and salt and white pepper.

Heat the olive oil in a large skillet over medium heat and sauté the minced onions, stirring occasionally, until light golden, about 6 minutes. Add the shrimp and sauté, stirring frequently, until bright pink, about 4 minutes.

Roll 2 generous tablespoons of the mashed potatoes into a ball. Poke a hole in the ball and stuff with about a tablespoon of the shrimp-and-onion mixture. Seal the croquette

by patting the potato over the stuffing. Form the rest of the croquettes in the same way.

Put the flour, beaten eggs, and bread crumbs in 3 separate shallow bowls. One by one, dredge the croquettes in the flour, dip in the egg, then roll in the bread crumbs until evenly coated. Place the croquettes on plates, cover loosely in plastic wrap, and refrigerate for 30 minutes.

Heat about 1 inch canola oil in a large skillet to 375°F. Fry the croquettes, 3 at a time, turning once until golden brown, about 1½ minutes per side. Transfer the croquettes with a slotted spoon to plates lined with paper towels to drain. Keep warm in a low oven while you fry the rest of the croquettes. Serve at once with lemon or lime wedges.

Makes about 16 croquettes;
serves 8 as a first course and 4 to 5 as a main dish

CRABMEAT AND AVOCADO SALAD WITH LIME MAYONNAISE

Ensalada de jueyes y aguacate con mayonesa de lima

Fresh lump crabmeat from blue crabs is always our choice for this salad, as we find it far sweeter and more succulent than that of any other crab, but Dungeness is also pleasing. Crabmeat and Avocado Salad with Lime Mayonnaise, or *Ensalada de jueyes y aguacate con mayonesa de lima,* comes from the Puerto Rican culinary repertoire, one that is rich in crab dishes, thanks to land crabs, which once found their way by the basketful to the kitchens of Puerto Rico. Commercial development and pollution have destroyed most of the crabs' natural habitat, and the species has all but disappeared from the island. Back in the days when crabs were plentiful, Puerto Ricans considered the crustaceans ordinary. Nowadays Puerto Ricans on the island depend on crabs shipped in from around the Caribbean, while mainlanders on the East Coast have adopted the Atlantic blue crab and on the West Coast the Dungeness crab.

In traditional *Ensalada de jueyes y aguacate,* the crab is mixed with a mayonnaise dressing and served with a garnish of avocado and tomato. We prefer to spoon the crabmeat on a bed of mixed greens, like a Louis salad, a popular California crabmeat or shrimp salad served with a chile-tomato mayonnaise dressing. This salad can be served alone as a first course, or with sesame breadsticks or oyster crackers for a light main entrée. A California chardonnay makes a fine companion.

I pound fresh lump crabmeat, from blue crabs or Dungeness crabs

½ cup mayonnaise, preferably homemade*

I tablespoon freshly squeezed lime or lemon juice

I tablespoon finely minced yellow onion

I small clove garlic, peeled and finely minced

2 tablespoons minced fresh parsley or cilantro

¼ teaspoon dried powdered oregano (not crumbled)

Salt and freshly ground black pepper, to taste

6 ounces mixed greens

2 medium ripe Hass avocados, halved, peeled, pitted, and cut into ¼-inch slices

2 small ripe tomatoes, cored and cut into 8 wedges each

See the recipe for cilantro mayonnaise on page 43. For this recipe simply omit the cilantro.

Pick over the crabmeat to remove any pieces of shell or cartilage. Mix together thoroughly the mayonnaise, lime or lemon juice, onion, garlic, parsley or cilantro, oregano, and salt and pepper in a medium mixing bowl. Fold in the crabmeat.

Arrange the mixed greens on large plates. Spoon the crabmeat in the center of each. Place the avocado slices and tomato wedges all around and serve at once.

Serves 4 or 5 as a first course and 3 as a main entrée

SHRIMP SEVICHE

Seviche de camarones

Seviche (also spelled sebiche, ceviche, and cebiche) is raw fish or shellfish that has been marinated for several hours in citrus juice, especially lime juice, until the acid in the juice "cooks" it, turning the flesh opaque, firm, tangy, and delicious. Shrimp, lobster, crayfish, octopus, squid, and clams made into a seviche must first be boiled and then may be marinated only for a short time, as the acid in the citrus juice breaks down their flesh.

Seviche originated in Peru and found its way to all corners of Latin America and the Caribbean colonized by the Spanish before reaching the United States, where it is prized among Latinos. Some of the world's finest seviches are prepared by Ecuadoran American cooks, who use the juice of Seville oranges (or a blend of sweet orange juice

and lime juice) as the basis for the marinade, as cooks do in Ecuador, rather than lemon or lime juice. While some Ecuadoran Americans serve seviche with the traditional accompaniment *maíz tostada,* corn nuts—large-kernel corn that is fried in lard and sprinkled with salt—for others the possibilities are endless.

As an appetizer or light main course, this Ecuadoran-style Shrimp Seviche is great with bruschetta or any crusty bread, or grilled polenta. Or serve it atop a mixed bed of leafy greens, such as arugula and lamb's lettuce, radicchio and frisee lettuce, or escarole and frisee; the shrimp marinade makes a delightful dressing. Shrimp Seviche is also marvelous with avocado, as Colombian Americans are apt to serve it, or with grilled vegetables, such as baby zucchini, artichokes, and Japanese eggplant, or the freshest steamed asparagus. For a more substantial main course, accompany Shrimp Seviche with tabbouleh or risotto or your favorite pasta salad or potato salad. Of course, Shrimp Seviche also stands on its own, especially as a cocktail party tidbit. Simply serve each shrimp on a small skewer.

2 dozen jumbo shrimp (about 1½ pounds), shelled and deveined, tail shells attached

1 cup sweet orange juice, freshly squeezed or from concentrate*

½ cup freshly squeezed lime juice*

¼ cup extra-virgin olive oil

Salt and freshly ground black pepper, to taste

1 medium ripe tomato, diced

½ cup minced red onion

1 tablespoon minced jalapeño chile, or to taste

3 tablespoons minced fresh cilantro, for garnish

* If Seville oranges are available, substitute 1½ cups Seville orange juice for the sweet orange juice and lime juice.

Bring 2 quarts water to a boil in a large saucepan. Add the shrimp and boil them over medium-high heat until they are bright pink, about 3 to 4 minutes. Drain the shrimp.

Mix thoroughly the orange juice, lime juice, olive oil, salt, and black pepper in a large stainless steel, glass, or ceramic bowl. Gently stir in the tomato, onion, and jalapeño. Add the shrimp and allow them to marinate, covered, in the refrigerator for at least 1 hour. Serve the Shrimp Seviche cold or at room temperature in individual decorative glass bowls with a garnish of minced fresh cilantro.

*Serves 8 to 10 as an hors d'oeuvre,
6 as an appetizer, and 4 as a main course*

PANAMA CANAL SEVICHE

Seviche del Canal de Panamá

I grew up in the Panama Canal Zone, where seviche, raw fish, or shellfish, marinated in citrus juice, is a way of life," says Jane Martin of Crawfordville, Florida. "My family partook of seviche at least once a week. When I was little, I would help my father make our favorite seviche—*seviche de corvina*. (Corvina, a fish related to striped bass, is found in the waters off most of Latin America.) After he meticulously boned and sliced the fish, he would let me help mix the citrus marinade and pour it over the fish. Then we would wait for what seemed like an eternity until the fish was opaque, which meant it had 'cooked' in the citrus juice. My father would arrange the pieces of fish in a beautiful pattern on a large serving platter and then decorate with parsley. He always placed a bottle of hot sauce on the table for those who liked their seviche hotter. Nowadays I make seviche often with striped bass or red snapper, and I garnish it with parsley as well as avocado slices, which afford a nice taste contrast to the firm, citrusy fish. I like to serve seviche on individual plates and with chopsticks. I usually serve it as a first course, but it is nice anytime with ice-cold beer."

I pound best-quality, fresh (not defrosted) striped bass fillets, or substitute another firm white-fleshed fish, such as red snapper, sole, or pompano, boned
¾ cup freshly squeezed lime juice
¼ cup freshly squeezed orange juice
I small ripe tomato, finely minced
I small yellow onion, peeled and finely minced
¼ cup finely minced green bell pepper
¼ teaspoon finely minced jalapeño chile, or to taste
I tablespoon finely minced fresh parsley
⅛ teaspoon each salt and freshly ground white pepper, or to taste
I ripe Hass avocado, halved, peeled, pitted, and thinly sliced
Sprigs of parsley, for garnish
Tabasco sauce, for serving (optional)

Rinse the fish fillets under cold running water. Lay them on a cutting board, one by one, and cut them into 1-inch pieces at a 45° angle with a sharp, nonserrated knife. Arrange the pieces of fish in a single layer, if possible, in a large shallow glass or ceramic baking dish.

Mix together the lime juice, orange juice, tomato, onion, bell pepper, jalapeño chile, parsley, and salt and white pepper in a medium bowl to make a marinade. Pour the marinade over the fish. Cover with plastic wrap and allow the fish to marinate in the refrigerator for about 3 hours, or until it is firm and opaque.

Arrange the pieces of fish on each of 4 large plates, and garnish with avocado slices and parsley sprigs. Serve at once with Tabasco sauce on the side and chopsticks, if desired.

Serves 4

OYSTERS HIMILCE

Ostras Himilce

One of my fondest childhood memories of Cuba is of Chinese Cuban vendors selling fresh oysters, plucked that morning from their beds in the Caribbean Sea, on the street corners of Old Havana. Every Thursday, after her morning business appointments, my mother would walk to Old Havana to buy me a dozen oysters. In the summer I would accompany her, but during the school year I would come home for lunch to find those oysters waiting for me on the half shell, garnished with a few lime wedges. I still love oysters, but nowadays I season them with a whole array of garnishes that I've picked up. —H.N.

It is best to serve the oysters without ice, since very cold temperatures merely numb their natural deep-sea taste.

FOR THE GARNISH:

3 tablespoons beluga caviar, or the caviar of your choice

3 tablespoons finely minced fresh lemongrass (cut away the leaves, wash the stalks, thinly slice crosswise, then mince)

3 tablespoons finely minced fresh chives

2 tablespoons whole pink peppercorns

1 lime or lemon, cut into wedges

26 fresh oysters live in the shell, Atlantic oysters such as Apalachicolas, Chincoteagues, Malpêques, or your favorite variety

Place the caviar, lemongrass, chives, and pink peppercorns in small individual serving bowls. Refrigerate the caviar, covered, but keep the rest of the garnishes at room temperature. Arrange the lime or lemon wedges on a small plate.

Shuck the oysters just before you plan to serve them. Hold one in a dish towel folded twice with the flat shell up and the hinge facing you. Carefully insert the tip of an oyster knife into the hinge, then twist the knife to open. Slide the oyster knife along the underside of the top shell to sever the muscle. Remove the top shell, taking care not to spill the liquid in the bottom oyster shell, and discard. Next slide the knife under the flesh to sever the small bottom muscle. Place the oyster on one of two large plates, again taking care not to spill the liquid. Repeat this process for each oyster until there are 13 oysters on each plate.

Arrange the bowls of garnishes with little spoons in each and the plate of lime or lemon wedges on the table, and serve the oysters on the half shell immediately. Allow each person to season the oysters with any combination of garnishes.

Serves 2

SWEET CLAMS ON THE HALF SHELL

Cocktail de almejas dulces en su ostra

Americans with roots in the Caribbean coastline of Colombia have a penchant for chilled seafood salads of either conch, lobster, shrimp, squid, octopus, or even freshly shucked oysters and clams. The seafood is first bathed in a choice of classic marinades that vary widely in their composition from a simple blend of oil, vinegar, and salt and pepper to more elaborate mixtures, like olive oil, tomato sauce, mayonnaise, coconut milk, and cumin, or in one of the countless *nuevo* marinades that mirror the vast range of flavors available in the United States.

One authentic marinade for seafood that Colombian Americans have preserved intact is composed of white wine, honey, and lemon juice. The lively sweet-sour taste of the marinade is a splendid counterpoint to the brine of plump, chilled cherrystone clams. While marinated seafood is traditionally served atop a bed of lettuce, many Colombian Americans return the clams to their half shells.

I cup sweet white wine, such as a
    Johannesberg Riesling or Muscat Canelli
2 tablespoons freshly squeezed lemon
    or lime juice

2 dozen cherrystone clams, or substitute
    Atlantic littleneck clams or any of
    the Atlantic (Eastern) varieties of
    oysters, live in the shell

Stir the wine and lemon or lime juice in a large mixing bowl until the ingredients are well blended. Set the marinade aside.

Shuck the clams: Holding a clam firmly, slide the blade of a clam knife between the shells. Move the blade toward the hinge until you can pry the clam open. Slide the blade under the clam to sever the muscle. Pour the clam and its liquid from the half shells into the marinade. Repeat this process for each clam and allow them to marinate for 5 minutes. Meanwhile, scrub the clam shells and pat them dry with paper towels.

Sweet Clams on the Half Shell (continued)

To serve, arrange a dozen empty half shells on a bed of ice, if you prefer, on each of 2 plates. Return the clams to the half shells and spoon 1 teaspoon marinade in each. Serve at once.

Serves 4 as a first course and 2 as a light meal

POTATO-CHEESE CAKES WITH PEANUT SAUCE AND AVOCADO

Llapingachos con salsa de maní

The Andes region of Ecuador, as far north as the capital city of Quito, once belonged to the vast Incan Empire. As early as 750 B.C. the Inca were cultivating on the temperate mountainsides of the Andes native varieties of potatoes in unexpected colors, such as blue, purple, and pink, and with unusual flavors and textures (see Sources, page 307). It was only in 1532, with the Spanish conquest of the Inca, that Europeans tasted potatoes for the first time. Many centuries after the demise of the Incan Empire, potatoes remain a mainstay in Ecuadoran highland cooking and find their way into countless dishes, such as *locro,* a creamy potato-and-cheese soup (see recipe on page 20), and *llapingachos,* luscious potato-and-cheese cakes, traditionally served with a sauce made of peanuts, another plant cultivated by the Inca.

Llapingachos are especially popular among America's approximately 191,000 people of Ecuadoran descent, since their traditional repertoire is somewhat limited due to the scarcity in the United States of the many other root vegetables native to the Andes, such as *oca,* which resembles a carrot with white flesh and with skin ranging in color from white to red; *yacón,* which tastes like jicama and is eaten raw or cooked, and *mashua,* which is reminiscent of hot radish when raw and mildly sweet potatoes when cooked (see Sources, page 307, for *yacón* and *mashua*). Ecuadoran Americans traditionally serve *llapingachos* as a main dish, sometimes with peanut sauce, as well as such adornments as fried eggs, sliced pork, sausage, rice, and fried sweet plantains, or as an appetizer with peanut sauce and avocado slices, and sometimes lettuce and tomato. We have discovered that children who love peanut butter find *llapingachos* irresistible.

FOR THE PEANUT SAUCE:

2 tablespoons olive oil

1 cup finely minced yellow onion

2 medium ripe tomatoes, coarsely
  chopped

¼ cup finely minced green bell pepper

1 cup chunky peanut butter, ground
  peanuts, or smooth peanut butter,
  if preferred

½ teaspoon salt, or to taste

¼ teaspoon freshly ground black pepper,
  or to taste

½ cup water

FOR THE POTATO-CHEESE CAKES:

2 pounds red-skinned (new) potatoes

Pinch of salt

1½ tablespoons butter

1 medium yellow onion, peeled and
  finely minced

1 cup grated Muenster cheese (about
  4 ounces), or 4 ounces cream cheese,
  cut into 12 pieces

Olive oil, for sautéing

FOR THE GARNISH:

1 medium ripe Hass avocado, halved,
  peeled, pitted, and sliced

3 tablespoons finely minced fresh
  cilantro

Prepare the peanut sauce: Heat the olive oil in a large skillet over medium-high heat. Sauté the minced onions until they are golden, about 5 minutes. Reduce the heat to medium, add the tomatoes and bell pepper, and cook, stirring occasionally, until the tomatoes break down, about 10 minutes. Stir in the peanut butter or ground peanuts, salt, and black pepper, then remove the skillet from the heat and add the water, a little at a time, to make a thick sauce. Test the sauce for seasoning and keep warm.

Prepare the potato-cheese cakes: Peel the potatoes and cut them into 1½-inch chunks. Put the potato chunks in a large saucepan with enough cold water to cover and a pinch of salt. Boil the potatoes until they are tender when pricked with a fork, about 20 minutes. Drain, transfer the potatoes to a large mixing bowl, and mash with a potato masher until smooth.

Melt the butter in a medium skillet over medium heat. Sauté the minced onions in the butter until they are golden brown, about 10 minutes. Remove the onions to a small mixing bowl.

Shape the mashed potatoes into 12 balls. Poke a hole in each ball and stuff it with sautéed onions and a heaping tablespoon grated Muenster cheese or 1 piece of cream cheese. Cover over the filling with potato and gently flatten each of the stuffed balls into patties approximately 3 inches in diameter.

Heat 1 tablespoon olive oil in a large nonstick skillet over medium-high heat. Sauté the potato cakes in batches of 3 or 4, turning them once, until they are golden brown

Potato-Cheese Cakes with Peanut Sauce and Avocado (continued)

on both sides, about 3 minutes per side. Transfer the potato cakes to a large plate lined with paper towels to drain. Add as much olive oil as needed throughout the sautéing process.

To assemble the dish, spoon the peanut sauce on each of 6 dinner plates to form pools of equal size. Place 2 potato cakes in the middle of each pool. Garnish the plates with avocado slices and minced cilantro and serve at once.

Serves 6 as an appetizer, side dish, or light lunch entrée

QUINOA | Quinoa (pronounced KEEN-wa), a grain native to the Andean region of South America, where it is known as *quinua,* was once a staple in the diet of the Inca, who called it "the mother grain." Nutritionists have proclaimed quinoa a supergrain, as it has fewer carbohydrates and more unsaturated fats than most grains, and it is the only one that is a complete protein. Uncooked quinoa takes the form of tiny ivory-colored beads that closely resemble millet. When cooked—just like rice but in half the time—the beads burst and expand to four times their size. Quinoa has a light texture and is rather bland, like most grains, and thus does not stand on its own. Americans with roots in the Andean region of South America, particularly of Bolivia, Ecuador, and Peru, have inherited a plethora of recipes for quinoa desserts, drinks, breads, salads, casseroles, and soups that enliven the grain.

QUINOA "TABBOULEH"

Salpicón de quinua

We have christened *Salpicón de quinua,* a salad of chewy, mild-tasting quinoa, sun-sweetened tomatoes, and crunchy cucumbers, Quinoa "Tabbouleh," as it bears a striking similarity to Middle Eastern tabbouleh, with the quinoa taking the place of bulgur wheat and hot chiles giving it a Peruvian accent. Traditional *Salpicón de quinua* has no garlic, but we like to add a little, as you would to tabbouleh.

Salpicón de quinua is commonly served on a bed of greens and adorned with a

whole array of garnishes, which may include wedges of hard-boiled eggs, little rounds of corn on the cob, capers, pitted black olives, and cubes of a zesty Peruvian cheese akin to feta. With all the cucumbers and herbs in the salad, we usually forgo the bed of greens and garnish with Bulgarian feta (it is creamier than Greek) and kalamata olives. Quinoa "Tabbouleh" is a complete meal with a crisp bread, like lavash or bruschetta, and a fruity white wine, but select any accompaniments that suit your fancy. A dessert of fresh tropical fruit slices and coconut custard pie or Three Milks Cake (see page 259) makes for a splendid finale.

2 cups quinoa*

4 cups water

¼ cup olive oil, preferably extra-virgin

3 tablespoons freshly squeezed lime or lemon juice

2 medium ripe tomatoes, diced

1 medium cucumber, peeled and diced

3 medium scallions, root ends trimmed, both white and green parts minced

1 large clove garlic, peeled and minced

1 serrano or jalapeño chile, seeded and finely minced, or to taste (optional)

¼ cup finely minced fresh Italian parsley or cilantro

¼ cup finely minced fresh dill or mint

Salt and freshly ground black pepper, to taste

1 cup Bulgarian or Greek feta cheese, crumbled or cubed, for garnish

½ cup kalamata olives, for garnish

*Quinoa is sold in some supermarkets and in most natural food stores.

Rinse the quinoa in a large bowl-strainer under cold running water, rubbing it with your fingertips until the water draining from the strainer runs clear. This will wash off any saponin, a naturally occurring soapy substance, that may adhere to the quinoa.

Bring the quinoa and the water to a boil in a medium saucepan over medium heat. Reduce the heat and simmer until the water has been absorbed and the grains are translucent, about 10 to 15 minutes.

Transfer the cooked quinoa to a large bowl, allow it to cool to room temperature, and then chill it, covered, in the refrigerator, for at least 1½ hours.

Mix together the olive oil and the lime or lemon juice in a small bowl. Stir the dressing into the quinoa. Add the tomatoes, cucumbers, scallions, garlic, serrano or jalapeño chile, parsley or cilantro, and dill or mint and toss gently. Taste and season with salt and black pepper, as needed. Spoon the quinoa salad on large plates, and garnish with feta cheese and kalamata olives or the garnish of your choice. Serve alone or with crisp bread, such as lavash or bruschetta.

Serves 6 to 8 as a first course and 4 as a main course

PINEAPPLE AND AVOCADO SALAD WITH CRISP WALNUTS

Ensalada de piña y aguacate con nueces fritas

This colorful and refreshing salad, an interpretation of a Cuban American classic, reflects tradition except for the embellishment of freshly shelled walnuts crisped in olive oil. It makes a fine accompaniment to grilled chicken or fish on a hot summer day. The quality of the pineapple is key, so make this salad only when the sweetest, juiciest fruit is available. Also prepare the salad close to serving time to preserve the integrity of the avocado, which browns when exposed to air for any length of time. As a variation, try garnishing with toasted shredded coconut or pine nuts instead of walnuts.

**2 cups fresh pineapple chunks
(¾-inch chunks)
1 tablespoon lime juice
3 tablespoons extra-virgin olive oil**

**1½ tablespoons granulated sugar
¼ cup walnuts, preferably freshly shelled,
for garnish
2 medium ripe Hass avocados**

Toss the pineapple chunks in a medium bowl with the lime juice, 2 tablespoons of the olive oil, and sugar. Taste and correct the seasoning. Cover and refrigerate for 1 hour.

Next heat the remaining tablespoon of olive oil in a small skillet over medium heat. Sauté the walnuts in the oil, turning them with a spatula, until they are crisp, about 4 minutes. Immediately remove the walnuts to a small bowl; they may burn if left in the skillet.

Cut the avocados in half lengthwise. Remove the pits and peel off the skin. Cut the avocado flesh lengthwise into thin slices and arrange the slices in a circular fashion on 4 dinner plates. Mound about ½ cup pineapple chunks, drained, in the center of each plate. Spoon the marinade left in the bowl over the avocado slices. Garnish the salad with the toasted walnuts and serve at once.

Serves 4

HEARTS OF PALM SALAD

Salada de palmito

Hearts of palm are the most voluptuous of foods. The tender pale ivory shoots, which bear an uncanny resemblance to white asparagus without the tips, are dear to the hearts of Brazilian Americans, who take advantage of their incredible versatility and flavor, and feature them as a complement to and centerpiece in soups, salads, stews, gratins, and turnovers. Hearts of Palm Salad is a Brazilian classic. Here is our version of it on a bed of arugula and radicchio, topped with Parmigiano-Reggiano shavings.

For the uninitiated, hearts of palm are the edible core of the stem of the young cabbage palm tree. In the United States, fresh hearts of palm are available only in Florida, home to the cabbage palm. Canned hearts of palm, packed in water, from either Florida or Brazil are sold in upscale markets and well-stocked supermarkets across the country. Whether fresh or canned, hearts of palm are on the expensive side, as the cabbage palm must be felled to reach the heart. Refrigerate opened hearts of palm in their own liquid in a nonmetal container for up to 1 week.

2 tablespoons freshly squeezed lime or
   lemon juice
4 teaspoons granulated sugar
½ teaspoon tamari sauce, or substitute
   soy sauce
Freshly ground black pepper, to taste
6 tablespoons extra-virgin olive oil
3 ounces radicchio, washed and dried

3 ounces arugula, washed, dried, and
   torn if the leaves are big
One 14-ounce can hearts of palm,
   drained and cut crosswise into
   1-inch rounds
¼ cup Parmigiano-Reggiano shavings, or
   another Parmesan cheese

Whisk together the lime or lemon juice, sugar, tamari sauce or soy sauce, and black pepper in a large salad bowl until the sugar dissolves. Gradually whisk in the olive oil to make a dressing.

Gently toss the radicchio and arugula in the dressing with your hands or a pair of salad servers. Arrange the greens on 4 large plates. Place several hearts-of-palm rounds in the center of each bed of greens. Garnish with the Parmigiano-Reggiano shavings and serve at once.

Serves 4

YUCA AND CABBAGE SLAW

Nuevo vigorón

Soft *yuca*, crunchy cabbage, and crisp bacon contrast marvelously in this dish, which derives its inspiration from *vigorón*, the most popular salad in Nicaraguan restaurants and homes across America. Authentic *vigorón*, which has a layer of tender *yuca* covered with cabbage in a citrus dressing, is garnished with *chicharrones*, pork rinds that have been twice deep-fried until they balloon into crispy, crunchy puffs. (*Chicharrones* come in many different sizes. We have seen entire glass cases filled with *chicharrones* three feet long or larger in Latin markets, inch-long little pork rinds packaged like potato chips, and every size in between.) Rather than layering the *yuca* and cabbage, we toss them together with a little fresh cilantro and top with diced avocado and crumbled bacon or *chicharrones* for *Nuevo vigorón*. (For a vegetarian version, this salad can be adorned with crumbled feta.)

Cooked *yuca* becomes somewhat dry and grainy when chilled (a little like cold french fries), so this dish should be prepared right before the meal and should not be refrigerated before serving. If you refrigerate any leftovers, bring to room temperature to restore the tenderness of the *yuca*. *Nuevo vigorón* is nice on its own or on the side with beef or pork.

1¼ pounds fresh **yuca**, peeled, cut into 1-inch chunks, and rinsed, or substitute frozen peeled **yuca** (see page 198 for information on **yuca** and page 189 for directions on peeling **yuca**)

¼ cup freshly squeezed lime or lemon juice, at room temperature

Pinch of salt

1 teaspoon granulated sugar

¼ cup extra-virgin olive oil

3 cups (about 10 ounces) firmly packed cabbage, sliced paper-thin, at room temperature

1 medium ripe tomato, cut into ¼-inch dice

2 tablespoons finely minced red or yellow onion

1 medium clove garlic, peeled and finely minced

2 tablespoons finely minced fresh cilantro

Freshly ground white pepper, to taste

1 medium ripe Hass avocado, cut in half, peeled, pitted, and cut into ½-inch dice (optional)

5 ounces **chicharrones**, broken into 1-inch pieces, or substitute 6 strips bacon, fried until crisp and crumbled

Put the *yuca* and enough cold water to cover in a large saucepan. Add ½ tablespoon of the lime or lemon juice and a pinch of salt. Cover and bring the *yuca* to a rolling boil, over medium-high heat, and then lower the heat and boil, still covered, until tender, about 25 minutes. Drain the *yuca*. Gently peel off any pinkish fibrous layers that may cling to the tuber and remove the fibrous core with a paring knife. Cut the *yuca* chunks into ½-inch dice.

Whisk together the remaining lime or lemon juice and the sugar in a large mixing bowl until the sugar dissolves. Whisk in the olive oil to make a dressing. Toss the *yuca*, cabbage, tomato, onion, garlic, and cilantro in the dressing to make a slaw. Add white pepper to taste.

To serve, divide the *Yuca* and Cabbage Slaw among 4 to 6 large plates. Garnish each with diced avocado and *chicharrones* or crumbled bacon, and serve at once.

Serves 6 as a first course or side dish and 4 as a light entrée

EGGPLANT CAVIAR

Caviar de berenjena

Meaty roasted eggplant, juicy red ripe tomatoes, aromatic onions and garlic, and lemon juice harmonize beautifully in eggplant caviar, one of the world's most popular eggplant tapenades or relishes. Of Georgian, Armenian, and Moldavian origin, this peasanty dish became a classic in the cuisines of Russia and Ukraine, where it is known as poor man's caviar, as well as in Latin America. Thanks to immigrants the world over who have brought this dish to our shores, there are as many subtle variations on eggplant caviar in America as there are cooks. With its cilantro, this version of the classic recipe is decidedly Latin.

Eggplant caviar is a refreshing summer condiment. Serve it as an hors d'oeuvre with thin slices of bread, such as Cuban Bread (see page 233), crostini, or pita-bread triangles, or as an accompaniment to grilled chicken, steak, or fish. Select only firm, glossy eggplants without blemishes or wrinkles, and allow the eggplant caviar to chill well, preferably overnight, to give the flavors time to marry.

2 eggplants (about 1 pound each)
2 tablespoons olive oil
1 medium yellow onion, peeled and
    finely minced
2 medium ripe tomatoes, minced
3 tablespoons tomato sauce

2 medium cloves garlic, peeled and finely
    minced
1 tablespoon freshly squeezed
    lemon juice
1½ tablespoons each finely minced
    fresh Italian parsley and cilantro
Salt and freshly ground black pepper,
    to taste

Eggplant Caviar (continued)

Prick the eggplants with a stainless steel fork, then roast them on a baking sheet on the middle rack of a preheated 375°F oven until the skins are wrinkled and charred in spots and the flesh is soft, about 1 hour. Allow the eggplants to cool enough to handle, then cut in half lengthwise, scoop out the pulp with a teaspoon, and finely chop. Put the chopped eggplant in a colander and press against it with a spoon or spatula to drain as much liquid as possible.

Heat the olive oil in a large skillet over medium heat and sauté the onions until they are golden brown, about 7 minutes. Stir in the eggplant, tomatoes, and tomato sauce, and continue to cook, stirring occasionally, for about 15 minutes, or until the tomatoes break down. Fold in the garlic and lemon juice, cover, and then remove from the heat. Allow the eggplant to sit, covered, for 10 minutes.

Stir in the parsley and cilantro, and season with salt and pepper to taste. Transfer the eggplant caviar to a serving bowl and chill in the refrigerator for at least 4 hours or overnight. Stir the eggplant caviar just before serving.

Serves 4 to 6 as an appetizer and 10 as an hors d'oeuvre

VENEZUELAN AMERICAN GUACAMOLE

Guasacaca

Venezuelan *Guasacaca*, a chile-laced creamy avocado sauce studded with minced tomato, sweet bell pepper, and onion, is reminiscent of Mexican guacamole, but it is enriched with extra-virgin olive oil. *Guasacaca* has countless uses as a marinade, spread, and relish in Venezuelan American cooking. In the traditional role of a marinade, it is slathered on chicken, beef, fish, and shellfish before grilling. As a spread, it typically accompanies *arepas,* those crusty corn cakes with a creamy center that are Venezuela's most beloved bread (see page 235). Americans of Venezuelan descent have discovered that *guasacaca* makes a marvelous substitute for mayonnaise or mustard on just about any sandwich, from BLTs and clubs to Reubens and hamburgers. We love the nutty, buttery spread in pita pockets stuffed with cubes of zesty goat's milk feta and tufts of alfalfa sprouts, and on sandwiches of rare roast beef or lamb and arugula between slices of pumpernickel. *Guasacaca* also works well as a dip for raw veg-

etables and as a dressing for a salad of mixed greens with toasted pine nuts and roasted garlic, or baby spinach with shavings of sharp Provolone.

Avocado flesh discolors rapidly once exposed to air, so be sure to prepare this dish just before serving (for more on avocados see page 23).

⅓ cup olive oil, preferably extra-virgin

1½ tablespoons red wine vinegar, or substitute freshly squeezed lime or lemon juice

2 medium ripe Hass avocados

1 medium ripe tomato, finely minced

¼ cup finely minced red or yellow bell pepper

2 tablespoons finely minced red onion

1 serrano or jalapeño chile, seeded and finely minced, or substitute ¼ teaspoon hot, medium, or mild ground dried red chile, or to taste (see the note on ground dried red chile on page 167)

Salt, to taste

Mix the olive oil and vinegar thoroughly in a medium mixing bowl to make a dressing.

Cut the avocados in half lengthwise, peel off the skin, then remove the pits. Cut the avocado flesh into chunks and fold into the dressing. Mash the avocados with a fork or potato masher until smooth.

Stir in the minced tomato, bell pepper, onion, and chile. Taste and add salt, if needed. Serve at once.

For Mexican American guacamole: Replace the olive oil and red wine vinegar dressing with 1½ teaspoons freshly squeezed lime or lemon juice. Omit the bell pepper and use only minced serrano or jalapeño chile (not ground dried red chile). Add 1 medium clove garlic, mashed into a paste, if desired.

FISH AND SHELLFISH—ALWAYS
FLAVORED WITH A VIBRANT
MARINADE OR SAUCE—MUST
DANCE THE MAMBO ON YOUR
TONGUE. BARE BROILED SCROD
IS ENTIRELY UNACCEPTABLE.

FISH AND
SHELLFISH

CRISTINA'S SHRIMP IN TOMATO-PIMIENTO SAUCE

Camarones enchilados Cristina

"**T**his is the dish I used to seduce my husband, Marcos Avila, a former musician and a founding member of Gloria Estefan's Miami Sound Machine," quips Cuban American Cristina Saralegui, or just Cristina, as she is known to her 100 million fans across Latino U.S.A., Latin America, and Europe, who tune in to her *El Show de Cristina,* the number one Spanish-language television talk show in the world, and her syndicated radio program *Cristina opina.* "Every weekend I prepared *Camarones enchilados,* Shrimp in Tomato-Pimiento Sauce, for Marcos, although occasionally I replaced the shrimp with lobster. After Marcos and I married, he said, 'Listen, we're married now. They're absolutely out of this world, but you don't have to cook those shrimp and lobster dishes anymore. I'll cook from now on.' Marcos, who also became my manager and producer, has done most of the cooking ever since. He is definitely Mr. Mom.

"What I like about *Camarones enchilados* is that it has little fat, but it is bursting with flavor. Performers eat differently from other people. They either have diverticulitis, like Celia Cruz, or they are afraid of getting fat, so they adapt their recipes. They go after low fat, low sugar, and high taste. For example, when we have dinner at Gloria Estefan's house, she cooks this marvelous *picadillo* (a Caribbean ground beef stew) with lean turkey instead of beef, and bananas. She cooks the bananas in the microwave without any oil, mashes them up, spoons them on a plate, and then heaps the turkey *picadillo* on top. She calls the dish *Tambor* ('Drum'). I have a similar banana dish. I combine ripe bananas, cloves, orange peel, and Equal, however much of each ingredient I like, and I microwave the mixture for 5 minutes. It is delicious! I call the dish Tempting Bananas or *Plátanos en tentación.*"

FOR THE SAUCE:

- 1 large green bell pepper, seeded, deribbed, and coarsely chopped
- 2 medium yellow onions, peeled and coarsely chopped
- 3 medium cloves garlic, peeled
- ½ cup coarsely chopped fresh parsley
- ½ cup bottled red pimientos, drained*
- 1 cup tomato sauce
- ½ cup tomato ketchup
- ½ cup dry white wine
- ½ tablespoon red wine vinegar
- 1 teaspoon Worcestershire sauce
- 1 teaspoon Mexican tomato salsa, mild, medium, or hot (your favorite brand or homemade)

FOR THE SHRIMP:

2 tablespoons olive oil (Cristina prefers
   light olive oil)
2 pounds medium or large shrimp,
   rinsed, peeled, and deveined

I bay leaf
3 teaspoons minced fresh parsley,
   for garnish

Pimientos packed in jars are sold in supermarkets.

Prepare the sauce: Purée all of the sauce ingredients in an electric blender or food processor until smooth. Taste the sauce and correct the seasoning.

Heat the olive oil in a large nonstick pot over medium heat. Sauté the shrimp, stirring frequently, until they turn pink, about 4 minutes. Remove the shrimp and their juices from the pot to a plate.

Add the sauce and the bay leaf to the pot, bring to a slow boil, then reduce the heat, cover, and simmer, stirring occasionally, for 25 minutes. Remove the sauce from the heat and stir in the shrimp and their juices. Continue cooking the sauce just until it is hot enough to serve. Discard the bay leaf. Serve the shrimp and sauce at once with steamed white rice and, if desired, Cristina's Tempting Bananas. Garnish each plate with the parsley.

Serves 6

SHRIMP STEW WITH COCONUT MILK, LEMON, AND CILANTRO

Moqueca de camarão

"Brazil's cuisine can be as subtly seductive as a bossa nova ballad or as irresistible as a feverish *Carnaval* anthem," notes Brazilian American Jayme Vasconcellos. "From tangy sausages and slab barbecue meats of the *gaucho* south, to savory pastries complementing pork and black bean stews of the middle states, to fiery palm oil and pepper-laced seafood dishes of Bahia, to Amazonian native dishes such as wild duck soup and tortoise stew—this continental giant's table promises originality and adventure." Jayme Vasconcellos should know. He spent a good deal of his life in Brazil with his Brazilian father and American mother. With America now his permanent home, Jayme runs Centro Latino Americano in Eugene, Oregon, the largest and old-

Shrimp Stew with Coconut Milk, Lemon, and Cilantro (continued)

Improvisation is a key ingredient in Jayme Vasconcellos's Brazilian American cooking.

est Latino social service agency in the state.

Jayme Vasconcellos has never forgotten the food of his past: "When the first aroma of *dendê* oil (a reddish orange oil extracted from the fruit of the African palm) strikes in my kitchen, the walls dissolve. I am in Salvador, that most beautiful and sad Brazilian city, with its extraordinary music, architecture, food. . . . Now I am surrounded by friends at an Ipanema beachside restaurant, a towel around my wet bathing suit, sipping an icy *cachaça* cocktail, stirring passionate discourse over a dismal national soccer team—and I am poised to consume the *moqueca* before me."

Moquecas are fragrant seafood stews that developed at the crossroads of indigenous, Portuguese, and African cultures in the Brazilian state of Bahia. Jayme Vasconcellos's recipe for *Moqueca de camarão,* a *moqueca* with shrimp, "represents equal parts remembrance, practicality, and improvisation." Improvisation is the key. While basic ingredients for the dish, such as cilantro and coconut milk, are widely available in the United States—thanks to the popularity of Mexican and Southwestern cooking and Southeast Asian cuisines, such as Thai—other integral ingredients in *moquecas,* and in Bahian cooking in general, are unavailable or hard to find. Vasconcellos advises making substitutions. For instance, if you do not have access to Brazilian markets that carry *dendê* oil, he suggests substituting olive oil or peanut oil, even though the flavors are dramatically different.

Jayme Vasconcellos typically serves *Moqueca de camarão* over aromatic basmati rice, with a salad, sliced avocado, and tender steamed asparagus or string beans. For those who like their *moqueca* a little hotter, as Brazilian Americans are apt to, he provides a little dish of spicy *môlho de pimenta e azeite de dendê* (malagueta chile peppers steeped in *dendê* oil), or *Môlho de pimenta e limão* (Malagueta Chile and Lime Salsa, see page 27).

2 cups water

1 pound medium shrimp, shelled and deveined, shells reserved

4 tablespoons Brazilian *dendê* oil, olive oil, peanut oil, or Polynesian palm oil (see Sources, page 307)

1 medium yellow onion, peeled and finely chopped

1 large clove garlic, peeled and minced

2 medium ripe tomatoes, diced

1 cup canned unsweetened coconut milk

½ teaspoon salt, or to taste

Freshly ground black pepper, to taste

2 tablespoons finely minced fresh cilantro

Juice of 1 medium lemon

Bring the water and the reserved shrimp shells to a boil in a medium heavy-bottomed saucepan, covered, over medium-high heat. Remove the lid and boil to reduce the liquid to 1 cup, about 20 minutes.

Meanwhile, heat the *dendê,* olive, peanut, or palm oil in a large skillet over medium heat and sauté the chopped onions until they are translucent, about 4 minutes. Stir in the garlic and then the tomatoes, and cook, stirring occasionally, until the tomatoes break down and the mixture thickens into a paste, about 10 minutes.

Pour the 1 cup shrimp stock and the coconut milk into the skillet with the tomato-onion-garlic paste. Add the salt, black pepper, and 1 tablespoon of the cilantro. Cook the sauce over medium heat until it is a little thicker than a cream soup, about 10 minutes.

While the sauce thickens, marinate the shrimp in the lemon juice. Add the shrimp with its lemon juice marinade to the sauce and cook until the shrimp turn pink, about another 5 minutes. Remove the *moqueca* to a serving bowl, sprinkle the remaining tablespoon of cilantro over the top, and serve at once.

Serves 4

SHRIMP AND ARTICHOKE HEART FRITTATA

Cuajado de camarones y corazones de alcachofa

Enrique Sandino, an independent film and television producer and director in Hollywood, has been experimenting in the kitchen ever since he left his native Colombia as a youth to study dance in London. To support himself, he worked as an au pair boy and was responsible for cooking his own meals between shifts. He frequently made traditional *cuajados,* a simple-to-prepare yet elegant Colombian skillet dish of eggs paired with either fruit, meat, or seafood that resembles a frittata, a thick, open-faced omelet. Now in Los Angeles he prepares more elaborate *cuajados,* employing unconventional ingredients and techniques. In this recipe Enrique revolutionizes the *cuajado de camarones* (shrimp frittata), by incorporating tender, meaty artichoke hearts and cooking with his own culinary creation, Sandino's Olive Oil with Garlic and Love, which he bottles for family and friends. (This recipe calls for olive oil and minced garlic instead.) And rather than boiling the potatoes that go into the dish beforehand, as is the usual practice, he sautés them in the skillet with the onions to intensify their earthy flavor and preserve their shape.

Enrique Sandino's Shrimp and Artichoke Heart Frittata is ideal for brunch, with glasses of freshly squeezed orange juice, a fresh fruit salad, and a basket piled high with lemon–poppy seed or banana nut muffins.

I tablespoon butter
I tablespoon olive oil
½ pound small waxy potatoes, such as red-skinned (new), rose fir, or German fingerling, peeled and cut into ¼-inch dice
I medium yellow onion, peeled and minced
2 large cloves garlic, peeled and minced

¾ pound Roma (plum) tomatoes, diced
Salt and freshly ground black pepper, to taste
4 large eggs
I pound small or medium shrimp, peeled and deveined
One 6½-ounce jar quartered marinated artichokes, drained and cut into ¼-inch pieces* (optional)

Available in most supermarkets.

Heat the butter and olive oil in a large nonstick skillet over medium heat. Sauté the potatoes, minced onions, and garlic, stirring occasionally, until the potatoes are tender and light brown, about 15 minutes. Add the tomatoes, and salt and pepper, and cook, stirring occasionally, until the tomatoes are quite soft, about 10 minutes.

Meanwhile, separate the eggs into 2 large mixing bowls. Beat the egg yolks with a spoon until they are well blended. Beat the egg whites with an electric mixer until stiff (do not overbeat). Fold one third of the egg whites into the egg yolks, and then stir in the remaining whites.

Add the shrimp and artichoke hearts to the skillet and cook, stirring frequently, until the shrimp are bright pink, about 4 minutes. Pour the eggs into the skillet, mix gently, and cook for about 5 minutes. Cover the skillet, remove it from the heat, and allow the eggs to set completely, about 5 minutes. Serve the *cuajado* warm or at room temperature right from the skillet, as it will be too loosely bound to transfer to a serving dish in one piece like a frittata.

Serves 4

TENDER CACTUS IN RED CHILE SAUCE WITH SHRIMP PATTIES

Nopalitos tiernos en chile rojo con tortas de camarón

"The *nopalito* symbolizes the desert. It thrives in the desert and so do I," notes Lupe Rulfo, a Mexican American with Papago Indian blood, whose family has inhabited the Papago ancestral lands of southern Arizona and the borderlands of Sonora, Mexico, for untold generations. "*Nopalitos* appear in spring," says Lupe. "Spring means Lent in the Catholic Church, and so we associate *nopalito* dishes like *Nopalitos tiernos en chile rojo con tortas de camarón*—shrimp patties in a red chile sauce studded with little strips of tender cactus—with Lent. These dishes also remind us how important the *nopal* cactus was to the Papago, who fermented the juice of the cactus fruit and then drank their fill of the cactus liquor during the rainmaking ceremony so that the earth might drink its fill of rain."

While she was growing up on the outskirts of Phoenix, Lupe learned from her Tía Rosa how to prepare *nopalitos tiernos,* a dish that has been cooked in the Americas for many hundreds and perhaps thousands of years. In the spring, they would drive to the open desert to cut *nopalitos,* the tender new cactus paddles of the *nopal* cactus,

Tender Cactus in Red Chile Sauce with Shrimp Patties (continued)

that would go into the sauce. "At home," says Lupe, "I would mix the batter for the golden, airy shrimp patties, which even today, despite the availability of fresh shrimp in supermarkets, are made with dried shrimp, just like in the old days. Tía Rosa would scrape the spines off the *nopalitos,* boil them, and then stir them into a fragrant red chile sauce that bubbled on the stove. Then she would assemble the dish on plates, floating the shrimp patties in the sauce. And after just one heavenly bite, Tía Rosa would speak animatedly about our next expedition to the desert for *nopalitos.*"

FOR THE RED CHILE SAUCE:

¼ cup olive oil

1 large yellow or white onion, peeled and finely minced

5 medium cloves garlic, peeled and finely minced

½ cup ground dried red chile, mild, medium, or hot (see the note on ground dried red chile on page 167)

1 cup cold water

¾ cup fresh *nopalitos,* cut into ¼-inch strips and boiled for 15 minutes, or substitute canned or bottled *nopalitos,* cut in strips (*nopalitos tiernos en rajas*), rinsed, and drained (see page 75 for information on *nopalitos*)

FOR THE SHRIMP PATTIES:

4 large eggs

½ cup ground dried shrimp*

Vegetable oil, for frying

Available in Mexican markets and in Chinese and Southeast Asian markets.

Prepare the red chile sauce: Heat the olive oil in a large skillet over medium heat. Sauté the minced onions and garlic in the oil until they are golden, about 8 to 10 minutes. Add the ground red chile, stirring constantly, for about 1 minute. Take care not to inhale the vapors from the chile. Stir in the water to make a sauce, then reduce the heat to medium-low. Next fold in the *nopalitos* and cook the sauce, stirring once or twice, for 5 minutes. Do not add salt to the sauce, since the shrimp patties are somewhat salty. Cover and keep the sauce warm.

Prepare the shrimp patties: Separate the eggs by putting the yolks in a little dish and the whites in a large mixing bowl. Beat the egg whites with an electric mixer until they are stiff. Continue to beat the stiffened egg whites as you add the ground

Nopalitos, the young paddles of the *nopal* (prickly-pear) cactus, are the pivotal ingredient in many Mexican American dishes.

NOPALES AND NOPALITOS

Nopales are the mature oval paddles that grow on the prickly-pear cactus, also known as the *nopal* cactus, and are best ignored by the cook. On the other hand, the cactus's young bright green paddles, known as *nopalitos,* have a refreshing, mild flavor reminiscent of string beans and asparagus with a touch of tartness and are marvelous alone, in salads, or integrated into a dish. In the spring, when the *nopalitos* are the tenderest, many Mexican Americans in southern California, Texas, and the Southwest cut their own *nopalitos* with a sharp knife from the *nopal* cactus that proliferate along the roadside. (They always wear gloves so that the small prickly spines do not become imbedded in their skin, and you should, too.) Back in the kitchen, they carefully scrape the spines off the *nopalitos* with a knife or vegetable peeler, taking care to preserve the skin, and then they rinse the paddles to remove the finer spines.

Nopalitos may be eaten raw, but they are most commonly cut into strips ¼ inch wide and then boiled until tender, about 15 minutes. (They are also tasty steamed, sautéed, roasted, or grilled.) Like okra, boiled *nopalitos* exude a slimy fluid, called *baba* in Spanish. The solution is to boil the *nopalitos* with a raw onion or two cloves garlic, which absorb the *baba.* Store uncooked *nopalitos* wrapped in plastic in the refrigerator for no longer than a week. Canned or bottled *nopalitos* cut in strips (*nopalitos tiernos en rajas*), packed in water or brine, sometimes with a jalapeño chile and sliced onions and garlic, may be substituted for fresh ones, although they taste different. Once opened, canned *nopalitos* and their liquid should be transferred to a glass or plastic container and stored in the refrigerator. *Nopalitos* packed in brine will keep indefinitely, while those packed in water will stay fresh for up to 1 week. Fresh *nopalitos* (available only in spring) and canned and bottled *nopalitos* cut in strips are sold in Mexican markets and in select supermarkets primarily in California, Texas, and the Southwest, and other regions of the United States with sizable Mexican American communities.

shrimp and then the egg yolks to make a batter. Beat only until all the ingredients are blended.

Heat ½ inch of vegetable oil in a small skillet over medium heat to approximately 400°F. Ladle ⅓ cup batter into the skillet. It should float and begin to sizzle immediately. Fry the shrimp patty, turning once with a spatula, until golden, about 1 minute per side. Remove the patty with a slotted spoon to a large plate lined with paper towels and drain. Repeat the procedure until all the batter is used. This makes about 9 or 10 patties.

To serve, pour the red chile sauce with the *nopalitos* on each of 4 plates to make a pool. Place 2 shrimp patties in the center of each pool. Serve at once with rice and beans and warmed flour or corn tortillas, if desired.

Serves 4 to 5

SEA BASS BAKED IN BEER

Peixe assado com cerveja

Brazilian Americans, especially those of the first generation, like to cook with whole fish as much as fillets. First the fish is usually steeped in one of an array of marinades that all have wine or beer as a pivotal ingredient, and then it is baked in the same marinade until tender. In this recipe for whole sea bass marinated and then baked in beer and lemon juice, we like to cook with an imported Brazilian beer, like Brahma Beer, a pilsner, or Xingu Black Beer, which is similar to a German Schwarzbier. Each beer imparts a unique flavor to the fish, so feel free to experiment with your favorite ones for this dish. We like to accompany Sea Bass Baked in Beer with steamed white rice and a robust romaine lettuce salad with warm goat cheese.

1 large or 2 medium sea bass (4 to 5 pounds in all), or substitute red snapper, gutted and scaled, head and tail intact	½ cup finely minced fresh parsley
	1 tablespoon olive oil
	1 serrano or jalapeño chile, seeded and finely minced, or to taste
1 medium yellow onion, peeled and minced	2 large cloves garlic, peeled and minced
¾ cup beer, your favorite brand	¼ teaspoon salt, or to taste
½ cup freshly squeezed lemon or lime juice	3 tablespoons butter

Place the fish on a work surface and make 6 diagonal slits on the top all the way to the bone.

Prepare a marinade by mixing together the minced onions, beer, lemon or lime juice, parsley, olive oil, chile, garlic, and salt in a baking dish just large enough to accommodate the fish. Put the fish in the marinade, cover, and marinate it in the refrigerator for 2 hours, turning occasionally.

Remove the fish from the marinade, dry with paper towels, and rub the outside with 1 tablespoon of the butter. Pour the marinade into a bowl. Rinse and dry the baking dish and rub it with the remaining 2 tablespoons of butter. Put the fish in the baking dish and pour the marinade over it. Bake the fish, uncovered, in a preheated 400°F oven, basting frequently, until the flesh is opaque to the bone (make an incision to check) and the dorsal fin comes off easily when pulled, about 20 to 30 minutes, depending on the size of the fish. Do not overcook.

Transfer the fish to a large serving platter and remove the skin from the top with a knife and your fingers. Pour the liquid from the baking dish over the fish and serve at once with steamed white rice.

Serves 6

DOG SAUCE

Salsa de perro

"**S**alsa de perro, literally 'Dog Sauce,' is a meaty fish stew from Cuba that is best known in my hometown of Caibarién, on the north shore of Villaclara Province. The fish, ideally grouper, is simmered in a full-bodied fish stock enhanced by a little white wine. Classic Mediterranean elements, like onion, garlic, and pepper, intensify the flavors of the stew, and potatoes make it hearty," says Cuban American playwright and poet Dolores Prida, some of whose works may be found in *Beautiful Señoritas and Other Plays* (1991). According to Dolores Prida, theories abound as to the origin of the name of this delicious dish. "Some say it comes from a type of fish formerly known as the *perro*. Others insist that the name was borrowed from the French Caribbean, where a chilled spicy condiment known as *Sauce chien* (Dog Sauce) accompanies poultry and fish."

Dolores Prida's eyes light up as she remembers her mother's *Salsa de perro*: "This was my mother Lola's favorite dish from back home, and she made it the best. She insisted that grouper (*mero* or *cherna* in Spanish) was the only fish to use in *Salsa de perro* because of its delicate flavor and rather firm flesh that stays intact in the stew pot. I agree, but unfortunately, grouper is not available consistently in fish markets in New York City, as it is in southern Florida and the Caribbean. Nowadays my sister Lourdes, my aunt Sylvia, and I substitute halibut, sea bass, or any other firm-fleshed fish if we can't find grouper."

FOR THE STOCK:

1 pound fresh fish heads and bones
1 large russet (Idaho) potato, peeled
1 medium yellow onion, peeled
1 medium green bell pepper

4 large cloves garlic, peeled
1 bay leaf
5 cups water

Dog Sauce (continued)

FOR THE STEW:

1 whole grouper (4 pounds), or substitute halibut, sea bass, or another firm-fleshed fish, gutted, skin and gills removed, and cut into 1-inch steaks, or 2 pounds grouper, red snapper, yellowtail snapper steaks or fillets, skinned

Salt and freshly ground black pepper, to taste

½ teaspoon ground cumin, or to taste

¼ cup olive oil

1 medium yellow onion, peeled and cut into ¼-inch slices

1 medium green bell pepper, seeded, deribbed, and cut into ¼-inch rings

4 large cloves garlic, peeled and mashed

2 medium leeks, root ends removed, halved lengthwise, rinsed thoroughly, and cut into ¾-inch slices

2 large russet (Idaho) potatoes (about 1¼ pounds), peeled and cut into ¼-inch slices

1 cup dry white wine

¼ cup finely minced fresh cilantro, for garnish

3 limes, cut into wedges, for garnish

Make a fish stock: Bring the fish heads and bones, the whole potato, the whole onion, the whole bell pepper, the 4 whole garlic cloves, the bay leaf, and the water to a boil in a large pot over medium-high heat. Reduce the heat and simmer the stock for 30 minutes. Remove the potato and mash it in a small bowl with a potato masher to make a purée that will add body to the stew. Strain the fish stock through a medium-mesh strainer. Discard the fish heads and bones, onion, bell pepper, garlic, and bay leaf.

Remove any pinbones from the fish steaks or fillets with tweezers, pincers, or needlenose pliers, and any backbones from the fish steaks with a small sharp knife. Season the fish with salt, black pepper, and cumin.

Layer the ingredients for the stew in a large pot in the following order: olive oil, onion slices, bell pepper rings, mashed garlic, leek slices, reserved potato purée, potato slices, and fish.

Cook the stew, covered, over medium heat for about 8 minutes so that the onions on the bottom are sautéed in the olive oil. Add the fish stock and white wine. The liquid should rise to the top of the fish. If it does not, add water until the liquid reaches the correct level.

Cover, bring the stew to a boil, then reduce the heat and continue cooking for 35 minutes, or until the potatoes are tender. Agitate the pot occasionally so that the ingredients do not stick to the bottom, but do not stir them. Reaching down to the bottom of the pot, ladle the stew into bowls. Garnish each with cilantro and lime wedges, and serve at once.

Serves 6

GOLDEN RED SNAPPER WITH COCONUT-LIME SAUCE

Pargo dorado con salsa de coco y lima

Golden fish fillets in a voluptuous coconut sauce spiked with lime is a classic dish that is revered in the Caribbean, Venezuela, Brazil, and Honduras. This traditional recipe for Golden Red Snapper with Coconut-Lime Sauce, from the Dominican American culinary repertoire, shows just how good a marriage of fish and coconut milk can be. The light-textured snapper is first steeped in a tangy *adobo,* a marinade of lime juice, garlic, and spices, then dusted with flour and sautéed in a little olive oil until crisp. The smooth, rich coconut-lime sauce acts as a marvelous counterpoint to the snapper. This dish is traditionally served with fluffy white rice and fragrant Fried Ripe Plantains (see page 182). An uncomplicated salad of mixed greens to start and fresh tropical fruit or Mango Sorbet (see page 278) for dessert round out the meal nicely. A pitcher of fresh limeade or Jamaican Red Stripe Lager is a wonderful companion to this dish.

FOR THE ADOBO:

¼ cup freshly squeezed lime juice

2 large cloves garlic, peeled and crushed

½ teaspoon dried powdered oregano
(not crumbled)

¼ teaspoon each salt and freshly ground
black pepper

FOR THE SNAPPER:

1½ pounds fresh skinless red snapper
fillets, or any other lean white
fish fillets such as sole, cut into 8
equal pieces

½ cup unbleached all-purpose flour

Olive oil, for sautéing

FOR THE COCONUT-LIME SAUCE:

1 small yellow onion, peeled and
finely minced

1 medium clove garlic, peeled and finely
minced

1 jalapeño or serrano chile, seeded
and diced, or to taste
(optional)

1 tablespoon olive oil

½ tablespoon light rum

One 14-ounce can unsweetened
coconut milk

1½ tablespoons tomato paste

1 bay leaf

¼ teaspoon salt, or to taste

1 tablespoon freshly squeezed lime juice

Fresh sprigs of parsley, for garnish

Mix together all the ingredients for the marinade in a large shallow glass baking dish. Arrange the snapper or other white fish fillets in the baking dish, cover with plastic wrap, and marinate in the refrigerator, turning once, for 1 hour, but no longer.

Meanwhile, make the coconut-lime sauce by sautéing the minced onions, garlic, and chile in the olive oil over medium heat until the onions are just golden, about 4 minutes. Pour in the rum and cook the vegetables for another minute. Add the coconut milk, tomato paste, bay leaf, and salt, and blend well. Reduce the heat to low and cook the sauce for 5 minutes. Add the lime juice, stir for 30 seconds, and then remove the sauce from the heat and keep warm.

Spread the ½ cup flour on waxed paper. Pat the snapper fillets dry with paper towels, and then coat each well in flour on both sides. Shake off the excess flour. Coat the bottom of a large skillet lightly with olive oil. Heat the olive oil over medium heat and sauté 3 or 4 snapper fillets at a time in a single layer, turning once, until golden brown, about 2½ minutes per side (1 minute longer for thicker fillets). Remove the fillets with a slotted spatula to a plate covered with paper towels and drain. Add more olive oil to the skillet as necessary during the sautéing.

To assemble the dish, pour an equal amount of coconut-lime sauce on each of 4 dinner plates. Arrange 2 snapper fillets on top of the sauce on each plate. Garnish each dish with a sprig of parsley and serve at once with steamed white rice and Little Havana Fried Ripe Plantains.

Serves 4

GOLDEN FRIED SMELTS

Pesca'itos fritos

"**M**y great-grandmother, Olympia Rosa Rodrigues, who hailed from Andalusia, was the ultimate Spanish matriarch—stern, tough, great as a mentor, fierce as an enemy," says Toni Flores, professor of Women's Studies and American Studies at Hobart and William Smith Colleges in Geneva, New York. "She ruled over my family in Brooklyn with an iron fist, running our boardinghouse for new immigrants and even helping them get jobs and wives. She was also a marvelous cook. I remember her, back erect, standing over the stove making a fragrant *potaje* of lamb and lima beans or a marvelous Cuban *picadillo,* a ground beef stew, which she learned from her dear Cuban sister-in-law Luga. Olympia loved to cook the most famous fish dish of Andalusia, Spain, *Pesca'itos fritos,* little golden fried smelts. She stuffed little smelts with a filling of bread crumbs and seasonings, and then fried them in olive oil until they turned as golden as her Andalusian earrings. The fish were always crisp and light, never oily, thanks to the olive oil. As Luga advised, she would garnish the little golden fried smelts the Caribbean way, with wedges of lime or lemon. She often served them as an appetizer or snack along with Luga's Fried Ripe Plantains (*Plátanos maduros fritos,* see page 182)."

This recipe is somewhat time-consuming, since each fish must be stuffed, but it is well worth the effort. Smelts are a little fish (they average 3 to 7 inches in length) and are always cooked with bones intact. We choose the littlest ones, since their bones disintegrate during frying, so you can eat them whole. (The larger ones

Toni Flores with her youngest sons, John and Anthony

must be boned after cooking.) Like her great-grandmother, Toni Flores fries the smelts with their heads attached, but you can remove them, if you wish. Note that olive oil has a low smoke point, and thus it cannot be heated to as high a temperature for frying as other oils, like corn, safflower, and peanut oil. Maintain a temperature of 260°F to 275°F for best results. We find that it is easiest to maneuver the little *pesca'itos* in the skillet with a pair of chopsticks.

1 ½ pounds small (about 3 inches in length) fresh or flash-frozen smelts, cleaned and heads removed or intact, depending on preference*

1 ½ cups bread crumbs

2 tablespoons hard cheese, such as Manchego, Parmesan, or Pecorino Romano, grated

¼ teaspoon salt, or to taste

Pinch of freshly ground black pepper, or to taste

2 large eggs, beaten

¼ cup olive oil, plus extra for frying

1 large clove garlic, peeled and finely minced

2 tablespoons finely minced fresh parsley

Lemon or lime wedges, for garnish

Smelt season runs from September to May. Since the fish are extremely perishable, they are flash-frozen.

Place the smelts in a colander and rinse them gently under cool running water. Allow them to drain while you make the stuffing.

Mix the bread crumbs, cheese, salt, and black pepper thoroughly in a medium bowl. Add the eggs, ¼ cup olive oil, garlic, and parsley to the dry ingredients and blend well with a spoon. The stuffing should appear crumbly, but when a little is pressed between your fingers, it should hold together. If it is too dry, add more olive oil, a teaspoon at a time.

Stuff the cavity of each smelt with about ¼ to ½ teaspoon stuffing, depending on the size of the fish. Squeeze the sides of the fish gently so that they both stick to the stuffing. Pat the smelts dry with paper towels and arrange them on a large plate.

Heat ¼ inch olive oil in a large heavy skillet over medium-high heat to 275°F. Pan-fry the smelts in batches of 12, turning them once with chopsticks or a fork until they are golden, about 3 minutes per side. Transfer the fried smelts with the chopsticks or a slotted spoon to paper towels to drain. Keep them warm in a 200°F oven until all the batches are fried. Serve the fried smelts at once, garnished with lemon or lime wedges and with Fried Ripe Plantains, if desired.

Serves 6 to 8 as a first course

FISH FLAN

Pudín de pescado

"Fish Flan is a gorgeous savory custard with delicate, finely flaked snapper throughout," says Ivette Sanchez, a student at Baylor University in Waco, Texas. "It was one of the specialties of my grandmother, Teresa Castillo de Sanchez, who was born in Matanzas, Cuba, and later settled in Miami, Florida. Her favorite things in all the world were cooking elegant and exotic Cuban dishes like Fish Flan, for my grandfather, José Angel Sanchez, and the family, reading the Bible, and entertaining friends. She always had marvelous dishes cooking on the stove for them, and she graciously shared her recipes. Starting at age six, I was constantly under my grandmother's wing in the kitchen, learning the basics and then the intricacies of Cuban cuisine. We made many, many flans together, fish flans, asparagus flans, vanilla flans, coconut flans, pineapple flans, chocolate flans, and she always insisted that they be made from scratch. Her motto was, Patience is a virtue no cook can do without when making flan or anything else."

Fish Flan has the moistness and gentle flavor of salmon mousse, but it is a bit denser, as it has a greater eggs-to-milk ratio and no cream. While it is traditionally served chilled, with a thin coating of mayonnaise, Fish Flan is also delicious warm. It makes an impressive first course or a light lunch with black bread or lavash and glasses of sauvignon blanc.

I pound skinless red snapper, sole, or sea bass fillets, or any lean white fish fillets
I small yellow onion, quartered
I laurel leaf
5 large eggs
1½ cups milk
5 ounces (about 6 regular slices) white bread, cut into I-inch cubes
2 tablespoons butter, melted, plus extra for greasing the dish
2 tablespoons chopped fresh parsley or dried parsley
⅛ teaspoon salt
Mayonnaise, for garnish

Put the fish fillets in one layer with the onion and laurel leaf in a large skillet with enough water to cover, and bring to a gentle simmer over medium-high heat. Reduce the heat and cook the fish, taking care that it does not boil, until it flakes when pierced with a fork, about 10 minutes.

Discard the laurel leaf and drain the fish in a colander, reserving the onion quarters and setting aside the fish stock for another use. Transfer the fish to a large mixing bowl, extract any bones, finely flake with a fork, and allow it to cool to room temperature.

Beat the eggs in a food processor or electric blender. Add the reserved onion quarters, the milk, bread, melted butter, parsley, and salt, and process until smooth. Pour the mixture into the large bowl with the fish and stir well.

Line the bottom of a 1½-quart soufflé dish or another ovenproof baking dish with straight sides with a waxed-paper circle cut to the diameter of the dish. (This will prevent the bottom of the flan from sticking.) Generously butter the sides of the soufflé dish and the waxed-paper bottom. Pour the fish mixture into the prepared soufflé dish and place in a bain-marie—any shallow pan large enough to hold the dish with room to spare and filled with 1 inch of hot water. Bake the flan in a preheated 325°F oven for 1 hour and 10 minutes, or until the top is light golden and a knife inserted off-center comes out clean.

Remove the flan from the oven and carefully lift it out of the bain-marie. Allow it to cool for 5 minutes. Unmold the flan by first running a sharp, nonserrated knife along the inside of the soufflé dish to loosen. Invert onto a large plate and peel off the waxed-paper circle. Gently invert again onto a serving platter so that the golden side of the flan is displayed. Serve warm, at room temperature, or chilled, cut into wedges. Before slicing, spread a thin layer of mayonnaise on top with a rubber spatula, if desired. Or serve with mayonnaise on the side.

Serves 8 as a first course and 6 as a light entrée

COLOMBIAN SEAFOOD STEW AMERICAN-STYLE

Cazuela de mariscos colombiano-americana

We experienced Colombian *Cazuela de mariscos,* a delectable bouillabaisselike stew with an abundance of lobster, shrimp, calamari, fish, and clams, for the first time at a lavish birthday dinner party at a Colombian American home in Miami. In the spirit of the great American mosaic, a perfectly Colombian *cazuela* was preceded by a classic Caesar salad and then accompanied by heaping plates of crusty garlic bread and a sauvignon blanc or a California Central Coast chardonnay. A lovely Bosc pear tart and all-American apple pie with homemade vanilla-bean ice cream ended this memorable dinner.

Cazuela de mariscos is a lovely dish for small dinner parties and other festive occasions. It looks dramatic, and the flavor is marvelous. For variation, we sometimes prepare this stew with mussels instead of clams, and sea bass or halibut instead of snapper. If you cannot find a live lobster, fresh or frozen lobster tails will do just fine.

I live lobster (1½ pounds), or 2 fresh or
defrosted ½-pound lobster tails
7 cups cold water
I dozen littleneck clams, well scrubbed
I cup finely diced celery
I medium green bell pepper, seeded,
deribbed, and finely diced
I medium red bell pepper, seeded,
deribbed, and finely diced
I cup grated carrots
One 6-ounce can tomato paste

I cup finely minced fresh parsley
½ teaspoon salt, or to taste
¾ pound jumbo shrimp, peeled
and deveined
1½ pounds snapper (either red snapper
or yellowtail) fillets, cut into
1½-inch pieces
I pound fresh squid, cleaned and cut into
½-inch rings*
I cup dry white wine
I cup heavy cream

See the recipe on page 88 for instructions on cleaning squid.

To prepare the lobster, place it on a cutting board, belly up, and insert the tip of a large sharp knife at the cross-shaped mark behind the head to kill it instantly. Draw the knife through the lobster to the tail, cutting it in half lengthwise. With a paring knife, remove the stomach (a hard sac below the head), the intestines, and the vein running the length of the crustacean. (Set aside the soft green substance, called tomalley, in the lobster's midsection. Once cooked, it is marvelous spread on a cracker or dipped in melted butter.) Cut off the claws. Separate the tail section from the rest of the body, and then slice the tail into 4 pieces, leaving the shell intact. You should now have 2 lobster claws, 4 tail pieces, and 2 pieces of the head and midsection.

Bring the 7 cups cold water to a boil over medium-high heat in a large pot. Add the clams, cover, and steam them for 5 minutes, or until they have opened. Carefully remove the clams, making sure that all the clam broth drains back into the pot. Discard any clams that did not open. To remove the sand from the clam broth, pour it through a cheesecloth-lined sieve and into a large bowl. Rinse the pot, and then return the broth to it.

Bring the clam broth to a boil once again over medium-high heat, add the celery, green pepper, red pepper, and carrots, cover, and boil for 5 minutes. Add the pieces of lobster, the tomato paste, parsley, and salt, and allow the stew to simmer, covered, for another 5 minutes. Add the shrimp and red snapper or yellowtail, and cook gently, covered, for 5 minutes more. Then add the squid, steamed clams, and wine, and cook, uncovered, for 2 minutes. Stir the cream into the stew and allow it to return to a simmer, about 5 minutes. Serve the stew immediately in large soup bowls, accompanied by garlic bread.

Serves 6 to 8

JACOBO DE LA SERNA'S
PARTY PAELLA

Paella festiva Jacobo de la Serna

"**A**lthough variations of this dish are plenty (and there are those purists), the uniqueness of this paella is what will make it run out at your next gathering," says Jacobo de la Serna, an historian and nationally recognized *santero,* or maker of *santos,* paintings and statues that depict the Catholic saints in the Spanish colonial style that evolved over the centuries in northern New Mexico. Jacobo de la Serna encourages cooks to experiment with seasonings for paella just as the artist contemplates different colors and elements in his or her works. "Spices are the spice of life," he notes, "and you can subtly change this dish by adding more garlic, or cayenne, cumin, or nutmeg. Also, different chiles add yet another range of possibilities."

Artist Jacobo de la Serna displays his masterpiece paella.

About ⅓ cup olive oil

10 large shrimp, shelled and deveined

2 dozen bay scallops

2 medium whole boneless, skinless chicken breasts

1 pound pork link sausage, preferably Spanish-style chorizo or hot Italian link sausage, sliced into ¾-inch rounds

1 medium yellow onion, peeled and finely chopped

2 medium red bell peppers, seeded, deribbed, and julienned

5 medium cloves garlic, peeled and minced

2 cups fresh ripe tomatoes or canned tomatoes, diced

¼ cup finely minced fresh parsley

3 cups short-grain white rice

5½ cups homemade or canned chicken stock

1 cup dry white wine to which a pinch of saffron threads or powder has been added

Sea salt and freshly ground black pepper, to taste

10 medium asparagus tips, lightly steamed	1 roasted red bell pepper, cut in julienne strips (see the directions for roasting peppers on page 167)

Heat 2 tablespoons of the olive oil in a paella pan or large pot over medium-high heat. Sauté the shrimp in the oil just until they are bright pink, about 4 minutes. Remove the shrimp to a plate.

Add olive oil, a little at a time, as needed to prevent sticking throughout the rest of the sautéing process. Sauté the scallops in one layer, turning once, for approximately 1 minute per side, then remove them to the plate with the shrimp. Next add the chicken breasts and sauté until golden brown on both sides, about 8 minutes. Add the sausage to the chicken and brown on all sides, about 8 minutes. Remove the chicken and the sausage to a plate. Slice the chicken into 1-inch wide strips.

Reduce the heat to medium and add 2 more tablespoons olive oil to the paella pan or pot. Sauté the chopped onions and bell peppers until the onions are limp, about 5 minutes. Add the garlic, tomatoes, and parsley, and cook them until all the liquid has evaporated.

Meanwhile, wash the rice under cold running water and drain. Raise the heat to medium-high and pour the chicken stock into the paella pan or pot. Add the rice, making sure that all the grains are immersed in the stock. Add the reserved chicken and sausage. Stir in the saffron-infused wine and season with sea salt and black pepper to taste. Bring to a boil, reduce the heat to low, cover, and simmer the paella, stirring occasionally, until the liquid is absorbed and the rice is tender, about 30 minutes.

When the rice is nearly ready, arrange the reserved shrimp and scallops on top. Remove the paella from the heat and garnish it with the steamed asparagus tips and the red bell pepper strips. Serve at once.

Serves 8 to 10

PAELLA: THE QUEEN OF THE TABLE IN SPAIN AND ITS EMPIRE

Paella, the classic rice dish that is queen of the Spanish and Spanish colonial table, marks the crossroads of two great civilizations that left their imprint upon the Iberian Peninsula. Over one thousand years ago the Romans brought irrigation to Valencia, and later, in the eighth century, the Moors introduced rice to the region. The Romans are also responsible for bringing pans to Spain, which profoundly influenced the manner in which foods were cooked. The Valencians combined the rice they grew in the irrigated fields with whatever foods were available—namely, rabbit, chicken, and vegetables—and named the dish after the all-important *paella*, the "pan," derived from the Latin word *patella*.

When the Spanish conquistadors set up colonies in the Caribbean in the fifteenth and sixteenth centuries, they planted new crops, such as beans, citrus, sugarcane, coffee, wheat, and rice. Wheat did not survive in the soils of the Caribbean islands, so Spanish rice dishes became particularly popular as staples of Cuban, Puerto Rican, and Dominican cooking. New World paellas evolved dramatically from the classic Valencian dish. Most Caribbean paellas are teeming with shellfish taken from the local waters. Depending on the day's catch and the chef's whim, they may contain an array of clams, mussels, scallops, lobster, shrimp, crabs, or squid. *Paella a la criolla,* a Puerto Rican version, combines Old World ingredients, such as chicken and Spanish-style chorizo, the spicy sausage, with the bounty of the New World. Cubans invented an adventuresome version of paella called *borracha,* or "drunken" paella, in which golden, bubbly lager beer is used instead of water. All of the New World paellas, be they from the Caribbean, Mexico, or Central or South America, have made their way into recipe books, cook's notes, and the memories of Latin American immigrants in the United States, where they are again undergoing an inevitable transformation.

PANFRIED CALAMARI IN LEMON-SHERRY SAUCE

Calamares en salsa verde

Calamari panfried in butter until tender and golden are a great delicacy, particularly with a vibrant sauce accented with lemon, parsley, and sherry. That is the essence of *Calamares en salsa verde,* literally "Calamari in Green Sauce," an Argentine American masterpiece proving that although beef is the staff of life to Argentines, who flock to *parrillas*—restaurants serving grilled meats, found in cities like New York, Los Angeles, and Miami—they also have a way with the fruits of the sea. Panfried Calamari in Lemon-Sherry Sauce is invariably descended from *Calamares al jerez* (Squid in Sherry Sauce), a popular method of preparing squid in Jerez, the city in Andalusia, Spain, renowned for its sherry and cognac.

Despite all the calamari on the menu in America's good Italian restaurants, many Americans squirm at the thought of preparing squid. It is probably because this mollusk with the internal shell is rather aesthetically displeasing and has an unearned reputation for being hard to clean, though it is just as easy to dismantle as shrimp. For those who cannot face the task, calamari are sold already prepared in many fish markets and supermarkets. Note: When buying squid, choose little whole ones with clear eyes and a sweet, not fishy, smell, and store them in an airtight plastic bag in the refrigerator for no more than a day.

2 pounds fresh or frozen (defrosted) squid	About 7 tablespoons butter
1 tablespoon freshly squeezed lemon juice	½ cup finely minced shallots
	1 cup chicken stock, preferably homemade
Salt and freshly ground white pepper, to taste	½ cup dry (fino) sherry
¾ cup unbleached all-purpose flour	½ cup finely minced fresh parsley

Rinse each squid under cold running water. Cut the tentacles off the squid just above the eyes. Cut off the eyes and remove the small hard beak (mouth) from the center of the tentacles. Run your fingers along the body cavity, squeezing from the closed end and moving toward the opening, to extract the entrails. Pull the transparent quill (cartilage) out of the body cavity and scrape the thin, mottled skin off the body with a paring knife. Thoroughly rinse out the body cavity and wash the tentacles under cold running water and drain.

Cut the squid bodies crosswise into ½-inch rings and slice the tentacles in half or in quarters if they are large. Sprinkle the squid with the lemon juice and season lightly with salt and white pepper. Pour the flour into a shallow bowl. Lightly dredge the squid in the flour. Melt 1 tablespoon of the butter in a large skillet over medium heat and panfry a small batch of the squid, turning once, until golden brown, about 1½ minutes per side. Transfer the squid from the skillet with a slotted spatula to a cookie sheet and keep warm in a 200°F oven while you cook the other batches. You will need to add a tablespoon of butter to the skillet with each new batch.

Sauté the shallots in the butter remaining in the skillet (if no butter remains, add 1 tablespoon) over medium-low heat until they have softened, about 5 minutes. Add the chicken stock, sherry, and parsley, and scrape up all the browned bits from the bottom of the skillet. Simmer the sauce for about 5 minutes, or until the parsley is soft. Taste and correct the seasoning. Transfer the squid from the baking sheet to the skillet, stir gently, and serve at once with steamed white rice.

Serves 4 to 6

MUSSELS IN *SALSA CARIBE* AND WHITE WINE

Mejillones en salsa caribe y vino blanco

"**M**y father, Pedro Rivera, makes the most incredible salsa, which we call *salsa caribe*. It is not a salsa in the Mexican sense, but rather a thick, crimson spread or marinade composed of Puerto Rican *adobo* (an oregano-rich spice rub), tomato, onion, garlic, lemon juice, and olive oil," began Gibrán X. Rivera, a senior majoring in International Studies at Boston College and a Woodrow Wilson Fellow. "We slather it on roasted chicken, grilled steak, and broiled fish during the final minutes of cooking, and on anything that strikes our imagination. My dad perfected the salsa recipe while we were still living in Puerto Rico. I remember that a jar of the *salsita* was always tucked in the picnic basket on our trips to the beach. After we moved to the Boston area, my dad continued to make *salsa caribe* often, especially during the long, snowy winter months, so that we would not forget the island we love. Whenever I go home from college and bring my Sri Lankan and Senegalese roommates or my Arab girlfriend along, my dad is sure to fix a batch of the salsa because he is proud to share a taste of Puerto Rico with the world."

"*Salsa caribe* is a great foundation for steamed mussels, a shellfish I have grown fond of in New England," says Gibrán. "In my recipe the salsa is added to mussels, tomatoes, and white wine to create a kind of Puerto Rican Mussels Marseillaise. I serve the mussels and sauce on a bed of al dente linguine with a heaping plate of my dad's garlic bread. It's just one more way we enjoy *salsa caribe* at my house."

4 dozen large live mussels

FOR THE ADOBO:

6 medium cloves garlic, peeled and left whole

½ tablespoon dried powdered oregano (not crumbled)

½ teaspoon salt, or to taste

⅛ teaspoon freshly ground black pepper, or to taste

2 tablespoons freshly squeezed lemon juice or distilled white vinegar

1 tablespoon olive oil

FOR THE *SALSA CARIBE:*

2½ tablespoons olive oil

2 medium yellow onions, peeled and
    minced

4 large cloves garlic, peeled and minced

4 tablespoons tomato paste

2 tablespoons freshly squeezed lemon
    juice or distilled white vinegar

½ teaspoon granulated sugar

FOR THE SAUCE:

5 medium ripe tomatoes, or 1½ cups
    canned peeled tomatoes, chopped

1½ cups dry white wine

¼ cup finely minced fresh parsley or
    cilantro, for garnish

Prepare the mussels: Discard any mussels that are not closed or feel much lighter (the mussel is dead) or much heavier (the shells are filled with sand) than the rest. Scrub the mussels under cool running water with a stiff brush to rid them of any dirt or barnacles. Debeard with a knife or scissors by cutting off any threads that protrude from the shells. Place the mussels in a bucket filled with cool water and soak them for 1 hour so they release any sand. Rinse the mussels in a colander and drain.

Make the *adobo:* Process the garlic, oregano, salt, pepper, and lemon juice or distilled white vinegar in a food processor or electric blender until blended. Add the olive oil and blend well.

Make the *salsa caribe:* Heat the olive oil in a large stockpot over medium heat and sauté the onions and garlic, stirring occasionally, until the onions are limp, about 6 minutes. Stir in the tomato paste, lemon juice or distilled white vinegar, sugar, and 2 teaspoons of the reserved *adobo.*

Add the tomatoes and white wine to the *salsa caribe,* and cook, covered, for 10 minutes. Raise the heat to medium-high, add the mussels, and cook, covered, until they open, about 5 minutes. (Discard any mussels that remain shut.)

Divide the mussels among 4 large bowls. Ladle the sauce over each and sprinkle with minced parsley or cilantro. (You may also serve the mussels and sauce on a bed of linguine.) Serve at once with garlic bread or crusty Italian bread and place a large bowl in the center of the table for discarding the mussel shells.

Serves 4

POULTRY AND GAME TASTE BEST

IN THE GOOD COMPANY OF CHILE

AND OTHER SPIRITED SAUCES.

TO THE LATIN AMERICAN PALATE

THERE'S NOTHING SADDER THAN

A LONELY CHICKEN ON A PLATE.

POULTRY

AND GAME

PIRI THOMAS'S CHICKEN *ASOPAO*

Asopao de pollo Piri Thomas

"*A sopao de pollo,* a comforting chicken stew that is a cross between a regal chicken paella and a thick, homey chicken-and-rice soup, is one dish that stirs the emotions of nearly every Puerto Rican— another is *arroz con gandules,*" says Puerto Rican–Cuban American writer Piri Thomas, who has written three highly acclaimed auto-biographical narratives all about life in New York City's Puerto Rican barrio, including his well-known *Down These Mean Streets* (1967), as well as the short story collection *Stories from El Barrio* (1978). Piri learned to cook *asopao* while he was growing up, the first of seven children, in New York City. His mother, Dolores Montañez, who was born in Bayamón, Puerto Rico, chose him as her ap-prentice in the kitchen and passed on to Piri all of her secrets, including the key to a su-perb *Asopao de pollo.*

Piri Thomas, author of *Down These Mean Streets*, makes a great *asopao*.

The key, Piri revealed to us, is the quality of the *sofrito,* an aromatic blend of herbs, spices, onions, garlic, bell pepper, and tomato—to Puerto Rican cooking what mire-poix is to classic French, five-spice powder is to Chinese, and garam masala is to Indian. (*Sofrito* is used so frequently at the Puerto Rican stove that most Puerto Ricans keep a batch on hand in a jar in the refrigerator or in ice-cube trays in the freezer.) Piri maintains that the *sofrito* must be infused with lemon juice to elevate an *asopao* from the everyday to the extraordinary.

FOR THE SOFRITO:

- 1 medium yellow onion, peeled and finely minced
- 2 large cloves garlic, peeled and finely minced
- 1 tablespoon olive oil
- 3 medium ripe tomatoes, finely chopped

- 1 medium green bell pepper, seeded, deribbed, and finely minced
- 3 tablespoons freshly squeezed lemon juice
- ½ teaspoon dried powdered oregano (not crumbled)

1 chicken (3 to 3½ pounds), cut
  into 8 pieces
2 tablespoons olive oil
1½ tablespoons *achiote* seeds (also
  called annatto), or substitute
  1 teaspoon saffron threads or
  ½ teaspoon sweet paprika*
¼ pound lean cured ham, cut into
  ½-inch dice
¼ pound Spanish-style chorizo, or
  substitute Italian link sausage, cut
  into ½-inch slices

2 cups long-grain white rice
7 cups water
¾ cup frozen green peas
½ cup chopped pimiento-stuffed
  green olives
3 tablespoons capers, drained
2 tablespoons finely minced
  fresh cilantro
Salt and freshly ground black pepper,
  to taste
One 4-ounce jar sliced red pimientos,
  drained, for garnish

*Achiote *seeds, called "poor man's saffron," are used to color food, though they also impart a faint smoky flavor. They are available in Latin grocery stores and some Asian markets and supermarkets. Choose* achiote *seeds that are brick red in color; a brownish hue indicates that they are old and have lost their flavor.*

Make the *sofrito:* Sauté the minced onions and garlic in the 1 tablespoon olive oil in a large skillet over medium heat, stirring occasionally, until the onions are limp, about 7 minutes. Add the tomatoes, bell pepper, lemon juice, and oregano, and cook the *sofrito* until the tomatoes are quite soft, about 10 minutes.

Rinse the chicken pieces under cold running water, and then pat them dry with paper towels. Heat the 2 tablespoons olive oil in a large pot over medium heat. Stir the *achiote* seeds into the oil and cook for 1 minute. Remove the oil from the heat and let it sit for 5 minutes or until it turns reddish orange. Remove the *achiote* seeds from the oil with a spoon or spatula. (If you are using saffron threads or paprika, skip this step and add the saffron or paprika with the *sofrito* in the next step.)

Sauté the chicken in the oil, turning occasionally, until golden brown, about 20 minutes. Add the ham and chorizo, and brown, stirring a few times, for 5 minutes. Spoon off all but about 2 tablespoons of the pan drippings. Mix in the *sofrito* and cook for 5 minutes.

Stir in the rice and water. Raise the heat to medium-high, bring the *asopao* to a boil, and then reduce the heat and simmer, covered, until the rice is cooked, about 20 to 25 minutes. Add the peas, olives, capers, cilantro, and salt and black pepper to taste, and simmer the *asopao* for 5 minutes more. (Note that the stew should be rather soupy.) Taste and adjust the seasoning. Ladle the *asopao* into serving bowls, garnish each with strips of red pimiento, and serve at once.

Serves 5

FRICASSEE OF CHICKEN WITH TOMATOES, RAISINS, AND OLIVES

Pollo estofado con tomates, pasas y aceitunas

Fricassee of Chicken with Tomatoes, Raisins, and Olives, or *Pollo estofado con tomates, pasas, y aceitunas,* is the Panamanian version of the age-old Spanish dish known as *pollo fricasé,* which features chicken in a glorious sauce combining fresh vegetables, herbs, and white wine, punctuated by salty green olives and sweet raisins. Since this dish is both elegant and cozy, Panamanian Americans serve it at casual gatherings of family or friends and at more formal dinners. To achieve a nice mix of flavors and colors, we like to start a meal spotlighting fricassee of chicken with a salad of radicchio with shaved Parmesan, or Bibb lettuce with warm goat cheese. This fricassee is typically served over rice, but since potatoes are cooked in the dish, we usually opt to skip the grain.

Panamanian Americans are not the only ones to inherit this jewel from the Spanish kitchen. The conquistadors brought *pollo fricasé* to all of Latin America, and as a result, Mexican Americans have their own version, which is served with potatoes cooked separately or rice. A classic Cuban American version, called *fricasé de pollo,* is embellished with peas, red pimientos, and capers, and is accompanied by rice. Guatemalan Americans have inherited a version of *pollo fricasé* that clearly reflects the crossroads of Spanish and indigenous cultures in Guatemala. The dish is replete with chayote, a tropical squash, and *chicha,* an alcoholic beverage made from fermented tamarind and pineapple peel.

4 tablespoons olive oil

1 chicken (3 to 3½ pounds), cut into 8 pieces, rinsed and dried

1 medium yellow onion, peeled and finely chopped

1 medium green bell pepper, seeded, deribbed, and finely chopped

3 medium ripe tomatoes, coarsely chopped

2 medium cloves garlic, peeled and finely minced

2 medium red-skinned (new) potatoes, cut into ½-inch chunks

1 slice white bread, toasted and cut into 1-inch pieces

1 cup dry white wine

1 cup chicken stock

½ teaspoon dried rosemary or, if available, 1 teaspoon finely minced fresh rosemary

½ teaspoon dried oregano or, if available, 1 teaspoon finely minced fresh oregano	Salt and freshly ground black pepper, to taste
¼ teaspoon cayenne pepper	¼ cup pitted green olives, cut in half
¼ teaspoon sweet paprika	1 tablespoon seedless black raisins

Heat 2 tablespoons of the olive oil in a large skillet over medium-high heat. Sauté the chicken legs and thighs for 5 minutes. Add the breasts and the wings, and brown the chicken on all sides, about 10 minutes.

Heat the remaining 2 tablespoons of olive oil in a large pot over medium-high heat, and sauté the chopped onions and green bell pepper until soft, about 5 minutes. Stir in the tomatoes and minced garlic, and cook for 10 minutes. Add the browned chicken, potatoes, bread, white wine, chicken stock, rosemary, oregano, cayenne pepper, paprika, and salt and black pepper. Reduce the heat and simmer the fricassee, covered, for 40 minutes.

Adjust the seasoning, add the green olives and raisins, and simmer the fricassee for another 5 minutes. Serve at once.

Serves 4

For Cuban American Fricassee of Chicken (*Fricasé de pollo*): Omit the rosemary. Add ¼ cup fresh or defrosted green peas along with the browned chicken, potatoes, etc. Add 1½ tablespoons drained capers along with the green olives and raisins. Garnish each serving with a few strips of bottled red pimientos (drained).

BRAISED CHICKEN IN SPICY FRUIT SAUCE

Manchamanteles de pollo

" **I** believe Mexican regional food is going to be one of the next culinary waves in the United States," says Zarela Martínez, one of the world's foremost experts on Mexican cuisine, a former head chef at New York City's Café Marimba, and the owner of and inspiration behind Zarela, a highly acclaimed Mexican restaurant in Manhattan that opened its doors in 1987. Many of the dishes on the Zarela menu, which brings together the best of Mexico's regional cuisines, have undergone subtle transformations in Martínez's kitchen. For instance, she has altered the original recipe for Braised Chicken in Spicy Fruit Sauce that comes out of Chiapas, Mexico, by browning the chicken rather than boiling it, to improve its look and texture.

Zarela Martínez first discovered *manchamanteles,* meaning "tablecloth stainer," back in Agua Prieta, Mexico, when family friends from the southern state of Chiapas, Mexico, served a young Zarela and her parents the succulent dish at a Sunday dinner. She was captivated by the dramatic taste and aroma of *manchamanteles*—until that time she had known only the more rustic, straightforward flavors of northern Mexican cooking. Zarela's mother, Aída Gabilondo, re-created the dish at home, then taught it to Zarela, who immediately went about improving on it. At that instant her eyes opened to the multitude of "exotic" cuisines in central and southern Mexico, and she was inspired to embark upon gastronomic "explorations" of her homeland.

According to Zarela Martínez, numerous versions of *manchamanteles* have been handed down throughout the ages; some call for pork or both pork and chicken, combined with fruit, and even ground nuts. Zarela Martínez's recipe marries chicken and fruit, and can be found in her cookery book entitled *Food from My Heart: Cuisines of Mexico Remembered and Reimagined* (Macmillan, 1992).

⅔ to ¾ cup vegetable oil

1 medium yellow onion, sliced into thin
    half-moons (1 cup)

2 large cloves garlic, peeled and minced

1 can (28 ounces) whole tomatoes,
    with juice

2 bay leaves

½ to 1 teaspoon freshly ground black
    pepper, or to taste, plus a little extra
    for seasoning the chicken

1 to 2 teaspoons salt, or to taste

¼ to ⅓ teaspoon ground cloves

1½ teaspoons ground cinnamon

1 teaspoon ground cumin

1 teaspoon dried Mexican
    oregano, crumbled

½ cup dried apricots, sliced

¾ cup pitted dried prunes, whole
    or sliced

½ cup golden raisins

One 20-ounce can unsweetened
    pineapple chunks, with juice

½ cup dry sherry or red wine

1 tablespoon cider vinegar

¾ cup *Adobo de chile colorado* (see box)

2 chickens (about 3½ pounds each), each
    cut into 6 to 8 pieces

1 to 2 medium tart apples, such
    as Granny Smith, cored and cut
    into eighths

1 to 2 tablespoons butter (optional)

1 large ripe plantain, peeled and sliced
    (optional)

Cinnamon sugar, made with 1
    tablespoon granulated sugar to 1
    teaspoon (or to taste) ground
    cinnamon (optional)

Heat 2 tablespoons of the vegetable oil in a heavy, medium-sized saucepan over medium-high heat until hot but not quite smoking. Add the sliced onions and garlic,

and cook, stirring, until the onions are golden and translucent, 3 to 4 minutes. Add the tomatoes, breaking them up with your hand. Add the bay leaves, ½ teaspoon of the black pepper, 1 teaspoon of the salt, the cloves, cinnamon, cumin, and oregano. Bring to a boil, then reduce the heat to low and simmer, uncovered, 10 to 12 minutes. Working in batches, if necessary, purée the mixture in a blender and transfer it to a large Dutch oven.

Bring the puréed sauce to a boil over high heat, adding the dried fruits, pineapple with its juice, sherry or red wine, and vinegar while it heats. Let simmer a minute, then add the *adobo*. Taste for seasoning and add more salt, if desired. Reduce the heat to medium-low and simmer the sauce, uncovered, about 10 minutes. While it cooks, heat about ½ cup vegetable oil in a large heavy skillet over high heat until almost smoking. Sprinkle the chicken pieces on all sides with salt and pepper. Working with 3 to 4 pieces at a time, brown the chicken on both sides (add a little more oil to the skillet, if necessary). As they are browned, add them to the simmering sauce. Add the apple pieces to the sauce and chicken. Let the sauce return to a boil and simmer, covered, until the chicken is cooked through, 25 to 30 minutes. Serve with corn tortillas.

If you wish to garnish, melt the butter in a medium-sized skillet over medium heat. When the butter begins to bubble, add the plantain slices and cook, stirring, until golden on both sides. Sprinkle with the cinnamon sugar and arrange over the *manchamanteles*.

Serves 8

RED CHILE *ADOBO*

Adobo de chile colorado

2 tablespoons lard or vegetable oil
4 medium hot whole dried red chiles, either ancho, guajillo, or dried Anaheim, stems intact (see pages 165, 166, and 167 for information on these chiles)

1½ cups boiling water
1 large clove garlic, peeled and finely minced
1 teaspoon dried Mexican oregano
1 cup water

Heat the lard or vegetable oil in a small or medium-sized heavy skillet over medium heat until rippling. Fry the whole chiles, one at a time, turning several times with tongs, until puffed and red or slightly orange in color, 30 to 60 seconds. *Be careful not to let them burn!*

As the chiles are done, add them to the boiling water in a bowl. Let soak until softened, about 10 minutes. Push them down if they float. Drain.

Pull or cut off the chile tops and scrape out the seeds. Discard the tops and seeds. Place the soaked chile pods in a blender with the garlic, oregano, and 1 cup water. Process to a smooth purée. Add a little more water, if desired, to facilitate blending, but the sauce should be thick.

Place a medium-mesh sieve over a bowl. Pour the paste into the sieve and force it through with a wooden spoon, scraping and rubbing to push through as much of the solids as possible. Discard any bits that won't go through. The *adobo* can be stored, tightly covered, in the refrigerator up to a month, or indefinitely in the freezer.

Yield: ¾ to 1 cup
(depending on the amount lost in sieving)

PUERTO RICAN CHICKEN IN ALMOND SAUCE

Gallina en pepitoria a la puertorriqueña

Puerto Ricans on the mainland as well as the island, where poultry reigns supreme and is served almost every day, adore one-pot chicken stews with rice and have developed a vast repertoire of such dishes. One of our favorite Puerto Rican chicken stews is Chicken in Almond Sauce. The key to this recipe is the sauce, which is made rich and creamy with lots of ground almonds and aromatic with cinnamon and cloves. The almond sauce transforms ordinary stewed chicken into a subtle and elegant dish. All that is needed with Chicken in Almond Sauce is a small salad to start, perhaps of radicchio and arugula for a splash of color, and for the ending, a vibrant dessert such as Passion Fruit Sorbet (see page 277).

Puerto Ricans are not the only Americans of Latin American descent who pair chicken and a sauce of ground nuts or seeds. In fact, nuts are the basis of sauces for chicken all across Latino America. Dominican Americans make a marvelous dish called Chicken in Almond and Hazelnut Sauce (*Pollo en salsa de almendras y avellanas*), in which a hot chile pepper is added to enhance the flavor and heat. Mexican Americans put hot chiles in a handful of chicken in almond sauce dishes, such as *Pollo verde almendrado* (Chicken in Green Almond Sauce), and *Pollo en pipián de almendra* (Chicken Stew with Almonds).

Americans with roots in Bahia, Brazil, pair chicken and fresh and dried shrimp in a nut sauce made with ground almonds or cashews and ground peanuts for *Xin-Xin*. Ecuadoran Americans are most likely to cook chicken in a nut sauce of either almonds, for *Pollo en salsa de almendras,* or ground walnuts, as in the dish *Pollo en salsa de nuez* (Chicken in Nut Sauce). Peruvian Americans are more apt to garnish chicken with a nut sauce made from ground peanuts or walnuts rather than almonds. A popular Peruvian chicken and nut dish is *Carapulcra* (Chicken, Pork, and Potatoes in Peanut Sauce). Guatemalan Americans prepare chicken in a sauce made with ground sesame seeds and pumpkin seeds (*pepitas*) for *Pollo en pepián*.

1 medium yellow onion, peeled and minced	2 cups water
2 large cloves garlic, peeled and minced	1 cinnamon stick
3½ tablespoons olive oil	6 whole cloves
½ cup blanched almonds	½ teaspoon salt, or to taste
⅓ cup unbleached all-purpose flour	2 medium eggs, lightly beaten
⅛ teaspoon freshly ground black pepper	2 teaspoons freshly squeezed lime or lemon juice
1 chicken (3½ to 4 pounds), cut into 8 pieces	2 tablespoons finely minced fresh parsley, for garnish
3 Roma (plum) tomatoes (about ½ pound), diced	

Sauté the minced onions and garlic in 1½ tablespoons of the olive oil in a large skillet over medium heat, stirring occasionally, until limp, about 6 minutes. Remove the onions and garlic from the heat.

Meanwhile, grind the blanched almonds into a fine powder in an electric blender or food processor.

Mix together the flour and pepper in a shallow bowl. Rinse the chicken pieces under cold running water and pat them dry with paper towels. Dredge the chicken in the seasoned flour and shake off the excess.

Heat the remaining 2 tablespoons of olive oil in a large pot over medium-high heat. Brown the chicken thighs and legs on one side, about 5 minutes, and then turn them over and add the chicken breasts and wings. Continue to sauté all the chicken pieces until they are golden brown, about 6 minutes per side.

Stir in the reserved onions and garlic, the ground almonds, tomatoes, water, cinnamon stick, and cloves. Bring the chicken to a boil, covered. Lower the heat and simmer, covered, stirring occasionally until the chicken is tender, about 35 minutes. Transfer the chicken pieces to a warm ovenproof plate or baking dish, cover them loosely with aluminum foil, and keep warm in a low oven while you prepare the sauce.

Skim the fat off the sauce. Bring the sauce to a boil over medium-high heat and cook it, stirring frequently with a spoon, until it has reduced to 1½ cups in about 8 minutes.

Season the sauce with salt and remove it from the heat. Remove the cinnamon stick and cloves from the sauce and discard. In a small bowl, quickly whisk together the eggs and citrus juice, and then whisk the mixture into the sauce until well blended. The sauce should thicken instantly. Return the chicken pieces to the sauce and serve at once with steamed white rice and a garnish of minced parsley.

Serves 4

For Mexican American Chicken Stew with Almonds (*Pollo en pipián de almendra*): Prepare the above recipe through sautéing the chicken. Then instead of tomatoes, cinnamon, cloves, raw eggs, lime or lemon juice, and parsley, add 1 seeded green or red serrano chile to the sautéed chicken, along with the reserved onions and garlic, ground almonds, and water. Simmer for about 35 minutes, then transfer the chicken to a baking dish and keep warm as above. Skim the fat off the sauce and add 2 chopped hard-boiled eggs, 1 cup bread crumbs, and 1 more cup water to it. Purée the sauce in an electric blender or food processor until smooth, then return it to the pot. Add more water, a little at a time, if it seems too thick. Add salt and freshly ground black pepper to taste. Return the chicken pieces to the sauce, and serve at once with steamed white rice.

SHREDDED CHICKEN AND CHILE ENCHILADAS

Enchiladas tapatías

Gabriela Navarro Guttry, a freelance television producer in Los Angeles, says this recipe for *Enchiladas tapatías,* corn tortillas dipped in a chile sauce, lightly sautéed, and then filled with shredded chicken, was her grandmother Ernestina's from Guadalajara, Mexico. "Of my grandmother's thirteen children, over half were girls. They would all gather in the kitchen to share laughter, love, heartache, and hope as they prepared, under the tutelage of Grandmother Ernestina, scrumptious dishes such as *Enchiladas tapatías* for holidays, birthdays, graduations, baptisms, and funerals. Later my sisters, my *primas* (female cousins), and I joined them in this exchange of culinary culture and family history. It won't be long before my three-year-old daughter, Caitlin, is helping out in the kitchen. I hope that she too will enjoy this facet of her family's history and will preserve for future generations Ernestina's recipes like this one for *Enchiladas tapatías.*"

¾ cup sour cream
¼ cup milk
I large whole boneless and skinless
   chicken breast
½ small yellow onion
4 large cloves garlic, peeled
I tablespoon finely minced fresh Italian
   parsley or cilantro
⅛ teaspoon dried powdered oregano
   (not crumbled)
Salt, to taste
6 poblano chiles, seeded and deribbed
   (see page 165 for information
   on poblanos)

3 medium ripe tomatoes
Olive oil, for sautéing
8 corn tortillas
I small yellow onion, peeled and finely
   minced (optional)
4 large lettuce leaves, shredded
I medium ripe Hass avocado, halved,
   peeled, pitted, and thinly sliced
I cup (about 6 ounces) *queso fresco*
   (a Mexican cheese also called *queso
   ranchero*), crumbled, or substitute
   I cup (about 4 ounces) grated
   Monterey Jack cheese

Make the sour cream topping: Mix together thoroughly the sour cream and milk in a small bowl. Cover with plastic wrap and refrigerate.

Put the chicken breast, the ½ onion, 2 of the garlic cloves, the parsley or cilantro, oregano, and salt with 1 quart water into a large saucepan. Cover, bring to a boil over medium-high heat, then reduce the heat and simmer until the chicken is very tender, about 15 minutes.

Remove the chicken to a large plate, shred it with two forks or your fingers, and keep it warm. Pour the contents of the saucepan through a fine wire-mesh strainer into a bowl.

Combine the poblano chiles, the tomatoes, and the 2 remaining garlic cloves with 2 cups water in the large saucepan. Cover, bring to a boil over medium-high heat, then reduce the heat and simmer for 15 minutes. Drain the chiles, tomatoes, and garlic, and then transfer them to a blender. Add ¼ cup of the reserved chicken cooking liquid and process until smooth. The chile sauce should be quite thick, almost like a paste. If it is too thick, add a little more chicken cooking liquid. Spoon the sauce into a large shallow bowl.

Heat 1 tablespoon olive oil in a medium skillet. Dip a tortilla into the chile sauce, then place it in the skillet and sauté it, turning once, for about 10 seconds per side. Transfer the tortilla with a spatula to a large plate and keep warm. Sauté the rest of the tortillas in the same way, adding more olive oil to the skillet as needed.

Spoon about 1 tablespoon shredded chicken in the center of a tortilla and add a little minced onion, if desired. Roll up the tortilla tightly. Fill the remaining tortillas and arrange 2 on each of 4 large plates. Spoon any remaining chile sauce over the tortillas, then garnish each with shredded lettuce, avocado slices, any remaining minced onions, and *queso fresco* or Monterey Jack cheese. Spoon a dollop of sour cream topping on the tortillas and serve at once.

Serves 4

CHICKEN POT PIE WITH CORN CRUST

Pastel de choclo con pollo

This hearty chicken pot pie with a buttery corn crust is the Chilean equivalent of the Mexican American tamale pie. The pie filling is a classic Latin fusion of chicken, raisins, and olives, with a touch of cumin and oregano. Some Chilean Americans also add ground beef to the filling, but we prefer the simplicity of chicken sans beef. A layer of corn purée enriched with eggs and butter goes over the filling, and then the top is dusted with sugar to add a sweet note. In the oven the corn purée turns crisp and golden brown on the outside but stays moist underneath. One of the marvels of this chicken pot pie is that all of the ingredients that go into it are commonplace in the American kitchen, but their juxtaposition is novel and appealing. *Pastel de choclo* is a potluck lover's dream, as it can be made in advance, travels well, and, above all, will delight.

We first sampled this pot pie (the chicken–ground beef version) at Rincón Chileno on Melrose Avenue in Los Angeles, a Chilean restaurant and deli that does a brisk take-out business. Demand is highest for *Pastel de choclo* to go, so owners Ricardo and Christina Florez always have a big supply on hand, as well as a whole selection of Chilean wines to complement the dish. Follow up this homey chicken pot pie and glasses of a Chilean white wine or a pilsner beer, like Brazilian Brahma, with a light, jazzy dessert, like mango slices and raspberries with Devonshire cream, Brazilian Rum-Soaked Sponge Cake (see page 263), or chocolate biscotti with macadamia nuts.

FOR THE CHICKEN FILLING:

1½ pounds bone-in chicken breasts

1 pound chicken thighs

1 small yellow onion, peeled

2 cups chicken broth, preferably homemade

1 bay leaf

¼ cup golden seedless raisins

3 tablespoons olive oil

2 medium yellow onions, peeled and minced

1 medium clove garlic, peeled and minced

½ teaspoon each sweet paprika and dried powdered oregano (not crumbled)

¼ teaspoon ground cumin

Salt and freshly ground white pepper, to taste

2 hard-boiled eggs, each cut into 8 wedges (optional)

1 dozen medium pitted black olives, coarsely chopped

FOR THE CORN TOPPING:

5 cups fresh or frozen (defrosted)
    corn kernels

I cup milk

½ cup (1 stick) butter, plus 1 tablespoon
    for greasing the casserole

¼ teaspoon salt, or to taste

⅛ teaspoon freshly ground black pepper,
    or to taste

I teaspoon sweet paprika

I tablespoon confectioners' sugar,
    or to taste

Prepare the chicken filling: Put the chicken breasts and thighs, the whole onion, chicken broth, and bay leaf in a large stockpot, and bring to a low boil over medium-high heat. Reduce the heat, cover, and simmer until the chicken is tender, about 30 minutes. Transfer the chicken pieces to a large plate. Once the chicken is cool, remove the skin and pull the meat from the bones. Discard the skin and bones, and the bay leaf, and dice the chicken meat. Reserve the chicken cooking liquid and the onion.

Soak the raisins in a small mixing bowl with enough warm water to cover so that they soften. Meanwhile, heat the olive oil in a large skillet over medium heat and sauté the minced onions and garlic, stirring occasionally, until just brown, about 10 minutes. Drain the raisins and stir them in along with the diced chicken, ½ cup of the reserved chicken cooking liquid, the paprika, oregano, and cumin. Cook for 5 minutes. Taste and season with salt and white pepper, as needed. Remove the filling from the heat and keep warm.

Prepare the corn topping: Purée the corn kernels and milk with the reserved onion in a food processor or electric blender until smooth. Melt the ½ cup butter in a large skillet over medium-high heat. Stir in the corn purée and cook, stirring occasionally, for 5 minutes, or until it is as thick as oatmeal. Taste, and season with salt and black pepper as needed.

Assemble the chicken pie: Butter a shallow 2-quart casserole with the remaining 1 tablespoon of butter. Spread the chicken filling on the bottom of the casserole. Press the egg wedges and chopped olives into the filling. Spread the corn topping over the chicken and smooth it with a rubber spatula. Sprinkle the top of the pie with the paprika and then the confectioners' sugar.

Bake the chicken pot pie in a preheated 350°F oven until the top is firm and light golden, about 45 minutes. Broil the pie under a preheated broiler about 4 inches from the heat until the top has browned, about 4 minutes. Serve at once.

Serves 4 to 6

CARIBE CHICKEN CROQUETTES WITH PEACH-HABANERO SALSA

Croquetas de pollo caribe con salsa de durazno y chile habanero

These homey, comforting chicken croquettes with a touch of smoked ham hail from the Dominican American kitchen, though variations may be found all across Caribbean America. As with many Caribbean-style fried morsels, Dominican croquettes are traditionally complemented by lime or lemon wedges, not the white sauce that so many Americans have learned to expect. In this recipe we dress the croquettes up with a Peach-Habanero Salsa to create a nice color contrast and a sweet counterpoint. Naturally, the sweeter and juicier the peaches, the more flavorful the salsa. So if fuzzy yellow or white peaches are not at their peak, pass them by and substitute another vibrant, sweet fruit, like the mango.

Cooks throughout the ages have recognized that croquettes are a marvelous way to use up leftovers. If your refrigerator is still bulging with turkey after Thanksgiving guests have all gone home, feel free to substitute it for the chicken in this recipe. Caribe Chicken Croquettes are nice with a tossed salad for a simple, light meal, and garlic mashed potatoes or wild rice with pecans or pine nuts for a grand feast.

2 tablespoons butter
1½ tablespoons finely minced yellow onion
2 tablespoons finely minced red or yellow bell pepper
2 tablespoons finely minced fresh parsley
½ teaspoon ground nutmeg
¼ teaspoon salt, or to taste
⅛ teaspoon freshly ground black pepper, or to taste
1¼ cups unbleached all-purpose flour

1 cup milk
1½ cups ground cooked chicken
¼ cup finely minced cooked country ham (optional)
2 large eggs, lightly beaten
1 cup seasoned dry bread crumbs
Canola oil, for frying
Peach-Habanero Salsa, chilled (see page 30)
Lime or lemon wedges, for garnish (optional)

Melt the butter in a large saucepan over medium heat. Sauté the minced onions until limp, about 3 minutes. Add the bell pepper, parsley, nutmeg, salt, and black pepper, and sauté an additional 3 minutes. Stir in ½ cup of the flour, but do not let it brown. Add the milk, reduce the heat to low, and cook, stirring constantly, until the mixture thickens, about 5 minutes. (Any lumps will dissolve as you stir and when you mix in the chicken and ham.)

Remove the saucepan from the heat, stir in the chicken and ham, if desired, transfer the mixture to a medium bowl, and allow it to cool to room temperature.

Shape the chicken mixture into croquettes by rolling about 2 generous tablespoons at a time into small rounds, ovals, or cylinders. Put the remaining ¾ cup flour, the lightly beaten eggs, and the bread crumbs into individual shallow dishes. One by one dredge the croquettes in the flour, then dip them in the egg, and then roll in the bread crumbs.

Heat 1 inch of canola oil to 375°F in a large deep skillet. Fry the croquettes, 4 or 5 at a time, until golden, about 1½ minutes per side. Transfer the croquettes with a slotted spoon to plates lined with paper towels to drain. Keep warm in a low oven while you fry the remaining batches. Serve the croquettes with the Peach-Habanero Salsa or with lime or lemon wedges.

Makes about 12 croquettes;
serves 6 as a first course and 4 as a main dish

GRILLED CITRUS-MARINATED CHICKEN

Pechugas de pollo español a la parrilla adobado en jugo de limón

Mexican American Dr. Ruth Gonzalez, a geophysical mathematician with Exxon in Houston, Texas, and her sister, Sylvia Gonzalez Cardwell, design director at KRON-TV in San Francisco, used to host marvelous dinner parties together until Sylvia relocated to California. Thousands of miles apart now, the two sisters still entertain "together" by preparing the same dishes for dinner parties. For casual weekend gatherings in summer, Ruth and Sylvia like to grill chicken breasts that have first been marinated in lime, lemon, and orange juice and spices—a Yucatecan technique for tenderizing and adding flavor to meat. They serve the moist chicken bursting with flavor with either a Caesar salad and warm corn tortillas; grilled vegetables, such as summer squash, baby Italian eggplant, cherry tomatoes, onions, and mushrooms; or sliced avocados and tabbouleh. Whether it's grilled in Houston or San Francisco, the sisters' chicken always has guests lining up for more.

Grilled Citrus-Marinated Chicken (continued)

- **3 large whole boneless, skinless chicken breasts**
- **Juice of 2 freshly squeezed limes**
- **Juice of 1 freshly squeezed medium lemon**
- **Juice of 1 freshly squeezed orange**
- **1 tablespoon olive oil**
- **½ jalapeño chile, seeded and finely minced, or to taste**

- **1 large clove garlic, peeled and mashed**
- **¼ teaspoon ground dried mild New Mexico chile or ancho chile (see the note on ground dried red chile on page 167)**
- **¼ teaspoon ground cumin**
- **¼ teaspoon dried basil**
- **¼ teaspoon ground oregano**
- **⅛ teaspoon salt, or to taste**

Place the chicken breasts in a large nonreactive shallow dish or bowl. Blend all the other ingredients in a small mixing bowl to make a marinade. Pour the marinade over the chicken and marinate it in the refrigerator, covered in plastic wrap, for 2 to 3 hours.

Prepare a grill with charcoal or wood chips. When the fire is ready, place the chicken breasts on the oiled grill. Grill the chicken until the juices run clear, about 3 to 4 minutes per side, depending on the thickness of the breasts. Transfer the chicken to serving plates and serve at once with the accompaniments of your choice.

Serves 4 to 6

CELIA CRUZ'S FRIED CHICKEN "GUARACHERO"

Pollo guarachero de Celia Cruz

In an illustrious music career that has spanned four decades, Celia Cruz, the reigning Queen of Salsa, those Afro-Cuban rhythms, has recorded over seventy-five albums, twenty of which have gone gold, and has been honored with over one thousand awards, including a star on the Hollywood Walk of Fame. Celia Cruz escaped Fidel Castro's revolution by defecting in 1960 during a music tour abroad with her orchestra, La Sonora Matancera. In retaliation the Cuban government has denied her permission to visit the island—even to bury her mother, who passed away in 1962—and has banned her music. Despite the devastation that has plagued Cuba since Castro rose

Celia Cruz, the reigning Queen of Salsa—and Latin fried chicken

to power, Celia Cruz still longs to return someday. In the meantime, she preserves Cuba in memory through her singing and her love of Cuban cultural traditions.

Celia Cruz also keeps her memories of the island alive in the kitchen. She is as fond of Cuban sugar and spice as she is of salsa. In fact, during her performances she likes to cry "*Azúcar!* (Sugar!)," to the sheer delight of audiences. This practice got started in the 1970s, when Celia Cruz and her husband, Pedro Knight (who is also her manager and musical director), were dining in a restaurant and the singer was asked if she wanted coffee with or without sugar. She was taken aback, since Cubans never drink coffee without sugar. Celia Cruz related the episode to her musicians, and they began to joke with her about sugar. The rest is history.

Celia Cruz's recipe for fried chicken may not call for *azúcar,* but it has a dash of Cuban spice and is juicy and tender. The singer has christened her dish *Pollo guarachero* after the title her Cuban American compatriots have given her: *Guarachera del mundo,* meaning "the world's greatest singer of *guaracha,*" a popular Caribbean song style and folk dance. Celia Cruz serves her fried chicken with steamed white rice and a tossed salad.

3½ pounds chicken thighs (no drumsticks attached), skinned and well rinsed	2 bay leaves
	1 teaspoon freshly squeezed lemon juice
	2 large eggs
1 teaspoon dried powdered oregano (not crumbled)	Seasoned dry bread crumbs of your choice
	Vegetable oil, for frying

Place the chicken in a large pot with just enough water to cover. Add the oregano, bay leaves, and lemon juice. Bring the chicken to a boil over medium-high heat and cook for 8 minutes, so it is cooked on the outside and still pink on the inside. Remove the chicken to a plate with a slotted spoon.

Beat the eggs in a small bowl and pour the bread crumbs into a shallow dish. Dip the chicken thighs, one by one, in the beaten egg, then dredge them in the bread crumbs until they are well coated.

Heat about ¾ inch vegetable oil over medium-high heat to 320°F in a large heavy-bottomed skillet. Gently slip 4 chicken thighs into the hot oil. Do not allow them to touch. Fry the chicken thighs, turning once, until they are golden brown and thoroughly cooked, about 7 minutes per side. Remove the fried chicken with a fork, slotted spoon, or wire skimmer to a large plate or tray lined with paper towels to drain. Fry the rest of the chicken thighs in batches of 4 in the same manner.

Serves 4

CHINO-LATINO CHICKEN WITH BLACK MUSHROOMS AND CLOUD EARS

*Pollo guisado con hongos y algas
wangi al estilo chino-latino*

In this Chinese-Peruvian dish, whose aroma and taste evoke Peking duck, chicken is steeped in a sauce that is entirely Chinese except for the shot of *pisco,* Peruvian grape brandy. Woodsy black mushrooms, satiny cloud ears, and pungent star anise—all quintessential Asian ingredients—intensify the flavor and diversify the texture. We first sampled this recipe, which we have dubbed Chino-Latino Chicken, at the Santa Barbara, California, home of Rogger and Diana Vivar. Rogger is a Peruvian American pastor of an independent evangelical church and a producer of Spanish-language television shows, and Diana, who is half Chinese and half Peruvian, is a translator. As Diana and Rogger explained, Chino-Latino Chicken, and hybrid dishes like it, came about when Peruvian and Chinese cuisine crossed paths in the nineteenth century, when Peru, like other Latin American countries, experienced waves of Chinese immigration.

Diana inherited this recipe from her Chinese maternal great-grandmother, who was born in Hawaii and later settled in Peru. Since potatoes are considered an inte-

gral part of a Peruvian American meal, she frequently serves Chino-Latino Chicken alongside Peru's most prized potato dish, *Papas a la huancaina*—scalloped potatoes with a mild cheese, egg, and chile sauce.

5 large dried Chinese black mushrooms (about 1 ounce)*

½ ounce dried cloud ears (otherwise known as tree ears, tree fungus, wood ears, and black fungus)†

1 chicken (3½ to 4 pounds), cut into 8 pieces

3 tablespoons olive oil

3 large cloves garlic, peeled and minced

2 tablespoons soy sauce

1 tablespoon *pisco,* or substitute grappa or brandy‡ (optional)

1 teaspoon granulated sugar

1 star anise

Freshly ground black pepper, to taste

1 cup chicken stock or water

3 medium scallions, root ends removed and cut into ½-inch slices

Dried Chinese black mushrooms are sold in most Asian markets.

†*Dried cloud ears are available in Chinese and Southeast Asian markets. They expand to five times their size when soaked in water. Purchase the smallest available (they will look like little dry black flakes), as they are the tenderest and you do not have to cut them once they are reconstituted.*

‡*Imported* pisco *is available in specialty liquor stores (see Sources, page 308).*

Reconstitute the dried black mushrooms and cloud ears by steeping them in separate bowls of enough boiling water to cover for 30 minutes. Rinse the mushrooms, drain, squeeze out the excess water, slice off their woody stems, and then cut the caps in half diagonally. Rinse the cloud ears thoroughly and drain. If they are large, cut off their stems and slice them into 1-inch pieces.

Rinse the chicken pieces under cold running water and pat them dry with paper towels. Heat the olive oil in a large pot over medium-high heat. Sauté the chicken pieces, turning once, until brown, about 8 minutes per side.

Stir in the garlic and sauté for 1 minute. Stir in the reconstituted mushrooms and cloud ears, soy sauce, *pisco* or grappa or brandy, sugar, star anise, pepper, and chicken stock or water. Reduce the heat and simmer the chicken for 30 minutes. Add the scallions and cook the chicken for 10 minutes more. Serve at once with steamed white rice.

Serves 4

CARMEN'S TURKEY *PICADILLO*

Picadillo Carmen

"Love comes in through the kitchen, goes a Cuban saying. My mother showed her love for her seven children and husband with her exquisitely prepared dishes like *picadillo*, a sensational ground beef stew studded with golden raisins and pimiento-stuffed olives," says Cuban-born Carmen Alea Paz, a university professor and author of a poetry collection entitled *El caracol y el tiempo,* and a forthcoming novel, *Hilos de silencio.* "Mama served *picadillo* with rice, fried eggs, avocado slices, and tomato slices or a tossed salad. Sometimes she made fried ripe plantains, which were fried just right so that their sugary edges caramelized and they melted in your mouth. Since there were so many of us children, we would each fix a plate as we pleased. How we delighted in those leisurely meals and the wonderful conversations we had before our world changed so radically."

Despite the diverse culinary influences all around her in multicultural Los Angeles, where she has resided since 1962, Carmen Paz has remained faithful to her mother's *picadillo,* except that nowadays she adds Worcestershire sauce and capers and, like many Cuban Americans, she substitutes turkey on occasion for beef. Carmen serves her *picadillo* with steamed white rice and Little Havana Fried Ripe Plantains (see page 182), and all who sit at her table, including her husband, Carlos, delight in the feast set before them.

I **pound ground turkey, or substitute lean ground beef**	2 **tablespoons olive oil, preferably extra-virgin**
4 **tablespoons freshly squeezed lemon juice**	One 8-ounce can tomato sauce
3 **tablespoons dry white wine**	½ **cup (loosely packed) seedless golden raisins**
I **cup minced yellow onion**	½ **cup pimiento-stuffed green olives, drained and sliced in half crosswise**
I **small green bell pepper, seeded, deribbed, and finely diced**	I **tablespoon capers, drained**
3 **medium cloves garlic, peeled and finely minced**	I **tablespoon Worcestershire sauce**
	Freshly ground black pepper, to taste

Marinate the turkey or ground beef in the lemon juice and wine in a medium stainless steel, glass, or ceramic bowl. Cover with plastic wrap and refrigerate for at least 1 hour.

Sauté the onion, green pepper, and garlic in the olive oil in a large skillet, covered,

over medium heat for 3 minutes. Add the turkey and its marinade to the skillet. Cook the turkey, uncovered, over medium heat, stirring constantly with a fork to break it up, until it loses its redness, about 5 minutes.

Stir in the tomato sauce, raisins, green olives, capers, Worcestershire sauce, and black pepper. Reduce the heat and simmer the *picadillo,* covered, for 25 minutes, stirring occasionally. Serve the *picadillo* at once, with steamed white rice and Little Havana Fried Ripe Plantains.

Serves 4

PICADILLO | *Picadillo,* a savory ground meat stew with tomatoes, onions, garlic, and other ingredients, was one of numerous Spanish dishes (like flan and paella) that made its way into most of the cuisines of Latin America. As a result, many of the Latino groups in America have their own versions of *picadillo.* Some Americans of Latin American descent, depending on their ethnicity, favor ground beef or turkey, while others cook with pork or veal. Some serve *picadillo* not only with rice but also with mashed potatoes or as a filling for empanadas, tamales, peppers, eggplants, pumpkins, and plantains.

CRISTINA'S WINE-INFUSED STUFFED TURKEY

Pavo relleno con infusión de vino a la Cristina

Cristina Saralegui, the Cuban American host of *El Show de Cristina,* the world's number one Spanish-language talk show, discovered this method for roasting turkey on a trip to Colombia with her husband and producer-manager, Marcos Avila. It has become one of their favorite ways to prepare turkey during winter holidays. "The secret to the success of the turkey," says Cristina, "is to inject it, without tearing the skin, with red wine the night before you cook it. The wine makes the turkey incredibly moist and flavorful. (Colombians are not the only ones to inject turkeys. Brazilians do so, but with beer, wine, or *cachaça,* a rumlike liquor.) Then you rub it inside and out with an *adobo,* a marinade that intensifies the flavor even more. The first time Marcos, the family chef, prepared this dish, he cooked a forty-pound turkey. It was so huge that it didn't fit in our oven, so we had to roast it with the oven door open!"

FOR THE TURKEY:

1 fresh turkey (10 to 12 pounds)

½ cup red wine

FOR THE *ADOBO*:

1 medium yellow onion, peeled and
    minced

3 large cloves garlic, peeled and
    mashed

¾ cup sweet sherry

¼ cup red wine vinegar

Freshly squeezed juice of 1 medium
    lemon for every 3 pounds of turkey

2 tablespoons Dijon mustard

1 tablespoon unsalted butter, melted

Salt and freshly ground black pepper, to
    taste

FOR THE STUFFING:

2 pounds ground lean pork

⅓ pound sliced bacon, cut into 1-inch
    pieces

2 medium yellow onions, peeled and
    coarsely chopped

3 Roma (plum) tomatoes, peeled,
    seeded, and diced

3 large red bell peppers, seeded,
    deribbed, and diced

1 bay leaf

½ cup water

¾ cup sweet sherry

3 slices French bread, or any white
    bread, cut into 1-inch cubes

⅓ cup slivered almonds

¼ cup pitted green olives, drained and
    sliced

¼ cup capers, drained

**FOR ROASTING WITH THE
TURKEY:**

1 cup dry white wine

3 Roma (plum) tomatoes, coarsely
    chopped

1 medium yellow onion, peeled and
    coarsely chopped

Salt and freshly ground black pepper, to
    taste

Prepare the turkey the evening before. Remove the innards and set them aside for another use or discard. Remove any excess fat from around the cavity opening and discard. Rinse the turkey inside and out under cold running water and pat it dry with paper towels. Place the turkey, breast side up, in a shallow, preferably nonstick, roasting pan. Fill a turkey baster with the red wine, make a small hole in the skin at the top of the turkey breast, and squirt the wine through the hole.

Make the *adobo:* Combine all the *adobo* ingredients in a large mixing bowl. Rub the inside and the outside of the turkey with the *adobo,* wrap it completely in plastic, and refrigerate overnight.

Prepare the stuffing: Mix together the ground pork, bacon, onions, tomatoes, bell peppers, bay leaf, and water in a large pot. Cook the mixture over medium heat, breaking the meat up with a fork, for 20 minutes. Cover, reduce the heat to low, and cook for an additional 40 minutes, stirring occasionally. Discard the bay leaf, and allow the mixture to cool enough to be handled.

Mix the cooked meat and vegetables, sherry, bread, almonds, olives, and capers in a large mixing bowl, kneading gently with your hands until well blended. If you think the stuffing is too dry, add a little more

Cristina Saralegui and Marcos Avila with their children

water. Remove the plastic wrap from the turkey, fill the body cavity loosely with stuffing, and sew it up or close it with small trussing skewers. If any stuffing is left over, bake it in a covered casserole with the turkey during the last 35 minutes of roasting.

Add the ingredients for roasting with the turkey to the *adobo* in the roasting pan and mix them around so they are evenly distributed. Put the turkey in the roasting pan, then set the roasting pan on the middle rack of a preheated 450°F oven. Roast the turkey for 30 minutes, basting with the pan juices, and then reduce the heat to 325°F. Continue to roast, basting with the pan juices about every 20 minutes, for approximately 3 to 3½ hours more, depending on the turkey's size, or until an instant-read meat thermometer measures the internal temperature at 180°F, or the turkey juices run clear when the thigh is pricked with a skewer. Be sure to add water to the pan as the pan juices evaporate. If the breast is golden brown before the turkey has finished cooking, cover it with aluminum foil during the last stage of roasting.

Remove the turkey from the oven, then transfer it from the roasting pan to a large serving platter. Remove and discard the skewers or thread. Cover the turkey with aluminum foil and allow it to rest in a warm spot for 20 minutes before carving. Meanwhile, make the gravy by deglazing the roasting pan. Skim the fat off the pan juices and place the roasting pan over moderate heat. Stir ½ to 1 cup water into the juices (depending on what is left in the pan) and scrape the solidified juices from the bottom and sides of the pan. Simmer the gravy until it has thickened. Spoon the stuffing into a serving bowl. Serve the turkey, stuffing, and gravy at once with any other accompaniments you choose.

Serves 10 to 14

TROPICAL DUCK WITH PINEAPPLE SAUCE

Pato tropical en salsa de piña

Long before the eighteenth century, when pineapples became emblems of wealth and hospitality in Europe and the United States to the extent that they even ornamented dining-room furniture, doors, and gateposts, pre-Incan peoples were carving pineapple artifacts in Latin America. So began Latin Americans' love affair with the tropical fruit. In fact, the Paraguayans so admired the pineapple that they gave it the name *nana*, which means "exquisite fruit." Central Americans and South Americans early on discovered that pineapple accentuates the rich, mouth-watering meat of roast duckling, and to this day they commonly pair the fruit and fowl. This recipe for Tropical Duck with Pineapple Sauce is a classic in the Panamanian repertoire. Nowadays it is made on festive occasions in Panamanian American homes.

We prefer to cook with fresh pineapple, but canned fruit may be substituted in this recipe. If you are using fresh pineapple, select a fruit that is a little soft to the touch and has no green spots. The leaves should be green with no brown or yellow tips. If the pineapple is a little underripe, keep it at room temperature for a few days to reduce the level of acidity.

- 1 tablespoon olive oil
- 1 cup minced green bell pepper
- 1 medium yellow onion, peeled and thinly sliced
- ½ cup pancetta (an Italian bacon cured with salt and spices but not smoked), diced, or substitute sliced bacon
- 1 teaspoon unbleached all-purpose flour
- 1 cup fresh or canned pineapple, cut into 1-inch cubes
- 1 cup pineapple juice
- ⅓ cup dry white wine
- 1 teaspoon red wine vinegar
- 1 teaspoon granulated sugar
- Salt and freshly ground black pepper, to taste
- 2 fresh or thoroughly defrosted plump Peking or robust-flavored Muscovy ducklings (4½ to 5 pounds each)
- ¼ cup toasted sesame seeds

Heat the olive oil in a large skillet over medium heat. Sauté the bell pepper and sliced onions until the onions are limp, about 5 minutes. Add the pancetta and sauté, stirring often, for an additional 4 minutes. Stir in the flour and allow it to brown. Next stir in the pineapple, pineapple juice, wine, vinegar, and sugar, and simmer the sauce over medium heat, stirring occasionally, until the pineapple becomes stewed, about 10 minutes. Taste, and season with salt and black pepper as needed.

Meanwhile, remove the innards and trim the excess fat from the cavities of the ducks. Wash the birds and pat them dry with paper towels. Prick the skin of the ducks all over with a fork, salt them inside and out, and place the ducks in a large roasting pan. Roast the ducks on the middle rack of a preheated 450°F oven for 15 minutes, then reduce the heat to 375°F and roast for another 10 minutes. Remove the ducks from the oven and pour off the fat.

Spoon the pineapple sauce around the ducks and continue roasting them in the center of the middle rack, uncovered, in a 375°F oven for approximately another 45 minutes, or until tender when pierced with a fork.

Remove the ducks from the oven and transfer them to a large serving platter. Let them stand for a few minutes before carving. Carve the ducks into serving pieces. Spoon the pineapple sauce over the ducks and garnish with the toasted sesame seeds. Serve at once with steamed white rice or the accompaniments of your choice.

Serves 4

CITRUS-MARINATED RABBIT IN WINE SAUCE

Conejo rosado

When Peruvian Americans have a hankering for richly flavored rabbit, they often prepare this dazzling dish, in which the delicate meat is marinated in citrus juice and pungent spices, sautéed until golden, and then simmered in an elegant white wine sauce until tender. Of all Americans of South American descent, first-generation Peruvian Americans seem to experience the most intense craving for succulent rabbit (although many light up at the mere mention of the Peruvian delicacies *charqui,* dried llama meat, and *cuy,* an Andean guinea pig). They have such enthusiasm for rabbit that they cook it in every way imaginable, as they might chicken: roasted, baked, fried, sautéed, and braised in myriad sauces. Most feast on rabbit less often now because it is not sold widely in the United States and their children and grandchildren share America's soft spot for bunnies and thus shun the would-be pet on the dinner plate. Thankfully, old culinary ways die hard, and Peruvian Americans still compare notes on the preparation of rabbit. Most would agree that Citrus-Marinated Rabbit in Wine Sauce is the most fabulous and foolproof way to prepare the small game animal.

We like to start a dinner of Citrus-Marinated Rabbit in Wine Sauce with a radicchio and Belgian endive salad, garnished with crumbled Danish blue cheese and walnuts and drizzled with a vinaigrette. The rabbit is teamed with a favorite potato dish, such as roasted red-skinned potatoes, Potatoes Anna, or potato pancakes, and glasses of the same dry white wine we use in the sauce. After the seductive citrus-spice high notes of the rabbit, a serene dessert such as Pumpkin Flan Under a Palm Tree (see page 251), perhaps with a dollop of whipped cream or a scoop of vanilla ice cream, makes an ideal finish to the meal.

I rabbit (3 to 3½ pounds), cut into 8 serving pieces, available in many meat markets and in some supermarkets and gourmet markets
½ cup freshly squeezed lime or lemon juice

½ cup fresh or frozen (defrosted) orange juice
I medium white onion, peeled and finely minced
I large clove garlic, peeled and finely minced

¼ teaspoon each ground cumin, ground
    oregano, and paprika
1 bay leaf
½ cup unbleached all-purpose flour

¼ teaspoon each salt and freshly ground
    black pepper
5 tablespoons olive oil
1 cup dry white wine

Rinse the rabbit pieces under cold running water and pat them dry with paper towels. Mix thoroughly the lime or lemon juice, orange juice, minced onions, garlic, cumin, oregano, paprika, and bay leaf in a nonreactive shallow pan to make a marinade. Marinate the rabbit pieces, covered in plastic wrap, in the refrigerator for at least 4 hours, turning every hour.

Remove the rabbit pieces from the marinade and blot them with paper towels until they are almost dry. Discard the bay leaf. Reserve the marinade. Mix together the flour, salt, and pepper in a shallow dish. Roll the rabbit pieces in the seasoned flour so that they are lightly coated.

Heat the olive oil in a large heavy pot over medium heat and sauté the rabbit pieces in one layer, turning once, until they are golden brown, about 5 to 7 minutes per side. Add the reserved marinade and the wine, reduce the heat, cover, and simmer until the rabbit is tender, about 1 hour.

With a slotted spoon, remove the pieces of rabbit to a platter and keep warm. If the sauce is too thin, mix a little flour with a few tablespoons water to make a paste and whisk the paste into the sauce. Simmer the sauce for a few minutes until it thickens, then pour it over the rabbit. Serve the rabbit at once, along with the potatoes of your choice.

Serves 4

MEAT IS KING, AND AMERI-
CANS WITH LATIN AMERICAN
ROOTS ARE AS LIKELY TO
ASK "WHERE'S THE PORK?" AS
"WHERE'S THE BEEF?"

MEATS

BEEF STEW WITH PEACHES AND PUMPKIN

Carbonada criolla

Beef is the staff of life not only in Argentina but in Argentine America. Many Americans of Argentine descent, who are among the newest immigrants in the United States, not only have a penchant for beef, they also prefer it prepared Argentine ways. For instance, *asado criollo*—steaks, short ribs, blood sausage, and organs such as calf's liver, and beef kidneys, udders, and intestines—grilled over hot coals is as much an institution in Argentine homes and *parrillas* (restaurants serving grilled meats) in America as it is in Argentina. So, too, are *matambre,* meaning "hunger killer," flank steak stuffed with hearts of palm, spinach, and ham or hard-boiled eggs; and *Carbonada criolla,* a magnificent beef stew made fragrant and flavorful with peaches and pumpkin.

Unless it is summer and farm stands and greengrocers are laden with sweet, juicy fresh peaches, it is best to prepare *Carbonada criolla* with canned peaches. For festive occasions in autumn and winter, Argentine Americans may serve this stew *en zapallo,* in a carved pumpkin that has been baked separately. Some of the pumpkin flesh is scooped out when the stew is ladled into bowls. For less fuss, many dispense with the pumpkin container and, instead, cook chunks of pumpkin right in the stew as in this recipe. In Argentina the pumpkin used in this dish is the *zapallo,* which bears a resemblance to the West Indian pumpkin (also known as *calabaza,* green pumpkin, and Cuban squash) available in Latin markets. If you cannot find this pumpkin variety, substitute the more common sugar pumpkin, Hubbard squash, or butternut squash, but avoid the common American pumpkin, as it tends to be bland tasting. Argentine Americans sometimes serve *Carbonada criolla* with white rice, but we find that this stew is quite hearty and needs no accompaniment.

2 pounds lean beef chuck, in stewing pieces	1 cup fresh ripe tomatoes, peeled, seeded, and chopped, or canned tomatoes, drained
2 tablespoons olive oil	1 tablespoon red wine vinegar
½ cup minced yellow onion	½ teaspoon fresh oregano
2 medium cloves garlic, peeled and finely minced	¼ teaspoon dried thyme
1½ cups beef stock, canned beef bouillon, or water	Salt and freshly ground black pepper, to taste

2½ cups (about 13 ounces) sugar
   pumpkin, Hubbard squash, or
   butternut squash, peeled, seeded, and
   cut into 1-inch dice
1 medium carrot, peeled and cut on the
   diagonal in ½-inch slices
3 medium full-flavored ripe peaches,
   peeled, halved, pitted, and cut into
   1-inch dice, or 6 canned peach halves,
   drained and cut into 1-inch dice

¾ cup fresh, frozen, or canned corn
   kernels (drained, if canned)
½ cup seedless black or golden raisins
2 tablespoons finely minced fresh
   cilantro, for garnish

Pat the meat dry with paper towels. Heat the olive oil in a large pot over medium-high heat. Sauté the beef with the minced onions and garlic, stirring occasionally, until it is brown on all sides, about 10 minutes. Stir in the beef stock, beef bouillon, or water, tomatoes, red wine vinegar, oregano, thyme, and salt and pepper, reduce the heat, and simmer the stew, covered, for 1 hour, stirring occasionally.

Raise the heat so that the stew boils moderately, add the pumpkin or squash and carrot, cover, and cook for an additional 20 minutes. Stir the stew. Next add the peaches, corn, and raisins, cover, and cook for 10 minutes more. Ladle the stew into soup bowls, or over a bed of rice if you prefer, garnish with cilantro, and serve at once.

Serves 4 without rice and 6 with rice

BORSCHT BELT BRISKET WITH A MEXICAN TWIST

Carne de pecho de res para asar a la
"Borscht Belt" con acento mexicano

"The beauty of this brisket dish," says novelist Montserrat Fontes, author of *First Confession* (1991) and *Dreams of the Centaur* (1996), "is that it's not only a whole meal in a casserole, it's easy to prepare yet tastes like you've slaved away in the kitchen." Montserrat Fontes learned her way around the kitchen from her maternal grandmother, Encarnación Elías de Gómez, who came to Los Angeles from Mexico with her two children in the mid-1920s at the urging of Montserrat's maternal grandfather, General Arnulfo R. Gómez, a presidential candidate. In 1927 General Gómez was executed in Mexico, and to support her family, Encarnación opened El Carmen Café, a Mexican restaurant at 3rd Street and La Brea Avenue in Los Angeles, a neighborhood that was home to a number of L.A.'s Jews and would later become known as the Borscht Belt. Many of her customers conversed in Yiddish, and to the day she died, at age ninety-six, Encarnación spoke English with a Yiddish accent. She also incorporated Eastern European Jewish dishes into her menu, such as brisket, or *gedempta brust,* which was a *Shabbas* dinner staple.

Montserrat got her love of *gedempta brust* from her grandmother, but an actual recipe for the dish from her friend Norine Dresser, a folklorist who shares her passion for matching favorite foods from different cultures. She has given a Mexican twist to Norine's classic Jewish brisket made with onion soup mix by adding the spices and corn of Mexico that she says are in her blood. Brisket should be cooked slowly in the oven to tenderize the meat and enhance the flavor. It is even tastier the next day, when all the spices have permeated the beef. Montserrat Fontes serves her Mexican-style Borscht Belt Brisket with warmed corn or flour tortillas or, to add yet another cultural dimension to the recipe, toasty pita bread.

2 cups canned crushed tomatoes	6 small red-skinned (new) potatoes, or
2 cups tomato salsa, homemade or your	3 medium, cut in half
favorite commercial brand	I medium red onion, thinly sliced and
I package onion soup mix	the rings separated
I beef brisket (3 pounds), most of the	2 large red bell peppers, seeded,
fat trimmed	deribbed, and thinly sliced
4 large cloves garlic, peeled and thinly	One 7-ounce can whole kernel corn,
sliced lengthwise	drained

Mix together the tomatoes, salsa, and onion soup mix in a large bowl. Make numerous ¼-inch slits in the brisket with a sharp knife and insert 1 garlic slice in each.

Place the brisket, fat side up, in a large casserole with a tight-fitting lid. Smother the brisket with the sauce and marinate it, covered, in the refrigerator for 3 hours or overnight.

Cook the brisket with its marinade, covered, in a preheated 350°F oven for 30 minutes. Remove the brisket from the oven, baste it with the sauce, and place the potatoes and onion slices all around, making sure to immerse them in the sauce. Return the brisket, covered, to the oven, and continue cooking for 1½ hours. Remove the brisket from the oven once again, skim off any excess fat, baste it with the sauce again, and add the bell peppers and corn. Return it, covered, to the oven, and cook it for 1 hour more, or until tender.

Remove the casserole from the oven and transfer the brisket to a cutting board.

With a sharp knife, cut the brisket across the grain into thin slices. Arrange the slices on a large serving platter, and then spoon the vegetables and sauce over the top. Serve at once with warmed corn or flour tortillas or pita bread if desired.

Serves 6 to 8

OLD CLOTHES

Ropa vieja

In the sixteenth century, Spanish colonizers introduced to the Americas *Ropa vieja,* literally "Old Clothes," a marvelous Iberian beef stew with a richly flavored sauce spiced with cinnamon and cloves and adorned with briny capers and sweet pimiento. *Ropa vieja* easily found a permanent place, sometimes under a different name, in the culinary repertoires of many Latin American countries, including Cuba, Puerto Rico, Mexico, Peru, Chile, Venezuela, and Brazil. Each country has its own take on the dish, but all have preserved the process of shredding the beef or in some cases pork, until, with a little imagination, it resembles old, tattered clothes—hence the recipe's name. Through shifting borders and centuries of immigration, Latin American variations on the original Spanish *Ropa vieja* eventually wound up in kitchens across the United States, where they once again were transformed.

At Versailles in L.A. (actually there are three), *Ropa vieja* ("Old Clothes") is a popular item on the menu.

Ropa vieja is a regular on the menus at Cuban restaurants around the country, like Versailles in Miami, Versailles in Los Angeles, and Victor's Café 52 in New York City, where it is cleverly served nestled in a tropical vegetable basket. *Ropa vieja* is also an old favorite among Cuban American home cooks, as the ingredients for the dish are readily available in supermarkets, the recipe is fairly simple, and the results are a bon vivant's dream. As is the custom in Cuba, most Cuban Americans serve *Ropa vieja* with steamed or boiled white rice, a grain the Spanish introduced to the Caribbean and that flourished in the soils of the New World. *Tostones* (Fried Green Plantains, see

Old Clothes (continued)

page 185); *Plátanos maduros fritos* (Little Havana Fried Ripe Plantains, see page 182); or *Yuca con mojo* (*Yuca* with Garlic-Lime Oil, see page 188) are sometimes served on the side. Flank steak, a popular cut throughout Latin America, works best for *Ropa vieja* since it is fairly lean and shreds easily after it is slowly simmered. *Ropa vieja* tastes even better the next day.

1 flank steak (1¾ pounds)	1 cup tomato purée
2 large yellow onions, peeled, 1 cut in half and the other minced	¼ teaspoon ground cinnamon
	¼ teaspoon ground cloves
1 small bay leaf	½ teaspoon salt, or to taste
1 medium green bell pepper, seeded, deribbed, and diced	3 tablespoons capers, drained
	One 4-ounce jar sliced red pimientos, drained
2 large cloves garlic, peeled and minced	
4 tablespoons olive oil	

Lay the flank steak flat in a large pot. Add the onion halves, bay leaf, and enough cold water to cover, and bring to a boil over medium-high heat. Cover, reduce the heat, and simmer the flank steak for 1½ hours, or until it is tender.

Transfer the flank steak to a cutting board, let it cool for 20 minutes, and then slice it across the grain into 2-inch-wide strips. Shred the strips into fine strands with the tines of two forks, then place the shredded steak on a large serving dish and keep warm. Discard the onion halves and the bay leaf, and reserve the stock.

Make the sauce: Sauté the bell pepper, the minced onions, and garlic in the olive oil in a large skillet over medium heat, stirring occasionally, until the onions are quite limp, about 10 minutes. Stir in the tomato purée, 1½ cups reserved stock, cinnamon, cloves, and salt, reduce the heat, and simmer the sauce, covered, for about 15 minutes. Add the capers and simmer an additional 5 minutes.

Pour the sauce over the shredded flank steak. Stir the steak with a fork to coat it evenly with the sauce and garnish the *Ropa vieja* with the sliced pimientos. Serve at once with white rice.

Serves 4

For a Brazilian American version of *Ropa vieja* (called *Roupa velha*): Simmer the flank steak with 1 medium peeled carrot, 1 medium stalk celery, and 4 peppercorns in addition to the onion halves and bay leaf. Discard the carrot, celery, and peppercorns, along with the onion and bay leaf. Omit the bell pepper, cinnamon, cloves, and capers from the sauce. Add ¼ cup minced fresh parsley to the sauce, along with the tomato purée. Just before pouring the sauce over the shredded steak, stir in 1½ tablespoons apple cider vinegar or freshly squeezed lemon juice, and Tabasco sauce (optional). Omit the pimientos.

For a Venezuelan American version of *Ropa vieja* (called *Pabellón criollo,* which means "Creole Flag"): Omit the bell pepper, cinnamon, cloves, capers, and pimientos. Serve with Venezuelan *Tajados de plátano,* fried ripe plantains prepared much like Cuban ones (see page 182), and *caroatas,* black beans similar to Cuban *Frijoles negros* (see page 177), for an entreé called *Pabellón con baranda,* or "Flag with a Railing."

BRAISED BEEF STUFFED WITH CARROTS, PARSLEY, AND GARLIC

Estofado argentino

"**E**stofado argentino,* hearty beef stuffed with grated carrots, fresh parsley, and lots of pungent garlic, and then braised in a tomato sauce redolent of sweet basil, thyme, nutmeg, and marjoram, ranks among our favorite comfort foods," say Roberto and Anita Cano, owners of Cultura Latina Bookstore and Art Gallery in Long Beach, California, one of the country's finest Latino and Latin American specialty bookstores. Cooking in the Cano household could best be described as Pan-Latin, since Roberto hails from Argentina and Anita from Mexico. But on the days that the couple prepares *Estofado argentino,* the mood is undeniably Argentine. Out of the kitchen come traditional Argentine accompaniments to the beef that reflect the Italian roots of half of Argentina's population—a warm, crusty loaf of Italian bread, a tossed salad, polenta, or ravioli or tortellini with freshly grated Parmesan or perhaps some *gnocchi,* known to Argentines as *ñoquis,* and an intense Argentine red wine like a Fabre-Montmayou merlot.

Roberto and Anita Cano learned to prepare *Estofado argentino* together, during a visit to Roberto's beloved grandmother, Doña Elvira, at her home in Barrio Boedo, an old section of Buenos Aires. Anita remembers how, in preparation for cooking, they made morning rounds to the green-

Anita Cano and Roberto Cano are passing on their Argentine and Mexican culinary secrets to their daughter, Andrea.

Braised Beef Stuffed with Carrots, Parsley, and Garlic (continued)

grocer, the butcher, and the pasta factory—an Old World way of shopping that, sadly, has virtually disappeared in America. Back at their house by the beach in southern California, Roberto and Anita recently taught their daughter Andrea, a student at Berkeley, how to prepare *Estofado argentino*. Six thousand miles from Barrio Boedo and two generations later, the tradition continues.

1 ½ cups peeled and grated carrots	2 bay leaves
1 ½ cups finely minced fresh parsley	½ teaspoon dried oregano
4 large cloves garlic, peeled and	½ teaspoon sweet paprika
finely minced	½ teaspoon dried sweet basil
1 tip roast (about 3 pounds), visible	¼ teaspoon ground marjoram
fat trimmed*	¼ teaspoon ground thyme
4 tablespoons olive oil	¼ teaspoon ground nutmeg
½ cup diced green bell pepper	½ teaspoon crushed red pepper
½ cup diced red bell pepper	(optional)
Two 28-ounce cans crushed tomatoes	Salt and freshly ground black pepper,
½ teaspoon granulated sugar	to taste

A tip roast is a triangular cut of beef that comes from the area right below the sirloin steak cuts of a steer. In California, tip roast is known as tri tip because of its shape.

Mix together ½ cup of the carrots, ½ cup of the parsley, and 2 of the minced garlic cloves in a small bowl. Pierce the roast lengthwise with a long, sharp knife so that the tip of the knife emerges at the other end. Slice the inside of the roast in any direction with the knife to make a 1½-inch-wide cavity that runs the whole length of the roast. (Do not cut through any of the sides; the roast should remain intact.) Stuff the cavity with the mixed vegetables. (There is no need to tie up the roast—the vegetables will remain snugly inside the cavity.)

Heat the olive oil in a large pot over medium-low heat. Sauté the remaining 1 cup of carrots, the remaining 1 cup of parsley, 2 remaining minced garlic cloves, and the green and red bell peppers in the oil, stirring occasionally, until the carrots are soft, about 8 minutes.

Add the crushed tomatoes. Cook the sauce until it begins to bubble, and then stir in the sugar, spices, and salt and pepper. Next add the stuffed roast to the sauce. Spoon some of the sauce over the roast, and then cover and simmer it, turning occasionally with a fork, until it is tender, about 1½ hours.

Remove the roast to a cutting board, cut it into ½-inch slices, and arrange the slices on a serving platter. Serve the roast at once with pasta or polenta, the sauce, and freshly grated Parmesan.

Serves 6

LOS GAUCHITOS' FAMOUS ARGENTINE AND URUGUAYAN PIZZA MENU

Uruguayans and Argentines love pasta and pizza almost as much meat. In Miami they rely on Los Gauchitos for heavenly homemade ravioli stuffed with such fillings as beef and ricotta or brain and spinach. For pizzas, Los Gauchitos offers a wide range of toppings that at first glance seem very California but are actually authentic. Whenever we make pizza at home, we consult Los Gauchitos' pizza menu for ideas about toppings.

Los Gauchitos special: ham, hearts of palm, eggs, cheese, tomato, mushrooms, mozzarella, and *salsa golf* (Thousand Island dressing)
mussels
anchovies
asparagus, onions, tomatoes, and peppers
eggplant, white sauce, and grated cheese
Neapolitan
spinach and ricotta
chorizo, onions, and mushrooms
ham, eggs, and cheese
hearts of palm, ham, and mozzarella
chick-pea-flour pizza crust smothered in olive oil and salt (called *faina*)
seasoned onion and mozzarella
mozzarella

CARIBBEAN BEAT BURGERS

Hamburguesas con ritmo caribeño

Caribbean Beat Burgers are the outrageously delicious invention of Puerto Rican Max Norat of Rockland County, New York, a character actor whom you can catch on the silver screen in the motion picture *Faithful*. Max got the idea for the burgers from Charlie Squires, a dear friend from Barbados, who told him about how his Barbadian burgers made people dance the calypso. Max figured that if he added ingredients from various Caribbean islands to his own hamburger recipe, he'd have people dancing the calypso, mambo, salsa, and merengue all at once! When he tried his Caribbean Beat Burgers out on his wife, Acté Norat (a.k.a. Dr. Acté Maldonado), Dean of Continuing Education at Borough of Manhattan Community College CUNY, and their teenage son, Eric, "it was as if the kitchen turned into New York City's Palladium, and both the Tito Puente Orchestra and Celia Cruz were headlining!"

Max prefers to grill his burgers and to serve them on Kaiser rolls or buns, with a side of french fries, potato salad, or *platanitos* (fried ripe plantains)—a favorite nosh throughout the Caribbean. *Viva el Caribe!*

FOR THE JERK SEASONING:
¼ **Scotch bonnet chile, or substitute**
   ½ **serrano or jalapeño chile, seeded**
   and mashed, or to taste
2 **medium scallions, root ends removed**
   and coarsely chopped

1 **teaspoon red wine vinegar**
1 **teaspoon soy sauce**
¼ **teaspoon ground cinnamon**
⅛ **teaspoon ground nutmeg**
⅛ **teaspoon freshly ground black pepper**

FOR THE *MOJO CRIOLLO*
(MARINADE):
2 **cups canned tomato sauce**
¼ **cup olive oil**
1 **small yellow onion, peeled and diced**
2 **tablespoons *alcaparrado* with liquid,**
   or substitute 1 tablespoon each
   capers and pimiento-stuffed olives
   with liquid*

1 **tablespoon red wine vinegar**
½ **teaspoon salt**
2 **laurel leaves**

FOR THE BURGERS:

2 pounds lean ground beef
¼ cup finely minced yellow onion
I large clove garlic, peeled and mashed

½ teaspoon dried powdered oregano
(not crumbled)

* Alcaparrado *is a mixture of olives, capers, and diced pimientos. It is available in Latin markets that serve a Caribbean clientele.*

Prepare the jerk seasoning: Process all the ingredients in an electric blender or food processor until mashed. Cover and refrigerate.

Prepare the *mojo criollo:* Combine all the ingredients in a medium saucepan. Bring the *mojo* to a boil over medium-high heat, then reduce the heat and simmer, covered, for 45 minutes. Pour the *mojo* into a shallow pan.

Make the burgers: Mix together all of the ingredients in a medium bowl with the jerk seasoning. Shape the ground beef into 6 hamburgers of equal size. Place the hamburgers in the pan of *mojo criollo* and cover tightly with plastic wrap. Marinate the burgers in the refrigerator, turning once, for at least 2 hours.

Grill, panfry, or broil the burgers to the doneness you desire. Serve Caribbean Beat Burgers on Kaiser rolls or hamburger buns with the condiments you like and with lettuce and tomato, if desired. Serve the burgers with Little Havana Fried Ripe Plantains (see page 182), french fries, or potato salad, or the accompaniment of your choice.

Serves 6

HEAVENLY POTATO PIE WITH MINCED BEEF, RAISINS, AND OLIVES

Pastel de papas celestial

"Heavenly *Pastel de papas*—minced beef, raisins, and olives in a nutmeg-scented potato crust—was a regular dish at home in Chile," remembers Santiago Daydí-Tolson, a professor of Hispanic Studies in the Department of Spanish and Portuguese at the University of Wisconsin, Milwaukee. "It combines the creamy softness and elegant simplicity of mashed potatoes with the more robust, lively flavors of *pino de carne,* the minced beef stuffing that went into the empanadas (turnovers) we enjoyed each Sunday. In our house, *Pastel de papas* was always served for lunch on cold, dark winter days. Whenever that golden potato dome appeared on the table, the household instantly brimmed with warmth and tranquillity. I treasure those moments when the potato crust was pierced for serving and the aroma of the steaming-hot stuffing drifted through the house, beckoning. No less joyful was the simple ritual—practiced all over Chile—of sprinkling a bit of sugar on one's piece of *pastel.*"

Santiago Daydí-Tolson has taught courses on food and gluttony in Latin American literature, in the works of such writers as Gabriela Mistral and Pablo Neruda, but at the stove he focuses on Chilean flavors, reconstructing dishes from home with a dash of imagination. "I've changed *Pastel de papas* in subtle ways. In Chile the dish always had wedges of hard-boiled egg in the stuffing, but I often replace the egg with sun-dried tomatoes or another adventuresome ingredient. But I always serve the *pastel* with a semidry white wine, in contrast to beef empanadas, which must be followed by a good full-bodied red wine. And I always begin a meal of *Pastel de papas* with a traditional Chilean tomato salad, composed of thinly sliced, juicy red tomatoes and white or purple onions cut in the thinnest of half-moons, which in Chile are called *cebollas plumas,* or 'feathered onions,' dressed with olive oil and salt and pepper. Of course, sometimes I throw tradition to the wind and sprinkle some crumbled goat cheese and minced fresh sweet basil on the salad."

FOR THE *PINO DE CARNE*
(MINCED BEEF FILLING):

½ cup black seedless raisins

2 tablespoons olive oil

2 medium yellow onions, peeled
   and minced

2 large cloves garlic, peeled and minced

I pound lean ground beef

I tablespoon sweet paprika

I teaspoon ground cumin

½ cup sun-dried tomatoes packed in
   olive oil (drained), minced

Salt and freshly ground black pepper,
   to taste

FOR THE POTATO CRUST:

3 pounds russet (Idaho) potatoes*

2 tablespoons butter

½ cup milk

I teaspoon ground nutmeg

Salt and freshly ground white pepper,
   to taste

FOR THE GARNISH:

One 6-ounce can ripe pitted medium
   black olives

Granulated sugar (optional)

*Avoid waxy potatoes such as red-skinned or White Rose, as they do not have the fluffy texture of starchy potatoes like the russet that makes for excellent mashed potatoes.

Prepare the filling: Soak the raisins in a small mixing bowl with enough warm water to cover so that they plump. Meanwhile, heat the olive oil in a large skillet over medium heat, and sauté the onions and garlic, stirring occasionally, until limp, about 6 minutes. Add the ground beef and cook it, breaking it up with a fork as it browns, about 10 minutes.

Stir in the paprika and cumin. Drain the raisins and stir them in along with the sun-dried tomatoes. Taste and season with salt and black pepper, as needed. Remove the filling from the heat and keep warm.

Prepare the potato crust: Peel the potatoes and cut them into 1-inch chunks, dropping them into a large pot of salted water as they are cut. Bring the potatoes to a boil and cook them until tender when pierced with a fork, about 20 to 25 minutes.

Drain the potatoes thoroughly and transfer them to a large mixing bowl. Add 1 tablespoon of the butter and coarsely mash the potatoes with a fork or potato masher. Add the milk and the nutmeg, and beat the potatoes with an electric mixer until smooth. (Or force the potato chunks through a potato ricer and simply mix in the butter and then the milk and nutmeg.) The mashed potatoes should be rather stiff so that they hold their shape when molded. Taste and season with salt and white pepper, as needed.

Assemble the potato pie: Butter a soufflé dish or another deep baking dish with a 2-quart capacity with the remaining tablespoon of butter. Spread a 1-inch layer of mashed potatoes with a spatula on the bottom and up the sides of the dish, leaving a ½-inch edge at the top. (You should have enough potatoes remaining for a ½- to 1-inch top crust.) Smooth the potatoes with the spatula.

Spoon the minced beef filling into the well in the center of the potatoes. The filling should reach to the top edge of the potatoes. Press the olives into the beef filling so that they are evenly distributed. Spread the remaining mashed potatoes over the beef filling. (The top can be flat or have a domed shape.) Smooth the potatoes with the spatula. For a sugared crust, sprinkle the top of the pie with 1 teaspoon granulated sugar.

Bake the potato pie in a preheated 350°F oven until the top is light brown and crusty, about 35 minutes. Cut the potato pie into 6 wedges with a knife and serve at once with a Chilean tomato salad or the salad of your choice. Pass around a bowl of sugar for sprinkling, if desired.

Serves 6

NEW MEXICO–STYLE
CHILES RELLENOS

Chiles rellenos a la Nuevo México

To most Americans *chiles rellenos* conjure up images of crisp, golden, batter-fried, whole long green chile peppers stuffed with molten Monterey Jack or Colby cheese in a pool of tomato sauce. In Mexican American kitchens, *chiles rellenos* are also commonly stuffed with refried beans or *picadillo,* a blend of minced beef, onions, and spices. All across New Mexico, Mexican American cooks make yet another version of *chiles rellenos* with *picadillo* in which the chiles—always beloved New Mexico green chiles—are diced, mixed in with the *picadillo,* and then shaped into croquettes that are dipped in egg batter and fried. These *chiles rellenos* are served alone or with a tomato or red chile sauce, or cinnamon-sugar syrup. Some Mexican Americans also sweeten the croquettes by adding brown sugar, pine nuts, or pecans, and cinnamon and allspice to the basic recipe. Sweetened *chiles rellenos* are commonly served as an appetizer or dessert at holiday celebrations and on other festive occasions.

Potter Margaret Duran of Albuquerque, New Mexico, makes some of the best savory *chiles rellenos* we have ever tried. "The basic recipe for my *chiles rellenos,*" Margaret told us, "is a family heirloom; it was handed down from my great-grandmother Stackpole of Socorro, New Mexico, to my grandmother Armijo of Albuquerque, and then to my mother, Isabel Duran. Whenever I have time away from my pottery, my job at the University of New Mexico Development Office, and the local track, where my jockeys race the horses I breed, I like to prepare these *chiles rellenos* for friends and family." We find Margaret's savory *chiles rellenos* irresistible—especially with New Mexican–style Spanish rice and slow-simmered pinto beans.

FOR THE TOMATO SAUCE:
- 1½ pounds ripe Roma (plum) tomatoes
- 1 tablespoon olive oil
- 1 small yellow onion, peeled and finely minced
- 1 large clove garlic, peeled and finely minced
- ¾ cup chicken stock
- Salt and freshly ground black pepper, to taste

FOR THE *CHILES RELLENOS:*
- 1½ pounds fresh New Mexico green chiles, or substitute green Anaheim chiles, roasted, peeled, and seeded
- (see pages 164, 162, and 167 for information on these chiles and for directions on roasting peppers)

½ tablespoon olive oil

½ pound lean ground sirloin beef

¼ cup finely minced onion

¼ teaspoon salt, or to taste

Approximately ½ cup unbleached all-purpose flour

5 large eggs, separated, with the egg whites in a large mixing bowl and the yolks in a small bowl

2½ cups vegetable oil, or as needed, for frying

Prepare the tomato sauce: Cut the tomatoes in quarters and purée them in an electric blender or food processor until smooth. Heat the olive oil in a large saucepan over medium heat. Sauté the minced onions and the garlic until the onions are limp, about 4 minutes. Stir in the puréed tomatoes and the chicken stock, bring to a boil, then reduce the heat and simmer the sauce, stirring occasionally, for 15 minutes. Taste and season with salt and pepper, if needed. Keep the sauce warm.

Prepare the *chiles rellenos:* Dice the roasted chiles. Heat the ½ tablespoon olive oil in a 10-inch skillet over medium heat. Sauté the ground beef in the oil until it has browned, about 5 minutes. Stir in the minced onions and sauté until they have softened. Next add the diced chiles and sauté over medium-low heat, stirring constantly, for approximately 5 minutes. Stir in the salt, then remove from the heat. Transfer the mixture to a medium mixing bowl (so that it cools faster) and allow it to cool to room temperature.

Lightly flour 2 baking sheets and then your hands. Roll 1 heaping tablespoon of the beef-chile mixture between your palms into a plump croquette about 1½ inches long. Place the croquette on one of the baking sheets. (The croquettes may not hold together too well at first, but shape them the best you can. They will hold together like a meatball once they have cooled further on the baking sheet.) Lightly flour your hands as often as necessary as you roll the rest of the croquettes.

Beat the egg whites until stiff with an electric mixer. Add the egg yolks and 1 teaspoon of the flour, and blend until smooth to make a batter.

Heat the vegetable oil to 400°F in a large skillet or electric fryer. Put a croquette on a tablespoon and dip it into the egg batter so that it is completely covered. Gently drop the croquette into the hot oil. If the top of the croquette has a bare spot, spoon some batter on it. Repeat with 2 more of the croquettes quickly. Fry them for approximately 1 minute, or until golden on the underside, and then gently flip with a wire skimmer or a fork and fry until golden on the other side. With a wire skimmer or slotted spoon, transfer the *chiles rellenos* from the skillet to a plate lined with paper towels to drain. Continue with the remaining croquettes, frying only 3 at the same time.

Spoon the tomato sauce on each of 4 plates. Place 2 or 3 croquettes in the pool of the tomato sauce on each of the plates and serve at once, alone, with Spanish rice and beans, or the accompaniments of your choice.

Serves 4

New Mexico–Style Chiles Rellenos *(continued)*

For variation, Semisweet *Chiles Rellenos*: We crossed Margaret's savory *chiles rellenos* with sweetened ones to arrive at what we call semisweet. These croquettes, perfumed with cinnamon and allspice and earthy with nuts, are not all that sweet, so they can still be served with tomato sauce. Simply add ½ cup finely chopped pine nuts or pecans, 2 teaspoons brown sugar, I teaspoon cinnamon, and ½ teaspoon ground allspice, along with the salt, to the ground beef mixture and prepare as directed.

EDDIE'S PUERTO RICAN ROAST PORK

Pernil de cerdo al horno Eddie

Whenever he wants to dazzle his friends, Puerto Rican actor Eddie Castrodad cooks up his mother's recipe for Puerto Rican Roast Pork—pork shoulder rubbed with an *adobo,* a blend of olive oil, garlic, and spices, and then roasted until a crisp outer layer gives way to flavorful, juicy meat. Eddie, like most Puerto Ricans, insists that the cut of choice for the roast is the pork shoulder rather than the loin or the leg, as its higher fat content renders the meat all the more succulent.

Roast pork is usually featured at Christmas dinner and on other special occasions in Puerto Rican homes, as well as in Cuban, Guyanese, and other Caribbean American households. Puerto Ricans have their own unique traditional accompaniments, which include *Arroz con gandules* (Rice and Pigeon Peas, see page 179), *Pasteles* (Stuffed Plantain Rectangles, see page 221), and *acapurrias* (green bananas stuffed with ground beef). Instead of a pork roast, some Puerto Rican mainlanders serve roasted suckling pig (*lechón asado*), a whole pig weighing 12 pounds on average that has been rubbed with *adobo* and roasted in the oven. (In Puerto Rico, pigs weighing up to 100 pounds are commonly spit-roasted over an open fire, which imparts a marvelous smoky flavor and aroma to the pork.) Most Puerto Ricans in the northeast, like Nuyoricans (Puerto Rican New Yorkers), indulge in *lechón asado* at *lechoneras,* restaurants that specialize in roasted suckling pig, rather than at home, as it is difficult to haul a whole pig into a New York apartment, though some manage to do it.

1 bone-in pork shoulder roast (4½ to 5 pounds)

12 medium cloves garlic (1 medium bulb), peeled and left whole

1 tablespoon dried powdered oregano (not crumbled)

1 teaspoon salt, or to taste

½ teaspoon freshly ground black pepper, or to taste

¼ cup distilled white vinegar*

2 tablespoons olive oil

*Some prefer an equal amount of freshly squeezed lime juice.

Rinse the pork shoulder under cold running water. Pat it dry with paper towels. Cut shallow slits with a small sharp knife all over the pork shoulder.

Make an *adobo*, a garlic-spice rub: Purée the garlic with the oregano, salt, black pepper, and distilled white vinegar in a food processor or electric blender. Pour in the olive oil and blend well. (Or make the *adobo* the old-fashioned way by crushing the garlic, oregano, and salt and pepper with a mortar and pestle, and then combining the crushed garlic mixture and the vinegar and oil.)

Place the pork in a shallow roasting pan, then pour the *adobo* over it. Rub the *adobo* into the pork with your fingers, forcing it into the slits. Cover the pork with plastic wrap and marinate it in the refrigerator overnight.

Roast the pork in a 350°F oven, basting regularly with pan juices, until tender, about 2½ to 3 hours. Remove the pork from the pan to a carving board and let it rest for 10 minutes before slicing. Serve the pork hot or warm, with Puerto Rican Rice and Pigeon Peas or the accompaniments of your choice.

Serves 6 to 8

PORK CUTLETS STUFFED WITH PRUNES AND OLIVES

Lomitos de cerdo rellenos

"**A**rgentine and Uruguayan Americans have a passion for meat. I guess it's in their Italian and Spanish gaucho blood," says Uruguayan American Carlos Petkovich, who, with his wife, Maria, works culinary magic at Los Gauchitos, a much lauded Argentine and Uruguayan restaurant, meat market, and pastry shop in Miami. "Our customers from the old country order a lot of filet mignon that is massaged with coarse salt to seal in the juices and then seared on the grill. *Chivitos*—authentic Uruguayan sandwiches piled a mile high with sliced steak, ham, pancetta, mozzarella, lettuce, tomato, and even an egg on Catalan bread—are big, too. Another dish in high demand, which I happen to love, is *Lomitos de cerdo rellenos,* succulent pork cutlets with a prune-and-green-olive stuffing in a fruity cream sauce. To me, the dish is like romance: it's sweet, savory, intense, and you hope it lasts forever. Uruguayans and Argentines cannot have enough fruit, so I serve the stuffed pork cutlets with a soothing homemade applesauce made from crisp, tart Granny Smith apples tamed with a little sugar and cinnamon. Roasted new potatoes are a good accompaniment, too."

4 boneless lean pork loin cutlets (1 inch thick), trimmed of any fat	½ cup water
Freshly ground black pepper, to taste	½ cup dry (fino) sherry
1 cup finely chopped pitted prunes	½ cup heavy cream
¾ cup pimiento-stuffed green olives, ½ cup minced and ¼ cup whole	1 small bouquet garni (a bundle of 1 bay leaf, 2 fresh thyme sprigs, and 3 fresh parsley sprigs held together with string)
1 dozen toothpicks	
3 tablespoons olive oil	1 teaspoon Dijon mustard

Cut pockets in each pork loin cutlet for the stuffing. Season the cutlets inside and out with pepper, and stuff each with 1 tablespoon of the prunes and 2 tablespoons of the minced olives. Close the cutlets and secure by inserting 3 toothpicks in each along the opening.

Heat the olive oil in a large heavy skillet over medium-high heat and brown the pork cutlets on both sides, about 10 minutes. Add the water, sherry, cream, and bouquet garni, and simmer, covered, over low heat until the pork is cooked, about 35 minutes.

Stir in the mustard. Add the remaining prunes and olives, and continue cooking, uncovered, for 5 to 10 minutes, or until the sauce has thickened. Transfer the stuffed pork to a serving platter and remove the toothpicks. Remove the bouquet ~ the sauce and discard. Pour the sauce over the cutlets and serve at once with applesauce and roasted new potatoes or the accompaniments of your choice.

Serves 4

PORK AND *CHILE VERDE* WITH *NOPALITOS*

Chile verde con nopalitos

"In the centuries-old tradition of desert Southwest cooking, my maternal grandmother, Elvira De La Rosa, made hundreds of dishes with wild foods, including *nopalitos*—the young paddles on prickly-pear cactus, which she collected right in her backyard in Phoenix," says Virginia Widing (née Rojas), a superb cook who grew up next door to her maternal grandparents. "My grandparents came to the United States from Santa Ana, Sonora, Mexico, and so I was raised on authentic Mexican dishes—and values. I spent endless hours in the kitchen at my grandmother's side, as she taught me not only to cook without measuring and to always select foods in season but to love God, family, and all humankind.

"One of my grandmother's favorite dishes in spring when the vivid green *nopalitos* burst forth was *Chile colorado con nopalitos,* beef and *nopalitos* simmered in a red chile sauce," says Virginia. "Over time I altered the recipe by adding cilantro and substituting pork for beef, and poblano and jalapeño chiles for red Anaheim chiles and yellow Santa Fe Grande chiles to make a *chile verde* (green chile sauce) instead of *chile colorado*." (See pages 162–3 for information on these chiles.) Virginia serves Pork and *Chile Verde* with *Nopalitos* just as her grandmother did, with Spanish rice, refried beans or pinto beans sprinkled with freshly diced onions, homemade flour tortillas, and fresh salsa. Her husband, Bob Widing, a real estate agent, is passionate about the tortillas, so she always makes huge batches. To drink, Virginia suggests limeade or lemonade from freshly squeezed citrus.

Pork and Chile Verde *with* Nopalitos *(continued)*

½ cup unbleached all-purpose flour

¼ teaspoon each salt and freshly ground black pepper, or to taste

2 pounds boneless pork loin or shoulder, cut into 1-inch cubes

3 tablespoons olive oil

1 medium yellow onion, peeled and diced

3 medium scallions, root ends cut off and diced

4 large cloves garlic, peeled and minced

3 poblano chiles, roasted, peeled, seeded, and diced (see page 165 for information on poblanos and page 167 for directions on roasting peppers)

3 jalapeño chiles, seeded and minced, or to taste

5 medium ripe tomatoes, diced, or one 28-ounce can chopped tomatoes

2 cups boiled fresh *nopalitos,* or substitute canned or bottled *nopalitos* cut in strips (*nopalitos tiernos en rajas*), rinsed, and drained (see page 75 for information on *nopalitos*)

¼ cup finely minced fresh cilantro

Mix together the flour, salt, and black pepper in a shallow bowl. Dredge the pork cubes in the seasoned flour.

Heat the olive oil in a large pot over medium-high heat. Sauté the pork cubes, about one third at a time, in the oil until they are brown on all sides. Remove them to a large plate as they brown. When all the pork cubes are cooked, spoon off all but 3 tablespoons of the pan drippings, if necessary. Add the onions, scallions, garlic, roasted poblano chiles, and jalapeños, and sauté for 3 minutes. Add the tomatoes and sauté for an additional minute.

Return the pork to the pot, and then pour in enough water to just cover. Bring to a boil, reduce the heat, and simmer the pork, covered, stirring occasionally, until tender, about 1 hour. Stir in the *nopalitos* and cilantro, and simmer the stew for an additional 15 minutes. The sauce should have a thick gravy consistency. Add more water, if needed, and cook until heated through. Taste and adjust the seasoning, if necessary. Serve Pork and *Chile Verde* with *Nopalitos* at once, with the accompaniments of your choice.

Serves 4 to 6

PORK CHOPS IN ORANGE GRAVY WITH GARLIC, CAPERS, AND RAISINS

Costillas de cerdo con ajo, alcaparras y pasas

In this Guatemalan American recipe, the orange juice marinade laced with cinnamon and cloves tenderizes the pork and lends a sweet-tart contrast, while the pungent garlic, salty capers, and soft, plump raisins add vibrant accents of flavor and texture. Guatemalan Americans prepare this fragrant dish with either pork loin roast or pork chops. We prefer to use pork chops for casual suppers for four, or even fewer. (See the directions below for cooking a pork roast.) Mashed potatoes or potato pancakes are the traditional accompaniments; steamed white rice or couscous is also nice. Since the essence of this dish is citrus, sugar, and spice, we always end the meal with a subtle, understated dessert, like hazelnut biscotti, Almond Cookies (see page 271), old-fashioned pound cake, or scoops of gentle green-tea ice cream.

1 ½ cups orange juice
¼ teaspoon ground cinnamon
⅛ teaspoon ground cloves
4 center-cut pork chops, about 1 inch thick
Salt and freshly ground black pepper, to taste
1 ½ tablespoons olive oil
1 cup finely minced yellow onion

2 large cloves garlic, peeled and finely minced
½ cup cold water
½ tablespoon Worcestershire sauce
2 tablespoons capers, drained
¼ cup seedless golden raisins
2 tablespoons slivered almonds, for garnish (optional)

Mix the orange juice, cinnamon, and cloves in a shallow dish, and add the pork chops in a single layer. Cover with plastic wrap and leave the chops to marinate in the refrigerator for at least 2 hours.

Remove the pork chops from the marinade and drain, reserving the marinade. Season them with salt and pepper. Heat ½ tablespoon of the olive oil over medium-high heat in a skillet just large enough to hold the chops in a single layer. Brown them on both sides in the oil, about 5 minutes per side, and then transfer the chops with the pan juices to a plate.

Sauté the minced onions and garlic in the remaining tablespoon of oil in the skillet over medium-high heat, stirring occasionally, until they are just golden, about 4 minutes.

Pork Chops in Orange Gravy with Garlic, Capers, and Raisins (continued)

Return the pork chops to the skillet, then add the orange juice marinade, the cold water, and the Worcestershire sauce. Cover and simmer the pork, stirring occasionally, for 45 minutes.

Add the capers and raisins to the skillet, cover, and cook the pork chops for 10 minutes more. Serve the pork chops in their sauce at once, with the potato pancakes, mashed potatoes, steamed white rice, or couscous, garnished with slivered almonds, if desired.

Serves 4

For a pork roast: Place a 4½- to 5-pound bone-in pork shoulder roast in a shallow roasting pan, just large enough to accommodate it comfortably, and then pour the orange juice marinade over it. (If the pan is too large the marinade will burn.) Cover the pork with plastic wrap and marinate it, turning once, in the refrigerator for at least 4 hours. Stir in the minced onions, garlic, and the ½ cup water. Roast in a preheated 350°F oven, basting regularly with the marinade, until tender, about 2½ to 3 hours. Remove the pork from the pan to a carving board and let it rest for 10 minutes before slicing. Skim off the fat from the juices. Make a gravy by scraping the bottom of the pan to loosen any brown bits. Stir in the Worcestershire sauce, capers, and raisins. Place the pan over moderate heat and boil for 2 minutes. Serve the pork with the gravy and steamed rice or mashed potatoes. Serves 6 to 8

PUERTO RICAN SPANISH RICE WITH PORK

Arroz con carne de cerdo a la puertorriqueña

This recipe for *arroz con carne de cerdo* comes from the Puerto Rican kitchen of architect Artemio Paz, Jr. of Springfield, Oregon. His mother, María Rosa Carballo de Paz, who was born in Vega Baja, Perto Rico, taught him how to cook this delicious dish. Growing up in New York City, Artemio vividly recalls the aroma of the grain boiling in Chicken broth that greeted him each day after school. On weekdays his mother would dress the rice with little more than onion or garlic, but on Sundays and holidays she would add pork, chicken, or vegetables, and capers or green olives, and green peppers to the dish, as her grandmother had shown her.

Today Artemio and his wife, Edana Paz often serve *Arroz con carne de cerdo,* which they affectionately call Grandma's Rice, making it with olive oil instead of the traditional bacon to brown the onions, garlic, and green pepper. Artemio and Edana Paz ritually serve Spanish Rice with Pork at holiday meals, along with a dish of garbanzo beans and potatoes and a sweet bread.

Traditional Puerto Rican *arroz con carne de cerdo* is similar to Dominican *arroz con carne de cerdo*—pork with rice flavored with bacon, green olives, hot pepper, capers, and parsley; Peruvian *arroz con chancho*—pork and rice spiced with ground annatto and hot red chiles and studded with peas; and Brazilian *arroz con porco*—rice and pork embellished with ham, bell peppers, hot chiles, garlic, and cilantro. Like the Paz family's Spanish Rice with Pork, all of these dishes have undergone a transformation in Latin American communities across America.

1 pound lean boneless pork loin, cut into
   1-inch cubes
1 tablespoon olive oil
1 large yellow onion, peeled and finely
   minced
½ cup diced green bell pepper
2 large cloves garlic, peeled and minced
2 cups long-grain white rice
4 cups hot homemade or canned
   chicken broth

½ cup canned tomato sauce
2½ dozen pimiento-stuffed green olives,
   or ⅓ cup capers, drained
Salt and freshly ground black pepper, to
   taste
½ cup finely minced fresh parsley, for
   garnish

Sauté the pork in ½ tablespoon of the olive oil in a large pot over medium heat, turning several times, until cooked on the outside, about 10 minutes. Remove the pork to a plate with a slotted spoon. Add the remaining ½ tablespoon of olive oil to the pan juices. Sauté the minced onions, bell pepper, and garlic in the oil over medium heat until the onions are golden brown, about 8 minutes.

Add the rice and sauté it, stirring, for 3 to 4 minutes. Stir in the chicken broth and tomato sauce, and bring to a boil over medium-high heat. Reduce the heat, add the sautéed pork, cover, and simmer until the rice is tender, and all the liquid has been absorbed, about 25 minutes. Stir in the green olives or capers, and salt and black pepper to taste, keeping in mind that the olives are salty. Serve at once, garnished with parsley.

Serves 6

For variation, Brazilian American Rice with Pork (*Arroz con porco*): Before sautéing the pork, marinate it for at least 2 hours in a marinade of ¼ cup each distilled white vinegar and dry white wine, 3 tablespoons finely minced onion, 1 finely minced garlic clove, and hot sauce to taste. Substitute ⅓ cup marinade for the tomato sauce in the above recipe, ½ cup diced ham for the olives, and ½ cup finely minced cilantro for the parsley.

PORK ENCHILADAS WITH POBLANO CHILE CREAM SAUCE

Enchiladas zacatecanas

"**T**hese enchiladas, bathed like crêpes in a wonderfully rich cream sauce laced with poblano chile purée, are as popular among those who dine at my table as *Carmen* is among opera lovers," says opera singer Juan Sanchez Lozano, who got his musical start in his native Mexico City. In 1985 the tenor came to the United States to study under opera master Georgio Tozzi. Since his arrival in America, Sanchez Lozano has performed with numerous opera companies throughout California, where he makes his home, as well as internationally. He is as talented at the stove as he is on the stage, and his dishes have all the grandeur and magnificence of great opera. "This," in-

sists Sanchez Lozano, "I owe to my aunt Mary, 'Tita,' who taught me not only to cook well but to appreciate cooking as an art."

FOR THE ENCHILADAS:

- I pound boneless lean pork loin or shoulder cutlets (¼ inch thick)
- 2 medium (about 4 inches long) poblano chile peppers, roasted, seeded, and peeled (see page 165 for information on poblanos and page 167 for directions on roasting peppers)
- ½ small yellow onion, peeled and minced
- I large clove garlic, peeled and minced
- I tablespoon olive oil, and a little extra for sautéing the tortillas
- 1½ cups half-and-half
- I cup (6 ounces) *queso fresco* (a Mexican cheese also known as *queso ranchero*), crumbled
- 8 corn tortillas

FOR THE GARNISH:

- 4 large red- or green-leaf lettuce leaves, shredded
- I ripe avocado, halved, pitted, peeled, and cut into ¼-inch slices
- I medium ripe tomato, sliced

Place the pork loin or shoulder cutlets in a large skillet with ½ inch water and bring to a boil over medium-high heat. Reduce the heat and simmer the pork, covered, until tender, about 25 minutes. Remove the pork from the broth to a plate and shred it with two forks. Cover the shredded pork with aluminum foil.

Prepare the poblano chile cream sauce: Purée the roasted chiles in a food processor or electric blender until smooth. Sauté the minced onions and garlic in the olive oil in a large skillet over medium heat until the onions are limp, about 3 minutes. Reduce the heat to medium-low and add the puréed chiles, the half-and-half, and half of the *queso.* Simmer the sauce, stirring frequently, until it thickens, about 10 minutes.

While the sauce thickens, prepare the tortillas. Heat about ½ teaspoon olive oil in a small skillet over medium heat. Sauté a tortilla in the oil, turning once, until it is pliable and light golden, about 40 seconds per side. Transfer the tortilla with tongs or a pair of wooden chopsticks to paper towels to drain. Cook the rest of the tortillas, adding more olive oil to the skillet as needed.

Assemble the enchiladas by dipping a tortilla into the sauce so that it is coated on both sides. Lay the tortilla on a dinner plate and place about 2 tablespoons shredded pork on one side of it. Fold the other side of the tortilla over the pork.

The green-black, thick-fleshed poblano chile, which turns red when mature, is often mislabeled an ancho or a pasilla.

Pork Enchiladas with Poblano Chile Cream Sauce (continued)

Assemble the rest of the enchiladas in the same manner and arrange 2 on each plate. Spoon any remaining sauce over the enchiladas. Garnish each plate with shredded lettuce, avocado slices, tomato slices, and the remaining *queso*, and serve at once.

Serves 4

POSOLE

Posole

This rich stew gets its name from the pivotal ingredient *posole,* otherwise known as hominy—dried whole corn kernels that have been treated with slaked lime. *Posole* (*pozole* in Mexico) was originally a staple food of the Pueblo Indians of the Southwest. The Spanish who settled in the region adopted it as their own and over time combined it with various ingredients, such as red chile, lamb, beef, and pork, in stews (that are frequently served as side dishes in the Southwest) or ground it into *masa harina* for tortillas and tamales. In Mexican American families not only in the Southwest but all across the United States, *posole* with pork (and sometimes chicken) is a traditional dish for Christmas and Las Posadas, processions re-creating the story of Mary and Joseph's journey to Bethlehem, which take place each of the nine nights before Christmas. Gabriel Peña of Carpinteria Middle School in Carpinteria, California, captures its significance in Mexican American culture in an essay he wrote for a school project on family traditions:

> My tradition is *posole.* The recipe is from my grandmother. She brought it from Mexico to Carpinteria in 1980, and the tradition has been going on for twelve years, and it will go on longer than that. I remember in 1990 all of my family was at my house and all of us were eating *posole.* I remembered the first time I had *posole.* It was so good. Christmas is a perfect time to have *posole.*

> **POSOLE RECIPE**
> 1 pork roast, boiled with seasoning. 1 chicken boiled with seasoning. When chicken is done, remove bones. Add 2 cans hominy. Serve in a soup bowl and top with cabbage, radishes, or about anything. It is usually served with tostadas.

Our *posole* recipe has no chicken and requires just a few more steps than Gabriel's. If you use dried hominy, start the recipe the evening before or in the morning. We

like to serve *posole* with a selection of garnishes that might include shredded green-leaf lettuce, minced radishes, grated Cheddar or Monterey Jack cheese, avocado slices, lime wedges, and finely minced fresh cilantro, each in a separate small bowl for passing around the table.

I cup dried white, yellow, or blue
    hominy, or substitute 3 cups canned
    hominy, drained and rinsed under
    cold running water*
I boneless pork roast (2 pounds)
I large ripe tomato, chopped, or
    substitute 3 canned tomatoes,
    chopped
I small yellow onion, peeled and
    finely minced
I red or green Anaheim chile or New
    Mexico green chile, roasted, peeled,
    seeded, and chopped (see page 162
    for information on the Anaheim, page
    164 for the New Mexico chile, and
    page 167 for instructions on roasting
    peppers)

I green or red jalapeño chile, seeded and
    finely minced
I large clove garlic, peeled and finely
    minced
I teaspoon dried powdered oregano
    (not crumbled)
Salt and freshly ground black pepper,
    to taste

Dried and canned hominy are available in some supermarkets and in Mexican markets. You can also order dried hominy by mail order (see Sources, page 302). Do not use hominy grits for this recipe.

To cook the dried hominy (if you are using canned hominy, skip this step), rinse it under cold running water, and then soak it in enough water to cover for at least 4 hours or overnight. Drain and rinse again. Put the hominy in a large pot with enough fresh water to cover, bring to a boil over medium heat, then reduce the heat to low and simmer, covered, until it is puffed, about 1 hour. Use 3 cups of the cooked hominy in this recipe. (Note that cooked hominy will keep in the refrigerator for up to 5 days.)

Add enough water to cover the hominy, then add the pork, tomato, onion, Anaheim and jalapeño chiles, garlic, oregano, and salt and black pepper, as needed, to the hominy, and simmer, covered, for 2 hours, or until the pork is tender. Remove the roast from the pot to a cutting board, allow it to cool enough to be handled, and shred it with two forks or your fingers. Return the pork with ½ cup water to the pot and simmer for another 30 minutes. Taste and correct the seasoning. Serve the *posole* at once, with the garnishes of your choice.

Serves 4

JERK LAMB SHISH KEBABS

"First comes a blast of chile heat, then a glow of spice, and then the flavors just dance on your tongue," says Terry Lindsay, Director of the Office of African American Student Development at Olivet College in Michigan. He is talking about Jamaican jerk. "The secret to great jerk is a marinade that balances the key elements: Scotch bonnet peppers, onions, garlic, thyme, allspice. The Scotch bonnets make the jerk fiery hot; turn down the heat, if you want, by just adding less. From there on in, the recipe's a breeze, and you can marinate just about anything—pork, chicken, beef, lamb, fish. Jerk lamb is one of my favorites. I have found that jerk lamb and summer vegetables go great together, as the mild, sweet vegetables offset the spiciness and tanginess of the meat. To simplify matters, I string the meat and vegetables on skewers like shish kebab and cook them on the grill or under the broiler. I love when the lamb and onions are a little charred on the edges and the tomatoes and red peppers are just bursting with concentrated juices."

There are many theories as to the origin of the term "jerk," says Terry. Some speculate that it has to do with the way you jerk (turn) slabs of meat on a grill, or you jerk (cut) them apart for serving. Terry came to appreciate jerk all the more when he realized that Lansing, Michigan, is devoid of Jamaican restaurants: "I was born in Jamaica

AMERICA'S MOST FAMOUS JERK | Janet's Original Jerk Chicken Pit in Los

Angeles and Vernon's Jerk Paradise in New York City are without question America's most famous jerk houses. Los Angelenos make a beeline to Janet's for the jerk chicken with crisp, crunchy skin scented with cracked black pepper, allspice, and thyme, and succulent meat. At Janet's the chicken is massaged with a dry jerk rub, grilled over aromatic hardwood on a gigantic open grill, and served with fried plantains, festival (a mildly sweet fried cornmeal bread that resembles johnnycake), and a choice of other scrumptious sides.

New Yorkers with longings for jerk find their way to the original Vernon's Jerk Paradise, which opened in 1982 on East 233rd Street in the Bronx (Vernon recently closed the swankier Vernon's on West 29th Street in Manhattan so that he could spend some time in warmer climes). At Vernon's the moist and flavorful jerk is served alongside Jamaican rice and peas (actually rice and red beans cooked with coconut milk) and steamed cabbage. Vernon's also offers exotic drinks like Irish Moss, which is supposed to enhance virility and the growth of hair. While Janet's subscribes to the dry-rub school, Vernon's has found fame in jerk sauce—so much fame that those addicted to Vernon's lively jerk sauce can purchase it all around town, including at Zabar's on the Upper West Side, and by mail order (see Sources, page 306).

but grew up in Brooklyn, just a subway ride from Vernon's Jerk Paradise in either the Bronx or Manhattan, the best jerk houses in New York City. Of course, my mother and my sisters also make fabulous jerk. On my first visit back to Brooklyn, they gave me jerk lessons, so now I can prepare jerk lamb in my island-style kitchen in Lansing. I will survive."

Terry serves his jerk lamb shish kebabs with "Jamaican coat of arms" (rice and beans steeped in coconut milk, see recipe on page 175) or a simple rice pilaf. To cool the lips, he pours several rounds of Jamaican pine-ginger, a tasty concoction of non-alcoholic ginger beer (made with fresh ginger, sugar, and water) and pineapple juice. Ice cream, baked bananas, or pinch-me-rounds (coconut tarts) provide the final flourish to a meal as upbeat as reggae.

FOR THE JERK PASTE:

- I small white onion, peeled and quartered
- 2 medium cloves garlic, peeled
- I Scotch bonnet chile, or substitute a 1-inch-long habanero, stem removed, halved and seeded, or to taste (see pages 165 and 163 for information on these chiles)
- I tablespoon coarsely chopped fresh ginger
- I teaspoon ground allspice
- 2 teaspoons fresh thyme, or I teaspoon dried thyme
- I teaspoon freshly ground black pepper
- 2 tablespoons freshly squeezed lime juice, or substitute white wine vinegar
- I tablespoon soy sauce

FOR THE KEBABS:

- 2 pounds boneless lean lamb shoulder or leg, trimmed of any excess fat and cut into 1½-inch cubes
- I large onion, peeled and cut into 1½-inch wedges
- I large red or yellow bell pepper, stem removed, seeded, deribbed, and cut into 2-inch pieces
- I medium zucchini, cut into ¾-inch slices
- I dozen ripe cherry tomatoes
- 2 tablespoons olive oil
- 6 long metal skewers

Purée all the ingredients for the jerk paste in a blender or food processor until smooth. Transfer the jerk paste to a medium glass, ceramic, or stainless steel mixing bowl.

Fold the lamb into the jerk paste, coating all the cubes. Cover and marinate in the refrigerator, stirring once, for at least 3 hours.

Put the onion wedges, bell pepper, zucchini, and cherry tomatoes in a large mixing bowl and toss them with the olive oil until they are well coated. Thread equal amounts of marinated lamb and vegetables, alternating the ingredients, on the 6 metal skewers.

Broil the kebabs 1 to 2 inches from a preheated broiler, rotating them as they cook, until well browned on all sides. (Or prepare a grill with charcoal or wood chips. When the fire is ready, place the kebabs on an oiled grill and cook until well browned.) Transfer the kebabs to serving plates and serve at once with "Jamaican coat of arms," a rice pilaf, or the rice dish of your choice.

Serves 6

CURRY GOAT OR LAMB

Some of the most tantalizing flavors of Jamaica, like aromatic allspice, spirited curry powder, fiery Scotch bonnet peppers, and creamy coconut, commingle in this rich bronze stew that adorns the table at most festive occasions in traditional Jamaican America. Curry Goat came to be when East Indian indentured laborers descended on Jamaica at the invitation of the British, who recruited them to work the fields after the abolition of African slavery in 1838. The curry recipes the East Indians carried with them called for lamb, but sheep were nonexistent in early-nineteenth-century Jamaica, so they turned to goat instead. Nowadays, kid—a baby goat no more than six months old—is the meat of choice for this Jamaican curry, as mature goats have tough, gamy meat. The scarcity of kid meat in the United States has led Jamaican Americans to come full circle and use lamb. If you are lucky enough to find kid in a specialty meat market, give it a try. It is just as tender as lamb and actually tastes less gamy.

Every Jamaican American family has its own special take on Curry Goat or Lamb, though most agree that the meat should first be marinated in a spice rub. Many insist that allspice, a spice native to Jamaica that comes from the dried berries of the pimiento tree, is a necessary ingredient in the spice rub, but a minority does without it. Some Jamaican Americans prepare a simple curry that hinges on the spices and broth, while others enrich the curry with coconut milk and lime juice, or with tomatoes. Since the flavors of coconut, lime juice, and tomatoes fuse so delightfully, this version of curry goat sidesteps tradition and includes all three. Jamaican Americans serve Curry Goat or Lamb over white rice, sometimes with traditional accompaniments of Fried Green Plantains (see page 185) and mango chutney. Curry Goat or Lamb is also used as a stuffing for *roti,* an East Indian griddle-fried bread that has also found a place in the Jamaican kitchen.

2 pounds boneless goat or lamb,
trimmed of all excess fat and cut into
1-inch cubes

1 Scotch bonnet chile, or substitute a
1-inch-long habanero chile, seeded,
stems removed, and minced, or to
taste (see page 165 for information
on Scotch bonnets)

1½ tablespoons curry powder (if you use
Madras curry powder, cut the amount
of chile in half)

½ teaspoon ground allspice

¼ teaspoon salt, or to taste

⅛ teaspoon freshly ground black pepper,
or to taste

1 tablespoon butter

1 tablespoon olive oil

1 large white onion, peeled and minced

1 large clove garlic, peeled and minced

1 medium ripe tomato, finely diced

1 cup canned unsweetened coconut milk

½ cup chicken stock, or substitute water

1 tablespoon freshly squeezed lime or
lemon juice

2 medium scallions, root ends removed
and minced

1 bay leaf

2 tablespoons finely minced fresh parsley
or cilantro, for garnish

Season the goat or lamb with the chile pepper, curry powder, allspice, salt, and black pepper in a large nonreactive mixing bowl. Cover with plastic wrap and allow the meat to marinate in the refrigerator for 1 hour.

Heat the butter and olive oil in a large skillet over medium heat. Sauté the meat in 2 batches until the pieces are browned on all sides, about 7 minutes per batch, removing them to a large plate when they have browned.

Raise the heat to medium-high and sauté the minced onions in the oil remaining in the skillet, stirring often, until the onions are lightly browned, about 4 minutes. Add the garlic and sauté an additional minute. Stir in the diced tomatoes and continue cooking for 2 minutes. Return the meat and its juices to the skillet. Add the coconut milk, chicken stock or water, lime or lemon juice, scallions, and bay leaf. Bring to a boil, then reduce the heat, cover, and simmer until the meat is very tender, 45 minutes to 1 hour. Taste and adjust the seasonings. Serve the dish, garnished with fresh parsley or cilantro, with steamed white rice.

Serves 4

BEEF TONGUE IN TOMATO SAUCE A LA BLANCA

Lengua en salsa de tomate a la Blanca

B eef tongue dishes are enjoyed by Americans of Latin American descent no matter what their country of origin, although those who grew up in Latin America tend to favor the delicacy more. Each culture has its own special ways of cooking tongue. For instance, Chilean Americans might prepare subtly sweet *lengua con ciruelas* (tongue with plums), or *lengua fiambre* (cold tongue), while Venezuelan Americans might serve *lengua de res en escabeche* (beef tongue in *escabeche*). *Escabeche* is a sauce with a base of vinegar, oil, and garlic. Brazilian Americans would be apt to dish up *lingua fresca* (Tongue in White Wine–Parsley Sauce). Chilean Americans and Ecuadoran Americans might bring a spicy tongue dish called *lengua en salsa picante* (tongue in chile sauce) to the table. A specialty among Puerto Ricans and Cuban Americans is *Lengua en salsa de tomate* (Tongue in Tomato Sauce). This is a wonderful Cuban American version, which Himilce bases on her memories of the tongue dish that Blanca, the family cook in Havana, used to make.

1 fresh beef tongue (approximately 3 pounds)	2 bay leaves
5 tablespoons olive oil	One 8-ounce can tomato sauce
1 medium yellow onion, peeled and thinly sliced	¼ cup seedless black raisins
½ cup minced celery	Salt and freshly ground black pepper, to taste
5 medium cloves garlic, peeled and left whole	Pinch of sugar
3 shallots, peeled and minced	12 pitted green olives, for garnish
2½ tablespoons unbleached all-purpose flour	6 sprigs of parsley, for garnish

Rinse the tongue under cold running water and place it in a large stockpot with enough water to cover plus 2 inches. Bring the water to a boil, then reduce the heat and simmer the tongue, covered, until tender, about 2 hours. Remove 2 cups of the cooking liquid and reserve. Transfer the tongue to a large plate and peel the skin off, beginning at the thick end, and discard.

Heat 3 tablespoons of the olive oil in the pot and sauté the onion slices, celery, garlic, and shallots over medium heat until the onions begin to brown, about 8 minutes. Transfer the vegetables to a plate.

Heat the remaining 2 tablespoons of olive oil in the pot over medium-low heat. Add the flour and cook, whisking constantly, until it turns golden. Slowly pour the reserved cooking liquid into the flour mixture, whisking constantly. Add the bay leaves and simmer for 5 minutes. Add the cooked tongue, sautéed vegetables, tomato sauce, raisins, salt and pepper, and sugar, and simmer for about 20 minutes, so the tongue absorbs all the flavors.

Remove the tongue to a cutting board and cool. Trim off and discard the gristle and small bones at the thick end of the tongue, and then cut it into ½-inch slices. Discard the bay leaves. Arrange the slices of tongue on a large serving platter, spoon on the sauce, and garnish with green olives and sprigs of parsley. Serve at once with yellow rice.

Serves 6

For Brazilian American Tongue in White Wine–Parsley Sauce (*Lingua fresca*):
Cook the tongue as instructed above, but omit all the other ingredients. After removing the skin from the cooked tongue, make about a dozen ½-inch incisions in it. Cut 2 strips of bacon into 1-inch pieces. Stuff each incision with a piece of bacon. Heat 1 tablespoon olive oil in a small roaster over medium heat. Sauté 1 small onion and 1 large garlic clove, both finely minced, in the oil for 4 minutes. Add 3 small chopped tomatoes and 2 tablespoons finely minced fresh parsley, and cook for 5 minutes more. Add 1½ cups dry white wine, ¼ teaspoon freshly ground black pepper, and salt to taste. Bring to a boil, and then remove from the heat. Put the tongue in the roaster and bake in a preheated 375°F oven for 1 hour, basting frequently with the sauce. Remove the tongue to a cutting board, trim off and discard the gristle and small bones at the thick end, and then cut it into ½-inch slices. Arrange the slices of tongue on a large serving platter, spoon on the sauce, and serve with mashed potatoes (the traditional accompaniment) or steamed rice.

"TAIL ON FIRE" OXTAIL STEW

Rabo encendido

Oxtails with meat so tender that it falls off the bone in a scrumptious deep brown winy sauce is the essence of Cuban *Rabo encendido*, which means "tail on fire." Long, slow simmering on the stove develops the wonderfully complex flavors of the oxtails and softens their gelatinous cartilage, thickening the stew. Cuban Americans traditionally serve oxtail stew with fluffy steamed rice, but it is also delicious the Brazilian American way, with squares of polenta that have been sautéed golden brown. Like most stews, this one is good reheated.

4 pounds oxtails (firm, with bright red meat), trimmed of fat and cut into 2-inch pieces
¾ cup unbleached all-purpose flour
¼ teaspoon salt, or to taste
⅛ teaspoon freshly ground black pepper, or to taste
¼ cup olive oil
3 cups homemade or canned beef broth
1 cup dry red wine

1 large green bell pepper, seeded, deribbed, and chopped
1 medium yellow onion, peeled and minced
3 large cloves garlic, peeled and minced
3 tablespoons tomato paste
½ teaspoon dried thyme
½ teaspoon cayenne pepper
A few sprigs of parsley, for garnish

Rinse the oxtail pieces under cold running water and pat dry with paper towels. Mix together the flour and salt and pepper in a shallow dish. Dredge the oxtails in the seasoned flour. Heat the olive oil in a large pot over medium-high heat. Brown the oxtails in 3 batches in the oil, turning once, about 3 minutes per side. When they have browned, remove them to a large plate.

Return all the oxtails to the pot with the beef broth, wine, bell pepper, minced onions, garlic, tomato paste, thyme, and cayenne pepper. Bring to a boil, then reduce the heat, cover, and simmer, stirring occasionally, until the oxtails are very tender, about 3 hours. Skim off the fat with a ladle or serving spoon. Taste and correct the seasoning.

Transfer the oxtails with a slotted spoon to a large serving bowl and keep warm. Bring the sauce to a boil over medium-high heat and reduce it until it is thick, about 10 to 15 minutes. Pour the sauce over the oxtails, garnish with parsley, and serve at once with steamed white rice or squares of golden brown polenta.

Serves 6

DOMINICAN AMERICAN STEW WITH TARO, *CALABAZA*, AND YELLOW PLANTAINS

Sancocho dominicano-americano

"One of my fondest childhood memories is of my twelve aunts preparing *sancocho,* a fragrant Dominican stew filled with a variety of tender tropical tubers and meats, in my grandmother Tina's kitchen in San Cristóbal," says Nicomedes E. Suriel, an attorney practicing immigration law in Phoenix. "All day long the aroma of *sancocho* would waft from the kitchen while we played with our twenty-two cousins by the little creek behind the house. We kids got really excited when my aunts made the *sancocho* in a *cambumbo* (the biggest pot in the house), which meant there would be leftovers for the next few days." These days Nicomedes Suriel visits his sister Victoria Suriel-Nelson, an artist and entrepreneur, at her home in Ahwatukee, Arizona, to enjoy *sancocho.* Victoria's version is based on their grandmother Tina's recipe, which the Suriel family brought with them in 1969 when they immigrated to the United States from Santo Domingo, Dominican Republic.

Sancocho, the quintessential Sunday meal in Dominican American households, gets its voluptuous flavor from an assortment of at least three meats, the choices being goat, beef, chicken, pork, sausage, or bacon, and a minimum of two tropical tubers (which Dominicans call *víveres*), from a selection that includes *yuca* (cassava), *ñame* (West African yam), taro, *yautía* (*malanga*), and potatoes. *Calabaza* (West Indian pumpkin) and yellow plantains are added to most *sancochos* to lend even more taste. Dominican Americans, like Cuban Americans and Puerto Ricans, enjoy a mild cuisine, but occasionally Dominican *sancocho* is laced with hot chiles. The Suriels omit the hot chiles, and they serve *sancocho* with the traditional side dishes—white rice and avocado slices.

½ cup unbleached all-purpose flour

½ teaspoon freshly ground black pepper, or to taste

½ teaspoon salt, or to taste

1 pound boneless beef chuck roast, trimmed of excess fat and cut into 2-inch cubes

1 pound skinless chicken thighs

4 thick bone-in pork loin chops (about 8 ounces each), trimmed of fat

3 tablespoons olive oil

2 quarts water

1 large green bell pepper, seeded, deribbed, and finely chopped

1 large yellow onion, peeled and finely chopped

2 large cloves garlic, peeled and minced

Dominican American Stew with Taro, Calabaza, and Yellow Plantains (continued)

2 yellow plantains, cut into 2-inch rounds and peeled (see page 183 for information on plantains and page 184 for instructions on peeling and cutting plantains)

1 large russet (Idaho) potato (about ¾ pound), peeled and cut into 1-inch chunks

1 pound taro, peeled and cut into 1-inch chunks (see page 198 for information on taro)

¾ pound *calabaza*, or substitute butternut squash, Hubbard squash, or sugar pumpkin, peeled, seeded, and cut into 1-inch pieces*

¼ cup minced fresh cilantro

2 ripe Hass avocados, peeled, pitted, and cut into thin slices (optional)

*Calabaza (also known as West Indian pumpkin, green pumpkin, or Cuban squash) is available in Latin markets and select supermarkets in regions of the country with sizable Latin American communities. Do not substitute the common American pumpkin (used for carving jack-o'-lanterns), as it tends to be bland and watery.

Mix together the flour, pepper, and salt in a large shallow bowl. Dredge the beef, chicken, and pork in the seasoned flour. Lightly brown the beef cubes in 1 tablespoon of the olive oil in a large skillet over medium-high heat, about 10 minutes. Transfer the beef to a large pot. Add another tablespoon of oil to the skillet and brown the chicken thighs until they are golden on both sides, about 10 minutes. Transfer the chicken to the pot. Next sauté the pork chops in the skillet until brown on both sides, about 8 minutes, and transfer to the pot. Set aside the skillet to use later. Add the water to the pot, bring it to a boil, and then reduce the heat and simmer the meats, covered, until tender, about 1 hour.

Remove the chicken and pork chops to a large plate with a slotted spoon, then cut the meat from the bones, discarding them. Cut the chicken and the pork meat into 1-inch pieces and stir them into the pot.

Sauté the bell pepper, chopped onions, and garlic in the remaining tablespoon of oil in the skillet over medium heat until the onions are limp, about 7 minutes. Transfer the sautéed vegetables, along with the plantains, potato, taro, and *calabaza* to the pot. Simmer the stew, covered, until all the tubers are quite tender, about 45 minutes. The *calabaza* will disintegrate, and the plantains will get very soft, thickening the stew. Stir the cilantro into the stew. Taste and correct the seasoning. Remove the *sancocho* from the heat and serve at once with white rice and avocado slices, if desired.

Serves 8

ASSORTED SMOKED AND FRESH MEATS WITH BLACK BEANS

Feijoada

"While growing up in Argentina, I was captivated by the ads for Coca-Cola portraying an idyllic American landscape that I saw in the *Saturday Evening Post.* I dreamed of one day going to America," recalls Brian Dyson, a corporate executive, nationally ranked squash player, and author of a sports novel entitled *Pepper in the Blood.* Not only did he fulfill his dream, but he landed a job with Coca-Cola and later served as president and CEO of Coca-Cola Enterprises, Inc. As a young Coca-Cola executive, Brian Dyson spent three years in Rio de Janeiro, where he fell in love with Brazilian cuisine. There he learned to make *Feijoada,* the national dish of Brazil, which includes a variety of smoked and fresh meats that are stewed until moist and tender in earthy black beans. It is usually served as *Feijoada completa,* with Brazilian rice (*arroz brasileiro*), shredded kale (*Couve a mineira,* see page 191), toasted manioc (*yuca*) meal (*farofa de manteiga*) for garnish, Malagueta Chile and Lime Salsa (*Môlho de pimenta e limão,* see page 27), and fresh fruit.

Cabana Carioca, a Brazilian restaurant in Little Brazil, New York City, serves one of the best *feijoadas* (a black bean stew with assorted meats) in town.

Assembling a meal of such a grand scale requires an entire afternoon of communal effort. Whenever he prepares *Feijoada completa* at his house in Atlanta, Brian enlists friends and family to make the side dishes while he minds the meats and beans. As in Brazil, the cooking is done to music and laughter, and the meal commences with *Caipirinhas,* the legendary Brazilian cocktail made with *cachaça,* sugar, and lime (see page 297). Nowadays his busy work schedule and his involvement in organizing sporting events (he was instrumental in bringing the 1996 Olympic Summer Games to Atlanta and served as attaché for Argentina during the games) doesn't allow Brian enough free time to prepare *Feijoada completa,* so he trims the meal to this version, served with steamed white rice.

4 cups dried black beans

1 smoked or pickled beef tongue
   (3 pounds)

1 pound fresh spareribs

½ pound whole Canadian bacon

½ pound lean slab (unsliced) bacon, rind
   removed*

½ pound *linguiça* sausage, or substitute
   kielbasa (Polish sausage)†

1 pound Spanish-style chorizo or Italian
   sweet (not hot) link sausage

1 pound filet mignon, cut into 2-inch-
   thick steaks

2 tablespoons olive oil

Freshly ground black pepper,
   to taste

2 medium yellow onions, peeled and
   finely chopped

2 large cloves garlic, peeled and minced

3 medium ripe tomatoes, peeled,
   seeded, and coarsely chopped

1 fresh hot chile, such as the jalapeño,
   seeded and minced, or to taste, or
   Tabasco sauce, to taste (optional)

Salt, to taste

Available from select butcher shops and specialty markets.
†Linguiça *sausage is available in Latin markets and many supermarkets.*

Pick over the black beans for any stones or debris and rinse them thoroughly under cold running water. Soak the beans overnight in enough cold water to cover in a large mixing bowl.

Rinse the tongue under cold running water and soak it overnight in the refrigerator in enough cold water to cover.

Drain the tongue, place it in a large pot with enough water to cover, bring to a boil over medium-high heat, then reduce the heat and simmer, covered, until tender, about 2½ hours. For the last 45 minutes of cooking, add the spareribs, Canadian bacon, slab bacon, and *linguiça* sausage to the tongue. Remove the meats from the pot to a large plate to cool. Once the tongue is cool enough to handle, peel off the skin and cut away the bones, gristle, and fat.

Meanwhile, drain the beans, then put them in a large pot with enough fresh water to cover. Bring to a boil, covered, over medium-high heat, then reduce the heat and simmer the beans, covered, for 30 minutes. Add the cooked meats to the beans and simmer, covered, for another 45 minutes, adding water, as necessary, so that the beans are always covered.

While the beans and meats simmer, sauté the chorizo or Italian sweet sausage in a large skillet over medium heat until brown on all sides, about 15 minutes.

Remove the ribs and slab bacon from the beans to the large plate. Continue to sim-

mer the beans. Slice the ribs and slab bacon, and place the pieces on a broiler pan. Rub the filet mignon lightly with ½ tablespoon of the olive oil, season with black pepper, and place the beef on the broiler pan.

Heat the remaining 1½ tablespoons of olive oil in a large skillet and sauté the onions and garlic over medium heat until the onions are limp, about 5 minutes. Stir in the tomatoes and chile or Tabasco sauce, and cook for 5 minutes. Add 2 cups of the cooked beans, mash them in the skillet, and cook for 10 minutes more. Stir the bean mash into the beans in the pot, then add the sautéed chorizo.

Broil the ribs, slab bacon, and filet mignon 4 inches from the heat, turning once, until brown on both sides, about 4 minutes per side. Watch them carefully so that they do not burn. Remove the tongue from the pot, cut it into thin slices, and arrange the slices in the center of a large serving plate. Place the broiled meats on one side of the tongue. Remove the sausages and Canadian bacon from the pot and place them on the other side of the tongue. (You may also place the meats on separate plates.)

Season the black beans, as necessary, with salt and pepper, and pour them into a large serving bowl. Serve the meats and black beans at once, with steamed white rice.

Serves 10 to 12

VEGETABLES, LEGUMES, AND EGGS ARE USUALLY THE SUP-PORTING CAST IN STEWS, SOUPS, AND SAUCES. WHEN THEY PLAY THE LEAD, IT IS USUALLY OPPOSITE RICE OR TORTILLAS. RARELY ARE THEY A ONE-MAN LATIN SHOW.

RICE, BEANS, AND VEGETABLES

CHILES

There are countless varieties of Latin American chiles; this list is by no means comprehensive. The chiles outlined in the first section are fresh; if a dried version is used in cooking, it is discussed at the end of the entry.

Capsaicin is the compound in chiles that makes them hot, and it is concentrated in the ribs and seeds. Chile heat may be measured in Scoville units (the amount of water and time it takes to neutralize chile heat after ingestion), but since chile experts do not agree on the measurements for each chile, we have rated them according to another popular heat scale of 1 to 10, with 10 being the hottest. Note that the heat does not decrease as chiles mature or when they are dried.

Some of the fresh chiles and many of the dried whole and ground chiles, as well as pick-

Ristras, strands of dried red chiles

led chiles (known in Spanish as *chiles en escabeche*), chipotle chiles in *adobo* sauce, and chile hot sauces, can be ordered by mail (see Sources, page 302). Consider growing your own. Some chile seeds are available in gardening shops; the more exotic ones are available by mail order (see Sources, page 308).

Ají

This fiery hot (7–8), fruity yellow chile, also called **ají amarillo,** is a favorite among Peruvian Americans and other Americans of South American descent. The thin-fleshed ají measures about ¾ inch in diameter and 3 to 5 inches in length. It can be found in some gourmet shops and in South American and Pan-Latin markets (see Sources, pages 306–7), along with jars of puréed ají chiles. The dried ají is known as the **ají mirasol.**

Fresh chiles vary enormously in size, shape, color, flavor, and heat quotient.

Anaheim

The green Anaheim, also called the **California chile pepper,** the **long green chile,** *chile verde,* and *chile verde del norte,* ranges in color from pale to bright green. This mildly hot (2–3) chile measures about 6 inches in length and 2 inches in diameter. Named after Anaheim, California, where it was first cultivated, this chile is available year-round in Mexican markets and supermarkets in California and the Southwest, and on a more limited basis in other parts of the country. Red Anaheim chiles, which are mature green ones, also go by the names **long red chiles** or *chiles colorados* and have a sweeter flavor. Dried red Anaheims are available whole and are also pulverized to make a mild **ground dried red chile.**

Güero

Güero is the generic name given to pale yellow chiles that range from 3 to 5 inches in length and 1½ to 2 inches in diameter. Güeros, such as the hot (6) **Santa Fe Grande,** are used primarily to make Mexican yellow moles and salsas, and they are available in Mexican markets and some supermarkets.

Habanero

Thirty times hotter than the jalapeño, the capsaicin-rich habanero is the hottest chile in the world (10+). This lantern-shape chile is 2 inches long on average and ranges in color from deep green, yellow, and red to completely ripe crimson. The habanero, which means "from Havana," is actually never used in Cuban cooking (nor for that matter is any hot chile), and is featured most in Mexican and some Central American and Caribbean cuisines. This chile is sold in Pan-Latin, Mexican, and Caribbean markets and in supermarkets in some parts of the United States. Golden yellow dried habaneros are available ground and flaked in some Mexican markets. The green, yellow, and ripe red *ají dulce* closely resembles its relative the habanero, but it is not as hot (7–8.5). It is used in some South American cuisines and is harder to find than the habanero.

Green and red Anaheim chiles (background), a yellow güero chile, and a jalapeño.

Jalapeño

The green jalapeño, which originated in Jalapa, Veracruz, Mexico, is the most widely recognized chile in the United States and is sold in most supermarkets. It measures about 1 inch to 1½ inches in diameter and 2 to 3 inches in length, and has medium-hot (5.5), thick flesh. Red jalapeños are the ripe version of green ones and have a sweeter flavor. Smoked, dried red jalapeños, which are used whole or ground and pickled, are called **chipotle chile peppers.** Often the green or red **Fresno chile** (also called *chile caribe* and *chile cera*) is mistaken for a jalapeño. The two look almost alike, but the Fresno is hotter (6.5).

Malagueta

These inch-long fiery hot (9) chiles are Brazil's most beloved. They are light green to medium green in color and should not be confused with **West African malagueta peppers,** seeds of a ginger relative also known as false cardamom. Fresh malaguetas are not available in the United States, but malaguetas bottled in *cachaça* (a Brazilian rumlike liquor) or vinegar are sold at Brazilian American shops (see Sources, page 305). Substitute Scotch bonnets for malaguetas.

New Mexico

Closely related to the Anaheim, medium-hot (3–5) New Mexico chiles are green when immature and red when mature, and measure 6 to 9 inches in length and about 2 inches in diameter. New Mexico chiles are grown almost exclusively in New Mexico, where they originated. They are available fresh in supermarkets and at vegetable stands in the state during the harvest from August through October only, and thus many New Mexicans freeze a supply to last throughout the year. New Mexico green chiles are one of the few immature chiles that are dried; they are

Chiles at the Santa Fe farmers' market, where gardeners and small farmers from across northern New Mexico sell vegetables and fruits in season, salsas, spices, and baked goods

usually ground and added to soups and stews. Dried New Mexico red chiles are used whole or ground. Whole dried New Mexico red chiles (as well as brown, gold, and orange ones that are available dried only) are also strung to make decorative *ristras* and chile wreaths. New Mexico companies ship fresh green chiles during the season and frozen ones (that have been roasted, peeled, and chopped) year-round, as well as dried whole and ground New Mexico green and red chiles (see Sources, page 302). Fresh Anaheim chiles may be substituted for fresh New Mexico chiles. **New Mexico miniatures** (2 to 3 inches long), in gold, orange, red, and reddish brown, were developed for small *ristras* and wreaths.

Peruvian

These green, yellow, and ripe red chiles measure about 1½ inches in diameter and 2½ inches in length. They are quite hot (7–8) and have a tropical fruit flavor. The Peruvian is commonly used in Peruvian, Colombian, and Venezuelan American kitchens, and is available in some Pan-Latin markets.

Poblano

This mildly hot (3), green-black chile with thick flesh measures about 2½ to 3 inches in diameter and 4 to 5 inches in length. The ripe red poblanos have a sweeter flavor. The poblano is one chile that changes names completely when it is dried, and this has caused much confusion. Dried red poblanos that are dark brown and have a licorice flavor are called **mulato chiles.** Brick red to mahogany dried poblanos with a sweet, fruity flavor are called **ancho chiles** and are commonly used whole or ground. In California, poblanos are sometimes mistakenly referred to as ancho chiles or **pasilla chiles.** The mild to medium-hot (3–4) chocolaty pasilla, also known as *chile negro* and *chile pasa,* is entirely unrelated to the poblano; it is a dried, long black **chilaca chile.** Poblanos, mulatos, anchos, and pasillas are sold in Mexican markets and some supermarkets. The chilaca is rarely available.

Rocoto

This slightly fruity and very hot (7–8) chile is popular among Americans of South American descent. It ranges in color from pale green to golden yellow to deep red at its ripest and averages 1½ inches in diameter and 1 inch in length. The rocoto is sometimes called the **rocotillo** or **squash pepper.** This chile is not sold in markets in the United States, but it is cultivated by home gardeners.

Scotch Bonnet

Jamaica's most celebrated chile, the smoky-flavored Scotch bonnet, is a yellow, green, orange, or red inch-long chile that resembles a miniature bell pepper. Its heat (9–10) is surpassed only by the habanero. Scotch bonnets are available in Caribbean and Pan-Latin markets, and in some specialty shops and supermarkets. The bright red **Jamaican Hot** (9) looks remarkably similar to its relatives the Scotch bonnet and the habanero. Like the Scotch bonnet, the Jamaican Hot is used in Jamaican and other Caribbean cooking, but it is harder to find.

Serrano

The immature green and ripe red serrano, which means "mountain" or "highland," measures about ½ inch in diameter and 1 to 2 inches in length. It is the hottest chile (7) widely available in supermarkets in the United States. Jalapeños may be substituted for serranos. The dried red serrano is also called *serrano seco* or *chile seco.*

The small, thick-fleshed serrano is the hottest chile widely available in American supermarkets.

Tabasco

These inch-long, intensely hot (9) chiles range in color from pale yellow to orange to bright red. They are made almost exclusively into Tabasco Brand Pepper Sauce in the United States and are rarely available fresh.

Tepín

This very hot (8) chile, the size and shape of a cranberry, is also known as the **chiltecpín** or **chiltepín**. Tepíns range in color from immature green to orange to very ripe brick red. They grow wild in southerly regions of the Southwest. Dried red tepíns have a dusty flavor. The orange-red **pequín**, a chile also called *chile pequeño* or *chile piquín,* is related to the tepín but has a sweet, smoky flavor and is slightly hotter (8.5). Both tepíns and pequíns are featured in Mexican and some Central and South American cuisines. They can occasionally be found fresh in Mexican and Pan-Latin markets, but they are more commonly sold dried. Pequíns are also made into chile *ristras* and wreaths in the Southwest.

CHILES AVAILABLE DRIED ONLY

Cascabel

This dark reddish brown, medium-hot (4) chile is called cascabel, meaning "rattle," because it makes a rattling sound when shaken. Cascabels are round chiles about 1½ inches in diameter. Mexican American cooks use them, most often in powdered form.

Cayenne

These bright red chiles measure about ½ inch in diameter and 2 to 4 inches in length. They are quite hot (8) and have a tart, smoky flavor. Dried cayenne chiles are usually ground and used as a seasoning and in pepper sauces. On rare occasions, fresh cayenne peppers can be found in stores. The **chile de árbol** is closely related to the cayenne and is virtually as hot (7.5). It is green to ripe red in color when fresh (though it is seldom used this way) and bright red when dried, and measures 2 to 3 inches in length and about ¼ inch in diameter. Dried whole and ground *chiles de árbol* can be found in Mexican and Pan-Latin markets and some supermarkets.

Guajillo

This shiny, reddish brown chile, also known as **chile guaque,** measures ½ inch to 1¼ inches wide and 3 to 5 inches long, and is mild to medium-hot (2–4). Whole and ground guajillos are used often in Mexican and Central American cooking. Fresh guajillos are called **mirasol chiles** (not to be confused with the *ají mirasol*), but are not available in markets in the United States. Mexican American home gardeners in the Southwest grow them to use in hot sauces.

A WORD ABOUT HANDLING CHILES

It is recommended that you wear rubber gloves when handling chiles, as capsaicin can ir-ritate the skin. Be careful not to rub your eyes or touch your face with your hands when working with chiles. Wash your hands well when you have finished. When grinding dried chiles, make sure to open a window, as chile dust irritates the eyes, nose, and skin.

A NOTE ABOUT GROUND DRIED RED CHILE

Ground dried red chile consists of pure, unadulterated dried red chiles, such as dried New Mexico red chiles, dried red Anaheims, and dried *chiles de árbol*, that have been pulverized. The heat level of ground chile depends, of course, on the variety of chile that is ground. Do not confuse ground dried red chile with the commercial chile powders found in many supermarkets that are actually a blend of ground chile and any number of spices and season-ings, most commonly cumin, oregano, paprika, onion, and garlic. The amount of ground chile in the recipes may seem prodigious to those unaccustomed to chiles, but these measurements are normal for those Americans of Latin American descent who cook with chiles. We do not recommend using less chile in sauce recipes (the sauces will turn out watery); just help your-self to less sauce if it is too hot for you. The freshest (and least expensive) ground dried red chile is sold (often by the pound) in Pan-Latin and Mexican markets. Good-quality ground chile will have a lumpy consis-tency—an indication that the natural oils, which hold the flavors, have not evaporated.

Many fresh chile varieties are dried when they reach the mature stage, although a few, like the New Mexico chile, are also dried when still immature.

ROASTING CHILE PEPPERS

Roasting enhances the flavor of chiles and makes it much easier to remove their skin. (The skin turns bitter when roasted, so always remove it and discard.) To roast chiles: Arrange them on a baking sheet and broil them about 1½ inches from a preheated broiler until their skins are blistered and charred on one side. Rotate the chiles and broil them until they are blackened on all sides. You can also do this on a grill or on a rack over an open flame. Trans-fer the chiles to a paper or plastic bag, seal tightly, and let them steam in their own heat for 5 minutes. Remove the chiles from the bag and let them rest until they are cool enough to handle. Scrape the skin off the chiles with a paring knife or peel it off with your fingers, then cut the peppers in half lengthwise and remove the stems and seeds. Scrape off any stray seeds with a paring knife. (Do not rinse the chiles, as you will wash away some of their oils.)

NEW SOUTHWESTERN GNOCCHI DI PATATE IN RED CHILE CREAM SAUCE

Gnocchi di patate con salsa de crema y chile rojo
"New Southwestern"

New Southwestern Cuisine, also known as Nouvelle New Mexican Cuisine, based on the cooking of Mexican Americans and Native Americans in the Southwest, has incorporated not only French and Asian elements but Italian as well. It is no longer unusual to find on menus in restaurants featuring the cooking of the New American Southwest, which have sprouted up all across America, Italian pastas and pestos speckled with a host of quintessential southwestern ingredients, such as cilantro and varieties of chiles, with wonderful names and flavors like the chipotle, poblano, Santa Fe Grande, and the tepín.

In this New Southwestern dish, we float traditional Italian *gnocchi di patate*—dumplings made from potatoes—in an intoxicating red chile cream sauce, composed of slightly sweet, mild red chile, tomato, and cream—an improvisation inspired by traditional New Mexico red chile sauces. Our sauce, like traditional chile sauces, calls for a lot of chile, which helps to thicken it and gives it a rich flavor. This dish can be assembled in under half an hour if you make the *gnocchi* ahead of time and freeze them. Just shape the dumplings, dust them with a little flour, and then pack them in a plastic container and freeze. There is no need to defrost the *gnocchi* before cooking; simply boil them frozen.

FOR THE RED CHILE CREAM SAUCE:

2 tablespoons olive oil

2 tablespoons finely minced yellow onion

I large clove garlic, finely minced

²⁄₃ cup ground dried mild red chile (see the note on ground dried red chile on page 167)

¾ cup water

2 cups tomato sauce

½ teaspoon salt, or to taste

½ cup heavy cream

FOR THE GARNISH:

½ cup pine nuts

I dozen medium fresh basil leaves

FOR THE *GNOCCHI*:

2 pounds baking potatoes, scrubbed
but not peeled

1 large egg

About 2¼ cups unbleached
all-purpose flour

½ teaspoon salt

1 teaspoon olive oil, and a little extra for
tossing the *gnocchi*

Prepare the sauce: Heat the olive oil in a large skillet over medium heat. Sauté the minced onions and garlic in the oil until they are golden, about 3 to 4 minutes. Stir in the ground chile, and then the water, tomato sauce, and salt. Mix well, then reduce the heat to low and cook the sauce for about 3 minutes. Slowly pour the cream into the skillet, stirring constantly. Cook the sauce for about 5 minutes more. Remove the skillet from the heat, cover, and keep the sauce warm.

Make the pine nut garnish: Pour the pine nuts into a large dry skillet, then turn the heat on medium-low. Agitate the skillet a few times each minute until the pine nuts turn golden, about 8 to 10 minutes. To halt the browning, remove them from the skillet as soon as they are golden.

Make the *gnocchi:* Boil the potatoes whole in their skins in enough water to cover, plus 1 inch, until they are tender when pierced with a fork, about 30 to 40 minutes. Drain the potatoes, allow them to cool enough to be handled, peel, then put them through a potato ricer or a medium-mesh wire sieve.

Transfer the potato purée to a large bowl and add the egg, 1½ cups of the flour, and the salt. Knead the mixture with your fingers until it is smooth, adding more of the flour, a tablespoon at a time, until the dough loses its stickiness. Put 4 quarts of water with the teaspoon of olive oil on to boil in a large heavy pot.

Lightly flour a cutting board or tray, and then your hands. With your hand, scoop up the equivalent of a scant teaspoon of dough from the bowl. Rest the dough in one palm while you shape it with the fingertips of your other hand into a plump, oblong piece about 1¼ inches long. With your fingertips, press the oblong piece of dough against the tines of a fork hard enough to make indentations. Set the *gnocchi* on the lightly floured cutting board or tray. Shape the rest of the dough in the same manner.

Drop one third of the *gnocchi* into the boiling water. After they have risen to the surface, cook them for 30 seconds more, and then transfer them with a slotted spoon to a medium mixing bowl. Toss the cooked *gnocchi* in a little olive oil and cover the bowl to keep them warm. Cook the remaining batches of *gnocchi.*

To assemble the dish, spoon about ½ cup red chile cream sauce in the center of each of 6 dinner plates to make a wide pool. Arrange the *gnocchi* on top of the sauce and garnish each plate with about a tablespoon of the reserved pine nuts and 2 basil leaves.

Serves 6

HOME FRIES WITH ROASTED POBLANO CHILES

Papas con rajas

This dish commonly serves as one of myriad fillings for Mexican American quesadillas, but we think that it also makes fabulous home fries to accompany omelets, or fried or scrambled eggs. The basic ingredients in Home Fries with Roasted Poblano Chiles—namely potatoes, chiles, and onions—also go into Potato Salad with Roasted Poblano Chiles (*Ensalada de papas con chile poblano*), best described as classic potato salad with gusto (see recipe below).

1 pound medium red-skinned (new) potatoes	**2 tablespoons olive oil**
1 poblano chile, or substitute 1 Anaheim chile, roasted, peeled, and seeded (see pages 165 and 162 for information on these chiles and page 167 for instructions on roasting and peeling chiles)	**½ cup finely minced yellow onions**
	½ teaspoon ground cumin, or to taste
	Salt and freshly ground black pepper, to taste
1 large red or yellow bell pepper, roasted, peeled, and seeded	**½ cup crumbled *queso fresco* (a Mexican cheese also known as *queso ranchero*), or substitute farmer cheese (optional)**

Bring a medium saucepan of salted water to a boil. Add the potatoes (with skins attached), cover, and boil until just tender when pierced with a fork, about 20 to 25 minutes. Drain, allow the potatoes to cool enough to be handled, then peel and cut them into ½-inch chunks.

Cut the roasted poblano chile and bell pepper into strips ¼-inch wide and about 1½ inches long.

Heat the olive oil in a large skillet over medium heat. Sauté the potato chunks and minced onions, stirring occasionally, until the potatoes are quite brown, about 20 minutes.

Add the ½ teaspoon cumin, and salt and pepper, as needed. Fold in the poblano chile and bell pepper strips, then remove the skillet from the heat. Stir in the *queso fresco,* if desired, and serve at once.

Serves 4

For Potato Salad with Roasted Poblano Chiles (*Ensalada de papas con chile poblano*): Cook 2 pounds medium red-skinned potatoes in a large saucepan of salted water

until tender, about 30 minutes. Peel and cut as above. Roast 2 poblano chiles instead of 1, as well as the large red or yellow bell pepper. Seed and cut the roasted peppers as described above. Mix together ¼ teaspoon granulated sugar, 1 tablespoon olive oil, and 2 tablespoons freshly squeezed lemon or lime juice in a large bowl to make a marinade. Gently toss the potato chunks, poblano chile and bell pepper strips, and ½ cup finely minced yellow onion in the marinade. Mix together 1¼ cups mayonnaise and ½ teaspoon Dijon mustard in a small bowl. Stir the mayonnaise mixture into the potato salad and coat evenly. Add salt and freshly ground black pepper as needed. Serve warm or chilled. Serves 6.

CALIFORNIA LAND GRANT ENCHILADAS

Enchiladas a la encomiendas californianas

"My entire family history is rolled up in these rustic enchiladas stuffed with hard-boiled eggs, Cheddar, and black olives," says Elizabeth Erro Hvolboll, whose ancestors were instrumental in the founding of California. "On my paternal side, I am descended from Spanish conquistadors who sailed to the New World perhaps as early as the sixteenth century. During the Spanish colonization of Alta California that began in 1769, my *mestizo* (of mixed Spanish and native blood) forebears in Mexico made their way north. They brought with them this enchilada recipe."

In 1782 Elizabeth's great-great-great-grandfather Felipe Gonzalez founded, with others, the Spanish *presidio* at Santa Barbara, laying the groundwork for the creation in 1786 of Mission Santa Barbara. After control of California passed from New Spain (the Spanish Empire in the Americas) to Mexico in the 1820s, mission lands were given through land grants to the state's colonists, known as *Californios,* who established great cattle *ranchos.* In this way, Elizabeth Hvolboll's forebears gained possession of Mission Santa Barbara grazing land, which was eventually divided into many family *ranchos.* Elizabeth inherited her paternal grandmother's *rancho* called La Paloma, where, with her husband, Arne Hvolboll, she raises cattle, cultivates Hass avocados, prepares the dishes of her past, and practices the old Spanish folk songs of the *Californios* that she performs at events such as Santa Barbara's Old Spanish Days Fiesta.

"Egg enchiladas were a mainstay on the *ranchos* for many, many generations. They could be made in a flash, they satisfied big appetites, and they were a nourishing and

California Land Grant Enchiladas (continued)

delicious alternative when supplies of beef ran low," says Elizabeth. "The family recipe has changed very little over the centuries. I have probably revolutionized it the most by grinding the eggs coarsely with an old hand grinder on occasion and using olive oil instead of lard. But in keeping with family tradition, I use only flour tortillas—never corn—and I serve the enchiladas with refried pink beans, not pintos, on the side."

Elizabeth Erro Hvolboll and Arne Hvolboll at La Paloma

FOR THE ENCHILADA SAUCE:

2 tablespoons olive oil

3 tablespoons finely minced yellow onion

3 large cloves garlic, peeled and crushed

One 28-ounce can tomato purée

2 cups beef stock, preferably homemade

1½ tablespoons mild ground dried red chile, such as mild California chile (see the note on ground dried red chile on page 167)

½ teaspoon dried powdered oregano (not crumbled)

¼ teaspoon cumin

Salt, to taste

FOR THE ENCHILADAS:

2 tablespoons olive oil

1 large yellow onion, peeled and coarsely chopped

8 large fresh flour tortillas

2½ cups (about 8 ounces) grated sharp Cheddar cheese, loosely packed

6 large eggs, hard-boiled, cooled, and cut into quarters or coarsely chopped

2 dozen small pitted black olives, sliced in half, plus 8 whole black olives, for garnish

Prepare the enchilada sauce: Heat the olive oil over medium heat in a large skillet. Sauté the minced onions and garlic in the oil until they are golden brown, about 5 minutes. Stir in the tomato purée, beef stock, chile, oregano, cumin, and salt, and mix well.

Reduce the heat and simmer the enchilada sauce for about 15 minutes. Remove the sauce from the heat and keep warm.

Prepare the enchiladas: Heat the olive oil in a large skillet over medium-high heat.

Sauté the chopped onions for about 4 minutes, and then reduce the heat to low, cover, and steam the onions in their own moisture, stirring occasionally, until they are limp, about 10 minutes.

Dip one of the tortillas in the warm enchilada sauce with tongs or a fork, and then lay it in a large shallow pan or casserole. Spoon 2 tablespoons enchilada sauce, 1 tablespoon sautéed onions, 2 tablespoons Cheddar cheese, 3 egg quarters or the equivalent amount of chopped egg, and 6 olive halves, in that order, on one half of the tortilla. Gently roll the tortilla and place it at the end of the pan or casserole. Repeat the process until all the tortillas are filled and they are nestled against each other in a row in the pan or casserole.

Pour 1 cup enchilada sauce over the filled tortillas and sprinkle the remaining cheese over the top. Place a whole black olive in the top center of each enchilada to garnish. Warm the enchiladas in a preheated 350°F oven for 20 minutes and serve at once with refried beans, if desired.

Serves 4

LINDA CHAVEZ'S NEW MEXICO–STYLE STACKED ENCHILADAS WITH RED CHILE SAUCE

Enchiladas con salsa de chile rojo estilo Nuevo México de Linda Chavez

" These enchiladas, corn tortilla stacks laden with molten Cheddar, fragrant onions, juicy olives, and a rich, spicy red chile sauce, were a big hit at my son David's bar mitzvah," says Mexican American Linda Chavez, director of the White House Office of Public Liaison under the Reagan administration, author of *Out of the Barrio: Toward a New Politics of Hispanic Assimilation,* and currently president of the Center for Equal Opportunity. "I learned to make enchiladas from my grandmother Petra. When I was a child, I would sit at her kitchen table in Albuquerque and watch her cook. She always made her corn tortillas from scratch, and would soak her dried red chiles in water before kneading them into a thick paste for the sauce for the enchiladas. Her hands would become red and raw from the chiles, which she forbade me to touch. 'You might burn your eyes if you touch them after handling the chiles, *mi hija,*' she would warn."

Rather than roll tortillas for enchiladas, Linda Chavez dips them in the chile sauce and then stacks them—a traditional New Mexican method she learned from her grandmother. However, she has modified her grandmother's dish ever so slightly to conform to her busy schedule. "In the interests of time and safety, I've replaced Grandmother Petra's ingredients with store-bought corn tortillas and ground dried red chile. From New Mexico, of course. I accept no substitutes." The chile sauce in this recipe is quite intense, just as chile lovers like it. If you wish to have less chile in your enchiladas, just leave the middle tortillas in each stack plain and dip the other two in the sauce. Do not use less ground chile when making the sauce, or else it will turn out soupy.

1 medium clove garlic, peeled and minced	¼ teaspoon salt, or to taste
2 tablespoons olive oil	Vegetable oil, for cooking the tortillas
½ cup ground dried red chile, preferably New Mexico, hot, medium, or mild (see the note on ground dried red chile on page 167)	12 corn tortillas
	1 cup (about 5½ ounces) grated medium Cheddar or longhorn cheese, packed
	One 4¼-ounce can black olives, diced
1 cup water	1 small yellow onion, peeled and finely diced

Sauté the garlic in the olive oil in a large skillet over low heat until lightly golden, about 4 minutes. Stir in the red chile, and then quickly add the water and salt so that the chile does not burn. Raise the heat to medium-low and simmer the red chile sauce, stirring occasionally, until it has the consistency of a gravy, about 5 minutes.

Heat ½ inch vegetable oil in another large skillet over medium heat until a piece of tortilla sizzles upon contact. Slip a corn tortilla into the oil and cook it for about 10 seconds so that it becomes pliable but not brown and crunchy. Remove the tortilla with tongs to paper towels to drain. Repeat this process until all the tortillas are cooked.

Dip a tortilla in the red chile sauce and place it on a large, greased, shallow baking dish. (Note that as the sauce cools, it tends to thicken. If it is too thick to drip off the tortilla, thin it with a few tablespoons water.) Sprinkle about 1 tablespoon of the cheese, 1½ teaspoons olives, and 1 teaspoon diced onion on the tortilla. Dip another tortilla in the sauce and place it atop the first tortilla. Sprinkle the same amount of cheese, olives, and onion on the second tortilla and top it with one more dipped tortilla.

Repeat the process until you have made 4 stacks of 3 tortillas each.

Spoon the remaining red chile sauce over the enchiladas, then sprinkle the remaining cheese on top. Bake the enchiladas in a preheated 350°F oven until the cheese inside melts, about 10 minutes. Serve at once the New Mexican way, with refried beans and Spanish rice or *Posole,* a hominy stew (see page 146).

Serves 4

JAMAICAN RICE AND PEAS

Rice and Peas, popularly known as "Jamaican coat of arms," with its marvelous coconut aroma, is cherished by Jamaican Americans as a versatile side dish or as a main entrée. The name of this dish is somewhat misleading, as the "peas" in Jamaican Rice and Peas are not peas at all, but rather small red beans (*frijoles colorados chicos*). Another essential component of Rice and Peas is the hot, smoky-flavored Scotch bonnet pepper, Jamaica's most celebrated chile pepper (see page 165 for information on Scotch bonnet peppers). The Scotch bonnet is left whole in this recipe so that it can be extracted, and its flavor, but not its fury, comes through. If you cannot find Scotch bonnets locally, you can order the chiles by mail. You may want to consider growing your own from seeds also available by mail order (consult Sources, page 308).

Many Americans of Latin American descent, especially those with roots in the Caribbean, have rice and red bean dishes similar to Jamaican Rice and Peas. For instance, Dominican Americans prepare *arroz con frijoles,* red beans and rice flavored with garlic, tomato, hot chiles, cilantro, coconut milk, and boiled ham, while Colombian Americans with roots in the Caribbean region of Colombia fix *ocho ríos,* literally "eight rivers," which is embellished with onions, chiles, thyme, and coconut milk. Haitian Americans cook up *pois et riz* (peas and rice), pink beans or red kidneys with rice, onions, shallots, chiles, and bacon. The Cuban American equivalent to Jamaican Rice and Peas is *Congrí,* red beans and rice accented with onions and garlic, and sometimes uncured bacon or tomatoes, but never coconut milk and hot chiles. Nicaraguan American red beans and rice, or *Gallo pinto* ("Spotted Rooster"), does not have coconut milk or chiles either, and it calls for red kidney beans.

I cup dried small red beans

2 cups canned unsweetened
    coconut milk

2 cups long-grain rice

I medium yellow onion, peeled and
    finely diced

I large clove garlic, peeled and
    finely minced

I whole Scotch bonnet chile, or a I-inch
    long whole habanero, or any other
    very, very hot whole chile pepper
    (see pages 165 and 163 for
    information on these chiles)

½ teaspoon dried thyme

Salt and freshly ground black pepper,
    to taste

Pour the beans into a colander, pick over them, and discard any pebbles or malformed beans. Rinse the beans thoroughly with cold running water. Place them in a large pot and soak them overnight in enough water to cover.

Drain the beans, return them to the pot, and add 4 cups of water. Bring the beans to a boil, covered, over medium heat. Lower the heat and simmer the beans until they are not quite tender, about 30 minutes. Stir in the coconut milk, rice, diced onions, garlic, Scotch bonnet pepper or other hot chile if desired, thyme, and salt and pepper. Simmer the rice and beans, covered, until the rice is tender, about 20 minutes. Discard the Scotch bonnet and serve at once.

Serves 6 as a main dish and 10 to 12 as a side dish

For Cuban American Red Beans and Rice (*Congrí*): Add 4½ cups chicken stock to the beans instead of the 4 cups water. While the beans are simmering, trim the tough outer layer off a ¼-pound chunk salt pork (sold in many butcher shops), slice it into three strips, then sauté in a large skillet over medium heat, turning once, until brown on both sides. Drain on paper towels and cut into small pieces. Sauté the onions and garlic in the fat in the skillet over medium heat until golden. Stir the salt pork, sautéed onions and garlic, rice, pepper, and 2 cups water into the beans after they have simmered 30 minutes. Omit the coconut milk, Scotch bonnet, thyme, and salt. Simmer 20 to 25 minutes, or until the rice is tender, and serve.

For Nicaraguan American Red Kidney Beans and Rice (*Gallo pinto*): Substitute red kidney beans for the small red beans. Boil the beans with I bay leaf and I teaspoon finely minced fresh oregano until they are not quite tender, about 40 minutes. Sauté 5 slices bacon in a large skillet until brown. Remove the bacon from the skillet and cut it into small pieces. Pour off all but 1½ tablespoons fat from the skillet, and add the onions and garlic, as well as ⅓ cup finely minced red bell pepper and I cup diced ham. Sauté over medium heat for 5 minutes. Stir the bacon-ham mixture and rice, as well as 3 tablespoons tomato paste, 2 cups water, and I tea-spoon ground cumin into the beans. Omit the coconut milk, Scotch bonnet, thyme, salt, and black pepper. Simmer the rice and beans, covered, until the rice is tender, about 20 minutes, and serve at once.

CAROLA'S BLACK BEANS

Frijoles negros Carola

Carola Infante Ash, the daughter of the distinguished writer Guillermo Cabrera Infante, fled Castro's Cuba for London as a child with her family in 1967. There Carola received an English education, but nonetheless learned the rudiments of Cuban cooking from her stepmother, Miriam Gomez. "Cubans in London in 1967 were as exotic as the plants in Kew Gardens. This was the London of Mary Quant and Vidal Sassoon, the Rolling Stones, Biba, and Carnaby Street. To run into a Cuban was

Carola Infante Ash and Eddie Ash

rare, but to find Cuban ingredients . . . forget it!" remembers Carola. "However, in our house a traditional Cuban meal of roast pork, fried ripe plantains, black beans, and white rice on *Nochebuena* (Christmas Eve) was essential. My stepmother, Miriam, a wondrous cook, could usually track down plantains in the West Indian markets, but black beans were nowhere to be found. And so her mother in Miami always sent us a bag, which we would treasure till Christmas. Then it was my job—and one not taken lightly—to pick over the beans and reserve only the best ones for *Frijoles negros*."

Nowadays Carola Infante Ash works in Los Angeles as vice president of development and production at actor Andy Garcia's company Cineson. "In L.A. the only way I enjoy Cuban food 'like Miriam used to make' is to cook it myself, following her recipes. Luckily, Cuban ingredients are easy to find. I guess my cooking must be okay, because even Andy Garcia likes it! My husband, Eddie Ash, though he is English, has become a Cuban food convert. He is in the wine business, and his only regret is that the best accompaniment to a traditional Cuban meal of roast pork, Fried Ripe Plantains (see page 182), and black beans and rice is ice-cold beer."

When we received Carola's recipe for *Frijoles negros* in the mail, we were delighted to find a CD entitled *Cachao Master Sessions* by Cuban musician Israel López, otherwise known as Cachao. When we later spoke to Carola, she insisted that we try out her recipe while listening to the Afro-Cuban rhythms of Cachao.

Carola's Black Beans (continued)

1 pound dried black beans	1 bay leaf
2 large green bell peppers, 1 whole and 1 seeded, deribbed, and finely minced	¼ teaspoon dried powdered oregano (not crumbled)
⅔ cup olive oil	¼ teaspoon ground cumin
1 large yellow onion, peeled and finely chopped	Salt and freshly ground black pepper, to taste
5 large cloves garlic, peeled and minced	2 tablespoons red wine vinegar
2 teaspoons granulated sugar	2 tablespoons dry white wine

Pour the black beans into a large colander, pick over them, and discard any pebbles and malformed beans. Rinse the beans thoroughly with cold running water. Put the black beans, the whole green bell pepper, and 9 cups of water in a large heavy pot, and allow the beans to soak with the pepper, covered, overnight.

Just before cooking the beans, discard the whole green bell pepper. Bring the black beans and the soaking water to a boil, reduce the heat, and simmer the beans, covered, for 45 minutes, or until they are soft.

Heat the olive oil in a large skillet over medium-high heat. Sauté the chopped onions, minced green pepper, and the garlic in the olive oil until the onions begin to brown, about 10 minutes. Next remove 1 cup of the cooked black beans with a slotted spoon so that the liquid drains back into the large pot. Put the beans in the skillet with the sautéed vegetables and mash them with a potato masher or fork. Sauté the vegetable-bean mixture for about 2 minutes, then add it to the beans in the pot. Add the sugar, bay leaf, oregano, cumin, salt, and pepper to the beans. Simmer the black beans, covered, stirring occasionally, over low heat for 1 hour.

Next pour the red wine vinegar and white wine into the black beans and allow them to cook, stirring occasionally, over low heat for an additional hour. The beans will be rather soupy—the traditional way to serve them is over white rice—but if you wish to thicken them some more, remove the lid and continue to cook them over low heat for about 20 minutes more.

Serves 6 to 8

ISLE OF ENCHANTMENT RICE AND PIGEON PEAS

Arroz con gandules a la isla del encanto

"If there is one dish that sings to the heart of every Puerto Rican, it must be *Arroz con gandules* (Rice and Pigeon Peas), the national rice-and-bean dish of Puerto Rico," says child psychologist Judith Sandino, who learned the secrets of cooking with rice from her mother in Puerto Rico. Pigeon peas are small yellow beans, about the size of a garden pea, with gray-brown markings that are native to Africa. They also go by the names *gunga* peas, *cajan* peas, *congo* peas, red *gram,* and no-eyed peas, and can be found fresh and frozen in southern states where they grow, and canned and dried in many supermarkets elsewhere, as well as in Caribbean markets.

Nowadays Judith prepares Rice and Pigeon Peas in Los Angeles, thousands of miles from *la isla del encanto,* or "the isle of enchantment," but you would not know it from the incredible tropical aromas that emanate from her kitchen. She always serves the rice at Christmas dinner to complement the traditional *Pernil de cerdo* (Roast Pork, see page 136), *Pasteles* (Stuffed Plantain Rectangles, see page 221), and *alcapurrias* (green bananas stuffed with ground beef).

Over time, Judith has improvised on her mother's *Arroz con gandules.* The family recipe, which closely follows Puerto Rican culinary tradition, calls for annatto oil, oil steeped in annatto (also known as *achiote* seeds), which had replaced the saffron the Spanish use to impart color and flavor to rice. In her recipe Judith returns to the saffron of old. Tradition also dictates that cured ham be added to the dish, but Judith prefers to omit it, since *Arroz con gandules* is usually served with a meat dish anyway. She also seasons her *Arroz con gandules* with herbs and spices, namely basil and oregano, that are not found in traditional recipes.

3 tablespoons olive oil
1 large yellow onion, peeled and diced
3 large cloves garlic, peeled and minced
1 medium green bell pepper, seeded, deribbed, and diced
½ cup canned tomato sauce
½ cup pimiento-stuffed olives, drained
1 tablespoon capers, drained

1 teaspoon dried powdered oregano (not crumbled)
1 tablespoon finely minced fresh parsley
1 tablespoon finely minced fresh basil
¼ gram (1 vial) saffron threads, or substitute ¼ teaspoon turmeric
Salt and freshly ground black pepper, to taste

5 cups cold water

**One 16-ounce can pigeon peas
(*gandules*),* drained**

2½ cups long-grain rice

**I medium red bell pepper, diced, for
garnish**

* Available canned, dried, and frozen in Latin markets with a Caribbean clientele.

Heat the olive oil over medium-high heat in a large pot. Sauté the onions, garlic, and green bell pepper, stirring occasionally, for 5 minutes. Stir in the tomato sauce, olives, capers, oregano, parsley, basil, saffron threads or turmeric, and the salt and pepper, and then the water and pigeon peas.

Increase the heat to high, add the rice, stir once, and bring it to a boil. Cover and boil, without stirring, until most of the water has been absorbed, about 10 minutes. Reduce the heat to low, stir the rice once from the bottom to the top, cover, and cook for approximately 20 minutes more. Test the rice for doneness. If it is not tender add a little more water and cook it, covered, for 5 minutes more. Spoon the rice into a serving dish, garnish it with red bell pepper, and serve at once.

Serves 6 as a main dish and 10 to 12 as a side dish

✳

STEWED BEANS WITH CORN, PUMPKIN, AND SWEET BASIL

Porotos granados

Porotos granados, a robust and lively vegetable-and-bean stew perfumed with lots of sweet basil, marries the five essential flavors of the Americas—namely, corn, squash, beans, tomatoes, and chile peppers. It is a splendid dish to make as summer and autumn cross paths, those bittersweet days of fleeting light when sun-baked red tomatoes hang heavy on the vine and the corn still stands tall as the first pumpkins and winter squashes are hauled in from the field. *Porotos granados* originated with the Mapuche Indians in pre-Columbian Chile; nowadays it is celebrated as a Chilean national summer dish and is consumed with local white wine. In Chile, fresh or dried cranberry beans, with their mottled red markings that fade during cooking, are routinely featured in *Porotos granados*. Chilean Americans depend almost solely on dried navy beans, since cranberry beans are a rarity in the United States, though fresh ones may be tracked down at some Italian markets and farmers' markets in September and October. *Calabaza* (also called West Indian pumpkin, green pumpkin, and Cuban squash) is the unifying force in *Porotos granados,* as some of it breaks down to form a rich sauce that enhances the flavors and textures of the beans and corn. Take a trip to a Latin market for *calabaza,* or substitute a winter squash such as the Tahitian, butternut, or kabocha. The common American pumpkin variety (used for carving jack-o'-lanterns) will not do for this stew, as it is bland and watery.

Many Chilean Americans like piquant foods, and they enliven this stew with *Pebre,* a Chilean fresh tomato salsa. *Porotos granados* with or without *Pebre* makes a wonderful vegetarian meal served with brown rice, and is also a pleasing side dish for beef, pork, or lamb. It is especially good the next day, after all the flavors have melded completely.

I cup dried navy or cranberry beans,
    picked over to remove any pebbles
    and debris, soaked for 3 hours and
    drained, or 2 cups fresh shelled
    cranberry beans
I ½ tablespoons olive oil
I medium yellow onion, peeled and
    minced
I tablespoon sweet paprika
I ½ pounds *calabaza* (West Indian
    pumpkin), or substitute Tahitian,
    butternut, or kabocha squash, or
    sugar pumpkin, peeled and cut into
    I-inch cubes

½ cup fresh corn kernels (cut from
    I medium ear corn), or substitute
    frozen corn kernels
2 tablespoons minced fresh basil
Salt and freshly ground black pepper, to
    taste
Pebre (optional) (see page 27)

Put the soaked or fresh beans in a medium saucepan with enough cold water to cover by 2 inches. Bring to a boil over medium-high heat, then reduce the heat, cover, and simmer gently until just tender, about 40 minutes. Reserve the beans in their cooking liquid.

Heat the olive oil in a large saucepan over medium heat, stir in the minced onions and paprika, and sauté until the onions are soft, stirring occasionally, about 6 minutes. Add the reserved navy or cranberry beans, 2½ cups of the bean cooking liquid (if you do not have 2½ cups, add water to make up the difference), and the pumpkin or squash. Bring to a boil, then reduce the heat, cover, and simmer, stirring occasionally, until the pumpkin breaks down and the beans are very tender, about 30 minutes.

Stir in the corn and basil, and cook, uncovered, stirring often, for an additional 10 minutes. Taste and season with salt and black pepper, as needed. Serve warm as a main dish with brown or white rice, or as a side dish. Pass around the *Pebre* to spoon on top, if desired.

Serves 4 as a main dish and 8 as a side dish

LITTLE HAVANA FRIED RIPE PLANTAINS

Plátanos maduros fritos a la Calle Ocho

Cuban Americans in Miami's Little Havana, and all across the United States, are apt to serve a plate of fragrant Fried Ripe Plantains, caramelized brown on the edges and deliciously gooey on the inside, with just about any meal. Fried Ripe Plantains are essential with the traditional Cuban feast of *lechón asado* (roast suckling pig), *Frijoles negros* (black beans, see page 177), *arroz blanco* (steamed white rice), and *Yuca con mojo* (*Yuca* with Garlic-Lime Oil, see page 188), which Cuban Americans enjoy on festive occasions, and they are also served with more casual Cuban meals.

Unlike bananas, plantains never completely lose their tartness, so for this dish we allow the fruit to ripen until its skin is almost entirely black so that it will be as sweet as it is tart. According to Cuban American culinary tradition, ripe plantains may be sautéed in oil, butter, or a combination of the two. We always choose all butter for a richer taste. Do not be concerned if the butter turns brown during cooking, but do not let it smoke. The plantains are done when they are golden brown and a bit black on some of the edges. Cuban Americans usually sprinkle the sautéed plantains with salt and lime juice, but they are also good with garlic salt or plain. Leftover plantains, wrapped tightly in plastic, will keep for up to three days in the refrigerator and can be microwaved or warmed in the oven. They are also quite delicious cold.

4 medium very ripe (nearly all black) plantains	Salt or garlic salt, to taste (optional)
4 tablespoons butter	2 limes, cut into wedges, for garnish (optional)

Peel the plantains as you would a banana, then cut them on the diagonal into ¾-inch slices. Heat 2 tablespoons of the butter in a large nonstick skillet over medium heat.

Sauté half the plantain slices in a single layer until they are quite brown on the underside, about 4 minutes. Flip them over with a fork or spatula and sauté until brown on the other side, about 3 minutes. Leaning the slices against each other if necessary, stand each plantain slice on one of its edges in the skillet and sauté for 30 seconds. Next stand the slices on their opposite edges and sauté an additional 30 seconds.

Remove one slice from the skillet, cut it in half, and check to see that the plantain has lost its pale yellow, white, or pink tinge and has turned yellow all the way through.

If so, the plantains are ready. If not, continue sautéing them for another minute on the sides that are the least brown.

Gently remove the fried plantains from the skillet with a fork or spatula and place them on paper towels to drain. Add the remaining butter to the skillet and sauté the rest of the plantains in the same fashion and drain. Arrange the fried plantains in one layer on a large serving plate, sprinkle them with salt or garlic salt, if desired, and serve at once with lime wedges or plain.

Serves 6 to 8 as an appetizer or side dish

PLANTAINS | Beloved all over Latin America and Latino U.S.A. the plantain (also called the cooking banana and macho banana in English, and *plátano* and *plátano macho* in Spanish) is one of the four hundred varieties of bananas cultivated around the globe. Plantains must always be cooked before eating. Unlike most banana varieties, the large, thick-skinned plantain is used at all stages of ripeness, from unripe dark green to yellow to brown to fully-ripe black. The off-white, pale yellow, or pink-tinged flesh of plantains has a mild starchy flavor akin to potatoes or winter squash when the skin is green and yellow green. As plantains ripen, their flesh becomes sweeter and banana-flavored, but it does not soften like that of the Cavendish banana, America's favorite variety.

Plantains are available year-round in most Latin markets across the United States. In recent years they have found their way into many greengrocers and the produce departments of some supermarkets. Select plantains that are free of cracks, mold, or soft spots. Plantains tend naturally to look rather beat up compared to bananas, so do not shy away from those with bruises or brown or black streaks. Store plantains at room temperature, allowing them to ripen to the stage you desire. Ripening can be accelerated by placing the plantains in a warm place and decelerated by storing them in the refrigerator. Plantains are among the hardiest of all banana varieties; their flesh does not bruise easily, nor does it oxidize (blacken) when it comes in contact with the air, and thus plantains can be sliced and diced hours before cooking.

Cuban Americans, Puerto Ricans, Colombian Americans, Venezuelan Americans, Ecuadoran Americans, Guatemalan Americans, and others commonly serve slices of Fried Ripe Plantains (see opposite), or *Plátanos maduros fritos* (called *tajadas fritas de plátano* by Venezuelan Americans, who sometimes prepare them with cheese), and rounds of Fried Green Plantains (see opposite), called *Tostones* (they are known as *patacones* to Ecuadoran and Colombian Americans) as side dishes. Green plantain chips, the Latino equivalent to potato chips, are a popular snack and are available in most Latin markets and some supermarkets under such names as *tostoncitos* (Dominican), *mariquitas* (Cuban), *chifles* (Ecuadoran), *chicharritas de plátano verde* (Costa Rican), *tostados de plátano* (Colombian), and *platanutri* (Puerto Rican).

A plantain is a large, firm variety of banana. It can be used at any stage of maturity, from unripe green to very ripe brown-black.

Mexican Americans usually cook with only ripe plantains, which are sometimes used in the *masa* for tamales and in fillings for *chiles rellenos*. One popular plantain dish among Guatemalan Americans is known affectionately as *niños envueltos,* or "babies in a blanket"—mashed green plantain turnovers stuffed with black beans and then deep-fried. Another is the dessert *plátanos al horno,* ripe plantains sprinkled with sugar and cinnamon, dotted with butter, baked until golden brown, and served with fresh cream and honey. Puerto Ricans use plantains in a variety of ways, including in the paste for *Pasteles* (see page 221); in *tostones rellenos*—plantain "cups" filled with crabmeat, lobster, beef, or chicken; and in *mofongo*—balls of mashed fried green plantains, crushed garlic, and *chicharrones,* or pork cracklings. The Dominican American version of *mofongo* has scallions, coconut milk, and coconut oil.

HOW TO PEEL AND SLICE PLANTAINS

Yellow-brown, brown, and black plantains can be peeled as you would a banana, but it is virtually impossible to peel green and yellow plantains this way, and thus the skin must be cut off with a sharp knife.

First slice the plantain, skin attached, on the diagonal into ¾-inch rounds (or another length as indicated in the recipe). Peel the plantain rounds, one by one, by placing them on a cutting board, then starting with one side of a plantain round, cutting away the peel with a paring knife. Rotate and slice the skin off the other sides until the plantain round is completely peeled.

FRIED GREEN PLANTAINS WITH BACON-ONION-GARLIC GARNISH FOR HERMINIA DEL PORTAL

*Tostones con tocino,
cebolla, y ajo para Herminia del Portal*

This dish is for Herminia, my mother, who, though she never learned to cook in Havana, or later in Manhattan, adores *Tostones* (Fried Green Plantains), one of the riches of Cuban cuisine, especially with my invention—bacon-onion-garlic garnish. —H.N.

These Fried Green Plantains make a great first course or a side dish. Serve them with lemon wedges as a counterpoint to the bacon. If you are in a hurry, you may skip the garnish and serve the fried plantains plain, with lime or lemon wedges, and a sprinkling of salt, or bathed in a traditional manner with *mojo* (garlic-lime oil), as described in the recipe for *Yuca* with Garlic-Lime Oil on page 188. Simply substitute the fried plantains for the *yuca* in that recipe.

10 bacon strips, cut into 1-inch pieces
2 medium white onions, peeled and
   finely minced
3 medium cloves garlic, peeled and finely
   minced
Olive oil, for sautéing

4 medium green plantains, cut into
   ¾-inch rounds (see opposite for
   instructions on peeling and cutting
   plantains)
½ cup dry white wine

Fry the bacon pieces in a large skillet, stirring 2 or 3 times, over medium-high heat until they all turn translucent, about 4 minutes. Add the minced onions and garlic, and sauté with the bacon over medium-high heat until the bacon and the onions turn golden brown, about 15 minutes. Remove the bacon, onions, and garlic with a slotted spoon or spatula to a plate lined with paper towels.

Pour off all but ¼ inch of bacon grease from the skillet. If there is less, add enough olive oil to reach that level. Heat the fat over medium heat in the skillet. Sauté half the plantain slices until they turn brown on the bottom, about 5 minutes. Flip them over with a fork or spatula and sauté until brown on the other side, about 4 minutes. Leaning the slices against each other if necessary, stand each plantain slice on its side in the

skillet and sauté for 1 minute. Then stand the slices on another side and sauté an additional minute, and finally do the third side. Remove the plantains to a large serving plate. Repeat with the remaining plantains, adding 2 tablespoons of olive oil.

While the plantains are still warm, place one on a brown paper bag, fold the bag over it, and press on it with your palm to flatten it to three quarters its original thickness. (Some prefer their plantains thinner, in which case you may flatten to half the original thickness.) Do not press so hard that the plantain falls apart. Repeat for each of the plantains.

Heat the fat and 2 more tablespoons of olive oil over medium heat in the skillet, and sauté half of the flattened plantains about 2 minutes, and then flip them and sauté for 2 additional minutes. Remove the plantains to paper towels and drain. Sauté the second batch in the same way in the fat and another 2 tablespoons of olive oil.

Cook the reserved fried bacon, onions, and garlic with the white wine in a large nonreactive skillet until all the wine is absorbed, about 3 minutes. Arrange the fried plantains in one layer on the large serving plate, spoon the bacon-onion-garlic garnish evenly on top, and serve at once.

Serves 6 to 8 as an appetizer or side dish

YUCA FRIES

Yuca frita

Many Americans have already fallen in love with *yuca* chips—those ivory chips in that irresistible potpourri of crunchy, paper-thin exotic root vegetables known as Terra Chips, which are sold in gourmet shops around the country. *Yuca* fries—golden wedges that are crispier on the outside and more tender on the inside than any french fries—are just as appealing. In many ways *yuca* fries are the ultimate fry. They never ever get soggy. In fact, they absorb little oil, and their outsides stay crisp long after they cool. Nor do they have the graininess of potatoes; they are a little waxy, with a mild, soothing sweet and buttery flavor. *Yuca* fries are about as easy to prepare as french fries. They just require the additional step of boiling before frying. And if you use packaged frozen *yuca,* you don't have to do any peeling.

Yuca fries can be found across the board in the kitchens of Americans of Latin American descent, though Caribbean, Brazilian, Peruvian, and Colombian Americans

perhaps hanker for them most. They are salted like french fries and are served with the usual Latin accompaniments, like lemon or lime wedges, and with everything imaginable that adorns french fries, including ketchup, vinegar, barbecue sauce, ground dried red chile, or paprika—even tomato sauce and melted mozzarella (*yuca pizza fries*). *Yuca* fries go nicely as a side with Cuban Sandwiches (see page 39), Crabmeat and Avocado Salad (see page 50), grilled steak, or hamburgers.

1 ½ **pounds fresh** *yuca* **(cassava), peeled,**
    cut into 2-inch-long rounds, and
    rinsed, or substitute frozen *yuca* **(see**
    page 198 for more information on
    yuca **and page 189 for directions on**
    peeling *yuca*)

1 **teaspoon salt**
1 **teaspoon lemon juice**
Vegetable oil, for frying
Lime or lemon wedges, for garnish

Put the *yuca* and enough cold water to cover, plus 2 inches, in a large saucepan. Add the salt and lemon juice. Cover and bring to a rolling boil over medium-high heat, then lower the heat and boil until tender, about 25 minutes. (If the *yuca* boils longer, it will become mushy.) Drain through a colander and allow the *yuca* to cool enough to be handled.

Gently peel off any pinkish fibrous layers that may cling to the tuber. Cut the *yuca* into ¾-inch-wide wedges and remove the fibrous core with a paring knife and discard. If the *yuca* is wet (it probably will not be, as it tends to absorb water), dry thoroughly with paper towels.

Heat 2 inches vegetable oil in a large, deep skillet or deep-fat fryer to 375°F on a deep-fat thermometer. Fry the *yuca* wedges, one third at a time, turning once, until light golden, about 5 minutes. Transfer the fried *yuca* to a tray or large plate lined with paper towels to drain, sprinkle with salt—or salt and ground dried red chile or paprika, if desired—toss, and serve immediately with lime or lemon wedges, or with the accompaniment of your choice.

Serves 4 as a side dish

YUCA WITH GARLIC-LIME OIL

Yuca con mojo

"**A**fter mashed potatoes, boiled *yuca,* the tropical tuber many Americans of Latin American descent most prize, must be the world's greatest comfort food," says Esther De La Torre, a Cuban-Colombian American, who lives in Bowling Green, Ohio, with her husband, Felipe De La Torre, and their three children. "Colombian Americans and Cuban Americans adore tender chunks of boiled *yuca* with *mojo,* a sublime tangy, garlicky oil. Cuban *mojo* for *yuca* is a simple blend of oil, garlic, and the juice of Seville oranges. Since Seville oranges are not available in most supermarkets in the United States, we make do with lime juice. While all the *yuca* lovers I know can reach a consensus on the ratio of olive oil to lime juice in a *mojo,* I have found that they cannot agree on how long to boil *yuca.* Some prefer it boiled until tender when pierced with a fork but not so soft that it falls apart, whereas others find bliss in downright mushy *yuca.* My family likes it somewhere in between."

Cuban Americans and Colombian Americans are not alone in their love of *Yuca con mojo;* other Latinos have their own delicious versions of this dish. For instance, Puerto Ricans coat *yuca* with a *mojo* flavored with fresh thyme, while Venezuelan Americans add minced cilantro to their *mojo.* Nowadays we abandon tradition and season our *mojos* with whatever fresh herbs, such as parsley, sage, rosemary, dill, mint, or basil, are ready to pick in our garden or fill the stalls at the farmers' market. Whether you bathe *yuca* in a traditional Cuban *mojo* or one infused with herbs or other ingredients, *Yuca con mojo* is so delicious and so versatile that it can accompany just about any meat or poultry dish in this collection.

1½ pounds fresh *yuca,* peeled, cut into
   1½-inch chunks, and rinsed, or
   substitute frozen *yuca* (see page 198
   for information on *yuca* and see
   opposite for how to peel)
½ teaspoon salt
2½ tablespoons freshly squeezed lime
   juice

¼ cup olive oil, preferably extra-virgin
3 large cloves garlic, peeled and minced
1 tablespoon minced fresh herbs (such
   as cilantro, parsley, sage, rosemary,
   thyme, dill, mint, or basil)*

Omit this ingredient if you are making traditional Cuban mojo.

Put the *yuca* with enough cold water to cover in a large saucepan, along with the salt and ½ tablespoon of the lime juice. Cover, bring to a rolling boil over medium-high heat, then lower the heat and boil the *yuca,* covered, until tender, about 25 minutes.

(Boil it longer for mushy *yuca*.) Drain the *yuca*. Gently peel off any pinkish fibrous layers that may cling to the tuber, and remove the fibrous core with a paring knife. Arrange the *yuca* in a serving dish and keep it warm.

Heat the olive oil in a small skillet over medium heat. Remove the skillet from the heat and then add the garlic. Stir in the remaining 2 tablespoons of lime juice and then the herbs, and pour the *mojo* over the *yuca*. Toss gently and serve the *yuca* at once.

Serves 4 to 6 as a side dish

HOW TO PEEL YUCA

Cut the *yuca* crosswise into 3-inch sections with a sharp knife. (Be sure to use a sharp knife, as raw *yuca* is as hard to peel and cut as raw mature beets.) Stand a section upright on a cutting board. Starting at the top of the tuber, cut a strip of the bark and fibrous layer off with the downward motion of the knife. Rotating the *yuca*, cut off the rest of the bark in this manner. Repeat for the other sections. Immerse the *yuca* in cold water after peeling until ready to use.

PARMESAN ONION RINGS

Anel de cebola com queijo parmesão

Too often fried onion rings are overwhelmed by thick breading, but Brazilian Americans dip them in beaten eggs so that when the onion rings are fried, the egg forms a thin, wispy envelope and the onions caramelize on the edges. Typically, Brazilian recipes for onion rings call for adding grated cheese to the beaten egg batter. We have found that the flavor of the cheese gets lost during frying, so we prefer instead to dust the fried onion rings with the cheese. Our choice is usually Parmesan, since it can be grated fine and is so flavorful. (Grate the Parmesan yourself just before serving; do not use store-bought pre-grated Parmesan.)

For the sweetest onion rings, try cooking with Vidalia or Walla Walla onions. Vidalias are available in May and June, while Walla Wallas are harvested from June to September. (These onions are available primarily in the regions where they are grown,

Parmesan Onion Rings (continued)

but they can be obtained through mail-order sources.) Parmesan onion rings, like all onion rings, go great with a tall glass of mango iced tea or a frosted mug of ice-cold beer. Try an imported Brazilian brew like Xingu Black Beer (a rich-tasting brew based on German Schwarzbier) or Brahma Beer, a pilsner.

Vegetable oil, for frying   ¼ cup finely grated Parmesan cheese

3 large eggs

2 large mild white or yellow onions, such
  as Bermuda or Spanish onions,
  peeled and cut into ½-inch rings

Heat 1 inch vegetable oil in a large heavy skillet to 360°F. Beat the eggs in a shallow dish. Dip an onion ring into the eggs and then slip it into the hot oil. Add 3 or 4 more dipped onion rings and fry until golden on both sides, about 1½ minutes per side. Transfer the onion rings with a fork to trays lined with paper towels to drain. Keep warm on baking sheets in a 200°F oven while you cook the remaining batches.

Sprinkle the onion rings with the grated Parmesan and serve at once.

Serves 4

When his nostrils hit the good food smells in the hallway of the apartment, Arnaz slapped his hands together and declared, "*¡Qué bueno!* How wonderful!" He found himself moving along a hallway whose walls were covered with framed photographs of musicians and portraits of Jesus Christ and his saints.

"Make yourself at home, *compañero*," Cesar said in his normal friendly manner. "Now this is your home, you understand, Mr. Arnaz?"

"Sounds good to me. Now, Lucy, isn't this nice?"

"Yes, it is, Desi, just swell."

"Ah, do I smell some *plátanos*?"

"*Plátanos verdes*," a female voice called from the kitchen.

"And *yuca* with *ajo*?"

"Yes," said Cesar happily. "And we have wine, we have beer!" He raised up his hands. "We have rum!"

"*¡Qué bueno!*"

> It was around one in the morning and Delores Castillo was in the kitchen, heating up all the pots of rice and chicken and beans, and the fritters were sizzling in a frying pan. Her hair was in a bun and she had a stained apron around her waist. When they all jammed into the kitchen, Delores recognized the famous Arnaz and his wife.
>
> "*Dios mío!*" she cried. "If I had known they were coming, I would have cleaned the house up."
>
> —Oscar Hijuelos, *The Mambo Kings Play Songs of Love*, New York: Farrar, Straus and Giroux, 1989

SAUTÉED RIBBONS OF KALE

Couve a mineira

Brazilian Americans share with southern cooks a deep and abiding love of greens, and they prize kale above all. They are most passionate about *Couve a mineira*—kale sliced into fine ribbons and then sautéed in bacon fat so that the greens are slightly crisp, bacony, and bright. *Couve a mineira* is a traditional accompaniment to Brazilian *Feijoada,* a veritable feast of stewed black beans, steamed rice, and a vast assemblage of smoked and fresh meats, from grilled steak to sausages (see page 157). Brazilian-style kale also goes beautifully with any dish of pork or ham that you might serve with southern-cooked greens. For a vegetarian version of *Couve a mineira* that is authentically Brazilian and just as easy to prepare, sauté the tenderized and drained kale in 1½ tablespoons olive oil instead of the bacon fat. If you wish, do what some Brazilian Americans do and toss a little minced garlic into the sauté pan with the greens. Kale sautéed in olive oil is a nice vegetable accompaniment to rice pilaf, wild rice, couscous, and risotto.

Kale is a leafy green vegetable that is a nonheading member of the cabbage family. Its dark green, crinkled leaves have a mild cabbage flavor and grow in a loose bouquet. Fresh kale is available in many supermarkets year-round, but it is best from October through April. Choose relatively small bunches of kale with crisp, dark leaves and store it unwashed in a plastic bag in the refrigerator crisper. Tender collard greens, another nonheading member of the cabbage family, are a good substitute for kale.

¾ pound kale, or substitute collard greens

3 tablespoons bacon fat

Salt and freshly ground black pepper, to taste

Discard any wilted or yellow leaves from the kale, rinse in a colander under cool running water until the leaves are clean of sand and dirt, then drain. Trim off any tough stems and bruised spots on the leaves with a sharp knife and discard. Stack 6 leaves on top of each other, fold in half lengthwise, and cut crosswise into ⅛-inch ribbons.

Bring 2 quarts salted water to a boil in a large pot. Remove the pot from the heat, drop the kale into the water, and let it sit for 5 minutes. Drain the kale well, through the colander.

Heat the bacon fat in a large skillet over medium heat. Add the kale and sauté for 2 minutes. Cover the skillet and cook the kale, stirring occasionally, for 9 minutes, or until it is tender, yet slightly crisp. Season with salt and pepper to taste, and serve at once.

Serves 4 to 6

OLD SLIPPERS

Chancletas

In the Costa Rican American kitchen, chayote, a tropical squash that tastes like a cross between zucchini and string beans (see page 194), is customarily stuffed with a filling of Cheddar cheese, half-and-half, sugar, and raisins for a delicious side dish or entrée called *Chancletas,* or "Old Slippers," because that's what it looks like. We first sampled Old Slippers in a fabulous Latin American greasy spoon in Los Angeles that serves Mexican and Cuban food alongside assorted dishes from across Latino America. We later discovered that the chef had altered the traditional recipe by adding walnuts, and we tried to re-create his version. Here it is.

For Old Slippers, select average-size chayotes (weighing about ¾ to 1 pound). If you are unable to find chayote, substitute pattypan squash—a summer squash also known as cycling squash.

3 chayotes (¾ to 1 pound each)
1 tablespoon unsalted butter
½ cup coarsely grated mild white
   Cheddar cheese, Monterey Jack, or
   Muenster
1 tablespoon half-and-half

¼ cup chopped walnuts
¼ cup seedless golden raisins
1 teaspoon granulated sugar
1 teaspoon vanilla extract
¼ cup finely grated Parmesan cheese
2 tablespoons seasoned bread crumbs

Drop the chayotes into a large pot of boiling water. Reduce the heat, cover, and boil gently until the chayotes are very tender when pierced with a fork, about 45 to 50 minutes. Carefully remove them from the pot with a slotted spoon or tongs to a colander and drain. When they are cool enough to handle, cut the cooked chayotes in half lengthwise. Remove the flat seeds and any surrounding tough fiber with a paring knife. Scoop out the pulp with a sharp spoon (a grapefruit knife works well) into a large mixing bowl, taking care to preserve the skin and ½ inch of pulp to form shells. Set the 6 shells aside.

Purée the pulp in a food processor or electric blender, return it to the mixing bowl, and stir in the butter, grated cheese, half-and-half, walnuts, raisins, sugar, and vanilla extract. Carefully spoon the filling into the reserved chayote shells. Sprinkle the Parmesan cheese and bread crumbs over the filled shells, and bake them in a baking dish or pie pan in a preheated 375°F oven for 15 to 20 minutes, or until the tops of the *Chancletas* are golden brown. You may serve the stuffed chayotes at once or keep them warm.

The chayote, a tropical pear-shaped squash, has a zucchini-and-string-bean flavor. It was once a primary food of the Maya and Aztec, and now can be found in Latin kitchens across America.

Serves 6 as a side dish and 3 as an entrée

CHAYOTE | Chayote is a tropical pear-shaped squash native to the West Indies, with cream-colored flesh and dark green to ivory skin. (The variety most commonly sold in this country has light green skin.) Chayote grows on climbing vines, and each plant may bear up to three hundred to five hundred fruits. (In southern California we have seen chayote plants gone wild, growing over fences and up telephone poles!) While chayote is classified as a fruit, it ranks as a vegetable among cooks, since it is not sweet and is similar in flavor to zucchini and string beans.

Chayote is quite popular in many Latin American countries and in Latin U.S.A., where it is also known variously as *tayote, chuchu, cho-cho, xuxu, sousous,* and *christophene*. While Europeans consider it a gourmet treat and import it from North Africa, the fruit is just catching on across America (except in Louisiana, where it is well known as mirliton). Chayote is available primarily from October to April in select supermarkets, especially in southern California, Florida, Louisiana, Texas, and the Southwest, and in Latin grocery stores. Select firm fruit with unblemished, smooth skin, and store it in an airtight plastic bag in the refrigerator for up to 2 weeks.

Chayote can be served raw in salads with a vinaigrette, or it can be boiled or sautéed like summer squash. It can also be stuffed and baked like winter squash, as in Mexican *chayotes rellenos*—chayotes stuffed with mashed pound cake, eggs, and raisins, flavored with sugar and spices. A unique chayote dish is Dominican *tayotes revueltos con huevos*—an omelet punctuated with chunks of cooked chayote, tomatoes, onions, and chile peppers. Simply boil 1 half of a small chayote (about ¼ pound), peeled, in salted water until tender when pierced with a fork, about 15 minutes. Remove the seed and cut the chayote into ½-inch chunks. Heat 2 tablespoons olive oil over medium heat in a large skillet and sauté 1 finely minced small onion and 1 finely minced garlic clove until the onion is limp. Add 2 chopped Roma tomatoes and 1 finely minced jalapeño or serrano chile, or to taste, and cook until the mixture is almost dry. Stir in the chayote chunks and salt and freshly ground black pepper to taste. Add 4 beaten eggs and cook until the omelet has set. Serves 2.

MINGA'S CALABACITAS

Calabacitas Minga

"While many American gardeners are overwhelmed by a bumper crop of zucchini and resort to leaving stacks of the vegetable on their neighbors' doorsteps, Mexican Americans are overjoyed," says Mexican American Dominga Garcia, or Minga, who, with her husband, Robert Garcia, Sr., son Rudy, and daughter-in-law Patsy, owns and operates Minga's Mexican Food Restaurant in Phoenix, Arizona, a restaurant that has captured 25 culinary excellence awards in the last 7 years. "That's because we are passionate about zucchini, or *calabacitas*. At home I am always inventing and reinventing dishes. Recently I came up with a new *calabacitas* recipe. It features onion, garlic, zucchini, tomatoes, and corn sautéed in olive oil and seasoned with a little lime juice and cilantro. It's really quite marvelous and so simple. My *nuevo calabacitas* can be served as a light main dish or as a side dish with anything your heart desires."

1 tablespoon olive oil
1 small yellow onion, peeled and minced
1 large clove garlic, peeled and finely minced
2 medium zucchini, cut into ½-inch cubes
1 cup fresh corn kernels (cut from 1 large ear of corn), or substitute frozen (defrosted) corn kernels
1 small ripe tomato, cut into ½-inch cubes
1 medium scallion, root ends removed and finely minced
1 teaspoon freshly squeezed lime juice
1 tablespoon finely minced fresh cilantro
Salt and freshly ground black pepper, to taste

Heat the olive oil in a large skillet over medium heat, and sauté the minced onions and garlic until the onions are limp, about 5 minutes.

Stir in the zucchini, corn, tomato, and scallions, and sauté, stirring occasionally, until the zucchini is tender, about 10 minutes. Remove the vegetables from the heat and stir in the lime juice, cilantro, and salt and pepper. Serve at once.

Serves 6 as a side dish

LATIN AMERICAN ROOT VEGETABLES

Arracacha

Popular among South Americans, *arracacha* has light yellow flesh that tastes a bit like celery and has the texture of potatoes. The root vegetable *apio,* known in English as celeriac or celery root, is strikingly similar to *arracacha.* (The Spanish word for celery is also *apio,* and should not be confused with this tuber.) Both *arracacha* and *apio* are available in Pan-Latin markets. *Arracacha* is used much like potatoes, and is especially delicious boiled and mashed or baked in its skin in the oven.

Jerusalem Artichokes (also known as sunchokes in English and *topinambur* in Spanish South America)

A species of sunflower, the Jerusalem artichoke suffers from mistaken identity, since its name arose from linguistic confusion over its earlier Italian appellation, *girasole articiocco.* This small knobby tuber has tan skin and crisp ivory flesh. It has a mild, slightly sweet, nutty flavor whether it is eaten raw or cooked. Jerusalem artichokes are sold year-round in many large supermarkets as well as Latin markets, but they are at their best in fall and winter. Select the largest, smoothest Jerusalem artichokes, as they are the easiest to peel. Bake Jerusalem artichokes in their skins, or peel, slice, and sauté them. They are also marvelous steamed or boiled, then peeled and puréed. Raw Jerusalem artichokes may be sliced thin or grated and added to salads.

Jicama

Nicknamed "yam bean" and "Mexican potato," this low-cal tuber comes in many sizes and is usually shaped like a turnip. It has thin tan skin and crunchy, juicy, slightly sweet white flesh, reminiscent of water chestnuts, that may be eaten raw or cooked. Peel the skin and the layer of fiber underneath just before using, as peeled jicama dries out quickly. A favorite among Mexican Americans, jicama has crossed over to mainstream American cooking and is available in many large supermarkets from October through May, as well as in Mexican, Pan-Latin, and Asian markets. Select medium roots that are smooth, hard, and free of spots. Store jicama in a plastic bag in the refrigerator for up to 3 weeks. Peeled chunks will keep for a few days in a bowl of water set in the refrigerator.

Malanga (also known as *yautía* to Puerto Ricans and as *tannia, tannier,* and *cocoyam*)

A tropical tuber closely related to taro, *malanga* is the foundation of many Caribbean and Central American dishes. The tuber weighs in at anywhere from ½ to 2 pounds and grows leggy like a carrot or squat like a turnip. Underneath the hairy, barklike brown skin of *malanga* is ivory, pinkish, or yellowish starchy flesh that turns gray when cooked. *Malanga* is never eaten raw, but is peeled and cooked and has a mild nutty flavor. Americans of Latin American descent serve *malanga* boiled as an accompaniment to meats, sausages, and fish. They also add chunks of the tuber to stews, and slice and grate it for chips and fritters. It is available year-

Malanga, a tropical tuber related to taro

round in Caribbean, Central American, and Pan-Latin markets and in some green-grocers and supermarkets. *Malanga* should be firm with no moldy or soft spots. Store the root at room temperature for up to 1 week or peel and freeze it whole (or in chunks if the tuber is large) to have on hand.

Sweet Potatoes (known as *batata* in Spanish Latin America)

A member of the morning glory family and not a potato, as its name falsely suggests, the sweet potato grows in the tropics and subtropics and figures prominently in Latin American cooking. Many varieties of sweet potato exist, but the ones most available

Boniato, a subtly sweet variety of sweet potato

in the United States are the light-skinned sweet potato with yellow flesh and its dark-skinned cousin with bright orange, sweet flesh. This latter variety, called the Louisiana yam, bears no relation to the real yam. The white variety of sweet potatoes, known as *boniato*, is only faintly sweet and is preferred by Americans of Latin American descent, who cook it just as they might *yuca*. *Boniato* is available year-round (although it is hard to find in February and March) in Caribbean markets. Never place sweet potatoes in the refrigerator. Store them at room temperature in a well-ventilated spot for up to 2 weeks.

Taro (also called *dasheen* by most West Indians and South Americans, and *baddo* by Jamaicans)

This ancient brown-skinned starchy tuber, native to the East Indies, was eaten by prehistoric peoples. Taro grows from five inches to over a foot in length and has pure white or grayish white flesh with tan flecks. Some varieties of taro are bitter and highly toxic in the raw state, and thus the tuber should be cooked thoroughly before eating to destroy both the toxins and the bitterness. Cooked taro has a mild taste reminiscent of artichoke hearts or chestnuts. Americans of Latin American descent fortify soups and stews with taro, grate it for fritters, and slice it into chips that are deep-fried. Chunks of taro are also cooked in sugar syrup for a confection that resembles *marrons glacés*. Taro is rather unappealing boiled and mashed (it becomes like glue) and dries out when baked or roasted. Taro can be found in select supermarkets, Caribbean, and Pan-Latin markets, and in Japanese groceries, where it bears the name *sato-imo*. Choose tubers that are firm and free of mold. Never refrigerate taro. Store it at room temperature for up to 5 days. The leaves of the taro plant, called callaloo, are also edible.

Yam (also known as tropical yam, African yam, *ñame*, *yampi*, and *mapuey*; and as *inhame* in Brazil)

No relation to the sweet potato and the tuber Americans call yam, the 600 species of the true yam have brown or purplish skin and ivory or yellow flesh, and can range in weight from a few ounces to a whopping 100 pounds or more. Like potatoes, yams are never eaten raw. Cooked yams are sweeter and more flavorful than sweet potatoes but contain fewer nutrients. They are sold in Latin markets and in some large supermarkets. Select the smaller varieties with a more concentrated flavor and store them at room temperature for up to 1 week. If you wish to use a portion of a yam, simply cut it off and leave the rest uncovered—it will seal the exposed flesh itself.

Yuca (also called cassava and manioc in English, and mandioca in Portuguese)

Often confused with yucca, an evergreen plant with white blossoms that are the state flower of New Mexico, *yuca* (pronounced YOU-ka) is a dense, starchy tuber with origins in Brazil. Nowadays it is grown in Latin America, Florida, and other regions of the globe, and ranges from 6 to 24 inches in length. Peeling

Yuca, a starchy tuber that is never eaten raw

away the barklike skin of the *yuca* (usually waxed to retard spoilage) reveals the root's crisp stark-white flesh that must always be cooked to rid it of glucoside, a poisonous substance found in one type of the tuber. Cooked *yuca* tastes like buttery potatoes with a hint of sweetness. While most Americans of Latin American descent boil, bake, or fry *yuca,* Brazilian Americans also dry and grind the root into manioc meal (*farinha de mandioca*), which they then toast and mix with other ingredients to make the ubiquitous dish *farofa.* Americans of all ethnicities have been eating this root for decades without realizing it, since tapioca is pregelatinized starch extracted from *yuca.* Fresh *yuca* is available year-round in most Latin markets and select Asian markets and supermarkets. Some Latin markets also carry frozen peeled *yuca.* Choose firm roots that are odorless, hard, and free of cracks and soft, slimy, or moldy spots. *Yuca* tends to spoil rapidly, so keep it at room temperature for no longer than 3 days, or peel it and freeze it for longer storage. If you cut off a portion of the *yuca,* leave the rest uncovered to seal over.

TAMALES, EMPANADAS, AND OTHER TURNOVERS—NOT BREAD—ARE THE REAL STAFF OF LATIN LIFE.

TAMALES,

EMPANADAS,

AND OTHER

TURNOVERS

LITTLE BRAZIL SHRIMP TURNOVERS

Empadinhas de camarão

While Brazilian Americans are passionate about meat dishes like *feijoada completa,* which is actually a whole meal of assorted cuts, such as pork, bacon, pigs' ears, dried beef, smoked tongue, and sausage, served with black beans, rice, and manioc (*yuca*) meal, they also have a penchant for fish and shellfish. In New York City's Little Brazil restaurants, like Via Brasil and Brasilia, *moquecas* (stews with fish and shellfish, see page 69) and *bacalhau* (salt cod), served in myriad ways, are invariably on the menus. One of the most heavenly seafood dishes is *Empadinhas de camarão* (Shrimp Turnovers)—a marriage of succulent shrimp and silky hearts of palm, a Brazilian delicacy, inside a buttery crust.

Given their size, *empadinhas*—the diminutive name of *empadas*—make perfect hors d'oeuvres, snacks, or appetizers. Brazilian Americans also serve them with salad and sandwiches for a light supper. Main-course *empadas* may be made by cutting out six-inch rather than four-inch circles of dough. This recipe for *Empadinhas de camarão* adheres to tradition in every way except that the proportion of butter to vegetable shortening is greater, to achieve a crisper, buttery crust.

FOR THE FILLING:

2 tablespoons olive oil

1 medium onion, peeled and finely minced

2 medium cloves garlic, peeled and finely minced

2 medium ripe tomatoes, coarsely chopped

¼ teaspoon salt, or to taste

⅛ teaspoon freshly ground white pepper

¾ cup canned hearts of palm, drained and coarsely chopped

½ pound medium shrimp, peeled, deveined, cut in thirds, and rinsed

¼ cup canned unsweetened coconut milk

2 tablespoons finely minced fresh parsley (cilantro is a nice alternative)

FOR THE DOUGH:

2⅓ cups unbleached all-purpose flour

½ teaspoon turmeric

¼ teaspoon salt

6 tablespoons (¾ stick) unsalted butter, chilled

1 tablespoon vegetable shortening

1 large egg

1 large egg yolk, beaten with 3 tablespoons cold water

FOR THE GLAZE:

1 egg yolk   1 tablespoon water

Prepare the filling: Heat the olive oil in a large skillet over medium-high heat. Sauté the minced onions and garlic until golden, about 5 minutes. Add the tomatoes, salt, and white pepper, and cook, stirring occasionally, for about 5 minutes. Next add the hearts of palm, shrimp, and coconut milk, and cook, stirring constantly, for an additional 5 minutes, or until the shrimp turn bright pink. Stir in the parsley or cilantro, and then remove the skillet from the heat and allow the filling to cool completely.

Meanwhile, make the dough: Mix together thoroughly the flour, turmeric, and salt in a large bowl. Cut the chilled butter into ½-inch pieces with a sharp knife. Add the pieces of butter and the vegetable shortening to the flour. Blend the ingredients with your fingertips until the mixture resembles a coarse meal. Next mix in the whole egg and the egg yolk beaten with cold water, and knead into a stiff dough. Add more water, a teaspoon at a time, if necessary. Cover the dough with a dampened towel and set it aside to rest for at least 20 minutes.

While the dough rests, make the glaze. Blend the egg yolk and 1 tablespoon water in a small bowl.

To assemble the *empadinhas,* roll the dough out on a lightly floured work surface to a thickness of ⅛ inch. Cut the dough into 4-inch circles with a cookie cutter or mark the dough with a 4-inch plate or bowl and cut out the imprints with a sharp knife. Roll out the scraps and cut more circles until all of the dough is used. Spoon a heaping tablespoon of filling into the middle of each pastry circle, leaving a ¼-inch edge. Coat the edges of a filled circle with the egg glaze, and then carefully fold one side of the circle over the filling so that the edges meet, forming a half-moon. Seal the half-moon by pressing the edges lightly with your fingertips, and then press the edges with the tines of a fork. Repeat until all the *empadinhas* are folded and sealed. (You will probably have a little filling left over.)

Arrange the *empadinhas* on a baking sheet lined with parchment paper. Brush them with the egg glaze, then bake them on the top rack of a preheated 375°F oven for 20 minutes, or until they are golden brown. Remove the *empadinhas* from the oven and place them immediately on wire racks to cool. Serve the *empadinhas* warm.

Makes about 16 empadinhas

VARIETIES OF EMPANADAS

What's the difference between *empanadas de carne, empadas de carne, caldudas, salteñas,* and beef patties?

Essentially nothing. They are all wonderful variations of the Latin American beef empanada—a rich, golden turnover filled with succulent ground beef. Cuban American beef empanadas, known as *empanadas de carne,* are embellished with hard-boiled eggs, olives, and raisins, as well as chopped tomatoes and capers. The traditional Brazilian American version, called *empadas de carne,* is close to the Cuban, except that hot chiles replace the raisins. Beef empanadas are known as beef patties to Jamaican Americans, and are also quite *picante* thanks to Scotch bonnet chiles (see page 165). Argentine Americans traditionally embellish the beef filling for *Empanadas de carne* with green bell pepper, pears, and peaches instead of hard-boiled eggs, olives, and raisins (see page 206), while Puerto Ricans make a filling of ground beef, green peppers, and tomato sauce, and then deep-fry rather than bake their empanadas. The Bolivian American equivalent of the beef empanada is the *salteña,* and it may have rice in the filling, while the Chilean version is the *calduda* featured below.

Empanadas (savory or sweet Latin turnovers)

CHILEAN AMERICAN BEEF TURNOVERS

Caldudas al estilo chileno-americano

Chilean empanadas, sweet or savory turnovers, are stuffed with one of a whole scrumptious array of fillings, such as shrimp, fish, cheese, or vegetables. Of all the Chilean empanadas, perhaps the one most favored in America is the *calduda,* with its savory-sweet filling of moist ground beef, hard-boiled eggs, olives, and raisins encased in delicate, buttery dough. Some Chilean American cooks make only subtle alterations to the ground beef filling recipe, but the majority have revamped the pastry dough by replacing lard with butter and vegetable shortening, as in this ⟨…⟩ Most agree that *caldudas* are an ideal snack or casual lunch or supper fare, ⟨…⟩ salad of dark greens and glasses of red wine. We have found that Chile's Cousino-Macul merlot (finer than many California merlots) or the medium-bodied Cousino-Macul cabernet sauvignon make wonderful companions.

Like all empanadas, *caldudas* may be made in different sizes. For this recipe the dough is cut in circles 5 inches in diameter to make *caldudas* suitable as a main dish. To prepare *caldudas* as an appetizer, hors d'oeuvre, or snack, simply cut the dough in circles 3 inches in diameter and stuff each with about half the filling. Note that uncooked empanadas freeze very well if they are wrapped tightly in plastic and then placed in an airtight plastic bag. Allow them to thaw for 2 hours before baking. Leftover baked empanadas reheat nicely the next day in the microwave or in the oven.

FOR THE DOUGH:

2¼ cups unbleached all-purpose flour

½ teaspoon salt

½ cup (1 stick) unsalted butter, chilled

¼ cup vegetable shortening, chilled

About ⅓ cup cold water

FOR THE FILLING:

2 tablespoons olive oil

1 medium yellow onion, peeled and
   finely minced

½ pound lean ground beef

½ teaspoon ground cumin

1 teaspoon sweet paprika

⅛ teaspoon cayenne pepper

¼ cup beef broth, canned or homemade

2 hard-boiled eggs, coarsely chopped

½ cup brine- or salt-cured black olives,
   such as kalamata, niçoise, ponentine,
   or Greek-style olives, pitted
   and chopped

½ cup golden seedless raisins

FOR THE GLAZE:

1 egg yolk

1 tablespoon water

Make the dough: Mix together the flour and salt in a large mixing bowl. Cut the chilled butter into ½-inch pieces, and then add the butter pieces and the vegetable shortening to the flour. Blend the ingredients with your fingertips until the mixture resembles coarse meal. Add the cold water and knead into a stiff dough. If the dough is too dry, add a little more water, ½ teaspoon at a time. Cover the dough with plastic wrap and chill it in the refrigerator while you prepare the filling.

To make the filling, heat the olive oil over medium-high heat in a large skillet and sauté the minced onions until they begin to brown, about 5 minutes. Add the ground beef, cumin, paprika, and cayenne to the skillet, and cook, breaking up the beef with a fork as it browns, about 5 minutes. Add the beef broth and simmer the beef until al-

Chilean American Beef Turnovers (continued)

most all of the broth has been absorbed, about 8 minutes. Remove the ground beef filling to a medium mixing bowl to cool.

Meanwhile, roll out the dough on a lightly floured work surface to a thickness of ⅛ inch. Using a 5-inch diameter plate or a bowl, cut the dough into circles by following the outline with a sharp knife. Roll out the scraps and cut more circles until all the dough is used.

To assemble the *caldudas,* spoon about 2 teaspoons beef, ½ teaspoon hard-boiled eggs, ½ teaspoon olives, and a few raisins in the center of a circle, leaving a ¼-inch edge. Carefully fold one side of the circle over the filling so the edges meet, forming a half-moon. Seal the

Mexican Americans at a gristmill in Arizona, 1907

half-moon by pressing the edges between your forefinger and thumb, then press the edges with the tines of a fork. Repeat until all the *caldudas* are filled, folded, and sealed.

Beat the egg yolk with the water for the glaze. Transfer the *caldudas* to lightly greased baking sheets, brush them with the egg glaze, and bake on the top rack of a preheated 425°F oven for 12 to 15 minutes, or until golden. Remove the *caldudas* from the oven and transfer them to wire racks. Serve the *caldudas* while they are still warm.

Serves 4 to 6

For Argentine American Beef Empanadas (*Empanadas de carne*): Sauté ¼ cup finely minced green bell pepper along with the onions. Omit the cumin, paprika, and cayenne pepper. In place of beef broth, add 2 tablespoons dry white wine, 1 finely minced small ripe tomato, ½ medium pear, peeled, cored, and finely diced, and ½ medium peach, peeled, pitted, and finely diced. Cook for 5 minutes or until the fruit is soft. Taste the filling and add salt and freshly ground black pepper, as needed. Fill each dough circle with 3 teaspoons filling and omit the hard-boiled eggs, olives, and raisins.

HOW JAMAICAN BEEF PATTIES ENDED UP IN NEW YORK CITY'S PIZZERIAS

When Beryl Levi and her husband, Earl, a clothing designer, came to New York City from Jamaica over three decades ago, they were stunned by the shortage of Jamaican goodies in the Big Apple. So one day they started baking their own at home. Friends and neighbors took one little taste of Earl and Beryl's beef patties—ground beef turnovers spiced with curry—and began placing orders. Sensing they were on to something, the Levis launched Tower Isle's, a small Jamaican bakery in the Crown Heights section of Brooklyn in 1968. Tower Isle's did a modest business until the day it dawned on the Levis that New York City's hundreds of pizzerias were the ultimate venue for their beef patties. When pizzerias received their first shipment, they were promised that if the patties didn't sell, they could return them. But New Yorkers couldn't get enough, and the demand skyrocketed. By then the Levis had Americanized the recipe by toning down the spice and beefing up the beef so that the patties could rival hamburgers. Some pizzerias gave the patties a few of their own personal Italian touches, adding a little mozzarella here for Beef Patties Parmigiana and a little pepperoni there for Pepperoni Patties. Before long, Tower Isle's emerged as one of the world's largest beef patty factories; by the 1990s the company was producing over 100,000 beef patties a day to supply pizzerias, Latin bodegas, and the frozen food sections of warehouse supermarkets like Price Club. In 1990 Tower Isle's added vegetable patties, and in 1994 along came chicken patties, but the beef patties are still number one in New York City's pizzerias.

JAMAICAN BEEF PATTIES

Jamaican American Michael R. Hall, who works in the media department for theatrical marketing at MGM/United Artists Studios in Los Angeles, grew up in Troy, Ohio, where virtually the only West Indian food around was made in his mother's kitchen. As a child, Michael always looked forward to the Fourth of July, when his family would gather together with twenty other Jamaican American families from across three states for a huge picnic and a game of cricket. "My parents prepared for the picnic for weeks in advance," says Michael. "Dad checked over all the cricket equipment, while Mom tested and retested my grandmother's recipe for Jamaican Beef Patties, spicy ground beef turnovers, to prepare for the enormous batch she would bake for the picnic. Those beef patties were irresistible because they were made with sausage as well as beef and were flavored with lots of curry."

Michael Hall cannot wait for the day when Jamaican beef patties are as common in Los Angeles as they are in New York City, where many pizzerias showcase the spicy delicacies alongside pizza pies and calzones (see How Jamaican Beef Patties Ended Up in New York City's Pizzerias, page 207). In the meantime, he relies on his grand-mother's recipe for Jamaican Beef Patties, which he serves as a snack or appetizer, or as a light meal with a soup or salad.

FOR THE DOUGH:

2 cups unbleached all-purpose flour

½ tablespoon curry powder

½ teaspoon salt

½ cup vegetable shortening

5 tablespoons cold water

FOR THE FILLING:

½ pound lean ground beef

½ pound hot or sweet Italian link sausage, removed from its casings

I medium yellow onion, peeled and finely minced

I large clove garlic, peeled and finely minced

½ Scotch bonnet chile, or substitute I jalapeño, seeded and finely minced, or to taste (optional)

½ cup plain dry bread crumbs

I tablespoon curry powder

½ teaspoon dried thyme

½ teaspoon rubbed sage

I teaspoon salt, or to taste

¼ teaspoon freshly ground black pepper, or to taste

½ cup water

2 medium scallions, root ends removed and minced

I large egg yolk, beaten

Prepare the dough: Mix together the dry ingredients thoroughly in a medium mixing bowl. Add the vegetable shortening and the 5 tablespoons cold water, and rub them into the seasoned flour with your fingers until you have a stiff dough. If the dough is too dry to hold together, add more cold water, ½ teaspoon at a time. Wrap the dough in plastic and chill it in the refrigerator for at least 2 hours.

Meanwhile, make the filling: Sauté the ground beef, sausage, minced onions, gar-lic, and chile, if desired, in a large skillet over medium-high heat until brown, about 15 minutes, breaking the meats up with a fork as they cook. Reduce the heat to low, add the bread crumbs, curry powder, thyme, sage, salt, and pepper, and the ½ cup of water, and cook the filling, stirring frequently, for 5 minutes. Stir in the scallions. Re-move from the heat and allow the filling to cool to room temperature.

Roll out the dough on a lightly floured work surface to a thickness of ⅛ inch. Cut the dough into circles 5 inches in diameter. (We prefer to press the edges of a plate or bowl with a 5-inch diameter into the dough, and then follow the outline with a sharp knife to cut the circles.) Roll out the scraps and cut more circles until all the dough is used.

Assemble the beef patties: Spoon about 1½ tablespoons filling on one side of a pastry circle. Fold the other half of the circle over the filling so the edges meet, forming a half-moon. Seal the edges by pressing lightly with your fingertips and then with the tines of a fork, and place the beef patty on a baking sheet. Fold and seal the rest of the beef patties in the same fashion and arrange them on baking sheets.

Brush the tops of the beef patties with the beaten egg and bake them on the upper rack of a preheated 400°F oven until golden brown, about 15 minutes. Remove the beef patties from the oven and transfer them to wire racks. Serve them while they are still warm.

Makes approximately 1 dozen

FETA CHEESE, CHILE, AND ONION PASTRIES

Pukas

"Pukas are savory round pastries stuffed with a Bolivian farmer cheese, known as *quesillo,* and onions, and painted red with ground dried ají chiles. In fact, *pukas* is the Quechua (a predominant indigenous language of the Andes region) word for red," says Bolivian American José Sánchez-H., a professor of film and electronic arts at California State University, Long Beach. "*Pukas* remind me of a time gone by in Bolivia. Whenever I break a pastry, fresh from the oven with its chile-pepper-red domed crust, in two so that the cheese-and-onion-scented steam escapes, I envision the Bolivia of yesteryear and a whole world of family and friends, some who remain, some who are gone. I shall never forget how on Sundays my sister Carla and I would go to a place on the Cochabamba–Santa Cruz Road, where we would stuff ourselves with *pukas.*"

José Sánchez-H. has altered the traditional recipe for *pukas* by substituting feta, the salty farmer cheese, for *quesillo,* and jalapeños for locoto chiles, Bolivian ingredients that are unavailable in the United States. Bolivian Americans tend to use a generous amount of hot chiles in their cooking, and José Sánchez-H.'s *pukas* are no exception. We have taken the liberty of tempering his recipe just a bit by cutting the amount of ground dried red chile in the filling in half.

Feta Cheese, Chile, and Onion Pastries (continued)

FOR THE DOUGH:

2 cups unbleached all-purpose flour

1½ teaspoons baking powder

½ teaspoon granulated sugar

½ teaspoon salt

¼ cup (½ stick) butter, cut into
   small pieces

2 medium egg yolks

½ cup milk or water

FOR THE FILLING:

¼ cup (½ stick) butter

1½ cups finely minced yellow onion

2 cups (about ¾ pound) crumbled
   feta cheese

1 small hot fresh chile, such as the
   jalapeño, seeded, deribbed, and finely
   minced, or to taste (optional)

2 medium scallions, root ends removed
   and finely minced

2 tablespoons finely minced peeled
   ripe tomato

1½ tablespoons finely minced
   fresh parsley

2 tablespoons mild ground dried red
   chile, or to taste (see the note on
   ground dried red chile on page 167)

1 dozen large pitted black olives, cut
   in half

FOR THE RED CHILE GLAZE:

1 tablespoon mild ground dried red chile

1 tablespoon butter

1 tablespoon water

Make the dough: Mix together thoroughly the dry ingredients in a medium mixing bowl. Cut the butter into the flour mixture with two knives, a pastry blender, or your fingertips, until it resembles coarse meal. Blend in the egg yolks and then the milk or water. Gather the dough into a ball. Add more milk or water, ½ teaspoon at a time, if the dough is too dry. Do not knead the dough, or it will become tough. Wrap the dough with plastic and let it rest while you make the filling.

To make the filling, melt the butter in a large skillet over medium heat. Sauté the minced onions in the butter, stirring occasionally, until they are very soft, about 10 minutes. Remove the onions and any butter remaining in the skillet to a large mixing bowl. Stir in the feta cheese, minced chile, if desired, scallions, tomato, parsley, and ground dried red chile.

Make the red chile glaze: Combine the ground dried red chile, butter, and water in a small saucepan. Cook the glaze over low heat for 5 minutes, and then remove it from the heat.

Roll out the dough on a lightly floured surface to a thickness of ⅛ inch. Cut the dough into circles with a 4-inch cookie cutter, or mark the dough with a 4-inch plate or bowl and cut out the imprints with a sharp knife. Pile the pastry circles on a plate and cover them with plastic wrap. Roll out the dough scraps and cut more circles. Continue rolling and cutting until all the dough is used.

Spoon 1½ to 2 generous tablespoons of filling in the center of one of the pastry circles. (Use as much filling as possible because it cooks down during baking.) Press 2 olive halves into the filling. Lay another pastry circle on top, and seal the circles by pressing down on the edges first with your fingertips and then with the tines of a fork. (If the *pukas* are not sealed completely, a little bit of the filling will ooze out during baking.) Assemble the rest of the *pukas* in the same way.

Arrange the filled pastries on greased cookie sheets and brush the tops with the red chile glaze. Bake the *pukas* on the upper rack of a preheated 400°F oven until the edges are golden brown, about 12 minutes. Transfer the *pukas* to wire racks and serve them warm.

Makes about 10 pastries

GRIDDLE-FRIED BREAD STUFFED WITH YELLOW SPLIT PEAS

Dhal puri

East Indian foods have been brought to the United States by way of Latin America, thanks to Guyanese, Trinidadan, and Surinamese immigrants. After Great Britain and the Netherlands abolished slavery in the early 1800s, the English landowners in Guyana and Trinidad, and the Dutch in Suriname, contracted East Indian and Chinese laborers, among others, to replace the slaves. As a result, East Indians now account for about half the population in Guyana. They have profoundly influenced the country's gastronomic life, as spicy curries and Indian breads, like *roti* and *poori* (which the Guyanese call *roti* skins and *puri*), mingle with English puddings and pastries, African stews like pepperpot, and Chinese noodle dishes.

Nowadays, East Indian dishes that bear an inevitable Caribbean stamp can be found on the menu in Guyanese American restaurants, such as those in New York City's Guyanese community centered in the Flatbush and Crown Heights sections of Brooklyn. This recipe for *Dhal puri* (Griddle-Fried Bread Stuffed with Yellow Split Peas) is as popular among Guyanese Americans as its antecedent, *hari matar paratha*, is among Americans with direct roots to India. While *Dhal puri* is traditionally cooked on a dry griddle and served as a bread to accompany a main dish, we also serve it as an appetizer or snack the Italian way, with a little dish of extra-virgin olive oil for dipping. Rather than cook the bread on a dry griddle, we also sometimes sauté it in a tablespoon of olive oil in a skillet. This cooking method produces a totally different bread, crisped on the outside and tender on the inside—a cross between Navajo fry bread and pizza crust.

Griddle-Fried Bread Stuffed with Yellow Split Peas (continued)

FOR THE FILLING:

½ cup (4 ounces) dried yellow split peas*

2 cups water

¼ cup finely minced yellow onion

I tablespoon finely minced jalapeño
  chile, or to taste (optional)

I medium clove garlic, peeled and
  finely minced

I tablespoon olive oil

½ teaspoon cumin

½ teaspoon turmeric

Salt, to taste

FOR THE DOUGH:

4 cups unbleached all-purpose flour

½ tablespoon baking powder

¼ teaspoon salt

I ⅓ cups water

Vegetable oil or olive oil, for cooking

Yellow split peas are available in natural food markets and some supermarkets.

Prepare the filling: Rinse the split peas in a colander under cold running water. Drain, put them in a small saucepan with the 2 cups water, and bring to a boil over medium-high heat. Reduce the heat, and simmer, covered, until the peas are tender, about 20 minutes.

Drain the split peas thoroughly in the colander and let them cool to room temperature while you prepare the dough.

To make the dough, mix together the flour, baking powder, and salt in a large mixing bowl. Stir the 1⅓ cups water into the dry ingredients to form a soft dough. If the dough is too dry, add a little more water, ½ teaspoon at a time. Knead the dough on a lightly floured surface until silky smooth, about 10 minutes. Shape the dough into a ball, cover it with a dampened towel, and allow it to rest for 30 minutes.

Meanwhile, blot the split peas dry with paper towels. Mash them in a food processor or blender until they resemble coarse meal, then transfer them to a small mixing bowl. Sauté the minced onions, jalapeño, if desired, and garlic in the tablespoon olive oil over medium heat until the onions are limp, about 4 minutes. Mix the sautéed vegetables, the cumin, turmeric, and salt into the split peas. The filling will be very dry.

Knead the dough for 1 minute on a lightly floured work surface, then divide it into 8 pieces of equal size. Roll the pieces into smooth balls between your palms. Flatten a ball and then roll it with a rolling pin into a 4-inch circle. Spoon a generous tablespoon of filling in the center of the dough circle. Carefully fold the edges of the circle up and toward the middle to cover the filling and form a ball. Press the edges to seal. Repeat until all the dough circles are filled.

Heat a griddle or large cast-iron skillet over medium heat. Gently roll out one of the filled dough balls into a 7-inch circle, turning it over once and rolling on the other side. As you roll out the dough, a dough pocket should form with the filling on the in-

side. The filling should not poke through the dough. Cook the *dhal puri* on the dry griddle or in the skillet until it is lightly browned on the underside, about 4 minutes, then flip it over and brush the browned side lightly with vegetable or olive oil. Continue cooking the *dhal puri* until it becomes puffy and brown, about 4 minutes. (Or cook it in a skillet with 1 tablespoon olive oil until golden brown on the underside, about 4 minutes. Flip it and cook it on the other side until golden, about 4 minutes.) Remove it to a plate lined with a dish towel and cover it with another towel to keep it warm. Repeat the process for the remaining circles. Serve the *dhal puri* at once.

Makes 8 dhal puri

TAMALES WITH PORK, RAISINS, AND ALMONDS

Tamales de cerdo con pasas y almendras

"The very fragrance of tamales steaming on the stove brings back the most vivid memories of loving and joyous family gatherings during my childhood in Mexico," says Shirley Muller, owner of Bay Books, a charming bookstore in Coronado, California. "My maternal grandmother made the most marvelous savory tamales with fillings like zucchini, squash blossoms, and *epazote* (pigweed); sautéed mushrooms in mole or *adobo;* and chicken or beef *picadillo* (a ground meat stew) with almonds, raisins, and olives. Tamales with pork in a green or red tomato sauce were a particular favorite of mine, and over the years I have added almonds and raisins to my grandmother's recipe." Shirley Muller serves pork tamales for lunch or dinner the authentic way, with steaming cups of New Mexican Hot Chocolate (see page 291) or *atole,* an interesting drink

Mexican tamales for Christmas

made with *masa harina de maíz* (corn flour), milk, and sugar, and flavored with fruit, nuts, or chocolate or served plain.

Leftover tamales will keep in the refrigerator for up to two days and in the freezer for up to a month, and can be warmed in a microwave oven or in a steamer basket in a large saucepan. There is no need to defrost frozen tamales; just extend the cooking time.

One 6-ounce package dried corn husks

FOR THE FILLING:

1 pound boneless pork shoulder, trimmed of all fat and cut into 1-inch chunks	**½ teaspoon ground oregano**
	¼ teaspoon ground cumin
	Salt, to taste
3 tablespoons olive oil	**One 15-ounce can tomato sauce**
1½ cups water	**¼ cup seedless black raisins**
1 small yellow onion, peeled and minced	**¼ cup slivered almonds**
2 medium cloves garlic, peeled and minced	**2 teaspoons minced fresh cilantro**

FOR THE MASA (CORN DOUGH):*

4 cups *masa harina de maíz* (corn *masa* mix)†	**1 cup canola oil**
	1 tablespoon baking powder
3 cups water	**2 teaspoons salt, or to taste**

* Or purchase ready-made masa *for tamales (not* masa *for tortillas) at Mexican markets and select supermarkets in California, Texas, the Southwest, and regions of the country with a sizable Mexican American population.*
† Available at Latin markets catering to Mexican Americans and Americans with roots in Central and South America, and in select supermarkets, especially in California, Texas, and the Southwest.

Soak the corn husks in hot water to cover in a large pot until they are pliable, about 30 minutes. Separate the husks into single "sheets" and discard any that are torn. Rinse the husks under warm running water to remove any grit or silk, drain, and pile them on a large plate or tray. You can use husks of all sizes to make different-sized tamales or choose the largest husks for large tamales. Overlap husks too small to stuff alone to make larger envelopes for the tamales.

Make the pork filling: Pat the pork dry with paper towels. Heat 2 tablespoons of the olive oil in a large skillet over medium-high heat and brown the pork in the oil on all sides, about 12 minutes. Add the water and bring to a boil. Reduce the heat and simmer the pork, covered, until it is tender, about 45 minutes. Remove the pork from the skillet with a slotted spoon or spatula to a cutting board. Shred it with two forks or your fingers. Reserve the pork broth.

Heat the remaining 1 tablespoon of olive oil over medium heat in a large saucepan.

Sauté the onion and garlic in the oil until limp, about 7 minutes. Stir in the oregano, cumin, and salt. Pour in the tomato sauce and ½ cup reserved pork broth. Bring the sauce to a boil, then reduce the heat and simmer the sauce for 15 minutes. Add the shredded pork, raisins, almonds, and cilantro to the sauce, and remove it from the heat.

Make the *masa,* or corn dough: Blend the *masa harina* and the 3 cups water in a large mixing bowl with a rubber spatula. (This foolproof formula makes approximately 2¾ pounds *masa,* but only 2½ pounds are needed in this recipe. If you do not have a kitchen scale to weigh the *masa,* subtract about ½ cup *masa* to arrive at approximately 2½ pounds.) Add the canola oil, baking powder, and salt to the 2½ pounds *masa* and blend well.

Assemble the tamales: Pat 1 of the husks dry with paper towels, and then place it, smoother side up, with the tapered end pointing toward you, on a work surface. Spoon 1 or 2 heaping tablespoons *masa,* depending on the size of the husk, in the center of the husk and spread it into a small square. Place 1 tablespoon pork filling in the center of the *masa* square. Fold the sides of the corn husk over the *masa* so that they overlap to make a long package. Fold the empty part of the husk under so that it rests against the side of the tamal without a "seam."

Gently place the tamal on a large plate or tray so that the open end tilts upward slightly to ensure that the filling will not ooze out. Repeat this process until all the *masa* and filling are used, piling the tamales on top of each other, tilted upward. (Note that any leftover husks may be stored in a sealed zip-lock bag or wrapped tightly in plastic and frozen for later use. Simply defrost them on the counter a few hours before using.)

Place a steamer basket in a large pot and fill the pot with enough water to almost touch the bottom of the basket. Stand the tamales on their folded ends in the basket. They should all fit without being squeezed too tightly together. Bring the water to a boil over medium-high heat, cover, reduce the heat to medium, and steam the tamales until they set and the husks peel away easily from the *masa,* about 40 minutes. The cooking time may be longer, depending on how crowded together the tamales are.

Remove the tamales from the pot to a large platter or tray and allow them to stand for 15 minutes before serving. Serve the tamales warm in their husks.

Makes 2 dozen large tamales or 3 dozen medium tamales;
serves 10 to 12

VARIETIES OF TAMALES

Tamales have an undeserved reputation as a difficult dish, but the truth is, they are easy to make. The *masa* (a dough made of cornmeal, grated fresh corn, or mashed *yuca,* potatoes, or plantains) is prepared, a little is spread on a square of wrapping (such as fresh or dried corn husks, fresh or dried banana and plantain leaves, cabbage leaves, or parchment paper), a filling is spooned on top (or the tamales are left unstuffed), and the whole thing is folded. The little bundles are then steamed until the *masa* sets. Once you have wrapped your first tamal you will see that it is a simple procedure, almost as easy as wrapping a potato in foil for baking. Another myth about tamales is that they require hours and hours to assemble. This is not the case if they are made in small quantities to serve 6 to 8, rather than in bulk with upward of 15 pounds of dough.

Most Latin groups in the United States make their own unique tamales (often called by another name) with a wide variety of ingredients, and some have as many different tamal recipes as there are stars in the night sky. Some of these tamales (even imported ones) can be found in the freezer section of Latin markets. Here are just a few of the most popular tamales in America:

Nacatamales

These gargantuan Nicaraguan corn *masa* tamales are filled with rice, potato, marinated pork, prunes, raisins, and pimiento-stuffed olives and constitute a whole meal.

Chuchitos

These mellow Guatemalan tamales are made with corn *masa* and usually no filling, and are wrapped in corn husks. *Tamalitos de chilpiin* are *chuchitos* flavored with Guatemalan mint. *Paches quetzaltecos,* unusual Guatemalan tamales, are made with a mashed-potato *masa,* stained pink from red chiles. They have no filling and are wrapped in banana leaves. *Tamales negros* are Guatemalan corn tamales with a filling of chicken, prunes, olives, and chocolate sauce (see page 218).

Humitas

These Ecuadoran, Bolivian, Chilean, and Argentine savory or sweet corn tamales are stuffed with a whole array of fillings, such as shredded beef flavored with onions and parsley, hard-boiled eggs, and raisins, or have no filling at all. To Peruvian Americans, *humitas* are sweet-corn tamales flavored with cinnamon and rum.

Chapanas

These Peruvian tamales, with a *pisco*-flavored *yuca masa* mixed with raisins, sugar, cayenne, and cloves, have no filling and are wrapped in banana leaves.

Bollos

These Ecuadoran tamales, made with a plantain *masa* stuffed with paprika-infused chicken, potatoes, raisins, and peas (or another of many fillings), are wrapped in banana leaves.

Hallacas

These Venezuelan tamales are made with annatto- and tomato-flavored corn *masa* stuffed with a chicken, pork, potato, and pea filling (or another of many fillings), and wrapped in banana leaves.

Pamonhas

These Brazilian tamales made with a *masa* of grated fresh corn, *yuca*, and coconut and no filling are wrapped in fresh corn husks.

Pasteles

These Puerto Rican tamales made with a *masa* of mashed root vegetables and plantains (more lika a paste than a dough), with a pork, beef, or chicken filling, are wrapped up in plantain or banana leaves and boiled, not steamed (see page 221).

Assembling Mexican tamales

Tamales cubanos

These Cuban tamales are made with a *masa* of fresh corn kernels, cornmeal, sour cream, and milk, and flecked with bits of pork, cheese, or vegetables. They have no filling and are wrapped in fresh corn husks or banana leaves. (*Tamales de Oro* is a popular frozen brand found in Latin markets.)

Tamales de elote

These Salvadoran tamales are made with a *masa* of ground sweet corn and no filling and are wrapped in dried corn husks. They are traditionally served with tart sour cream and creamy puréed beans.

Tamales de queso y chile

These Mexican tamales, featuring corn *masa* stuffed with Monterey Jack or another semifirm cheese and roasted chiles, are wrapped in corn husks or aluminum foil. (They are one of countless Mexican American tamales.)

Nouveau tamales with French, Italian, and Asian elements are now part of the tamal scene, thanks to John Sedlar, of Abiquiu, a restaurant in Santa Monica, California, showcasing modern Southwest cuisine. Sedlar has revolutionized the tamal by fusing *masa* with unexpected fillings, as in such dishes as Salmon Mousse Tamales with Ground Nixtamal and Cilantro Cream Sauce, Tamales of Sweetbreads with Morels and Black Truffle, and Japanese Tamales of Pompano with Ginger Butter. All across America, chefs and home cooks alike now make exotic tamales with unusual *masas* and fillings.

✳

BLACK TAMALES

Tamales negros

While most people think of mole as a Mexican chocolate and chile sauce, the word is actually derived from the Spanish verb *moler,* "to crush," and is used in Latin American cultures (in Brazil it is called *môlho*) to refer to any sauce made of ground or mashed ingredients, as in guacamole, or "avocado sauce" (see page 64). Guatemalan Americans claim a rich inheritance of mole dishes, including *mole de conejo,* rabbit in a mashed tomato and tomatillo sauce, flavored with oregano and annatto; and *mole de plátano,* fried plantains in a thick sauce of bitter chocolate, chiles, squash seeds, and tomatoes spiced with cinnamon. Mole is also at the heart of Guatemalan *Tamales negros,* corn tamales filled with chicken, olives, raisins, and prunes, and tinted with virtually the same chocolate sauce as in *mole de plátano.*

Tamales negros are a specialty of the inland regions of Guatemala. (Along the country's Caribbean coast *bimenas*—tamales stuffed with pork, shredded green banana, and coconut milk—are preferred.) Guatemalan Americans, over half of whom live in Los Angeles, where many frequent the Guatemalan shops and restaurants in MacArthur Park, a Central American neighborhood, have for the most part preserved the old ways of preparing *Tamales negros*. We have altered the basic recipe just a bit to conform to American tastes, however, by adding sugar to the sauce to balance the bitterness of the chocolate and the acidity of the tomatoes.

While *Tamales negros* are usually served plain, some like to top them with sour cream, which frequently appears as a garnish in Guatemalan cooking. Chocolaty *Negra Modelo,* a beer from the Yucatán that is available in Mexican markets and some general liquor stores, is just the right beverage to accompany these tamales. If you still have room for dessert, Fried Ripe Plantains (see page 182) are an excellent finale to a Guatemalan meal. Or for something a little lighter and splashier, try Passion Fruit Sorbet (see page 277).

FOR THE *MASA* (CORN DOUGH):*

3 cups *masa harina de maíz* (corn *masa* mix)†

3 cups water

2 tablespoons granulated sugar

½ cup (1 stick) butter, melted

FOR THE SAUCE:

2 teaspoons sesame seeds

2 teaspoons squash seeds (*pepitas*), or substitute pumpkin seeds‡

1 pasilla chile, or substitute an ancho chile (see page 165 for information on these chiles)

1 pound ripe tomatoes, coarsely chopped

¼ cup water

1 ounce unsweetened baking chocolate, melted

2 tablespoons plain dry bread crumbs

1½ teaspoons granulated sugar, plus more to taste

½ teaspoon ground cinnamon

½ pound boneless skinless chicken breast, cut into 1-inch cubes

FOR THE FILLING:

Seven 12 × 10-inch sheets of parchment paper

7 pitted prunes (optional)

⅓ cup seedless black raisins

14 large pitted green olives, cut in half crosswise

Seven 12 × 10-inch sheets of aluminum foil

Sour cream, for garnish (optional)

Or purchase 2½ pounds prepared masa for tortillas *(not* masa for tamales, *which will have lard or vegetable shortening in it) at Mexican markets and select supermarkets, especially in California, Texas, the Southwest, and the Chicago metropolitan area.*
†*Available in Latin markets catering to Americans with roots in Mexico and Central and South America, and in select supermarkets, especially in California, Texas, and the Southwest.*
‡*Available in Latin markets and some health food stores.*

Mexican pork, corn, and chicken tamales for sale

Make the *masa* (corn dough): Mix together all the ingredients in a large saucepan. Cook the dough over low heat, stirring constantly for 10 minutes so that it thickens. Remove the *masa* from the heat, cover, and allow it to cool to room temperature.

Prepare the sauce: Toast the sesame seeds and squash or pumpkin seeds, stirring frequently, in a large dry skillet over medium-low heat until the sesame seeds are light brown, about 7 minutes. Reconstitute the dried chile by putting it in enough water to cover in a small saucepan. Bring to a boil, then remove from the heat and let the chile soak in the hot water until the pulp has softened (the skin will remain stiff), about 10 minutes. Cut off the stem. Slice open the chile with a sharp knife and scrape out the seeds. Purée the chile and the toasted sesame and squash seeds in a food processor or electric blender. Add the tomatoes, water, chocolate, bread crumbs, sugar, and cinnamon, and process until smooth. Pour the sauce into a large skillet. Add the chicken and cook, stirring occasionally, over medium-low heat for 15 minutes. Taste for acidity and add more sugar, if desired.

Assemble the tamales: Place a sheet of parchment paper flat on a work surface. Spread ½ cup *masa* in the center of the parchment paper to make a 5 × 5-inch rectangle. Spoon about 3 tablespoons sauce in the center of the *masa*. Place 3 cubes chicken, 1 prune, a few raisins, and 2 olive halves on top. Fold the parchment paper in half lengthwise. Fold it in half lengthwise once again. (All the filling should be on one side.) Fold the ends in as you would to wrap a gift. Then wrap the tamal in a sheet of foil and twist the ends of the "package" to seal. Assemble the rest of the tamales in the same way.

Place a steamer basket in a large pot and fill the pot with enough water to almost touch the bottom of the basket. Arrange the tamales flat in the basket. Bring the water to a boil over medium-high heat, cover, reduce the heat, and steam the tamales for 1 hour and 10 minutes, or until the *masa* is firm. Add boiling water, as needed, during the steaming process to maintain the original level of the water.

With a slotted spoon or tongs transfer the tamales to serving plates. Cut away the parchment paper and foil to expose the *masa* and filling, but leave the tamales inside the wrapping, like an opened foil-wrapped baked potato. Serve the *Tamales negros* warm, garnished with a dollop of sour cream, if desired.

Makes 7 main-course tamales

PUERTO RICAN STUFFED PLANTAIN RECTANGLES

Pasteles

Puerto Ricans love *pasteles,* their version of tamales, made with mashed root vegetables and plantains and a pork, beef, or poultry filling. *Pasteles* are traditionally served for Christmas dinner, *cena de Nochebuena,* along with *Lechón asado* (Roast Pork, see page 136), *Arroz con gandules* (Rice and Pigeon Peas, see page 179), and *Coquito* (Puerto Rican Coconut Eggnog, see page 298) spiked with lots of rum. Puerto Ricans also make *pasteles* for other special events, such as New Year's and Puerto Rican Day parades, like the one held each year in New York City, when Spanish Harlem sings and dances its way up Fifth Avenue. The parade brings Puerto

Sam Maldonado sampling *pasteles* and *cuchifritos* at a Puerto Rican parade in Newark, New Jersey

Ricans from all around the Northeast to the city, where they revel in the merry-making and savor the marvelous aroma of *pasteles* and other Puerto Rican treats that permeate the air from the Empire State Building north to the Metropolitan Museum of Art.

Pasteles are so delectable that many Puerto Ricans do not wait for a special occasion to serve them. In fact, there is such a demand that many Puerto Rican women in New York City run small year-round *pastel* businesses out of their homes. The Cubans knew a good thing when they tasted it, and at some point they borrowed the *pastel* recipe from the Puerto Ricans—though some substitute a cornmeal dough for the mashed root vegetables and plantains—and thus these savory tamales grace the table in Cuban American homes. Some stateside Puerto Ricans and Cuban Americans have been known to experiment with unconventional fillings such as seafood. According to custom, *pasteles* are wrapped and steamed in plantain or banana leaves, which are available in Caribbean, Chinese, and Southeast Asian markets. Parchment paper works just as well, except that the flavor that the leaves impart to the *pasteles* is lost. Uncooked *pasteles* freeze nicely. Rather than thawing them, simply extend the cooking time by 15 minutes.

FOR THE WRAPPING:

Eighteen 12 × 8-inch "sheets" of plantain or banana leaf, or substitute sheets of parchment paper

Olive oil, for greasing the plantain or banana leaves or parchment paper

Eighteen 30-inch pieces kitchen string for securing the *pasteles*

FOR THE FILLING:

2 tablespoons olive or vegetable oil

½ pound lean ground pork

¼ pound lean ground sirloin beef

¼ pound lean cured ham, cut into ½-inch dice

1 small yellow onion, peeled and finely minced

1 small ripe tomato or 2 canned tomatoes, diced

½ cup finely minced green bell pepper

1 medium clove garlic, peeled and finely minced

⅓ cup tomato sauce

½ cup chick-peas, cooked and drained

⅓ cup coarsely chopped pimiento-stuffed green olives

¼ cup seedless black raisins or currants

1 tablespoon finely minced fresh cilantro

½ teaspoon red wine vinegar

¼ teaspoon dried powdered oregano (not crumbled)

FOR THE PASTE:

1¼ pounds *yautía* (*malanga*), taro, or yuca (cassava), peeled (see the directions for peeling *yuca* on page 189; peel *yautía* and taro in the same way)*

1 large (about ½ pound) green banana

3 (about 1½ pounds) yellow plantains, cut into 1-inch rounds and peeled

(see page 183 for information on plantains and page 184 for directions on peeling plantains)

¼ cup olive oil

1½ tablespoons annatto, also called *achiote* seeds (available in Latin markets and some supermarkets)

Pinch of salt

See pages 196–9 for information on yautía, *taro, and* yuca.

Prepare the "sheets" of plantain or banana leaf: Clean both sides of each leaf with a damp cloth. Hold the leaves, one by one, over a flame, turning slowly so that they are heated but do not burn.

Prepare the filling: Heat the 2 tablespoons oil in a large skillet over medium-high heat. Sauté the pork, beef, and ham, stirring frequently to break up the meats, until brown, about 8 minutes. Reduce the heat to medium and add the minced onions, tomato, bell pepper, and garlic. Sauté, stirring occasionally, until the onions are limp, about 8 minutes. Next stir in the tomato sauce, chick-peas, olives, raisins or currants, cilantro, vinegar, and oregano. Cover, cook the filling over medium-low heat for 5 minutes, then remove it from the heat and let it cool.

Prepare the paste: Cut the peeled *yautía* into 1-inch chunks. Peel the green banana (as you would a yellow banana) and cut into 1-inch rounds. Put the *yautía* chunks and green banana and plantain rounds in a large bowl with enough cold water to cover, and soak them for 15 minutes. Drain, purée in a food processor or electric blender until smooth, and spoon the paste back into the bowl. (Or prepare the paste the old-fashioned way by soaking the *yautía,* plantains, and banana as above, then grating them with the coarse side of a grater into the large bowl and mashing them with a potato masher until smooth.)

Heat the ¼ cup olive oil in a small saucepan over medium heat. Add the annatto, reduce the heat to low, and sauté until the oil turns a deep orange-red, about 5 minutes. Remove the saucepan from the heat, strain the seeds from the annatto-flavored oil, and stir the oil and a pinch of salt into the paste.

Assemble the *pasteles:* Lightly grease one side of each plantain or banana leaf sheet, or parchment paper sheet, with olive oil. Place a sheet, oiled side up, on a work surface. Spoon 3 tablespoons paste in the center of the sheet and spread it into a 6 × 5-inch rectangle. Place 2 heaping tablespoons of filling in a line down the very center of the paste. Fold the sheet in half lengthwise. Gently push the filling with your fingertips toward the fold. Then fold the sheet in half lengthwise once again. (All the filling should be on one side.) Fold the ends in as you would to wrap a gift. Repeat until all the paste and filling are used up. (You should have about 16 to 18 *pasteles.*)

Stack 2 *pasteles* so that the sides with the folded ends touch. Tie them snugly together with a piece of string by wrapping it around all four sides as if the *pasteles* were a gift box. Repeat with the rest of the *pasteles.* At this point they may be frozen for later use.

Cook the *pasteles:* Bring 4 quarts of water to a boil in a large pot. Gently lower the *pasteles* into the pot, cover, and bring the water to a boil again. Reduce the heat and simmer the *pasteles,* covered, for about 50 minutes. Drain the *pasteles* and discard the string. Unfold the wrappings. The *pasteles* should hold together like Mexican tamales. Serve the *pasteles* at once in their wrappings.

Makes approximately 16 to 18 pasteles

Then, on Puerto Rican Day, he met Lydia and her two kids at the 59th Street station and took them over to Fifth Avenue to watch the big parade. On one of the floats, surrounded by pom-pom–twirling, pink puff–brassiered and mink-bikinied showgirls with plumed headdresses, stood Mr. Salsa himself, Tito Puente, white-haired and imperial, waving at his fans. Then processions of dancers and Channel 47 television personalities—a float featuring the winsome Iris Chacón, a Goya Foods float with conga players in black-bean costumes, then more floats with *salsa* bands, and a float in the shape of the island of Puerto Rico and on its throne the splendid Miss San Juan; country dancers and guitarists and vocalists singing mountain *pregones.*

After this great spectacle, they made their way through the park, visiting the beer stands again and again, and buying the children treats: *cuchifritos, pasteles,* and sausage sandwiches.

—Oscar Hijuelos, *The Mambo Kings Play Songs of Love,*
New York: Farrar, Straus and Giroux, 1989

CORN PATTIES STUFFED WITH REFRIED RED BEANS AND MONTEREY JACK

Pupusas revueltas

The most cherished comfort food of Salvadoran Americans is without a doubt *pupusas,* the moist and delicious stuffed corn patties that are El Salvador's national snack. They are made by sandwiching a savory filling between raw corn patties (very thick tortillas) that have been patted by hand to about an ⅛-inch thickness, never flattened in a tortilla press. The corn patties are then sealed along the edges, and the *pupusas* are grilled on a dry griddle until they are speckled golden brown.

Most *pupuserías* in America (restaurants specializing in *pupusas*—there are over a dozen chains in Los Angeles), as well as Salvadoran American home cooks, adhere to traditional fillings for *pupusas.* They stuff

Pupusas (stuffed corn tortillas), the number one Salvadoran snack

their corn patties with either *queso* (usually Monterey Jack); *queso* flavored with chopped *loroco,* a mild-tasting flower bud that is imported frozen or pickled in jars from El Salvador; *chicharrón,* a mixture of crisp fried pork, green bell pepper, tomato, onions, and garlic; or *frijoles,* refried red beans. Corn patties may also be stuffed with two or even three fillings, such as *queso* and *frijoles,* for *Pupusas revueltas,* literally "mixed *pupusas.*" Many Salvadoran Americans who live in cities with sizable Salvadoran communities have the luxury of purchasing ready-made *pupusa* fillings. The two Liborio Markets in Los Angeles are known far and wide for the fabulous Salvadoran *chicharrón* in their butcher sections.

Pupusas are traditionally served with a side of *curtido,* an invigorating Salvadoran carrot and cabbage slaw laced with hot chiles, and a smooth and mild *salsa de tomate.* Second-generation Salvadoran Americans have been known to eat their *pupusas* with Mexican salsa. *Tamarindo,* a sweet and sour drink made from tamarind pulp, or *horchata,* a sweet, cinnamony drink made from boiled rice, are great with *pupusas,* and are on the menu in virtually all *pupuserías* in America.

Corn Patties Stuffed with Refried Red Beans and Monterey Jack (continued)

**FOR THE REFRIED RED BEAN
AND MONTEREY JACK FILLING:**

¼ pound small red beans

1 tablespoon finely minced yellow onion

1 medium clove garlic, peeled and finely
   minced

⅛ teaspoon salt, or to taste

½ tablespoon olive oil

½ cup grated **Monterey Jack cheese**

FOR THE *MASA* (CORN DOUGH):

3 cups *masa harina de maíz* (corn *masa*
   mix)*

2 cups water

*Available in Latin markets catering to Americans with roots in Mexico and Central and South America, and in select supermarkets, especially in California, Texas, and the Southwest.

Prepare the *frijoles:* In a small bowl, soak the beans overnight in enough water to cover plus 3 inches. Drain the beans and put them in a medium saucepan, along with the onion, garlic, and enough water to cover plus 1 inch. Simmer the beans until they are quite soft, about 1 hour. Purée the beans with ¼ cup of the cooking liquid and the salt in a food processor or electric blender until smooth. Heat the olive oil in a medium

NEW YEAR'S FOOL *PASTELES*

In her book entitled *Silent Dancing: A Partial Remembrance of a Puerto Rican Childhood* (1990), poet and novelist Judith Ortiz Cofer provides a vivid account of her early years spent in the Puerto Rican barrio in Paterson, New Jersey. Among the many images of bygone days that she remembers are the gastronomic delights served at a New Year's Eve party that an uncle captured for posterity on film with his movie camera:

Even the home movie cannot fill in the sensory details such a gathering left imprinted in a child's brain. The thick sweetness of women's perfume mixing with the ever present smells of food cooking in the kitchen: meat and plantain *pasteles,* the ubiquitous rice dish made special with pigeon peas—*gandules*—and seasoned with the precious *sofrito* sent up from the island by somebody's mother or smuggled in by a recent traveler. . . . But what I remember most were the boiled *pasteles*— . . . the plantain or yuca rectangles stuffed with corned beef or other meats, olives, and many other savory ingredients, all wrapped in banana leaves. Everyone had to fish one out with a fork. There was always a "trick" *pastel*—one without stuffing—and whoever got that one was the "New Year's Fool."

skillet over medium-low heat and cook the red bean purée, stirring occasionally, until it thickens, about 15 minutes. Remove from the heat and cool to room temperature.

Prepare the *masa* (corn dough): Combine the *masa harina* and water in a large mixing bowl and mix well with a spoon. The *masa* should have the consistency of chocolate-chip cookie dough. Shape the dough into patties ⅛-inch thick and 3 inches in diameter and cover them with a dampened cloth.

Assemble the *pupusas:* Spoon about ½ tablespoon *frijoles* and ½ tablespoon Monterey Jack in the center of a patty. Put another patty on top and press the edges of the patties together with your fingertips to seal the *pupusa.* No filling should be exposed. If it is, cover it with a piece of *masa* and pat the spot smooth.

Cook the *pupusas* on a dry nonstick griddle or in a large nonstick skillet over medium-high heat, turning once, until they are browned, about 4 minutes per side. If you use a griddle or skillet that is not nonstick, brown the *pupusas* in a tablespoon of butter heated over medium-high heat. Serve at once with *curtido* or your favorite cole slaw, and tomato salsa (see page 27).

Makes about 14 pupusas; serves 4 to 6 as a snack or lunch

For *Pupusas* with Cheese (*Pupusas de queso*): Omit the bean filling, and use 1 cup grated Monterey Jack instead of ½ cup. Spoon 1 tablespoon cheese in the center of each *pupusa* and cook as directed.

FRUIT BREAD, FRIED BREAD,

CORN BREAD, CUBAN BREAD,

STUFFED BREAD, BREAD OF THE

DEAD . . . INCREDIBLE BREAD.

BREADS

HAM-AND-OLIVE-STUFFED BREAD

Pan de jamón

"**I** am very proud of Venezuela, *mi tierra bella*," beams Omaira Gibens of Bowling Green, Ohio, who, with her husband, Guillermo Gibens, and daughter Vanessa, performs classic Venezuelan dances, like the *joropo*, at local festivals in her spare time. "I seize every opportunity to share Venezuela's rich culture and exquisite cuisine. I like nothing more than to have a houseful of guests—who have never sampled Venezuelan cooking—over for dinner. I introduce them to such Venezuelan master-pieces as *Pan de jamón*, a long golden loaf of ultrasoft white bread, as soft as challah but not sweet and with the same shiny crust, that is swirled with thin slices of ham, pimiento-stuffed olives, and raisins. The dough around the swirls of ham is nice and buttery, which makes the bread all the moister, as moist as a ham croissant. *Pan de jamón* traditionally graces the Christmas and New Year's dinner table, along with *hallacas*—tamales stuffed with chicken, beef, tomatoes, peppers, onions, and capers, and wrapped in banana leaves; *ensalada de gallina*—a Venezuelan-style Olivier salad, with diced chicken, potatoes, and carrots, peas, hard-boiled eggs, and mayonnaise; and *pernil horneado*—marinated roast pork that is quite similar to oregano-infused Puerto Rican *pernil* (see page 136)."

Pan de jamón is wonderful any time of year. Since it is a whole sandwich inside a loaf, it is great alone for lunch or a snack, or with a bowl of soup for a light supper. We like to pack a loaf in the picnic basket, since it is a good traveler. Store any left-over bread in a zip-lock bag in the refrigerator for up to 3 days. To reheat, cut the loaves into three slices, place the slices without any wrapping on a baking sheet, and let them warm in a preheated 250°F oven for 20 minutes.

2½ teaspoons or 1 (¼-ounce) package
   active dry yeast
1 tablespoon granulated sugar
½ cup warm water (105°F to 115°F)
2 large eggs
1 cup warm milk (105°F to 115°F)
½ teaspoon salt
4 cups unbleached all-purpose flour

1 tablespoon butter, melted
¾ pound Virginia ham, thinly sliced
2 dozen pimiento-stuffed green olives,
   cut in half
½ cup seedless golden raisins
Vegetable oil, for greasing a bowl, a
   surface, and the baking sheets
1 tablespoon water

Dissolve the yeast and sugar in the warm water in a large bowl. Let stand until soft, about 5 minutes.

Separate the eggs into small bowls and reserve the egg yolks for the glaze. Mix together the egg whites, warm milk, and salt in the small bowl and add to the yeast mixture. Stir in 2 cups of the flour and beat with a mixer on low, or with a spoon, until smooth, about 2 minutes.

Gradually add the remaining 2 cups of flour, ¼ cup at a time, to form a soft dough. Turn the dough out onto a lightly floured surface and knead, adding just a little flour when the dough starts to stick, until it is satiny smooth and elastic, about 8 minutes. Turn the dough in a lightly oiled large bowl, cover with a towel, and let rise in a warm place for about 1 hour, or until doubled in bulk.

Omaira Gibens and Guillermo Gibens in traditional Venezuelan costumes

Punch down the dough and turn it out onto a lightly oiled surface. Do not knead. Divide the dough into 3 equal portions. Roll one of the portions with a rolling pin into a 12 × 15-inch rectangle. Brush the whole surface of the dough with one third of the melted butter and cover with one third of the ham slices spread out in a single layer. Sprinkle one third of the olives and raisins evenly over the ham. Roll up the dough starting from one of the longer sides. Pinch the ends to seal. Place the rolled loaf on 1 of 2 lightly greased baking sheets. Repeat for the remaining portions of dough and arrange them on the second baking sheet at least 2 inches apart. Cover the loaves with towels and let rise for 30 minutes.

Mix together the egg yolks and the 1 tablespoon water, and brush the tops of the loaves lightly with the egg glaze. Bake on the upper racks of a 375°F oven until the tops of the loaves are golden brown, about 15 minutes. Remove the bread from the oven and cool on wire racks for 5 minutes. Cut each loaf into 6 slices and serve warm.

Makes 3 long loaves; serves 8 to 10

AUSTRALIAN DAMPER CUBAN-STYLE

Damper australiano a la cubana

"My children and I adopted damper, the famous Australian country bread that resembles baking-powder biscuits in color, taste, and texture, after eight years of living in Australia, a country discovered by Latinos in 1606, when Luis Báez de Torres became the first European to sight the southern continent," says Cuban American Miguel Bretos, Counselor for Community Affairs and Special Services at the Smithsonian Institution in Washington, D.C. "In my family, damper has crossed over to Cuban culture, as we adore piping hot slices of the puffy bread slathered with butter and Cuban *dulce de guayaba* (guava preserves). The recipe for damper is very simple and quick (it can be prepared in about 40 minutes), and it is a lifesaver on weekends when there is a little bit of time to cook breakfast and enjoy it with the children, but not enough for a leisurely brunch out. Traditionally, damper is baked in the raked embers of a campfire, but I cook it in a regular oven. It's a lot simpler and less messy!"

Damper is also fabulous with butter and other tropical spreads, like pineapple, papaya, or mango preserves. Since this quick bread is best appreciated hot out of the oven, brew a nice pot of tea or coffee while it bakes.

2½ cups unbleached all-purpose flour
2½ tablespoons baking powder
⅛ teaspoon salt

1¼ cups milk
1½ teaspoons butter

Mix together the flour, baking powder, and salt in a large mixing bowl. Warm the milk in a small saucepan to 105°F. Add the butter and stir until it has melted. Reserve 1 teaspoon of the milk mixture to glaze the loaf, then pour the rest into the dry ingredients all at once. Stir to form a soft dough. Pat the dough into a round loaf, place it on a lightly buttered and floured baking sheet, and brush lightly with the reserved glaze.

Bake the loaf on the middle rack of a preheated 375°F oven for 20 minutes, or until lightly golden and puffed, and a toothpick inserted off center comes out clean. Serve damper hot from the oven with butter and preserves.

Makes 1 loaf; serves 6

CUBAN BREAD

Pan cubano

Cuban Bread is an easy and basic loaf that in Cuban American circles is baked almost solely for the legendary Cuban Sandwich, a grilled masterpiece piled high with tender ham, succulent roast pork, Swiss cheese, and thin pickle slices (see page 39). With its crunchy crust and light and airy interior, Cuban Bread is also marvelous sliced thin and served plain, smeared with butter, tapenade, *taramosalata,* Eggplant Caviar (see page 63), or your favorite spread.

A Latin American bakery in Elizabeth, New Jersey

Cuban Bread tastes best the day it is baked. If you do not plan on using the loaf right away, freeze it in a tightly sealed zip-lock bag just as soon as it has cooled completely, and store it for no more than 3 months. When defrosting, allow the bread to rest on the counter for about 25 minutes, then warm it in a preheated 350°F oven. As with all yeast breads, time is as essential an ingredient as flour, so plan on getting started about 3 hours before serving.

2½ teaspoons or 1 (¼-ounce) package active dry yeast	**2 tablespoons olive oil**
1½ cups warm (110°F) water	**1 teaspoon salt**
1½ teaspoons granulated sugar	**3¼ to 3½ cups bread flour**
	Vegetable oil, for greasing

Sprinkle the yeast over ½ cup of the warm water in a large mixing bowl, add the sugar, and let stand for 5 minutes. Stir in the remaining cup of water, the olive oil, and salt.

Slowly add the flour, 1 cup at a time, and mix to make a dough. Turn the dough out onto a lightly floured work surface and knead for about 4 minutes, or until the dough is satiny and elastic.

Place the dough in a lightly oiled bowl, cover with plastic wrap or a damp towel, and let rise in a warm place until doubled in bulk, about 1½ hours. Punch down the dough and shape it into an oblong loaf, about 12 inches long. Place the loaf on a lightly greased baking sheet (or one dusted with cornmeal), cover it with a towel, and allow it to rise for 30 minutes.

Brush the loaf lightly with warm water. Bake it on the baking sheet in a preheated 400°F oven until it is golden brown and sounds hollow when the bottom is tapped, about 35 minutes. Remove the bread and cool it on a wire rack before serving.

Makes 1 large loaf

VENEZUELAN AND COLOMBIAN AMERICAN CORN CAKES

Arepas

"There is nothing more heavenly than an *arepa,* a corn cake with a crisp crust and a snow-white or yellow creamy interior, slathered with butter or cream cheese while it's still steaming hot," asserts Venezuelan American Simón Contreras, a teacher at Washington-Lee High School in Arlington, Virginia, who was born in El Socorro, Guárico, Venezuela. "*Arepas* are the daily bread of both Venezuela and Colombia, as the countries were once one. They are such a part of everyday life that Venezuelan speech is filled with *arepa* sayings, such as 'No sirve ni para vender arepas,' literally 'That will never help you to sell *arepas,*' which means 'With that kind of voice, you'll never be a singer.' "

Arepas are made from fresh or dried corn that has been ground and then shaped as thin as a Mexican tortilla or as plump as a Parker House roll. "Most Venezuelan and Colombian American families have their own special *arepa* recipe, but not everyone has a grinder to grind the corn like families do in Venezuela and Colombia," says Simón Contreras. "Some mix butter or cheese into the dough or batter. Mexican *ranchero* or *panela,* or Muenster, usually takes the place of Venezuelan or Colombian cheeses, which are difficult to obtain in America. Many also stuff *arepas* with chicken, roast pork, ham, shredded beef, beans, or even avocado. Others make plain *arepas* and serve them with cheese, cream cheese, butter, or *Guasacaca,* a spicy avocado sauce (see page 64), on the side. A few insist that the best *arepas* are grilled over charcoal, but most cook them on a griddle or in the oven."

There are three basic varieties of *arepas.* One is the white *arepa,* made from dry corn kernels soaked overnight in water and then pounded in a *pilón*—a wooden mortar—with a stick until the hulls (*afrechos*) separate from the white interiors. The corn is then boiled until soft, mixed with cheese, molded into patties, and cooked on the grill or griddle. A second variety is the yellow *arepa,* or *arepa de choclo,* which is far easier to make. Corn kernels are cut from fresh ears of corn and ground, hull and all, in a small grinding machine. Brown sugar, cornmeal, butter, and sometimes cheese are added, and then the batter is poured into individual baking pans and baked until

Hornos, beehive-shaped ovens constructed of brick and mud, are still used for baking in northern New Mexico.

golden brown. A third variety is what some have dubbed quick *arepas*. Packaged, pre-cooked, finely ground white or yellow cornmeal, known as *areparina* and *masarepa,* is simply mixed with water to make a dough, which is shaped and cooked first on the griddle and then in the oven. In America some Venezuelan and Colombian restaurants still make *arepas* from dry corn kernels, but most home cooks prefer the less laborious fresh corn *arepas* and the no-fuss *arepas* from *areparina.*

FRESH CORN *AREPAS*

Arepas de choclo

4 medium ears of corn, or substitute
  1½ cups frozen corn kernels
  (defrosted) plus 1 tablespoon milk
¾ cup cornmeal for *arepas* (*areparina* or
  masarepa), or substitute extra-fine
  yellow cornmeal*

1 teaspoon light brown sugar
¼ cup (½ stick) butter, softened

Brands of areparina, *such as Goya, Iberia, and Pan, are sold in Pan-Latin and South American markets in the United States.*

If you are using fresh ears of corn, cut the kernels from the cobs with a knife or a corn kernel remover. Measure 1½ cups corn kernels, reserving the extra for another use, and coarsely grind in a meat grinder or food processor. Pour the ground corn and its liquid into a large mixing bowl. If you are using defrosted corn kernels, coarsely grind in a meat grinder or food processor, then place the ground kernels in a large mixing bowl and add the 1 tablespoon milk.

Stir the cornmeal and brown sugar into the ground kernels and their liquid. Mix in the butter thoroughly and stir the batter until it is smooth.

Spoon ⅓ cup batter into the lightly buttered cups of a standard muffin pan (2¾ inches wide at the top). Bake in a preheated 425°F oven until the *arepas* are lightly browned and have set, about 30 to 40 minutes. Serve warm with butter or cheese.

Makes 6 or 7 arepas

QUICK AREPAS

Arepas de areparina

1 cup precooked cornmeal for *arepas* (*areparina* or *masarepa*)*	1½ cups lukewarm water
¼ teaspoon salt	

Brands of areparina, *such as Goya, Iberia, and Pan, are sold in Pan-Latin and South American markets in the United States.*

Mix together the cornmeal and salt in a large mixing bowl. Slowly stir in the water to make a dough. Allow the dough to stand for 5 minutes.

Shape the dough with your hands into cakes about 2½ inches in diameter and 1 inch thick. Lightly butter a large heavy skillet or griddle. Cook the *arepas* over medium heat in two batches, turning once, until a golden crust forms on both sides, about 5 minutes per side. Arrange both batches of *arepas* on a baking sheet and bake in a preheated 350°F oven for 10 to 15 minutes, or until the *arepas* sound hollow when tapped. Wrap the *arepas* in a napkin placed in a basket or bowl to keep them warm, and serve at once plain, or with cheese or cream cheese, or butter.

Makes 6 arepas

BREAD OF THE DEAD

Pan de muerto

Mexican American Bread of the Dead is descended from the sweet altar breads, made with yeast, flour, sugar, eggs, and aromatic flavoring, that for centuries have been offerings on feast days in Europe. Spanish missionaries introduced altar bread to Mexico, where over time it became associated with the Day of the Dead (see The Party Starts at the Cemetery, page 238). Mexican bakers changed the appearance of the altar bread by shaping the loaves into human figures, or *muertitos,* meaning "dead ones," but most commonly into crosses or skulls and bones, and by decorating the bread with colored sugar crystals. For the most part, Mexican Americans have remained faithful to Mexican recipes, and in the week leading up to the Day of the Dead, traditional *Pan de muerto* can be found in bakeries throughout the Southwest, California, and other regions of the country with sizable Mexican American communities. Traditionally, Bread of the Dead is eaten only during Day of the Dead celebrations in both Mexico and the United States.

Fine-textured, airy, and mildly sweet, like brioche or Russian *baba,* Bread of the Dead is delicious on its own, with sweet butter, or with a citrus marmalade, which complements the flavor of the orange peel in the loaf. We cannot resist a slice with Busha Browne's Burnt Orange Marmalade made with Jamaican Seville oranges and caramelized raw cane sugar or Busha Browne's Guava Jelly. (These products are available in some gourmet shops.)

2½ teaspoons or 1 (¼-ounce) package active dry yeast
4 tablespoons granulated sugar
¾ cup warm milk (105°F to 115°F)
2 large eggs, plus 2 large egg yolks
¼ cup (½ stick) unsalted butter, softened
3 cups unbleached all-purpose flour, plus more as needed

1 teaspoon finely grated orange peel
½ teaspoon ground anise seed (optional)
½ teaspoon salt
2 tablespoons colored sugar crystals, for decoration (optional)

Dissolve the yeast and 1 tablespoon of the sugar in ½ cup of the warm milk in a small bowl and let it soften, about 5 minutes.

Beat 1 of the whole eggs and the egg yolks in a small bowl. Stir in the remaining ¼ cup milk, the butter, and the dissolved yeast.

Mix together the flour, the remaining 3 tablespoons of sugar, orange peel, anise seed, and salt in a large bowl. Stir in the egg-yeast mixture.

If the dough feels sticky, mix in a teaspoon more flour at a time until it is pliable enough to knead. Turn the dough out onto a lightly floured board and knead it for 8 to 10 minutes, until it is silky and elastic. Place the dough in a large, lightly greased bowl, cover it with a damp towel, and allow it to rise in a warm place for approximately 1 hour, or until it has doubled in size.

Punch down the dough and turn it out onto a lightly floured work surface. Allow the dough to rest while you grease and flour a cookie sheet. Cut off one third of the dough and place it back in the bowl. Plump the rest of the dough into a smooth round loaf and place in the center of the prepared cookie sheet.

Shape the remaining dough into a skull and crossbones by dividing it into 2 equal pieces. Lightly pat one of the pieces into a ball for the skull. Tear the remaining piece in half and roll the 2 halves between the palms of your hands to make 8-inch ropes for the crossbones. Flatten the ends of the ropes to form knobs for the bones. Then stretch

Bread of the Dead (continued)

An altar bedecked with loaves of Bread of the Dead for Day of the Dead celebrations in Santa Barbara, California

and crisscross the 2 bones over the loaf and press the skull onto the loaf right above the crossbones. Cover the loaf loosely with a cloth towel and let it rise in a warm spot for approximately 20 minutes.

While the dough is rising, preheat the oven to 375°F. Beat the remaining egg with 1 teaspoon water to make an egg glaze. Paint the risen loaf with the egg glaze, and then bake it for 30 minutes, or until it is golden and sounds hollow when tapped. Remove the bread from the oven, sprinkle it with the colored sugar crystals, and then return it to the oven for 1 minute to melt the crystals. Remove the loaf from the oven and immediately transfer it to a wire rack to cool. Store the completely cooled bread at room temperature, in an airtight plastic bag, or tightly wrapped in plastic wrap.

Makes 1 large loaf

THE PARTY STARTS AT THE CEMETERY

Many Mexican Americans observe the centuries-old Mexican holiday of *El día de los muertos*, literally "The Day of the Dead," held on All Saints' Day and All Souls' Day (November 1 and 2). *El día de los muertos* is rooted in pre-Columbian and Spanish Roman Catholic religious traditions that began to blend when the Spanish conquistadors set foot in Mexico in the sixteenth century. At the time of the Spanish conquest, numerous indigenous civilizations in Mexico adhered to the belief that death was but a peaceful phase in the perpetual cycle of existence, and they held celebrations for the souls of the departed. The Jesuit and Franciscan missionaries, who accompanied the Spanish explorers to Mexico to convert the native peoples, introduced the Catholicism of the Middle Ages, with its abhorrence of death and its concept of Purgatory for the unredeemed—a contrasting view of eternal life. They also introduced All Souls' Day to Mexico, the day that the faithful pray for the souls still suffering in Purgatory. As native religious traditions combined with Catholicism, All Souls' Day was transformed into the Day of the Dead, when Mexican families make merry with the souls of the deceased, rather than pray for those in Purgatory.

El día de los muertos is still observed in Mexico. It is a happy occasion on which Mexicans celebrate with the souls of deceased family members, who return home each year to commune with loved ones and to experience the pleasures of earthly existence. Families set up *ofrendas,* or altars, in their homes, which they adorn with gifts to please the souls and prepare them for their journey to heaven—favorite foods and clothing, toy skeletons, candles, plaster saints, incense burners, photographs, fruit, chocolate, bottles of tequila, and flowers such as *cempazuchitl,* or golden marigolds, the traditional pre-Columbian flowers of the dead. For the soul of a deceased child, they might place favorite toys, new clothing, candy, and even a bottle of Coca-Cola upon the *ofrenda.* In keeping with tradition, Mexicans give *calaveritas de azúcar*—sugar-candy skulls gaily decorated with tin-foil eyes and brightly colored icing, sometimes with the recipient's name written on foil across the foreheads—as gifts to friends in the community.

Beginning at dusk on October 31, families gather together in cemeteries to hold vigils for the souls. They tidy the plots of loved ones and decorate them with flowers, candles, photos, and assorted mementos. Then comes a picnic for the dead and the living—a focal point of the celebration, since both body and soul are nourished. The souls dine until the stroke of midnight, when they are presumed to have finished, making way for the living to feast on food and drink, pray, dance, talk, and sometimes sleep until the crack of dawn. Mexicans prepare aromatic, colorful dishes for the occasion, such as tamales, turkey with mole poblano, and *calabaza en tacha,* a pumpkin dessert. Another Day of the Dead specialty is *Pan de muerto,* literally "Bread of the Dead."

While Mexican Americans who observe the Day of the Dead often construct *ofrendas* in their homes, most have done away with nighttime festivities in the cemeteries. Instead, families come together in the cemeteries during daylight hours on All Saints' Day and All Souls' Day. They tidy the graves, replace the crosses and wreaths, and decorate with natural or paper flowers. Then they kneel in prayer or share in a picnic lunch in honor of deceased friends and relatives. Mexican Americans also give sugar-candy skulls to friends on the Day of the Dead. They often prepare traditional Mexican dishes for the holiday, including tamales and *Pan de muerto.* Nowadays jack-o'-lanterns and eager trick-or-treaters are a common sight at Day of the Dead celebrations as Mexican and American traditions fuse.

PARAGUAYAN CORN BREAD

Sopa paraguaya

Lightly scented with allspice and cumin, and enriched with cottage cheese and Muenster, this authentic corn bread is very moist and flavorful. In the homes of the approximately seven thousand Americans of Paraguayan ancestry, this beloved bread from the old country is always present on the holiday table and at special occasions, like birthdays and weddings. Paraguayan Corn Bread travels well, so you're apt to find it at potluck dinners and Fourth of July and Labor Day picnics.

Paraguayan Corn Bread makes a nice accompaniment to peasanty soups, stews, and casseroles. Like all corn breads, this one is at its peak when served fresh from the oven. Store any leftovers—if indeed there are any—in the refrigerator for up to 3 days; they will not dry out. Paraguayan Corn Bread may be warmed in a microwave or conventional oven.

I cup yellow cornmeal

I ½ cups hot water

I small yellow onion, peeled and minced

I tablespoon olive oil

3 tablespoons butter

3 large eggs, separated, with the yolks in a small bowl and the whites in a large mixing bowl

½ cup cottage cheese

I cup grated Muenster cheese

½ cup milk

One 8-ounce can corn kernels, drained

I teaspoon baking powder

¼ teaspoon ground allspice

¼ teaspoon ground cumin

¼ teaspoon sweet paprika

¼ teaspoon salt

Mix the cornmeal with the hot water in a medium bowl. Sauté the minced onions in the olive oil in a small skillet over medium heat until limp, about 3 minutes.

Cream the butter in a large mixing bowl with an electric mixer, and then blend in the egg yolks and cottage cheese. With a spoon, stir in the cornmeal, sautéed onions, Muenster cheese, milk, corn, baking powder, allspice, cumin, paprika, and salt.

Beat the egg whites with the electric mixer until they form soft peaks. Gently fold the beaten egg whites into the cornmeal batter with a rubber spatula. Do not beat. The finished batter will be soupy. Pour it into a greased 2-quart square or round baking pan. Bake the corn bread in a preheated 400°F oven until it is firm in the center, about 50 to 55 minutes. Cool the corn bread in the pan for 15 minutes, then cut it into squares or wedges.

Serves 6 to 8

MANGO PECAN BREAD

Americans of Jamaican origin have inherited a host of great recipes for tropical quick breads, such as banana bread, gingerbread, corn bread, pumpkin bread, and coconut bread. One winning bread that deserves more fanfare is enhanced with mango, a fruit that is the basis of numerous Jamaican sweets. While orange-yellow mango usually takes center stage in most versions of Jamaican mango bread, we have added pecans to create a play of tastes and textures. Moist and richly flavored, Mango Pecan Bread makes a superb brunch or coffee-break treat served plain or with a slathering of sweet butter or whipped cream cheese. For a pleasurable, tropical-tasting dessert, simply adorn slices of Mango Pecan Bread the Jamaican way, with scoops of vanilla ice cream. If wrapped tightly in plastic wrap when cool and stored on the counter, this bread will stay fresh for 3 to 4 days.

2 cups unbleached all-purpose flour
1 ½ teaspoons baking soda
2 teaspoons ground cinnamon
½ teaspoon salt
½ cup vegetable oil
3 medium eggs
¾ cup granulated sugar

1 teaspoon vanilla extract
2 cups ripe mango (about 2 to 3 mangos, depending on their size, peeled, sliced from the pit, and diced)
½ cup shelled pecans, coarsely chopped (optional)

Sift the flour, baking soda, cinnamon, and salt together in a large mixing bowl. Beat the vegetable oil, eggs, sugar, and vanilla extract in a medium mixing bowl until well blended. Add the oil-egg mixture to the dry ingredients, stirring just until they are blended. Lightly fold in the diced mango and pecans.

Pour the batter into a greased and lightly floured 4½ × 8½-inch loaf pan. Bake the bread on the center rack of a preheated 350°F oven for 1 hour to 1 hour and 10 minutes, or until a wooden skewer inserted in the center comes out clean. Remove the bread from the oven and cool it in the pan on a wire rack for 10 minutes. Turn the bread out onto the wire rack and allow it to cool completely. Serve Mango Pecan Bread plain or with the topping of your choice.

Makes 1 loaf

COLOMBIAN AMERICAN
GUAVA BREAD

Mojicón

his ring-shaped, wonderfully rich yeast bread, baked in Colombian American kitchens, is perfumed with guava, a tropical fruit that tastes at once of pineapple and ripe strawberries. The subtly sweet dough is stuffed with bits of guava—not the ripe fruit that is available only sporadically, and then primarily in the region where it grows, but guava paste (*pasta de guayaba*). During baking, the guava paste within the rings of dough melts a little, filling the bread with its lovely flavor and fragrance. (For more on the guava, see page 281.) Guava paste, which somewhat resembles the fig filling in a Fig Newton (but chewier, sweeter, and more citrusy), is sold in Latin markets. It is packaged as a long, neat rectangle wrapped in cellophane, or as little individually wrapped slices, fitted snugly into a box. Many Americans of Latin descent serve guava slices with cream cheese or a semifirm cheese as a dessert or snack. Colombian American Guava Bread is a marvelous way to enjoy guava at breakfast or brunch, or with a steaming cup of tea or coffee any time of day.

Guava bread freezes well. Just wrap the cooled rings individually in plastic wrap and then in aluminum foil. When ready to use, thaw the rings, remove the wrappings, and warm them in a 325°F oven for about 10 minutes.

2½ teaspoons or 1 (¼-ounce) package
    active dry yeast
¼ cup warm water (105°F to 115°F)
1 cup milk
¼ cup (½ stick) butter, softened
¼ cup granulated sugar
1 large egg
1 teaspoon salt

3¾ cups unbleached all-purpose flour,
    plus more as needed
6 ounces guava paste, cut into ¼-inch
    dice*
1 egg white, beaten with 1 teaspoon
    water for the glaze
About 1 tablespoon coarse sugar
    (decorator's sugar), for garnish

If you cannot obtain guava paste, cook 1¼ cups strawberry or seedless raspberry jam in a medium saucepan over medium heat, stirring constantly, until it is reduced to ¾ cup. Pour the jam into a buttered shallow dish and chill it until firm.

Sprinkle the yeast over the warm water in a large mixing bowl or the large bowl of an electric mixer. Let stand until soft, about 5 minutes.

Scald the milk in a small saucepan. Stir in the butter until it melts. Remove the milk from the heat and allow it to cool to about 110°F.

Mix the milk-butter mixture, sugar, egg, salt, and 1 cup of the flour into the yeast until blended, and then beat at medium speed with an electric mixer for 5 minutes. Gradually stir in the remaining flour with a plastic spatula to make a smooth, elastic dough.

Turn the dough out onto a lightly floured surface and knead until silky smooth, about 5 minutes. (If the dough is sticky, add a little more flour.) Put the dough in a large, lightly greased bowl, and then flip it over so that the top is greased. Cover the dough with plastic wrap and a towel, and let it rise in a warm place until doubled in bulk, about 1½ hours.

Punch down the dough, turn it out onto a floured surface, and divide it into 4 equal portions. Roll one into a 5 × 15-inch rectangle on a lightly floured surface. Leaving a ¼-inch border, sprinkle one fourth of the diced guava paste evenly over the dough. Roll up the dough from the long side, like a jelly roll, to form a long rope.

Transfer the rope to one end of a greased baking sheet, form it into a ring, and pinch the ends to seal. Repeat until all the dough pieces are shaped into rings. Place 2 rings on each baking sheet. Make 5 evenly spaced crosswise cuts, ¾ inch deep and 2 inches long, in each ring to expose the filling (as if you were cutting them each into 5 chunks, but do not cut through the bottom layer of dough).

Cover the rings with towels and let them rise in a warm place until almost doubled in bulk, about 40 minutes. Brush each with the egg white glaze and dust with the coarse sugar. Bake the rings on the upper rack of a preheated 350°F oven until they are golden brown and sound hollow when tapped gently, about 30 minutes. Transfer the bread to wire racks to cool and serve warm or at room temperature.

Makes 4 small bread rings; serves 8

SANTA FE TRAIL *SOPAIPILLAS* WITH HONEY

Sopaipillas Sendero de Santa Fe con miel

Sopaipillas, little fried bread pillows the color of amber, accompany many a meal in New Mexico. We tasted them for the first time in Santa Fe, at Little Anita's, a humble restaurant serving honest, old-fashioned New Mexican regional cooking. One of us ordered New Mexico Green Chile Stew, a quintessential New Mexican dish, and

Santa Fe Trail Sopaipillas *with Honey (continued)*

it arrived with freshly fried *sopaipillas*. Taking our cue from the table next to us, we smothered the *sopaipillas* with honey and consumed the airy puffs of dough in minutes and then ordered more. The next morning found us back at Little Anita's to sample the Stuffed *Sopaipilla* Skillet, a giant *sopaipilla* filled with scrambled eggs, cheese, ham, and topped with green chile sauce. It was delicious.

Traditional *sopaipillas* are made with either baking powder or yeast. They are dipped in honey or rolled in cinnamon sugar or stuffed with meat

Mexican Americans at a lunch counter in Brownsville, Texas, circa 1920

and beans and other savory or sweet fillings. Whenever we prepare *sopaipillas* for guests, we like to cut four or five squares of dough with cookie cutters into cactuses, cowboy boots, Valentine hearts, Christmas trees, and other shapes depending on the occasion. A heaping plate of warm traditional *sopaipillas* adorned with dough cactuses or Valentine hearts always delights.

4 cups unbleached all-purpose flour	½ cup evaporated milk
2 tablespoons baking powder	Canola oil, for frying
1 teaspoon salt	Cinnamon sugar (½ cup granulated
¼ cup (½ stick) unsalted butter	sugar and 2 teaspoons ground
1 large egg, beaten	cinnamon, mixed well) or your
1 cup lukewarm water	favorite honey

Sift together the flour, baking powder, and salt in a large mixing bowl. Cut the butter into the dry ingredients to blend until it resembles a coarse meal. Mix in the beaten egg, water, and evaporated milk. Turn the dough out onto a lightly floured work surface and knead it until smooth, about 1 minute. Cover the dough with a damp towel and allow it to rest for 30 minutes.

Divide the dough into 3 pieces. On a lightly floured work surface, roll each piece out into a rectangle ¼ inch thick. Since the dough is somewhat fragile, handle it as little as possible. Cut the dough into 3-inch squares with a sharp knife. Cut a few squares with a cookie cutter, if so desired. Roll out any scraps to make more squares. Cover the dough squares with a damp towel while you heat 2 inches of canola oil in a large skillet at least 2½ inches deep over medium-high heat to 400°F.

Carefully drop a dough square into the oil. It should sink and fry upon contact, and then float back up a few seconds later and puff. (If the dough refuses to puff up, the oil is not hot enough.) Drop in 3 more squares, one after the other. Fry the *sopaipillas* for about 20 seconds, or until they are all puffed up and the edges turn light golden, and then turn them over with a slotted spoon and fry them on the other side for another 20 seconds, or until they are golden brown. Remove the *sopaipillas* with a slotted spoon to a plate lined with paper towels to drain, and keep them warm in a pre-heated 150°F oven. Fry the rest of the squares in batches of 4. Once all the *sopaipillas* are fried, roll them in cinnamon sugar or serve them at once, plain or with your favorite honey.

Makes approximately 2 dozen sopaipillas

"I remember those many times in Oralia's kitchen, making empanadas, sealing the edges with fork grooves, or boiling oil to just the right heat so that the sopaipillas puffed up high once they touched the hot grease. Oralia's only attempts at cooking American were her donas, special doughnuts she made from canned biscuits, with the center punched out with a thimble. She fried them in hot grease and then turned them over in brown sugar."

—Denise Chávez, *Face of an Angel,* New York: Farrar, Straus and Giroux, 1994

THE DESSERTS ARE A LAND
OF THEIR OWN, OVERFLOWING
WITH MILK AND HONEY. FLANS,
PUDDINGS, WHIPPED-CREAM OR
MILK CAKES, AND MERINGUE
CONFECTIONS ABOUND.

DESSERTS

CHARLIE CARRILLO'S CUSTARD

Natillas Charlie Carrillo

"**A** large bowl of *natillas*, a dazzling creamy custard with a frothy topping as light as the clouds in the wide Santa Fe sky, is my most favorite dessert," says Mexican American Charlie Carrillo, who is considered the Leonardo da Vinci of contemporary New Mexican *santeros*—that is, makers of *santos,* Roman Catholic religious artifacts, such as statues carved from wood (*bultos*) and painted wood panels (*santo retablos*). Carrillo's *santos* have been displayed in galleries and museums across America. In the summer of 1995 we visited Charlie Carrillo at his home several days before Spanish Market—the annual exhibition of New Mexican *santos* in Santa Fe. He took many precious hours away from readying his pieces to tell us stories about his *santos,* his ancestors who first settled in New Mexico in the 1690s, and his artistically inclined

Charlie Carrillo in his art studio

children, Estrellita and Roán. He also told us of the passion he and his wife, Debbie, a talented potter who creates New Mexican clay bean pots and other traditional clay pieces, have for classic New Mexican cooking. "We always prepare traditional dishes from scratch, as our ancestors did. *Natillas,* which I consider a marvelous work of art, is just one of those dishes."

Natillas starts out as a stirred custard that is much thinner in consistency than *crème anglaise* because it has fewer egg yolks per cup of milk. Once the custard is cooked, in go crumbled saltine crackers, which give body to the custard. Stiff, sweetened egg whites are either folded into the custard or put on top like French floating islands. Since consuming raw eggs poses a health risk, Charlie suggests (though he does not do this for himself) folding the egg whites into the custard.

4 large eggs
1 quart whole milk
½ cup granulated sugar
3 tablespoons cornstarch
½ teaspoon vanilla extract

½ tablespoon confectioners' sugar
2¼ cups coarsely crumbled saltine
    crackers (about 36 single crackers)
Ground cinnamon or nutmeg, to taste

Separate the eggs, putting the whites in a large bowl and the yolks in a small bowl. Heat the milk, stirring often, in a medium saucepan over low heat until it is hot, but not boiling. Add the granulated sugar slowly, stirring constantly. Ladle about 1 cup of the hot milk into the bowl containing the egg yolks and stir until blended. Add the egg yolk–milk mixture to the hot milk in the saucepan. Whisk in the cornstarch. Cook the mixture slowly, stirring often, over low heat, about 25 minutes. The custard should be rather liquidy. Remove from the heat and stir in the vanilla extract.

Beat the egg whites until stiff with an electric mixer. Gently fold the confectioners' sugar into the stiffened egg whites. Next fold the hot custard and crumbled saltine crackers into the stiffened egg whites. Pour the custard into a serving bowl and sprinkle with cinnamon or nutmeg to taste. Serve warm or cold. Cookies, especially New Mexican *Biscochitos* (see page 268), are traditional accompaniments to *natillas*.

Serves 6

ABUELITA'S VANILLA FLAN

Flan de leche de abuelita

"Sometimes I daydream about Vanilla Flan (*Flan de leche*), a satiny smooth molded custard of eggs and milk cascading with deep amber caramelized sugar," says Josefina Ramirez, director of a government office in Tallahassee. "That's when I know it's time to head home to Miami for my *abuelita's* (grandmother's) glorious *Flan de leche,* which she bakes just for my visit. Before I moved north to Tallahassee, I never realized how, as a first-generation Cuban American, I took for granted the exquisite taste and aroma of *abuelita's* Cuban food, the loud conversations in rapid-fire Spanish around the dining table, and the Latin flavors and rhythms of Miami."

Classic Vanilla Flan, which traveled from Spain to every corner of the Americas, is the quintessential Latin dessert and comfort food for millions of Americans of Latin

American descent. It is among the easiest of desserts to prepare, as long as you follow each step of the recipe carefully and give the flan time to set in the refrigerator.

One 12-ounce can evaporated milk	**5 large eggs, plus 1 egg yolk**
One 14-ounce can sweetened condensed	**1 teaspoon vanilla extract**
milk	**1 cup granulated sugar**

Beat together the evaporated milk, condensed milk, eggs and egg yolk, and vanilla extract in a large bowl with an electric mixer, or process in a blender or food processor until smooth.

Caramelize the sugar: Cook it in a small heavy saucepan or a copper caramelizing pot over medium heat. Stir constantly until the sugar turns a honey color. As it begins to dissolve, stir only occasionally. Once the sugar dissolves, cook it without stirring (or the sugar will begin to crystallize), until it turns deep amber in color. The color will change rapidly, so watch the saucepan closely. Immediately after you remove the caramelized sugar from the burner, pour it into a 1-quart soufflé dish or another ovenproof baking dish. Quickly tilt the dish in various directions so that the caramelized sugar coats the bottom and sides.

Pour the milk mixture into the soufflé dish and then place it in a bain-marie—any shallow pan large enough to hold the soufflé dish with room to spare and filled with 1 inch of hot water. Bake the flan on the middle rack in a preheated 350°F oven for 1 hour, or until a knife inserted off center comes out clean. Check on the flan after 20 minutes. If the top is golden brown already, cover the flan loosely with aluminum foil so that it does not brown too much.

Remove the flan from the oven and carefully lift the soufflé dish out of the bain-marie. Cool the flan to room temperature, then chill it in the refrigerator for at least 3 hours. Unmold the flan by first running a sharp, nonserrated knife around the inside of the soufflé dish. Next invert the flan onto a serving platter. The flan should slide out easily onto the plate, and the caramelized sugar syrup should flow over it. Cut the flan into 6 wedges and serve.

Serves 6

PUMPKIN FLAN
UNDER A PALM TREE

Flan de calabaza bajo las palmas

As with every dish brought from Europe to the Americas, subtle and dramatic variations of classic Spanish vanilla flan arose at the crossroads of the Old World and the New World. All of the flans that were created in Latin America have reached our shores, and thus on any given day Mexican Americans in Houston might be found dishing up Coffee Flan; Chilean Americans in San Francisco, Chestnut Flan; Panamanian Americans in Miami, Chocolate Flan; Dominican Americans in New York City, Cream Cheese Flan (see page 253); Colombian Americans in Queens, Mango Flan; Peruvian Americans in L.A., Coconut Flan; and Puerto Ricans in Chicago, Pumpkin Flan.

All the New World flans are delicious and intriguing, but Puerto Rican Pumpkin Flan truly warms the heart, perhaps because it is so lovely, with its shades of deep orange and amber and its scent of cinnamon and clove. On special occasions we pair Puerto Rican Pumpkin Flan with New Mexican *Biscochitos* (see page 268), a crisp butter cookie with a touch of anise. We cut the *biscochitos* with palm tree–shaped cookie cutters in homage to the tropical homeland of Pumpkin Flan. Just before serving, we stick one palm tree *biscochito* in the top of each flan, as you would a birthday candle.

FOR THE PUMPKIN CUSTARD:

One 16-ounce can pumpkin purée
½ teaspoon ground cinnamon
¼ teaspoon ground cloves
⅔ cup evaporated milk

⅔ cup sweetened condensed milk
1 teaspoon vanilla extract
5 large eggs
¼ cup granulated sugar

FOR THE CARAMELIZED SUGAR:

1 cup granulated sugar

Mix together the pumpkin purée, cinnamon, and cloves in a large mixing bowl. Pour in the evaporated milk, condensed milk, and vanilla extract, and mix well. Next stir in the eggs, one at a time, and then the ¼ cup sugar, and mix until all the ingredients are well blended.

Caramelize the sugar: Cook the 1 cup sugar in a small heavy saucepan or a copper caramelizing pot over medium heat. Stir constantly until the sugar turns a honey color.

As the sugar begins to dissolve, stir only occasionally. Once it dissolves, continue cooking without stirring (or the sugar will begin to crystallize), until the caramelized sugar is deep amber in color. The color will change rapidly, so closely monitor the saucepan. Immediately after you remove the caramelized sugar from the burner, pour it into six 6-ounce (or seven 5-ounce) individual custard cups or an 8-inch soufflé dish. Quickly tilt the cups or dish in various directions so that the caramelized sugar coats the bottom and sides.

Carefully pour the pumpkin mixture into the custard cups or soufflé dish, and then place them in a bain-marie, any shallow pan large enough to hold the custard cups or soufflé dish with room to spare and filled with 1 inch of hot water. Bake the flan on the middle rack in a preheated 350°F oven for 40 minutes for the custard cups and 1 hour and 20 minutes for the soufflé dish, or until a knife inserted comes out clean.

Remove the flan from the oven and carefully lift the custard cups or soufflé dish out of the bain-marie. Allow the flan to cool to room temperature, and then chill it in the refrigerator for at least 3 hours. Unmold the flan by first running a nonserrated knife along the inside edge of the custard cups or soufflé dish. Next invert the flan onto individual plates or a serving platter. The caramelized sugar syrup will cascade over the flan. If you made the flan in a soufflé dish, cut it into 6 wedges. Garnish each portion with some of the sugar syrup and a *biscochito,* if you choose, and serve at once.

Serves 6 or 7

For Mexican American Coffee Flan (*Flan de café*): Beat together 5 large eggs, 2 large yolks, one 14-ounce can sweetened condensed milk, 1 cup whole milk, and ½ cup espresso at room temperature in a large bowl with an electric mixer, or process in a blender or food processor until smooth. Caramelize 1 cup granulated sugar, following the directions above. Coat an 8-inch soufflé dish with the caramelized sugar and pour in the coffee mixture. Place in a bain-marie and bake on the middle rack in a preheated 350°F oven for 1 hour, or until a knife inserted comes out clean. Chill the flan and unmold according to the instructions above.

For Peruvian American Coconut Flan (*Flan de coco*): Beat together one 14-ounce can sweetened condensed milk, ½ cup evaporated milk, ½ cup canned unsweetened coconut milk, and 5 large eggs plus 1 egg yolk in a large bowl with an electric mixer, or process in a blender or food processor until smooth. Stir in ½ cup firmly packed sweetened coconut flakes. Caramelize 1 cup granulated sugar following the directions above. Coat an 8-inch soufflé dish with the caramelized sugar and pour in the coconut mixture. Place in a bain-marie and bake on the middle rack in a preheated 350°F oven for 1 hour, or until a knife inserted comes out clean. Chill the flan and unmold according to the instructions above.

CREAM CHEESE FLAN WITH A DARK CHOCOLATE CRUMB CRUST

Flan de queso con galletas de chocolate en corteza

This satiny smooth, voluptuous flan, a national treasure to Puerto Ricans and Dominican and Guatemalan Americans, has a much denser custard than a vanilla flan, thanks to the cream cheese, but it is not as dense as cheesecake, since it has a greater egg-to-cream-cheese ratio. The top glistens with amber caramelized sugar syrup like a traditional flan, but like a New York cheesecake, beneath the cream-cheese custard lies a surprise dark chocolate crumb crust—a simple, uncooked blend of ground chocolate wafers and butter. Cream Cheese Flan with a Dark Chocolate Crumb Crust should be finished hours ahead of serving so that all can see this edible work of art before every last crumb disappears.

FOR THE CREAM CHEESE FLAN:
Two 8-ounce packages cream cheese, at room temperature
7 large eggs
One 14-ounce can sweetened condensed milk

I cup whole milk
I tablespoon granulated sugar
I teaspoon vanilla extract

FOR THE CARAMELIZED SUGAR:
I cup granulated sugar

FOR THE CHOCOLATE CRUMB CRUST:
8 ounces chocolate wafer cookies
6 tablespoons (¾ stick) lightly salted butter, melted

Whip the cream cheese, eggs, and condensed milk in an electric blender or food processor. Add the milk, sugar, and vanilla extract, and process until smooth.

Caramelize the sugar by cooking it in a small heavy saucepan or a copper caramelizing pot over medium heat. Stir constantly until the sugar turns a honey color. As the sugar begins to dissolve, stir only occasionally. Once it has dissolved, continue cooking without stirring (or the sugar will begin to crystallize), until it is deep amber in color. The color will change rapidly, so closely monitor the saucepan. Immediately

Cream Cheese Flan with a Dark Chocolate Crumb Crust (continued)

after you remove the caramelized sugar from the burner, pour it into a 2-quart soufflé dish. Quickly tilt the dish in various directions so that the caramelized sugar coats the bottom and sides.

Pour the cream cheese mixture into the soufflé dish, and then place it in a bain-marie—any shallow pan large enough to hold the dish with room to spare and filled with 1 inch of hot water. Bake the flan on the middle rack in a preheated 350°F oven for 1 hour and 20 minutes, or until a knife inserted off center comes out clean. (The flan will puff completely, like a pumpkin pie, when it has finished baking.) Remove the flan from the oven and carefully lift the soufflé dish out of the bain-marie.

Allow the flan to cool while you prepare the cookie crumb crust. Grind half of the cookies in a food processor to make fine crumbs. Add the other half of the cookies to the crumbs and grind those. Pour in the melted butter and process for a few seconds to blend. Spread the cookie-crumb mixture evenly over the flan (which will have deflated a bit by now). Press very gently on the crumb mixture to pack it down. Allow the flan to cool to room temperature, then chill in the refrigerator for at least 4 hours so that the crust sets.

Unmold the flan by first running a sharp, nonserrated knife around the inside of the soufflé dish. Next invert the flan onto a serving platter, cut it into 8 wedges, and serve.

Serves 8 to 10

Variation: If you are not a chocolate fan, substitute an equal amount of vanilla wafers, gingersnaps, or graham crackers for the chocolate wafer cookies, and proceed as directed.

RAIN OF GOLD TAMALES

Tamales lluvia de oro

We first tasted these sweet, moist tamales studded with golden corn kernels at a birthday party held in honor of Mexican American writer Victor Villaseñor, author of the best-selling novel *Rain of Gold*, at his hacienda in Oceanside, California. It was a delightful party that spilled from a Spanish-tiled patio off the main house, where a marvelous buffet of Mexican American delicacies was laid out, to picnic tables on the front lawn, where peacocks and other exotic birds oversaw the festivities from their cages. Rain of Gold Tamales are the creation of Victor Villaseñor's sister, Sita Paloma, an expert cook who runs a tamales business and holds classes in cooking, Spanish dance, and spiritual transformation.

Rain of Gold Tamales are easy to prepare, as they are not filled. If you wish, assemble the tamales hours in advance and store them in the refrigerator, covered tightly in plastic wrap, until cooking time. Leftover tamales will keep in the refrigerator for up to 2 days and in the freezer for up to a month, and can be warmed in a microwave oven or in a steamer basket in a large pot. We love Sita's Rain of Gold Tamales for breakfast or brunch instead of pancakes or waffles, and for dessert or a sweet snack. They are so moist and flavorful they need no accompaniment.

FOR THE MASA (CORN DOUGH):*

4 cups *masa harina de maíz* (corn *masa* mix)[†] 3 cups water

FOR THE TAMALES:

1¾ cups plus 1 tablespoon canola oil
1¾ cups plus 1 tablespoon honey
1½ teaspoons salt, preferably fine-grained sea salt, but table salt is fine

2¾ pounds frozen (defrosted) corn kernels
One 6-ounce bag dried corn husks, or substitute fresh corn husks

*Or purchase 2½ pounds prepared masa *for tortillas (not* masa *for tamales, which will have lard or vegetable shortening in it) at Mexican markets and select supermarkets, especially in California, Texas, and the Southwest.*
[†] *Available in Latin markets catering to Americans with roots in Mexico and Central and South America, and in select supermarkets, especially in California, Texas, and the Southwest.*

Make the *masa,* or corn dough: Mix thoroughly the *masa harina* and water in a large mixing bowl. This foolproof recipe makes approximately 2¾ pounds *masa,* but the tamales call for 2½ pounds. If you do not have a kitchen scale to weigh the *masa,* subtract about ½ cup *masa* to arrive at approximately 2½ pounds. Add the canola oil, honey, and salt to the *masa,* and mix well with a spoon. Gently stir in the corn kernels. Do not overmix or the corn kernels will break up.

If you are using dried corn husks, soak them in enough hot water to cover in a large pot until they are pliable, about 30 minutes. Separate the husks into single "sheets," discarding any tattered ones. Rinse the sheets under warm running water to remove any silk or grit. Pile the wet husks on a large plate or tray. At this point, Sita selects only the biggest husks to make large tamales, but you can use all sizes to make different-sized tamales. You may also overlap husks too small to stuff alone to make larger "sheets."

To assemble the tamales, pat a husk dry with paper towels, and then place it, smoother side up and tapered end pointing toward you, on a work surface. Spoon 2

Rain of Gold Tamales (continued)

to 4 heaping tablespoons *masa,* depending on the size of the husk, at the top center of the husk. Spread the *masa* with the spoon down to the middle center of the husk. (The lower part of the husk should be unfilled.) Fold the sides of the corn husk over the *masa* so that they overlap to make a long package. Fold the unfilled end of the husk under and up so that it touches the side of the tamal without a seam. The top of the tamal should be open.

Gently place the tamal on a large plate or tray so that the open end is tilted upward slightly to ensure that the filling will not ooze out. (You may want to set a butter knife or a chopstick on the tray and rest the first layer of tamales against it.) Fill the rest of the husks in the same manner and pile them on the plate or tray as you complete them. (Note, any leftover husks may be stored in a sealed zip-lock bag or wrapped tightly in plastic and frozen for later use. Simply defrost them a few hours before using.)

Place a steamer basket in a large wide pot and fill the pot with enough water to almost touch the bottom of the basket. Stand the tamales on their folded ends in the basket. They should all fit into the pot without being squeezed too tightly together. Bring the water to a boil over medium-high heat, cover, reduce the heat, and steam the tamales until they set and the husks peel away easily from the *masa,* about 1 hour. (It may take longer depending on how crowded the tamales are in the pot.) The *masa* will not become firm until the final stages of steaming. Add boiling water, as needed, throughout the steaming process to maintain the original level of the water but no more. Be careful not to soak any of the tamales when you add the water.

Remove the tamales from the pot to a large platter or tray and allow them to stand for 15 minutes before serving so that they become firmer. Serve the tamales warm in their husks.

Makes about 2½ dozen large tamales and 3½ to 4 dozen medium tamales or tamales of various sizes; serves 10 to 12

GISÈLE BEN-DOR'S RICE PUDDING

Arroz con leche Gisèle Ben-Dor

Gisèle Ben-Dor, music director and conductor of the Boston ProArte Chamber Orchestra, the Annapolis Symphony, and the Santa Barbara Symphony, was born in Montevideo, Uruguay, to Polish parents. She sometimes waxes nostalgic about the life she left behind before she set off on the road to an international music career: "Only now am I beginning to understand what a different world that was in Uruguay, compared to the one I live in now. I was part of a very large family, and we saw each other weekly, or at least very often. Everything revolved around the family. The family got together and ate marvelous foods. One of the dishes that I remember most from my childhood is rice pudding. I remember not only the delicious taste, but also the children's song that went with it. Song, after all, was the center of my life. It went like this:

> *"Arroz con leche, me quiero casar con una señorita del barrio oriental,*
> *Que sepa coser, que sepa bordar, que sepa abrir la puerta para ir a jugar.*
> (Rice pudding, I want to marry a girl from the east side of town
> Who knows how to sew, who knows how to embroider,
> who knows how to open the door and go out and play.)"

1 cup rice	1 teaspoon vanilla extract
2 cups water	1 teaspoon grated lemon peel
1 cup whole milk	1 teaspoon butter, for greasing the pan
2 large eggs	1 cup heavy cream
½ cup granulated sugar	Cinnamon, for dusting

Put the rice and the water in a medium saucepan and bring to a boil over medium-high heat, then reduce the heat to low and cook the rice, covered, until it is tender, about 20 minutes.

Stir the milk, eggs, sugar, vanilla extract, and lemon peel in a medium bowl until blended. Add the rice and gently stir until the ingredients are well mixed.

Butter a 9-inch pie pan and spoon the rice mixture into it. Bake in a preheated 350°F oven for 25 minutes. Remove the rice pudding from the oven, stir it well, and allow it to cool for 15 minutes. Meanwhile, whip the cream to soft peaks in a

Gisèle Ben-Dor

large bowl with an electric mixer. Fold the rice pudding into the whipped cream. Transfer to a serving dish, dust with cinnamon, and serve warm or chilled.

Serves 4 to 5

COCONUT BREAD PUDDING

Budín de pan de coco

Whenever we long for a simple, homey dessert, we reach for a loaf of French bread, some coconut milk, and a few basic ingredients, and whip up Puerto Rican Coconut Bread Pudding. Recipes for the island's bread pudding abound, but most combine the same ingredients, though some are made with half-and-half or heavy cream, and others with evaporated milk or condensed milk. When chopped fruit, such as oranges or fruit cocktail, is folded into basic Puerto Rican bread pudding, it is transformed into *Pudín diplomatico* (Diplomat Pudding), also a Cuban American favorite, which bears no resemblance to the classic molded dessert by the same name that is made with liqueur-soaked ladyfingers or sponge cake, custard, jam, and candied fruit.

In this recipe we add sweetened coconut flakes to traditional Puerto Rican bread pudding, an idea we got from Puerto Ricans Marcos Rivera and his wife, Carmen Rivera, who are both administrators at Bowling Green State University in Bowling Green, Ohio. The coconut flakes stay moist inside the pudding and get crispy on top, resulting in a marvelous pudding with lots of textures. We like to serve Coconut Bread Pudding with slices of fresh mango, but only when in season. Count on 1 mango for every 3 persons.

One 13½-ounce can unsweetened
  coconut milk
2 cups milk
½ cup half-and-half
1 loaf (1 pound) French bread, cut into
  1-inch cubes (do not remove
  the crusts)
3 large eggs

¾ cup granulated sugar
1½ teaspoons vanilla extract
½ cup plus 2 tablespoons firmly packed
  sweetened coconut flakes
⅓ cup golden raisins
1 tablespoon butter, for greasing the pan
3 or 4 ripe mangos, peeled and sliced
  (optional)

Mix together the coconut milk, milk, and half-and-half in a large mixing bowl. Fold the bread into the liquid, making certain all the cubes are moistened. Allow the bread to soak while you beat together the eggs, sugar, and vanilla extract in a small mixing bowl. Add the egg mixture to the soaked bread. Stir in ½ cup of the coconut flakes and the raisins.

Grease a 9 × 13-inch baking pan with the butter. Spoon the batter into the pan and sprinkle the remaining 2 tablespoons coconut flakes on top. Bake on the upper rack of a preheated 350°F oven until the bread pudding has set and is golden brown on top, about 45 minutes. Cut the bread pudding into squares and serve hot, warm, or chilled, on its own or with mango slices.

Serves 8 to 10

THREE MILKS CAKE

Tres leches

Very rich and moist with three kinds of milk, *Tres leches* is a quintessential Nicaraguan dessert, beloved not only by Nicaraguan Americans and Costa Rican Americans who have adopted the cake but also by all who experience it. To the typical American palate, traditional *Tres leches* is a bit too sugary. Thus we have toned down its sweetness by cutting most of the sugar out of the whipped cream topping. While traditionally *Tres leches* may also be topped with meringue, we have opted for whipped cream to minimize preparation time without sacrificing flavor. Some traditional recipes also call for the addition of light rum to the milk syrup, but Latinos also prepare *Tres leches* without the rum flavoring.

Carefully wrapped, *Tres leches* will keep in the refrigerator for up to 2 days. The cake is actually at its most delectable after it has been refrigerated for at least 8 hours and has set completely. Some Latino chefs and home cooks add a little extra pizzazz to traditional *Tres leches* by garnishing it with sliced fruit, such as mango or banana, or dusting with grated coconut. Or you can decorate it with plump raspberries, blueberries, blackberries, olallieberries, or loganberries.

FOR THE CAKE:

1½ cups cake flour	5 large eggs
1 teaspoon baking powder	½ teaspoon vanilla extract
1 cup granulated sugar	⅓ cup milk
½ cup (1 stick) butter, softened	

FOR THE MILK SYRUP:

1 cup sweetened condensed milk	1 tablespoon light rum or your favorite
1 cup evaporated milk	liqueur (optional)
1 cup whole milk	

FOR THE WHIPPED-CREAM TOPPING:

1 cup heavy cream	½ teaspoon vanilla extract
1 teaspoon granulated sugar	

Make the cake batter: Sift together the cake flour and baking powder. Cream the sugar and the butter in a large mixing bowl with an electric mixer until well blended. Add the eggs and the vanilla extract, and beat until foamy. With a rubber spatula, gently fold in the dry ingredients, alternating with the milk, until the batter is smooth.

Pour the cake batter into a lightly greased 7 × 11 × 2-inch cake pan or baking dish, and bake on the middle rack in a preheated 350°F oven for 30 minutes, or until a wooden toothpick inserted in the center comes out clean and the top springs back when gently pressed. Allow the cake to cool in the pan on a wire rack for 20 minutes, then invert it onto a serving platter. Pierce the cake with a fork in many places and allow it to cool completely.

Next make the syrup: Whisk all the syrup ingredients in a medium mixing bowl until well blended. Pour the syrup evenly over the cake and refrigerate the cake, covered in plastic wrap, for at least 3 hours.

Make the topping: First chill the cream, a large mixing bowl, and beaters or a whisk in the refrigerator. Beat the cream in the chilled mixing bowl with an electric mixer or the whisk until it begins to thicken. Add the sugar and vanilla extract, and continue beating until stiff peaks form. Cover the top and sides of the cake with the whipped-cream topping using a spatula or knife. Cut the cake and serve. You may also cut the cake first, and then garnish with whipped cream only those portions you plan to serve.

Serves 10 to 12

TÍA LULÚ'S MERINGUE CAKE

Torta de merengue Tía Lulú

"Whenever I yearn for a gooey, decadent dessert," says Chilean American M. Isabel Valdés, president of Hispanic Market Connections, Inc., "I consult the family recipe for Meringue Cake that my sister Luz María, who lives in Santiago, Chile, adapted for the American kitchen during a trip to the United States. Chilean Meringue Cake recalls Pavlova, that majestic New Zealand dessert honoring the Russian ballerina Anna Pavlova, in which a baked meringue shell is filled with whipped cream and decorated with ripe fruits, especially kiwi fruit, passion fruit, and strawberries. While Pavlova is created around a single meringue shell, Meringue Cake has three baked meringue circles, separated by a luscious layer of chestnut cream—a blend of *crème de marrons* and whipped cream—and a layer of juicy ruby-red strawberries or raspberries. The cake is coated with clouds of whipped cream and adorned with more berries. It sounds elaborate, but actually it is quite easy to make. Luz María, known affectionately as Tía Lulú, made the recipe so foolproof that even cooks with minimal experience with meringue will have great success. You should have a candy thermometer to help you."

According to Isabel Valdés, Meringue Cake was brought to Chile by the Spanish, who probably adopted it from the Arabs, during the many centuries that they inhabited Spain and influenced forever its culinary heritage. In fact, the sugar syrup that goes into the meringue is called *almíbar* in Spanish, a word derived from Arabic. If strawberries or raspberries are not at their peak of ripeness at the farmers' market, vegetable stand, or in your garden, Isabel suggests substituting 3 cups kiwi fruit, pineapple, banana, or mango slices.

Tía Lulú's Meringue Cake (continued)

FOR THE 3 MERINGUE LAYERS:

1½ cups granulated sugar

½ cup water

1 teaspoon vanilla extract

3 large egg whites, at room temperature

Three 10-inch-long sheets parchment
   paper

FOR THE TOPPING AND FILLING:

1 cup heavy cream

1 teaspoon confectioners' sugar

¾ cup chestnut spread, also known as
   *crème de marrons**

3 cups fresh ripe strawberries, washed
   and sliced, or fresh ripe
   raspberries, rinsed

*Canned crème de marrons *imported from France and Switzerland is available in gourmet shops and by mail order (see Sources, page 307).*

Make the meringue: Cook the sugar, water, and vanilla in a medium heavy-bottomed saucepan over low heat, stirring constantly, until all the sugar has dissolved. Increase the heat to medium and cook the sugar syrup, without stirring, until it reaches the firm-ball stage (244°F to 248°F on a candy thermometer).

As the sugar syrup cooks, beat the egg whites in a medium copper, stainless steel, or glass bowl with an electric mixer until they are very stiff. Slowly pour the sugar syrup in a thin stream into the stiffened egg whites as you beat them on high. Continue to beat the meringue until it cools, about 10 minutes.

Draw a 9-inch circle on each sheet of parchment paper. Divide the meringue evenly between the 3 circles. Spread it out with a spoon or spatula to fill the circles. Center the 3 sheets of parchment paper on 3 different baking sheets. Bake the meringues in a preheated 350°F oven for 2 minutes, then turn off the heat and leave them in the oven for 40 minutes. Remove the parchment paper from the backs of the meringue disks by gently pulling the paper off, as you would a sticker. Transfer the meringues to wire racks and allow them to cool away from drafts.

Make the topping just before assembling the cake: First chill the cream, a large mixing bowl, and beaters or a whisk in the refrigerator. Beat the cream in the chilled bowl with an electric mixer or the whisk until it begins to thicken. Add the confectioners' sugar and continue beating until it forms soft peaks. Next make the chestnut filling: Mix the chestnut spread with ½ cup of the whipped cream in a medium mixing bowl until well blended.

To assemble the cake, place 1 meringue disk on a cake plate, spread half the fruit evenly over the disk, and lay a second meringue disk on top. Spread the chestnut cream evenly on the second disk, and then place the third meringue disk on top. Spread the remaining whipped cream over the top and sides of the cake, decorate the top with the remaining fruit, and serve at once.

Serves 8 to 10

RUM-SOAKED SPONGE CAKE

Bôlo bêbado

This scrumptious Brazilian sponge cake, as yellow as the sun, is a favorite among many Brazilian Americans, who know it as *Bôlo bêbado,* or "Drunken Cake," because it is bathed in a rich rum-flavored syrup. The sponge cake itself is rather unorthodox, as it is made with a leavening agent and only a tablespoon of flour. It is very easy to prepare because the batter is whipped up in one easy step by blending the ingredients in a food processor or blender all at once. This method makes the cake quite porous and springy, but once it is soaked in the rum-flavored sugar syrup, it becomes soft and very moist.

Bôlo bêbado is traditionally embellished with nothing more than the rum-flavored syrup, but some Brazilian Americans go a step further and garnish with fresh fruit or fruit compote, crème chantilly, or ice cream. We often make just a simple design on the cake with confectioners' sugar using a parchment paper stencil or merely sift a little sugar on top. This must be done just before serving, or the moisture in the cake will dissolve the confectioners' sugar.

FOR THE CAKE BATTER:

¼ cup plus 2 tablespoons plain dry bread
crumbs

¼ cup plus 2 tablespoons granulated
sugar

1 tablespoon unbleached all-purpose flour

1 tablespoon baking powder

6 large eggs, at room temperature
(70°F)

FOR THE RUM-FLAVORED SYRUP:

½ cup granulated sugar
¼ cup water

¼ cup *cachaça,* or substitute white rum*

FOR THE GARNISH:

Fresh fruit, fruit compote, crème
chantilly, ice cream, or confectioners'
sugar (optional)

*Cachaça *is a Brazilian rumlike liquor distilled from the sap of fermented sugar cane (see page 297).*

Put all the cake batter ingredients into a food processor or electric blender and process until the batter is smooth and well blended. Grease the bottom and sides of a nonstick 8- or 9-inch square cake pan. Pour the batter into the prepared cake pan.

Bake the cake on the upper rack in a preheated 350°F oven until golden and a wooden skewer inserted in the center comes out clean, about 15 minutes. Remove the cake from the oven to a wire rack to cool for 15 minutes.

Meanwhile, make the rum-flavored syrup. Put all the syrup ingredients in a small saucepan, bring to a boil over medium-high heat, stirring occasionally, and then remove from the heat.

Run a knife around the edges of the cake to loosen it from the pan, and then turn the cake out onto a large serving plate. Pour the rum syrup over the cake and allow it to cool. Serve the sponge cake at room temperature or chilled, plain or with the garnish of your choice.

Serves 6

HEAVENLY CAKE

Torta del cielo

Almond cakes, such as the famous *tarta de Santiago* (Santiago almond torte), named after the Galician city of Santiago de Compostela, are popular all over the Iberian Peninsula. When the Age of Exploration dawned, almond cake recipes began to make their way to Latin America with Spanish and Portuguese explorers. For some reason, these almond cakes incorporated the word "heaven" in their names once in Latin America, as in an almond cake of the Yucatán, called *Torta del cielo*, or "Heavenly Cake." Cuban almond cake is similarly named *Tocino del cielo*, or "Bacon from Heaven"; a Brazilian almond cake bears the same name as the Cuban but in Portuguese, *Toucinho de céu*. Historians have conjectured that these cakes were first made by the devout in institutions such as convents in the New World. Shifting borders and immigration brought many versions of Heavenly Cake, Bacon from Heaven, and other Latin almond cakes to the United States. They are made with varying amounts of flour (or none at all) and eggs. This version of Heavenly Cake has rum as a flavoring, but some recipes call for vanilla extract instead. (For the vanilla version, substitute 1 teaspoon vanilla extract for the tablespoon rum.) Store any leftover cake in an airtight plastic storage bag in the refrigerator for up to 3 days.

Sheet of waxed paper

Vegetable oil, for greasing the waxed paper

1 ½ cups (8 ounces) unsalted almonds

2 cups water

½ cup cake flour

1 teaspoon baking powder

10 large eggs

1 ¼ cups granulated sugar

1 tablespoon rum, or substitute 1 teaspoon vanilla extract

¼ teaspoon cream of tartar

Pinch of salt

Confectioners' sugar, for dusting

¼ cup slivered or chopped almonds, for garnish

Cut a circle in the waxed paper to line the bottom of a 10-inch springform pan. Lightly grease the waxed paper with vegetable oil, but not the sides of the pan.

Blanch the almonds: Bring the water to a boil in a medium saucepan, add the almonds, and boil for 4 minutes. Drain and then press the almonds, one by one, between your thumb and forefinger to remove their skins. Or put them in the center of a dish towel and rub the skins off with the edges of the towel.

Grind the blanched almonds in a food processor or electric blender until very fine. Transfer to a medium mixing bowl and stir in the cake flour and baking powder.

Separate the eggs, putting the yolks in a large bowl and the whites in a large copper or stainless steel bowl. Beat the egg yolks and the sugar together with an electric mixer until the mixture falls from the beaters in a thin ribbon and leaves a trail on the surface that slowly disappears. Beat in the rum, or the vanilla extract, if you like. Fold in the flour-nut mixture with a spatula.

Beat the egg whites until just foamy and add the cream of tartar (omit if you are using a copper bowl) and the salt. Continue beating until stiff, glossy peaks form. Stir one third of the beaten whites into the nut mixture to lighten, then gently fold in the remaining whites until just blended. Do not overmix.

Spoon the batter into the springform pan and bake in a preheated 375°F oven for about 40 minutes, or until the top is quite brown and the cake has started to pull away from the sides of the pan. Remove the cake from the oven to a wire rack and let it cool completely in the pan. Run a knife along the inside edge of the pan to loosen the cake. Release the sides of the springform pan. Invert the cake on a large plate, remove the bottom of the pan, peel off the waxed paper, gently place another large plate on top, and flip again so the cake is top side up. Just before serving, dust with finely sifted confectioners' sugar, cut the cake into wedges, and garnish each wedge with slivered or chopped almonds.

Serves 8 to 10

For Cuban American Bacon from Heaven (*Tocino del cielo*): Dissolve 1¾ cups sugar in ½ cup water in a large saucepan over medium heat, stirring constantly. Stir in 1¾ cups ground blanched almonds. Remove from the heat. Beat together 8 egg yolks and 3 whole eggs, and slowly whisk into the sugar-almond mixture. Cook over low heat, stirring constantly, until thick,

about 10 minutes. Pour the batter into a greased and floured 8-inch cake pan and bake in a bain-marie on the middle rack of a preheated 350°F oven for about 30 minutes, or until the cake has set. Remove from the oven, unmold, cool on a wire rack, and serve.

For Brazilian American Bacon from Heaven (*Tocinho de céu*): Cook 1½ cups sugar and ½ cup water in a medium saucepan over medium heat, stirring constantly, until threads form when a spoon is dipped into the syrup and some of the syrup on the spoon is dripped into ice water. Remove from the heat and stir in ¾ cup butter. Mix together ¾ cup ground blanched almonds and ¾ cup unbleached all-purpose flour in a large bowl. Stir the sugar-butter mixture into the dry ingredients. Beat 3 egg whites in a large copper or stainless steel bowl until stiff peaks form, and then beat in 6 egg yolks. Slowly whisk the beaten eggs into the sugar-almond mixture. Pour the batter into a buttered 8-inch cake pan and bake in a preheated 350°F oven for about 20 minutes, or until the cake has set. Cover loosely with aluminum foil halfway through the baking process. Remove from the oven, unmold, cool on a wire rack, dust with finely sifted confectioners' sugar, and serve.

For Brazilian American Walnut Cake (*Bôlo de nozes*): While Mexicans, Cubans, and other Latin Americans have held fast to the almond, Brazilians and Brazilian Americans use an array of nuts in their cakes, including walnuts, peanuts, and Brazil nuts. This frosted cake calls for walnuts and is made with a simple filling of sugar and eggs, which we have omitted as it is quite sweet. Replace the almonds with 2 cups ground walnuts, use 8 eggs instead of 10, use 1 cup sugar instead of 1¼ cups, and 1 tablespoon flour plus 1 tablespoon plain bread crumbs in place of the ½ cup cake flour. Omit the baking powder and rum. Bake in 2 lightly greased and floured 9-inch cake pans in a preheated 350°F oven for 20 to 25 minutes. Turn out onto wire racks and cool completely.

Make the frosting (we use seven-minute frosting rather than traditional meringue frosting): Beat 1½ cups sugar, ¼ cup water, 2 egg whites, 1 tablespoon corn syrup, and ½ teaspoon cream of tartar with an electric mixer in a large mixing bowl resting atop a medium saucepan of simmering water until fluffy (7 minutes). Stir in 1 tablespoon vanilla extract. Frost the cake at once.

SWEET POTATO "BREAD"

Pain patate

With its seductive blend of sweet potatoes, bananas, cinnamon, and nutmeg, Haitian *Pain patate* (Sweet Potato "Bread") is really not a bread at all, though it is baked in a loaf pan. In fact, it has not an ounce of flour. It most resembles the moist, spiced pumpkin filling in a traditional Thanksgiving pumpkin pie. Haitian Americans in places like Miami's Little Haiti, Manhattan's Bois Verna (a Haitian colony on the Upper West Side), and Brooklyn's La Saline (a Haitian enclave centered around Rutland Road), wax lyrical, in English and melodic patois, about *Pain patate,* a favorite dessert, which they serve plain or garnished with whipped cream or a splash of rum.

Haitian Americans are not the only Americans of Caribbean descent to create delectable desserts from sweet potatoes. Dominican Americans make *tarta de batata* (sweet potato cake) flavored with coconut milk, cream, light rum, and spices. Jamaican Americans have their own sweet potato dessert flavored with coconut milk: Sweet Potato Pudding, made fragrant with ginger, nutmeg, vanilla, and raisins (see page 268). A long-standing favorite among Cuban Americans is *pastel de batata,* a moist cake made with *boniatillo,* a paste composed of *boniatos* (white sweet potatoes that are less sweet and drier than the yellow American variety, see page 197), sugar, egg yolks, sherry, and cinnamon.

2 cups sweet potatoes, peeled and boiled until tender	½ teaspoon vanilla extract
	½ teaspoon salt
2 medium ripe bananas, peeled	¼ teaspoon ground cinnamon
2 tablespoons butter, melted	¼ teaspoon ground nutmeg
3 medium eggs, beaten	I cup whole milk
¼ cup granulated sugar	¼ cup seedless golden raisins
¼ cup molasses	

Coarsely mash together the sweet potatoes and bananas with a potato masher or fork in a large mixing bowl, and then blend with an electric mixer until smooth.

Beat the butter and eggs into the sweet potato–banana paste with a wire whisk to combine. Add the sugar, molasses, vanilla extract, salt, cinnamon, and nutmeg, and whisk until well blended. Next whisk in the milk until it is incorporated. Stir in the raisins.

Pour the batter into a 2-quart loaf pan and bake it in a preheated 350°F oven until the center is firm and the top is golden brown, about 55 minutes. Remove the "bread" from the oven and let it cool in the pan for 10 minutes before turning it out onto a plate. Serve generous slices of *Pain patate* warm or chilled, with whipped cream or a little rum poured over the top, or plain.

Serves 6 to 8

Sweet Potato "Bread" (continued)

For Jamaican American Sweet Potato Pudding: Peel and grate 1 pound sweet potatoes. Mix together the sweet potatoes with ¼ cup melted butter, ¾ cup light brown sugar, and ½ teaspoon vanilla extract in a large mixing bowl. Mix thoroughly ¼ cup unbleached all-purpose flour with ¼ teaspoon each ground nutmeg and ginger, and a pinch of salt in a small bowl, then stir into the sweet potato mixture. Fold in 1 cup canned unsweetened coconut milk and ¼ cup seedless golden raisins. Spoon the batter into a lightly buttered baking dish and bake in a preheated 350°F oven for about 1 hour and 15 minutes, or until firm. Cut into squares and serve warm or chilled, drizzled with coconut milk, if desired.

NEW MEXICAN *BISCOCHITOS*

Biscochitos a la nuevomexicano

Mexican American *biscochitos,* crisp buttery cookies lightly spiced with anise seed and dusted with sugar and cinnamon, are simply divine. For the Mexican Americans of New Mexico, the Christmas season would not be complete without *biscochitos* (also spelled *bizcochitos*). But don't wait for winter holiday festivities to bake a few batches. Traditionally *biscochito* dough is made with lard, creating a flakier cookie akin to shortbread. While many Mexican Americans remain faithful to lard, in some homes in New Mexico lard has given way to butter in *biscochitos* with delicious results. If you have misgivings about anise seed, fear not; the sweet licorice scent and flavor of anise is so subtle and blends so well in these cookies that you will look anew at this spice.

A Mexican American gathering in Texas, circa 1920

1¾ cups unbleached all-purpose flour	½ cup granulated sugar
1 teaspoon baking powder	1 large egg
1 teaspoon anise seed	1 tablespoon brandy
⅛ teaspoon salt	Cinnamon sugar (¼ cup granulated
½ cup (1 stick) unsalted butter,	sugar and ½ teaspoon ground
softened	cinnamon mixed well)

Mix the flour, baking powder, anise seed, and salt together in a medium mixing bowl.

Cream the butter and sugar in a large mixing bowl. Stir in the egg and brandy until the ingredients are just blended. Gradually stir in the dry ingredients and mix well to make a smooth dough. Cover the bowl with plastic wrap and chill the dough in the refrigerator for 2 hours or overnight.

Roll out the dough, working with one third of it at a time, to a thickness of ⅛ inch (for really crisp cookies) on a lightly floured work surface. Cut the dough with fancy cookie cutters or use a handmade pattern.

Carefully transfer the cookie shapes to ungreased baking sheets and sprinkle with the cinnamon sugar. Bake the cookies in a preheated 350°F oven for 10 to 14 minutes, depending on their thickness, or until golden brown. Let the *biscochitos* stand for about a minute and then gently remove them with a spatula to wire racks to cool. Serve the *biscochitos,* or store them, once they are completely cooled, in an airtight tin at room temperature for up to 1 week.

Makes about 3 dozen 2½- to 3-inch cookies

MEXICAN WEDDING COOKIES

Polvorones

Tender, cinnamon-scented *Polvorones* (Mexican Wedding Cookies) are reminiscent of old-fashioned Snickerdoodles. This traditional recipe was given to us by U.S. Representative Henry B. González (D-Texas), the first Texan of Mexican ancestry elected to the House, where he has served for over three decades. Congressman González considers *polvorones* his favorite of all cookies. It's easy to see why. They are as quick and easy to make as they are irresistible. Simply mix the dough, shape it by hand into balls, bake, and coat the cookies in cinnamon sugar. Henry B. González prefers his *polvorones* made with lard, but we found that butter makes just as flavorful and tender a cookie.

2¼ cups unbleached all-purpose flour

¾ cup granulated sugar

2 teaspoons ground cinnamon

¼ teaspoon salt

⅔ cup (10 tablespoons) butter or lard,
cut into ½-inch pieces

2 large eggs

Cinnamon sugar (½ cup granulated
sugar and 1 teaspoon cinnamon
mixed in a small bowl)

Mix the flour, sugar, cinnamon, and salt together in a large bowl. Add the butter or lard and blend thoroughly with your fingers. Add the eggs and knead the cookie dough by hand until all the ingredients are blended and the dough is smooth.

U.S. Representative Henry B. González (D-Texas) working up an appetite for Mexican Wedding Cookies (*Polvorones*)

Pinch off small pieces of dough and roll them into balls the diameter of a quarter. Place the dough balls about 1 inch apart on ungreased baking sheets and bake them in a preheated 350°F oven until golden brown on the bottom, about 15 minutes.

Remove 2 or 3 cookies at a time with a spatula from the baking sheets to the bowl of cinnamon sugar. Coat the cookies generously with the cinnamon sugar, and then transfer them to wire racks to cool completely. Serve the *polvorones,* or store them, once they are completely cooled, in an airtight container at room temperature for up to 1 week.

Makes about 6 dozen

Variation of *Polvorones*: This version is also traditional, but it calls for pecans. Combine the flour, sugar, and salt with 1 cup finely chopped pecans, and proceed with the recipe above. The cinnamon is optional. The cookies are coated in either cinnamon sugar or confectioners' sugar.

ALMOND COOKIES

Alfafores de almendras

These crisp, nutty, butter-rich cookies from the Argentine American cookie jar are an almond lover's dream. Lots of ground almonds in the cookie dough and slivered almonds nestled on top are what make them taste great. Serve them at an afternoon tea, on a dessert buffet, or with a cup of espresso after dinner. Children, and adults too, love to dunk them in a tall glass of cold milk. These almond cookies will keep well, as long as you store them in an airtight container.

Almond cookie dough is rolled and cut with cookie cutters like traditional sugar cookies. Choose cookie cutters that spark your imagination. You can also make custom patterns by tracing shapes onto heavy cardboard and cutting them out with scissors.

1¾ cups unbleached all-purpose flour	¾ cup granulated sugar
¾ cup finely ground blanched almonds	1 large egg
1 teaspoon baking powder	1 tablespoon cognac
⅛ teaspoon salt	¼ teaspoon almond extract
½ cup (1 stick) unsalted butter, softened	4 tablespoons heavy cream
	¾ cup slivered almonds

Mix thoroughly the flour, ground almonds, baking powder, and salt in a medium mixing bowl.

Cream the butter and sugar in a large mixing bowl. Add the egg, cognac, and almond extract, and beat until light and fluffy. Gradually stir in the dry ingredients and mix well to make a smooth dough. Gather the cookie dough into a ball, wrap it in plastic, and chill in the refrigerator for 2 hours or overnight.

Roll out the dough to a thickness of ⅛ inch, working with one third of it at a time, on a lightly floured surface. Cut the dough with fancy cookie cutters. Carefully transfer the cookie shapes to buttered baking sheets. Brush lightly with cream and put a few slivered almonds on top of each.

Bake the cookies on the upper rack of a preheated 350°F oven for 6 to 8 minutes, or until they are golden brown. Gently remove the cookies with a spatula to wire racks to cool. Serve the almond cookies, or store them, once they are completely cooled, in an airtight tin at room temperature for up to 1 week.

Makes approximately 3 dozen 2½- to 3-inch cookies

BANANAS STUFFED WITH RUM BUTTER CREAM

Figues bananes fourrées

Banana halves piped with rich rum butter cream, dusted with rum-scented raisins and ground nuts, and topped with glacé cherries make a spectacular dessert prized by Haitian Americans. This banana dish is the chilled counterpart of Haitian *Bananes au rhum,* bananas baked in butter and sugar and then flamed with rum. It can be made ahead—just sprinkle the bananas with lemon juice after slicing them in half so that they do not turn brown.

2 tablespoons seedless black raisins

2 tablespoons plus 1 teaspoon dark rum

½ cup (1 stick) butter, softened

½ cup confectioners' sugar

3 large ripe bananas

¼ cup freshly squeezed lemon juice (if you will be serving the bananas later)

¼ cup coarsely ground peanuts, walnuts, almonds, or pecans

12 glacé cherries (candied cherries) (optional)

Soak the raisins in the 2 tablespoons of rum in a small bowl.

Cream the butter and the confectioners' sugar with an electric mixer in a small bowl. Beat in the remaining 1 teaspoon of rum.

Peel the bananas and cut them in half crosswise and then lengthwise. Arrange the bananas, flat side up, on a serving plate. If you are preparing the bananas ahead, sprinkle them with lemon juice to prevent them from turning brown. (If you will be serving them at once, omit this step.)

Fill a small pastry bag, fitted with the tip of your choice, with the rum butter cream. Pipe the rum butter cream along the length of each banana. (Or just spoon about 2 teaspoons rum butter cream on top of each banana.) Garnish each with the rum-soaked raisins and the nuts. (The leftover rum from the raisins can be sprinkled on the bananas, if desired.) Put a cherry on top of each banana and serve at once. Or refrigerate and serve within 8 hours.

Serves 6

SAUTÉED BANANAS IN GRAND MARNIER WITH CRÊPES

Guineos con licor de china en crêpes

Guineos con licor de china, ripe bananas sautéed or baked in butter and an orange-flavored liqueur, sometimes flambéed, and served either plain or with vanilla ice cream, is a popular dessert among Puerto Ricans on the mainland. It most certainly inspired the chefs at Brennan's restaurant in New Orleans, who in the 1950s created the famous Bananas Foster, bananas sautéed in rum, brown sugar, and banana liqueur, flambéed, and served à la mode. *Guineos con licor de china* is quick and easy to prepare and tastes exquisite, and so we make it often, especially with Grand Marnier, our favorite of the liqueurs. Sometimes we dress the sautéed bananas in classic French dessert crêpes. To ease the preparation of this dessert, you may make the crêpes up to 5 days ahead of time. Just stack them when they have completely cooled, wrap them in waxed paper and then aluminum foil, and refrigerate. Warm the crêpes in a low oven before assembling this dessert.

FOR THE DESSERT CRÊPES:

1 cup unbleached all-purpose flour, sifted	3 large eggs
4 tablespoons granulated sugar	1½ cups milk
Pinch of salt	Butter, for cooking the crêpes

FOR THE BANANAS:

4 small ripe bananas, peeled and sliced in half lengthwise and then crosswise	2 tablespoons brown sugar
3 tablespoons butter	2 tablespoons Grand Marnier

FOR THE GARNISH:

Confectioners' sugar	1 pint vanilla ice cream
Ground cinnamon	

Prepare the crêpes: Mix the flour, sugar, and salt in a large bowl. Whisk in the eggs and milk alternately, until the batter is smooth. Let the batter rest for 30 minutes. Melt about 1 teaspoon butter in a 7-inch nonstick skillet or crêpe pan over medium-high heat. When the butter bubbles, swirl it so that it coats the bottom of the skillet.

Add 3 to 4 tablespoons batter to the skillet and immediately tilt the pan so that the batter covers the bottom evenly. Cook the crêpe until it is light golden, about 1

Sautéed Bananas in Grand Marnier with Crêpes (continued)

minute, and then gently flip it and cook the other side for about 45 seconds. Remove the crêpe to a sheet of waxed paper or parchment paper. Repeat this process, adding butter as necessary, until all the batter is used. Cover the crêpes with waxed paper or parchment paper to prevent them from drying out.

Prepare the bananas: Melt the butter in a large skillet over medium heat. Stir in the brown sugar and Grand Marnier. Place the bananas in the skillet in 1 layer and sauté them, turning once, until soft and golden brown, about 2½ minutes per side.

To assemble the dish, lay a crêpe on a large plate and spoon 2 pieces of banana on one-quarter of the crêpe. Fold the crêpe in half over the bananas, and in half again, to make a triangle. Fold a second crêpe on the plate and arrange the crêpes in a decorative way. Repeat this process until 2 crêpes with bananas are arranged on each of 4 large plates. Dust each plate with confectioners' sugar and ground cinnamon. Working quickly, spoon about 6 balls of ice cream with a 1-inch melon baller on each plate, or simply garnish each with a large scoop of ice cream. Serve at once.

Serves 4

COCONUT-MERINGUE CONFECTION

Dulce de coco con merengue

"I was born in El Salvador to a Romanian father and a Chilean mother. Since my family is Jewish, our dining table was always overflowing with a multicultural array of marvelous Salvadoran, Chilean, Romanian, and Jewish dishes," says Eva Asher, Director of Hispanic Student Affairs at Florida State University in Tallahassee. "A typical meal in our house consisted of matzo ball soup; Chilean *Pastel de choclo*—Chicken Pot Pie with Corn Crust (see page 104); Romanian stuffed cabbage; Salvadoran *plátanos con crema*—fried plantains with sour cream; and vanilla flan for dessert. Once a year every Jewish family in El Salvador received a package of matzo meal and matzos that came by boat from the United States. When that ran out, there was no more matzo for the rest of the year. This presented a bit of a quandary when supplies ran out before Passover." Eva reminded us that "in memory of Exodus, leavening is forbidden during the eight days of Passover, and thus matzos are eaten in Jewish homes around the world. Ceremonial matzos, representing the three divisions of the Jewish people, adorn the Passover Seder table, and matzo meal is the basis for countless holiday cakes. Since Salvadoran Jews often had little or no matzo meal left in the pantry for Passover, some Salvadoran flourless desserts found their way to the Seder table. One such dessert is *Dulce de coco con merengue,* a sweet confection with layers of coconut and soft meringue. Interestingly this dessert is made with lots of grated coconut just like coconut macaroons, which are invariably an ancient Jewish *pareve* (made without milk, meat, or their derivatives) confection."

We have cut down on the amount of sugar, but this confection is still as sweet as candy and so it will serve many.

Sheet of waxed paper	I cup evaporated milk
3 large eggs	½ teaspoon grated lemon peel
I¾ cups granulated sugar	I teaspoon vanilla extract
I cup sweetened coconut flakes, firmly packed	

Cut a square of waxed paper to line the bottom of a 9 × 9-inch baking pan. Lightly grease the waxed paper and the sides of the pan.

Separate the eggs, putting the yolks in a medium bowl and the whites in a large stainless steel or copper bowl. Add ¾ cup of the sugar, the coconut, evaporated milk, and ¼ teaspoon of the lemon peel to the egg yolks and mix thoroughly. Pour the batter into the greased baking pan. Evenly distribute the coconut in the pan with a spoon. Bake the coconut layer in a preheated 375°F oven for 25 minutes, or until it has set and is speckled golden brown.

After the coconut layer comes out of the oven, raise the oven temperature to 425°F and make the meringue. Beat the egg whites to soft peaks. Add 1½ tablespoons of the remaining sugar and beat until stiff, glossy peaks form. Gently fold in the remaining sugar, the remaining ¼ teaspoon lemon peel, and the vanilla extract, taking care not to stir too much or the meringue will deflate.

Spoon the meringue evenly over the baked coconut layer. Bake in a preheated 425°F oven until the meringue is puffy and golden brown, about 5 to 6 minutes, watching carefully during the final minutes of cooking because it can burn easily. Remove the Coconut-Meringue Confection from the oven and allow it to cool to room temperature.

Makes about 16 small servings

PAPAYA IN SYRUP

Dulce de lechosa

"Puerto Ricans have a soft spot for tropical fruit stewed in syrup and served with cheese or ice cream for dessert," wrote cyberspace cook Nellie Casiano, a Puerto Rican mainlander, who loves to prepare island cuisine and to surf the Cooks Online Forum on Compuserve in her spare time. Nellie says that papaya in syrup is a favorite among Puerto Ricans on the mainland as well as on the island, and that the older generation serves it the old-fashioned way atop slices of cream cheese or a semisoft or semifirm cheese, while the younger set prefers it over ice cream. We like it with vanilla and coconut ice cream.

Puerto Rican children dressed in traditional costumes at the Puerto Rican Week Festival in Philadelphia

Store any leftover papaya in syrup in a tightly closed container in the refrigerator for up to five days.

¼ cup baking powder
2 pounds ripe papaya, any variety, peeled, seeded, and cut into 1-inch chunks
1 cup granulated sugar

1 teaspoon vanilla extract
1 cinnamon stick
Cream cheese, or vanilla or coconut ice cream (optional)

Dissolve the baking powder in 1½ quarts water in a large ceramic bowl. Add the papaya and soak it for 5 minutes. Drain the fruit and rinse it well under cold running water.

Cook the papaya with the sugar in a large pot, covered, over medium-high heat, stirring occasionally, for 20 minutes. (Do not add water. The papaya will cook in its own juice.)

Reduce the heat to very low, add the vanilla extract and the cinnamon stick, and simmer the papaya, uncovered, until the juice thickens into a thin syrup, about 30 minutes.

Remove the cinnamon stick and allow the papaya to cool. Serve it warm or chilled, plain or as a garnish, as suggested above.

Serves 10

PASSION FRUIT SORBET

Sorbete de granadilla

Passion Fruit Sorbet is one of the most voluptuous of sorbets, for it captures not only the sweetness and tartness of the fruit's golden pulp but its seductive tropical perfume as well. Passion Fruit Sorbet is loved by Latins with roots in tropical, sun-drenched regions of Latin America, where the fruit grows, and by all who venture to taste it.

When buying passion fruit, look for firm, heavy fruits with dimpled, withered skin—an indication of ripeness. (Unripe passion fruit will ripen if left at room temperature for a few days.) Store ripe fruit in the refrigerator for up to 2 weeks. Passion fruit can also be frozen whole in an airtight plastic bag, or the pulp may be spooned into freezer containers and stored in the freezer for several months. (For more information on passion fruit, see page 282.)

2 cups water
I cup granulated sugar

2¾ pounds passion fruit (about 42 passion fruits), or substitute one 14-ounce package frozen passion fruit pulp*

Frozen passion fruit pulp is available in Latin and Asian markets, and an occasional supermarket. Fresh passion fruit is available sporadically year-round except in June in Latin markets and some supermarkets, especially in California and Florida.

Bring the water and sugar to a boil in a large saucepan over medium heat. Boil for 2 minutes, or until the sugar dissolves. Remove the saucepan from the heat and let the sugar syrup cool to room temperature.

Meanwhile, if you are using fresh passion fruits, cut them in half, one by one, with a sharp knife over the container of a food processor or a blender to catch the juice that spills out. Spoon the pulp and seeds into the food processor or blender and purée with the sugar syrup until smooth.

Strain the passion fruit purée through a nonaluminum strainer with medium-gauge mesh to remove the seeds.

Freeze the passion fruit purée in an ice-cream maker according to the manufacturer's directions. Or pour it into a wide container and place it in the freezer. When frozen, purée in a food processor or blender until smooth, return it to the freezer, and freeze until stiff. Let the sorbet stand at room temperature for a few moments to soften before serving.

Makes about 5 cups

MANGO SORBET AND RASPBERRY SORBET

Sorbete de mango y sorbete de frambuesa

A peeled mango on a stick, with a pattern cut into the orange-yellow flesh, is a summertime treat that Americans of Latin American descent love. Another is Mango Sorbet, which captures the essence of those pure mangos on a stick in a refreshing chilled form. At the risk of gilding the lily, we like to mingle Mango Sorbet and Raspberry Sorbet, if we have the time to prepare both, since the colors of the sorbets harmonize so well. If you prepare both, put a little scoop of each in chilled glass bowls. If not, the vivid flavor of Mango Sorbet is all you need.

The best Mango Sorbet is made with the best-tasting fruit, so wait until domestic mangos are at their peak from May through September. Before proceeding with this recipe, cut a little slice off each fruit, skin and all, and take a taste of the flesh. If your senses do not sing from sweet, perfumey mango ambrosia, try another. If you are new to mangos, see the information on selecting the fruit on page 281.

FOR THE MANGO SORBET:

2 cups water

I cup granulated sugar

2 pounds ripe mangos (about 2 or
   3 mangos, depending on size)

½ cup freshly squeezed lime juice

I tablespoon white rum (optional)

FOR THE RASPBERRY SORBET:

2 cups granulated sugar

I cup water

2 pints fresh red raspberries, rinsed, or
   12 ounces frozen raspberries

1 ½ tablespoons freshly squeezed lemon
   juice

Prepare the mango sorbet: Bring the water and sugar to a boil in a small saucepan over medium heat. Boil for about 5 minutes, or until the sugar has dissolved completely. Remove from the heat and allow the sugar syrup to cool completely.

Peel the thin skin off the mangos with a sharp knife and slice the flesh from the flat pits. Cut the mango flesh into large chunks and purée in a food processor or electric blender until smooth. Add the cooled sugar syrup, lime juice, and white rum, if desired, and purée until well blended. Cover and chill in the refrigerator.

Transfer the chilled mango purée to an ice-cream maker and freeze according to the manufacturer's directions.

Prepare the raspberry sorbet: Make the sugar syrup following the instructions above, but with 2 cups sugar and 1 cup water. Purée the raspberries with the cooled sugar syrup and lemon juice in a food processor or blender.

Strain the raspberry purée through cheesecloth or a fine sieve to remove the seeds. Transfer to an ice-cream maker and freeze according to the manufacturer's directions.

Let the sorbets stand at room temperature for a few minutes to soften before serving.

*Makes about 3 cups mango sorbet and
about 1 quart raspberry sorbet*

There was a story about Cuban women—well, not a story, but a way of classifying them—which Esmeralda had heard Arnaldo tell. It divided women into three categories: Bananas, Mangos and Coconuts.

Bananas are the tall, thin ones: self-contained one-piece suits without curves to hang on to or blue grottos to navigate. You have to peel them back to eat them, and sometimes they are too green and sometimes too ripe. In either case, it's often hard to tell what you will get beforehand.

Mangos are the best kind because they are sweet and their skin is so thin you can prick it with your front teeth and let the juice run freely in your mouth. Mangos are firm and full of promise. They release all the fragrance of God's dewy earth as soon as you pluck them from the tree and float them on the palm of your hand.

Coconuts, on the other hand, are also good. Coconut women are the ones with round, firm breasts that have never nursed and consequently tremble with milk inside. Coconut women are hard to crack because they tend to be reserved. And, like the fruit, they fall in two distinct categories: the green ones, which are the ones swelling with thick clear milk; and the brown ones, which have no milk but nurse such cool silvery flesh, painted the color of the moon, that even the blade of a dull *machete* can melt their hearts with a single blow.

    —Himilce Novas, *Mangos, Bananas and Coconuts: A Cuban Love Story,*
    New York: Riverhead Books/Putnam, 1997

LATIN AMERICAN FRUITS

Immigrants from Latin America who cherish tastes from home have brought about an exchange of produce between the United States and their home countries, as well as the cultivation on our shores of "exotic" fruits. As a result, the American fruit basket now overflows with an unimaginable variety of subtropical and tropical fruits.

Ackee (also known as *akee* and *achee*)

A common Jamaican fruit, the *ackee* was introduced to the island from West Africa by Captain Bligh in 1793. When fully mature, the bright red and yellow tropical fruit bursts into three sections to reveal three large, shiny, black seeds and creamy white flesh. Canned *ackee* is subject to import restrictions because parts of the fruit are toxic when underripe. *Ackee* is an integral ingredient in one of Jamaica's national dishes known as saltfish and *ackee*. In this dish, the fruit is blended with salt cod, pork, eggs, tomatoes, onions, and green peppers, and served with **breadfruit,** a fruit native to the Pacific that Captain Bligh also introduced to Jamaica. Breadfruit is available fresh in some Latin markets and specialty produce stores.

Chirimoya (also known to English speakers as *cherimoya,* custard apple, and sherbet fruit, and to some Brazilian Americans as *fructa do conde*)

A native of Peru and Ecuador, the *chirimoya,* meaning "cold seeds" in Quechua, an Andean language, belongs to the Annonaceae family, one of the oldest families of New World fruits. In fact, terra-cotta urns fashioned after *chirimoya* have been unearthed at pre-Columbian ruins in Peru. The oval-shaped *chirimoya* grows to about the size of a grapefruit and has dull, olive-colored skin covered with "scales" or "thumbprints" and dark nodules. The cream-colored pulp of the *chirimoya* clings to many large inedible dark brown seeds and tastes like a mildly sweet custard of mango, banana, pineapple, and strawberry, with a hint of vanilla. This fruit is eaten raw (it is best well chilled) or made into ice cream, sorbet, or fruit drinks. In the United States the *chirimoya* is cultivated in Florida and California, but it does not travel well and is available in a limited number of supermarkets and Latin markets from September to May. The green-skinned **sweetsop,** so named for its sugary light yellow flesh, is another member

The olive-colored *chirimoya* (or *cherimoya*) has custardy, off-white flesh that tastes like a blend of pineapple, banana, mango, strawberry, and vanilla.

of the Annonaceae family. The **atemoya** is a hardy hybrid of the sweetsop and the *chirimoya.*

Guanábana (also known to English speakers as soursop)

Native to the West Indies and in the same family as the *chirimoya,* the *guanábana* usually reaches the size of a baseball or softball, and is oval or irregular in shape. This fruit has rough green skin and pure white juicy pulp containing shiny brown seeds. *Guanábana* pulp tastes like bananas but is too tart to eat as is, so it is usually strained and made into delectable fruit drinks, ice cream, sorbet, custards, jams, and jellies. *Guanábana* nectar is sold in Latin markets, particularly those catering to Caribbean Americans.

Guava (also known in English as the common guava and Mexican guava, to Spanish speakers as *guayaba* and to Portuguese speakers as *goiaba*)

In his *The Natural History of the Indies,* published in 1562, the Spaniard Gonzalo Fernández de Oviedo y Valdez wrote of his encounter with the guava: ". . . the fruit is beautiful and appetizing . . . persons who are used to it esteem it as a very good fruit, much better than the apple." The round, oval, or pear-shaped guava, 1 to 4 inches in diameter, still wins praises today, particularly when it is very ripe, yielding an intoxicating perfume and sweet pulp tasting like a cross between a strawberry and a pineapple. The thin, edible skin of the ripe guava may be yellow-green, purple, or red, and its pulp may be off-white, pale yellow, orange, or red, and it is dotted with small seeds. Guavas are often made into jam, jelly, paste, chutney, relish, fruit drinks, ice cream, and sorbet. In the United States the fruit is now grown commercially in Florida, California, and Hawaii, and usually makes it to market only in these states from September through January. Guavas imported from New Zealand are available from March through June.

Mamey (also known as mammee apple and Saint Domingo apricot to English speakers, as *zapote* in Colombia and Central America, and as *zapote mamey* in Venezuela)

The *mamey* is just one of four hundred varieties in the family of *zapotes,* meaning "soft fruit." With its large size and oblong shape, the *mamey* sets itself apart from other *zapotes.* It has leathery brown-yellow or grayish skin with a layer of bitter white fiber underneath, reminiscent of that of an orange or grapefruit. The luscious sweet flesh of the *mamey,* surrounding a large inedible jet-black pit, ranges in color from salmon to red and is eaten raw or cooked.

Mango (known as *manga* to Portuguese speakers)

Called "the apple of the tropics" and the "king of fruits," the mango is cultivated in temperate and subtropical regions, in such places as Mexico, Central and South America, the Caribbean, California, and Florida. The most common varieties of mango for sale in the United States are oval or round in shape, weigh a little less than a pound, and have bright yellow or yellow-green skin, with a blush of orange or crimson. The bright yellow-orange flesh of the mango must be cut away from the large, flat, off-white pit to which it clings. Domestic mangos are available in many large supermarkets and in Latin markets from May to September. During the rest of the year, imported mangos are sold. At its best, the mango is juicy, fragrant, and sweet when ripe, with an extraordinary taste. However, the quality of mangos varies greatly, especially when they are not in season in the United States, and some may appear promising only to reveal an insipid or tart flavor or a turpentine odor. Mangos are worth every ounce of patience, so try again during mango season and choose only those whose stem ends have a pleasant scent.

Papaya (known as *lechosa* in Puerto Rico and Venezuela, *melón papaya* in Mexico, *pawpaw* in Jamaica, *paw paw* in Brazil, and *fruta bomba,* "bomb fruit," in Cuba, since the word "papaya" is Cuban slang for female genitalia)

A New World native that dates back to prehistoric times, papayas may be oblong, oval, or pear-shaped and vary widely in size. The varieties of papaya commonly found in the United States include Hawaiian, Mexican, Strawberry, and Maradol. Most have smooth yellow or orange skin when ripe, and succulent golden yellow, orange, or rose flesh similar in taste to honeydew melon but more intensely flavored. The cavity in the center of the *papaya* is filled with hundreds of tiny grayish black seeds that look like beluga caviar. Though they are edible, the seeds are usually discarded. The juice of the papaya contains a digestive enzyme, papain, that is used in commercial meat tenderizers. Papayas are grown in Florida and Hawaii, and are sold at large supermarkets and Latin groceries sporadically throughout the year, with the summer months yielding the largest crop.

Passion Fruit (known in Brazil as *maracujá* and to Spanish speakers as *granadilla,* except in Venezuela and Puerto Rico, where it is called *parcha* or *parchita,* and in Colombia, where it is known as *maracuyá*)

Passion fruit earned its name not for its reputation as an aphrodisiac, but for markings on its blossoms that Spanish missionaries in the New World thought resembled symbols of the Crucifixion. Over 400 varieties of passion fruit in all shapes and sizes have been identified. Two common varieties—the purple passion fruit and the yellow passion fruit—are the size of plums. Both varieties have leathery skin, which becomes brittle

Ripe passion fruit, with its sweet-tart golden pulp beneath dimpled, leathery skin

and dimpled when the fruit is ripe, and liquidy golden pulp dotted with small, shiny, black edible seeds that resemble the collapsed eggs of salmon caviar. The pulp has a sweet and tart flavor and a tropical perfume. A native of the Amazon, passion fruit is now cultivated in California, Hawaii, and Florida, and can be found in some large supermarkets and Latin markets sporadically throughout the year except in the month of June. Frozen passion fruit pulp is also available at Latin and Asian markets.

Prickly Pear (known also as cactus pear, barbary fig, Indian pear, and Indian fig, and to Spanish speakers as *tuna*)

A native of the American Southwest and Mexico, the prickly-pear cactus bears fruit, called prickly pears, that are classified as berries, not pears. The ripe prickly pear is the size and shape of a chicken egg, with skin shaded green to red. It is covered with fine hairs, nearly invisible to the naked eye, that may become imbedded in the skin, causing irritation, and thus the fruit must be handled carefully. Luckily most of the prickly pears on sale in U.S. markets have had these hairs removed. The soft yellow, pink, or crimson pulp of the prickly pear has a mildly sweet taste, with hints of watermelon, pomegranates, strawberries, and cherries. The pulp is dotted with small black seeds that are edible but are usually removed. This fruit is sold in some large supermarkets and in Latin grocery stores from September to December. In California and the Southwest,

Prickly pears, or *tunas*, the fruit of the nopal (prickly-pear) cactus, have a sweet, mellow flavor akin to that of watermelon.

fans of the fruit pick, with gloved hands, the ripe prickly pears they find growing along the roadside, carefully maneuvering around the sharp spines of the prickly-pear cactus.

Sapodilla (also known as naseberry and dilly in the English Caribbean, as *níspero* in Venezuela, Colombia, and Central America, and as *chicozapote* in Mexico)

A native of the Yucatán Peninsula and Central America and a relative of the *zapotes,* the brown-skinned *sapodilla* varies greatly in size and shape. The creamy flesh of the ripe *sapodilla* ranges in color from yellow to reddish brown. The fruit has a delicious sweet taste, once described as "a pear dipped in brown sugar." Before indulging, be sure to remove the few glossy seeds of the *sapodilla* first, for they have small hooks on the ends. Americans are more familiar with the *sapodilla* tree than they might imagine. Following a process perfected over many centuries by the Maya of Central America, the sap of the tree is boiled until it thickens and is then molded into blocks of *chicle,* the rubbery main ingredient in chewing gum.

MOST LATIN DRINKS ARE MADE
WITH TWO OUT OF THREE KEY
INGREDIENTS: FRUIT, MILK,
AND RUM. IT'S FROM THE VARI-
OUS COMBINATIONS THEREOF
THAT MANY DELICIOUS LIBA-
TIONS ARE CREATED

DRINKS

TROPICAL FRUIT SHAKES

*Vitaminas, frescos, refrescos, jugos, batidos,
batidas y licuados*

While Americans of Latin American descent share the universal love of eating fruits in their natural state, they are also mad about tropical fruit shakes, which nowadays they make at home in a blender or order in Latin American restaurants or at fruit stands in barrios or Latino neighborhoods. These shakes carry an assortment of names, such as *vitaminas, frescos, refrescos, jugos, batidos, batidas,* and *licuados,* depending on the Latin American country represented, but they are all made with a base of milk (and occasionally water) and one or more of an array of tropical fruits. Pineapple, banana, mango, papaya, guava, avocado, coconut, passion fruit, *guanábana, chirimoya,* and *mamey* are much appreciated, as are fruits that are impossible to obtain fresh in the United States, such as the *lulo* or *naranjilla* from the Andes. Colombian Americans and Brazilian Americans relish avocado milk shakes made with fresh milk and sugar, an unsavory combination to most other Americans of Latin American descent. Puerto Ricans traditionally do not blend their fruit shakes, which they call *jugos.* Instead, they squeeze the juice from the pulp of a fruit and mix it by hand with evaporated milk (testimony to the time when fresh milk was unavailable), water, sugar, and a few drops of vanilla extract.

CUBAN AMERICAN
MANGO MILK SHAKE

Batido de mango al estilo cubano-americano

In his book entitled *Going to Miami: Exiles, Tourists, and Refugees in the New America,* David Rieff speaks of his childhood encounters with Cuban Americans in New York City: "I think I have always known Cubans. As a latchkey kid on the West Side of New York, I owed much of my security to the benign (and quite innocent) attentions of the two natty queens from next door, who used to appear almost magically and whisk me away to a Cuban restaurant on Amsterdam Avenue for those thick trop-

ical milk shakes called *batidos*. As I slurped my *mamey,* papaya, or mango shake (I remember thinking, the first time I encountered good old American strawberry, that there had been some terrible mistake), one or other of the men would feed dimes into the jukebox. They liked to play Nat 'King' Cole's version of 'Hit the Road, Jack.'"

This traditional Cuban mango shake has a lush tropical taste and aroma, and is frothy and filling. It takes only minutes to prepare in the blender.

3 medium or 2 large ripe mangos	½ cup crushed ice
2 cups milk	
2 tablespoons granulated sugar, or to taste	

Cut the mangos in half, peel off the skin with a sharp paring knife, and slice the flesh away from the pits. Combine all the ingredients in a blender and purée until smooth. Test the shake for sweetness and add more sugar, if desired, puréeing a few seconds more. Pour the mango milk shake into glasses and serve at once.

Makes four 8-ounce servings

PANAMANIAN AMERICAN PAPAYA SHAKE WITH VANILLA ICE CREAM

Batido de papaya con helado de vainilla al estilo panameño-americano

Papayas are available virtually year-round in southern California, so we like to make this shake in the late fall and early winter, when the days are short but warm and the winter rains have not yet begun. It is very creamy, thick, and delicious as is, and can be served with or without vanilla ice cream.

This recipe calls for less sugar than is in a traditional Panamanian *batido*. We find that by substituting lowfat evaporated milk or evaporated skim milk for the regular evaporated milk, we sacrifice little in the way of taste and consistency.

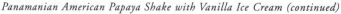

Panamanian American Papaya Shake with Vanilla Ice Cream (continued)

1 ¼ **pounds ripe papaya, any variety**	¼ **teaspoon salt**
1 **cup evaporated milk**	1 **cup crushed ice**
¼ **cup granulated sugar, or to taste**	1 **pint vanilla ice cream (optional)**

Slice the papaya or papayas in half, scoop out the seeds, cut the thin skin off the fruit with a paring knife, and slice the flesh into 1-inch chunks. Place the papaya chunks, evaporated milk, sugar, salt, and ice in a blender, and purée until smooth. Test the shake for sweetness and add more sugar if necessary, blending a few seconds more. Pour the papaya shake into glasses and top with a scoop of vanilla ice cream, if desired. Serve immediately.

Makes four 8-ounce servings

MEXICAN AMERICAN GUAVA MILK SHAKE

Licuado de guayaba y leche al estilo
mexicano-americano

In our opinion this is one of the best—and easiest—ways to enjoy the guava.

4 **medium ripe guavas**	1 **tablespoon granulated sugar,**
2 **cups milk**	**or to taste**

Cut the guavas in half and scoop the flesh into a blender, taking care to remove the seeds. Pour the milk and sugar into the blender and purée until smooth. Test the shake for sweetness and add more sugar if necessary, puréeing again for a few seconds. Pour the shake into glasses and serve at once.

Makes four 8-ounce servings

CHILEAN AMERICAN *CHIRIMOYA* AND BANANA MILK SHAKE

Batido de chirimoya y plátano al estilo chileño-americano

This shake has a marvelous silky texture, thanks to the banana. The flavors of the fruit marry beautifully. It is almost as delicious made with milk, if you are watching your waistline.

I large ripe *chirimoya*	2 cups half-and-half
I tablespoon fresh lemon juice	3 tablespoons granulated sugar,
I medium ripe banana	or to taste

Peel the *chirimoya,* cut it in half, remove the core, and cut the flesh into 1-inch chunks, eliminating the seeds. Sprinkle the lemon juice over the *chirimoya* chunks and toss them so that all the chunks are coated with the juice. Peel the banana and cut it into 4 pieces. Place the banana pieces and the *chirimoya* chunks in a blender and purée until smooth. Then add the half-and-half and sugar to the blender, and purée until the ingredients are blended. Pour the shake into glasses and serve immediately.

Makes four 8-ounce servings

JAMAICAN AMERICAN BANANA–ALLSPICE MILK SHAKE

This creamy milk shake sees us through the winter months when other tropical fruits are absent in the markets or not in peak shape. Banana shakes can be made without the ice cream with wonderful results, but vanilla ice cream and bananas are such a comforting and nostalgic pair that it is hard to resist. Sprinkle a little fragrant allspice—a spice native to Jamaica—on top to get in the island mood.

Jamaican American Banana-Allspice Milk Shake (continued)

3 ripe medium bananas
2 cups milk
½ pint vanilla ice cream
**1 tablespoon granulated sugar,
   or to taste**

**¼ teaspoon ground allspice, plus extra
   for sprinkling**

Peel the bananas and cut each in half. Place the banana halves, the milk, ice cream, sugar, and allspice in an electric blender, and purée until smooth. Test the shake for sweetness and add more sugar if necessary, then process a few seconds more. Pour the banana shake into glasses, sprinkle with additional allspice, and serve at once.

Makes four 8-ounce servings

COLOMBIAN AMERICAN AVOCADO MILK SHAKE

Fresco de aguacate al estilo colombiano-americano

I f you are an avocado fan, this milk shake's for you. Use only the finest-quality Hass avocados, as their flesh is creamier and tastier than that of Fuerte avocados.

1 ripe medium Hass avocado
3 cups milk

¼ cup granulated sugar, or to taste

Cut the avocado in half, remove the pit, and spoon the avocado flesh into a blender. Add the milk and sugar, and purée until smooth. Test the shake for sweetness and add more sugar, if desired, blending a few more seconds. Pour the avocado shake into glasses and serve at once.

Makes four 8-ounce servings

NEW MEXICAN HOT CHOCOLATE

Chocolate estilo Nuevo México

While etymologists still speculate about the origins of the word "*chocolate*," some attributing it to the Aztec *xocoatl,* meaning "bitter water," historians are quite certain that the first hot chocolate was served in pre-Columbian Mexico. In those days the cocoa bean was worth its weight in gold, and thus the nobility of Mexico alone partook of *chocolatl,* hot chocolate—then an aromatic unsweetened drink of ground cocoa beans, spices, and hot water. It is believed that the Aztec emperor Montezuma coveted hot chocolate for its aphrodisiacal qualities and in pursuit of passion drank 50 goblets of the rich beverage each day.

Before it was introduced in the United States, chocolate first made its way to Europe in the 1500s, where it lost its spice and became a fashionable drink and confection. In the mid-1600s the Dutch sent chocolate to the American colonies, and by the late 1760s Americans were manufacturing chocolate as a "European" luxury whose roots in Mexico were long forgotten. The Swiss and the Belgians first perfected the process of making milk chocolate and then created chocolate-filled and chocolate-covered candies in the latter half of the nineteenth century. Since that time Swiss and Belgian chocolates have been appraised as the world's finest.

While most Americans find satisfaction in hot chocolate without spice, Mexican Americans in New Mexico and elsewhere enjoy an aromatic, cinnamony cup that is closer to the drink Montezuma so relished. Rather than mixing cocoa, sugar, and spices, many make hot chocolate from special chocolate imported from Mexico, which is already sweetened and flavored with cinnamon, cloves, and ground almonds, and is usually formed into tablets. Ibarra and Abuelita are two of the most popular brands of Mexican chocolate sold in the United States, and they are available in Mexican and Pan-Latin grocery stores and some supermarkets, particularly in the Southwest, California, and Texas. Since Mexican chocolate is not sold everywhere, we offer a recipe for New Mexican Hot Chocolate made with unsweetened cocoa, sugar, and cinnamon.

½ cup water
⅓ cup fine-quality Dutch-process
   (European-style) unsweetened cocoa,
   such as Bensdorp, Droste, or
   Ghirardelli
½ cup granulated sugar

½ teaspoon ground cinnamon
4 cups milk
1 teaspoon vanilla extract
4 cinnamon sticks, for garnish

Heat the water to boiling in a large saucepan over medium-high heat. Add the cocoa, sugar, and cinnamon, and cook, stirring constantly, until the mixture is smooth. Add the milk and bring the hot chocolate to a boil, stirring constantly. Remove the saucepan from the heat and stir in the vanilla extract.

Beat the hot chocolate, either in the saucepan or in a large mixing bowl, with a portable electric mixer, a rotary eggbeater, a wire whisk, or a *molinillo* (a Mexican wooden chocolate beater) until it is frothy. Serve at once with a cinnamon stick in each cup.

Serves 4

HOT CHOCOLATE AND COCONUT

Chocolate con leche de coco

If you love creamy chocolate-coconut clusters, chewy chocolate-dipped or chocolate-chip coconut macaroons, Almond Joys and Mars Bars, or any confection for that matter with chocolate and coconut, Hot Chocolate and Coconut is sure to delight. This cocoa drink was brought to the United States by Colombian immigrants of the Pacific coast region of Colombia, where coconut finds its way into myriad savory and sweet dishes, particularly those featuring meat, poultry, seafood, and rice.

1½ cups canned unsweetened
    coconut milk
⅓ cup fine-quality Dutch-process
    (European-style) unsweetened cocoa,
    such as Bensdorp, Droste, or
    Ghirardelli

½ cup granulated sugar
3 cups milk

Heat the coconut milk, stirring constantly, in a large saucepan over medium heat, but do not let it boil. Whisk in the cocoa and the sugar, until dissolved. Pour in the milk and heat the hot chocolate, stirring constantly, but do not let it boil. Serve at once.

Serves 4

GUATEMALAN AMERICAN COFFEE WITH HOT CHOCOLATE AND CINNAMON

Champurrado

It is a toss-up as to whether this rich and creamy hot drink should be described as coffee with hot chocolate or hot chocolate with coffee. This is a perennial favorite among Guatemalan Americans with ties to their ancestral cuisine, who use chocolate in unexpected ways to transform the ordinary into the sublime. Pass around a plate of Scotch shortbread, biscotti, or another mildly sweet cookie with Guatemalan American Coffee with Hot Chocolate and Cinnamon.

½ cup granulated sugar
1 tablespoon cornstarch
2 squares (2 ounces) unsweetened
   baking chocolate, broken into pieces
3 cups hot milk
2 cups hot best-quality coffee,
   freshly brewed

1 teaspoon ground cinnamon
½ teaspoon vanilla extract
Pinch of salt
Whipped cream, for garnish
Ground cinnamon, for dusting

Mix together the sugar and cornstarch. Melt the chocolate pieces in the top of a 1½- or 2-quart double boiler over hot, but not boiling, water. Gradually stir in the sugar-cornstarch mixture to make a thick paste.

Add the hot milk, hot coffee, cinnamon, vanilla extract, and salt, and stir until the chocolate-sugar paste dissolves. Cook over low heat, stirring occasionally, until the drink thickens, about 30 minutes.

Pour the coffee with hot chocolate into 4 mugs, garnish with whipped cream and dust with cinnamon, and serve at once.

Makes four 8-ounce servings

JAMAICAN SORREL RUM PUNCH

This scarlet-colored punch gets its spicy aroma from fresh ginger and cloves and its subtle tanginess and vibrant hue from the dried calyxes of a tropical flower known to Caribbean Americans as sorrel (not to be confused with the perennial herb by the same name that resembles spinach) and to Mexican Americans as *flor de Jamaica, Jamaica,* and hibiscus. (It is what makes Red Zinger tea crimson.) The most common use of sorrel in the Latin kitchen is in making iced tea (known to Mexican Americans as *agua de Jamaica,* which is a staple on menus in authentic Mexican restaurants). The dried calyxes (the leafy parts that enfold the flower before it blooms) are steeped in boiling water, which is then strained and sweetened with sugar. Ginger, cloves, or cinnamon are occasionally boiled with the sorrel to add another flavor dimension to the tea. Sorrel iced tea flavored with ginger and cloves is the basis for Jamaican Sorrel Rum Punch, a favorite summertime drink of many Americans of Jamaican descent. The tea is strained into a pitcher, and then all that is added is dark rum. Lime and orange slices are floated on the punch for color.

Sorrel is sold under the names sorrel, *flor de Jamaica* and *Jamaica,* roselle or rosella in Latin markets, and as Jamaica flowers, Jamaica sorrel, roselle, rosella, or hibiscus in health food stores in the United States. It will keep for up to a year if stored in an airtight container in a cool, dry place.

6 cups water	¾ cup granulated sugar
2 cups (about 2¼ ounces) dried sorrel	1½ cups dark rum
2 ounces gingerroot, peeled and cut into ½-inch chunks	Ice cubes
	Lime and orange slices, for garnish
2 whole cloves	

Bring 5 cups of the water to a boil in a large saucepan. Remove the saucepan from the heat and stir in the sorrel, gingerroot, and cloves. Allow the mixture to steep for at least 4 hours.

Bring the remaining 1 cup water and the sugar to a boil in a small saucepan over medium heat. Boil, stirring constantly, until the sugar dissolves. Remove the sugar syrup from the heat and let it cool to room temperature.

Pour the sorrel mixture through a fine strainer into a pitcher. Stir in the sugar syrup, rum, and ice cubes. Garnish the punch with lime and orange slices and serve.

Makes about 2 quarts

YERBA MATÉ ICED TEA

Maté tetre

Tea seems to have taken a backseat to coffee in this era of tall café lattes and iced mocha javas, yet for many it marks the dawning of each new day. Countless Argentine, Uruguayan, Paraguayan, Chilean, and Brazilian Americans, especially of the first generation, prefer *Yerba maté* (also called Paraguayan tea) over Chinese or Indian teas. It is an aromatic caffeinated tea made from the pulverized leaves of the *Ilex paraguayensis,* a holly tree of South America. In South America the brew is poured into a small gourd and sipped through a wooden or metal straw called a *bombilla,* but in America most make do with a tea cup—and not just at breakfast time but all through the day. *Yerba maté* is packed with minerals and vitamins, and some have such faith in its restorative powers that they tote thermoses of hot and cold tea everywhere they go—shopping malls, airports, dentist's offices—just the way countless Californians carry their water bottles filled with Evian and other brands of filtered water.

Yerba maté has quite a following among the health conscious, Latin and not, in the United States, and loose tea and tea bags imported from Paraguay are sold in many health food stores, as well as in South American markets. This recipe is for iced *Yerba maté,* but if you prefer the tea hot, just let it steep in the teapot for 5 minutes, pour it through a fine strainer into tea cups, and serve plain (*maté amargo*), or with lemon slices or milk or cream, and sugar or honey (*maté dulce*). Like all tea leaves, *yerba maté* should be kept in an airtight container in a dark, cool, dry place. It can be stored for up to a year.

4 tablespoons *yerba maté* leaves	Granulated sugar, to taste
4 cups boiling water	4 lemon or lime wedges

Fill a kettle with fresh cold water and bring it to a rolling boil. Warm a teapot by swirling a little boiling water in it. Discard the water in the teapot and then put in the tea leaves. Add 4 cups boiling water. Cover and allow the tea to cool completely.

Pour the tea through a fine strainer into each of 4 tall ice-filled glasses. Serve with sugar and a wedge of lemon or lime perched on the top of each glass.

Serves 4

PISCO SOUR

Pisco agrio

Pisco is Peruvian brandy that bears a close resemblance to Italian grappa. It is made from Muscat grapes that are aged in containers lined with paraffin rather than in oak vessels, so that it does not imbibe the flavor or color of wood. Although local brands of *pisco* are produced throughout South America, Peru is considered *pisco* country, and the world's most celebrated *pisco* cocktail is the Peruvian *Pisco* Sour. This cocktail has a strong following among Americans of South American descent, particularly Peruvian, Chilean, and Bolivian Americans, some of whom rely on grappa if they cannot get their hands on *pisco*.

Imported *pisco*, with brand names such as Inca Pisco, Don César, and Pisco Control, are available in specialty liquor stores in the United States. If you cannot find *pisco* locally, order it by mail from one of the specialty liquor stores in the United States that ships (see Sources, page 308).

1½ ounces *pisco*, or grappa in a pinch	6 ice cubes
1 teaspoon egg white	A few drops of Angostura bitters
1 teaspoon superfine sugar	
2 teaspoons freshly squeezed lime or lemon juice	

Place all the ingredients except for the Angostura bitters into a cocktail shaker. Shake vigorously and then strain the cocktail into a chilled whiskey-sour glass. Sprinkle the Angostura bitters on top and serve at once.

Serves 1

For Bolivian *Pisco* and Orange Juice (*Yungueño*): Place 1½ ounces *pisco* or Italian grappa, 1½ ounces orange juice, ¼ teaspoon superfine sugar, and 2 or 3 ice cubes in a cocktail shaker. Shake vigorously and pour, without straining, into a cocktail glass. Serves 1

CACHAÇA AND LIME COCKTAIL

Caipirinha

Cachaça is a potent Brazilian rumlike liquor distilled from the sap of fermented sugarcane, which tastes like Haitian raw white rum and the white lightning of the American South. The more refined *cachaças* are also known as *aguardente de cana* (sugarcane brandy), and indeed they taste more like brandy than rum. Brazilians and Brazilian Americans swear by the restorative powers of *cachaça* to such a degree that many women drink *cachimbo,* a beverage made from *cachaça* and honey, just after giving birth. The liquor is so dear to Brazilians that when they speak colloquially about a passion or hobby, they refer to it as their *cachaça.*

Cachaça is served straight or with fruit juices in what are called *batidas* (not to be confused with the nonalcoholic ones), or sometimes it is paired with pieces of fruit in quite a number of Brazilian cocktails. Perhaps the most popular of the *cachaça* cocktails is the *Caipirinha,* literally the "little hillbilly," traditionally an unstrained cocktail featuring *cachaça,* sugar, and lime, rind and all. Nowadays Brazilian Americans are experimenting with other fruits in place of lime in their *caipirinhas*—oranges, tangerines, and grapefruits, and even grapes, mangos, and pineapple chunks also find their way into the drink.

Cachaça is just gaining in popularity among Americans with no Latin American roots, and thus imported Brazilian brands of *cachaça,* such as *Pitú* (Crayfish), *Nêga Fulô* (Young Slave), and *Blanca Fulô* (White Slave), are still available only in select liquor stores in the United States (see Sources, page 308). If you don't have *cachaça* on hand, substitute an equal amount of your favorite white rum in this recipe to make the Brazilian cocktail *Caipirissima,* or try a *Caipiroska,* the same drink prepared with vodka instead of *cachaça.*

½ fresh lime, or an equal amount of
   another citrus fruit
1 tablespoon superfine sugar

2 ounces *cachaça* or white rum or vodka
½ cup crushed ice

Cut the ½ lime into 2 wedges and squeeze the juice from the wedges into a small bowl. Slice the squeezed wedges crosswise into ¼-inch pieces. Combine the lime juice, lime pieces, sugar, *cachaça* (or white rum or vodka), and ice in a cocktail shaker. Shake vigorously until all the ingredients are blended. Pour the *Caipirinha* (or *Caipirissima* or *Caipiroska*), unstrained, into a cocktail glass and serve.

Serves 1

PUERTO RICAN COCONUT EGGNOG

Coquito

Puerto Ricans on the island and the U.S. mainland ring in the Feast of the Patron Saints and Christmas with *Coquito,* a scrumptious coconut-flavored eggnog. The traditional method of preparing the coconut milk that goes into *Coquito* entails cracking a whole ripe coconut into several pieces with a hammer to expose the coconut meat. The meat is then shredded with a hand grater or in a food processor, soaked in water, and then wrung in cheesecloth to extract the coconut milk. In the name of convenience and oftentimes necessity, many Puerto Ricans on the mainland have broken away from tradition and make their coconut milk for *Coquito* with packaged unsweetened shredded or flaked coconut and water. Still others take the easiest route of all and use canned coconut milk.

In this recipe we take the middle road and make the coconut milk from packaged coconut, but if you enjoy the art of opening coconuts, use 1 medium coconut, which will yield approximately 3 to 4 cups shredded or flaked coconut. If you do not wish to make the coconut milk, simply skip the first step of this recipe and substitute 1 cup canned unsweetened coconut milk in the second step.

**3 cups packaged unsweetened shredded
  or flaked coconut**
I cup hot water
I cup sweetened condensed milk
**I cup Puerto Rican white rum, such as
  Bacardi, or your favorite variety**

2 large egg yolks*
**Ground cinnamon or nutmeg,
  for garnish**

* If you are concerned about salmonella in raw eggs, substitute a pasteurized egg blend.

Combine the coconut and hot water in a large pitcher, and let the coconut steep for 10 minutes. Strain the liquid into a blender. Put the coconut pulp in a cheesecloth and squeeze it to extract as much coconut milk as possible, then add the extracted milk to the coconut milk in the blender. Discard the coconut pulp.

Add the condensed milk, rum, and egg yolks to the coconut milk in the blender, and process until the *Coquito* is well blended. Transfer the beverage to the pitcher, cover, and refrigerate it for at least 2 hours. Take the *Coquito* out of the refrigerator about 30 minutes before serving. When ready, stir it thoroughly and pour the *Coquito* into short glasses and add a dusting of cinnamon or nutmeg.

Serves 8

MOJITO

Mojito

This quintessential Cuban cocktail, flavored with fresh mint, was loved by Ernest Hemingway, who had a preference for the *mojitos* served at La Bodeguita del Medio, a restaurant in Old Havana. The *Mojito,* along with other legendary Cuban cocktails, like the *Cuba libre,* the *Periodista,* and the *Presidente,* remains a favorite among Cuban Americans in Miami, New York, L.A., and in between.

Juice of ½ lime
1 teaspoon granulated sugar
2 or 3 fresh mint leaves and 1 sprig of
  mint, for garnish

Crushed ice
1 ½ ounces white rum
Club soda

Stir the lime juice and sugar in a tall drink glass until the sugar dissolves. Add the mint leaves, the crushed ice, and the rum, then stir. Top off the drink with club soda. Stir again, garnish with the sprig of mint and serve.

Serves 1

SOURCES

Listed here are select retail stores and mail-order companies that carry Latin American products. (The number of Latin American establishments in the United States is tremendous, so this list is by no means exhaustive.) Those retail stores with no mail-order service (marked with an asterisk) are worth a visit if you are in the vicinity. Also note that if you live in an area where a particular Latin American group is well represented, local supermarkets may have a specialty section catering to that group.

MEXICAN

CHILES, SALSAS, HOT SAUCES

Colorado Spice
5030 Nome Street, Unit A
Denver, CO 80239
(800) 67-SPICE (800-677-7423)
FAX (303) 373-9215
TDD (For Hearing Impaired) (303) 373-2844

Mail-order company that carries *achiote* paste; dried chiles, such as the habanero, pasilla, ancho, and pequín; Caribbean hot sauces and chutneys; and exotic items, such as buffalo meat and elk seasoning. AMEX, VISA, MC, DC. Free catalog.

The Chile Shop
109 E. Water Street
Santa Fe, NM 87501
(505) 983-6080
FAX (505) 984-0737

Retail shop with mail-order service that sells salsas, dried whole and ground chiles, such as the ancho, chipotle, habanero, pasilla, pequín, tepín, and the New Mexico green and red, as well as jellies, mole, *achiote* paste, chile *ristras* and wreaths, and gourmet gift boxes. VISA, MC. Free catalog.

Coyote Cafe General Store
132 W. Water Street
Santa Fe, NM 87501
(800) 866-HOWL (800-866-4695)
FAX (505) 989-9026

Retail shop with mail order that carries whole and ground dried chiles, its own line of Southwest products that includes Tomatillo Serrano Salsa, New Mexico Red Chile Honey, and our favorite spread, Habanero Peach Preserves. Gift baskets and a Salsa of the Month Club. AMEX, VISA, MC, DC. Free Catalog.

A delivery truck for L.A.'s Liborio Markets, the Zabar's of the Pan-Latin set

Los Chileros de Nuevo Mexico
P.O. Box 6215
Santa Fe, NM 87502
(505) 471-6967
FAX (505) 473-7306

Mail-order company that ships fresh New Mexico chiles in season and frozen ones year-round, dried chiles, other typical Southwestern ingredients, and gift baskets. Cash, check, or money order only. Brochure available.

Salsa Express
P.O. Box 3985
Albuquerque, NM 87190
(800)-43-SALSA (800-437-2572)

Mail-order company that carries salsas, hot sauces, habanero pecan brittle, and chile peanut butter. They ship frozen *chiles rellenos* and green-chile-and-cheese tamales overnight. AMEX, VISA, MC, DC. Free catalog.

Santa Fe School of Cooking
116 West San Francisco Street
Santa Fe, NM 87501
(505) 983-4511
FAX (505) 983-7540

Cooking school and retail store with mail-order service that carries fresh New Mexican chiles (in season), dried chiles, white and blue *posole, piloncillo,* heirloom beans, tortilla presses, *molcajetes,* gift baskets, and much more. They also carry seeds for more than 21 varities of chiles, from the exotic to the popular New Mexico chile. AMEX, VISA, MC. Free catalog and cooking class schedule.

Kitchen Food Shop
218 Eighth Avenue
New York, NY 10011
(212) 243-4433

One of the few Mexican take-out places in New York City (and it has mail order), and one of the city's best sources for dried and fresh chiles, including chipotles, pasillas, and smoked jalapeños. Cash, check, or money order only.

The El Paso Chile Company
909 Texas Avenue
El Paso, TX 79901
(800) 274-7468
(915) 544-3434
FAX (915) 544-7552

Mail-order company that stocks whole and ground dried chiles (ancho, chipotle, New Mexico red, habanero, pasilla, pequín, de árbol), as well as pickled serrano and pequín chiles, chipotles in *adobo,* mole, *nopalitos,* salsas, barbecue sauces, bean dips, New Mexican–Italian Chipotle Chile and Basil Pesto, gift boxes, and more. AMEX, VISA, MC. Free catalog.

La Casa de Gourmet
514 West Commerce
San Antonio, TX 78207
(800) 972-3049
(210) 223-3047

Retail store and mail-order company that sells salsas, hot sauces, spice blends, dried chiles, mole, Mexican chocolate, *menudo* mix, taco fryers, *molcajetes,* and more. AMEX, VISA, MC, DC. Free brochure.

CORNMEAL, MASA, AND TORTILLAS

St. Mary's Mexican Food
1030 West St. Mary's Road
Tucson, AZ 85745
(520) 884-1629

Mexican restaurant that ships tortillas and tamales by Federal Express and UPS. Cash, check, or money order only.

Gallegos Brothers*
1424 Broadway
Santa Monica, CA 90404
(310) 395-0162

Family-owned Mexican *tortillería* that sells tortillas hot off the press, *masa preparada* for tamales, homemade salsas, chorizo, and Mexican cheeses, such as *asadero, cotija,* and *Oaxaca.* They also prepare *tortas,* soft tacos, and burritos for takeout.

Léona's de Chimayó
P.O. Box 579
Chimayó, NM 87522
(505) 351-4660 or (800) 4-LEONAS
FAX (505) 351-2189

Léona Medina-Tiede, the founder of this market with mail-order service, is famous far and wide for her vegetarian tamales and unique, flavored flour tortillas (blueberry, chocolate, jalapeño, garlic, pesto, and more). Look for her products in specialty markets and supermarkets in the Midwest, Southeast, Southwest, and West. Chimayó is such a tiny village that Leona's doesn't have (or need) a street address, so if you want to visit, pick up Highway 76 at Española (north of Santa Fe) and go 8 miles to the Manzana Center in Chimayó. You can't miss Léona's. VISA, MC. Free brochure.

Luna's Tortilla Factory
1615 McKinney Avenue
Dallas, TX 75202
(214) 747-2661
Retail store that sells *masa preparada* for tortillas and tamales, and many kinds of tamales and tortillas. Luna's will ship tortillas. Cash, check, or money order only.

MEXICAN AMERICAN SUPERMARKETS

Grand Central Market*
317 South Broadway
Los Angeles, CA 90013

The vendors at this enormous market in downtown L.A. carry a vast array of Mexican products, including mountains of ground dried red chile, as well as Guatemalan and Salvadoran foodstuffs. At Ana María's stall, sample some of the tastiest *gorditas,* stuffed corn cakes, in all of L.A.

La Casa del Pueblo*
1810 South Blue Island
Chicago, IL 60608
(312) 421-4640

Retail store that sells just about everything for the Mexican kitchen.

Hernandez Mexican Foods*
2120 Alamo Street
Dallas, TX 75202
(214) 742-2533

Since 1918 this retail store has been a great source for Mexican foodstuffs, meats, and medicinal herbs. They also carry prepared dishes like *carnitas* and tamales for takeout and can supply large quantities for parties. (They ship some products on request, but do not have a mail-order department.) Cash, check, or money order only.

The following supermarket chains carry Mexican products:

Vons, Albertson's, and Boys Markets in California
Tianguis in the Los Angeles area
Fiesta Mart in Texas
Safeway Supermarket in Colorado and Arizona
Cedanos Supermarket in Miami
Jewel and Dominics Supermarkets in the Chicago metropolitan area

CENTRAL AND SOUTH AMERICAN
STAPLES

Los Gauchitos*
4315 Northwest 7th Street
Miami, FL 33126
(305) 447-4651

Argentine and Uruguayan restaurant with attached pastry shop and market that carries an array of meats and sausages for the South American grill, homemade ravioli, breads, and sweets, as well as South American wines and other imported products.

International Market*
365 Somerville Avenue
Somerville, MA 02143
(617) 776-1880

Brazilian American market that carries Brazilian staples such as *carne seca,* fruit concentrates, manioc (*yuca*), and malagueta chiles.

Casa America*
102-04 Roosevelt Avenue
Jackson Heights, NY 11372
no phone

Retail market that stocks Colombian fruits and dry ingredients such as *yuca harina* (*yuca* flour).

Coisa Nossa
46 West 46th Street
New York, NY 10036
(212) 719-4779

Brazilian American grocery with mail-order service that sells staples such as passion fruit juice, guava paste, manioc (*yuca*), Brazilian sausage, *carne seca* (a dried Brazilian beef), as well as ingredients for *feijoada,* Brazil's national dish. Cash, check, or money order only.

La Gran Habana Carnicería*
76-17 Roosevelt Avenue
Jackson Heights, NY 11372
no phone

Meat market that sells Ecuadoran, Colombian, and Bolivian goods.

Los Paisanos*
79-16 Roosevelt Avenue
Jackson Heights, NY 11372
(718) 898-4141

Retail store that carries typical Ecuadoran, Peruvian and Colombian, as well as Central American and Mexican, products.

CARIBBEAN

Vernon's Jerk Paradise
987 E. 233rd Street
Bronx, NY 10466
(407) 726-0491 (for mail order)
(718) 655-8348 (for the restaurant)

Allan Vernon, known far and wide as the King of Jerk, has prepared his irresistible Jamaican jerk chicken and jerk pork for New Yorkers for over a decade. He ships his famous Vernon's Jamaican Jerk Sauce and Vernon's Seasoned Jamaican Curry. VISA, DC.

Isla
P.O. Box 9112
San Juan, PR 00908-0112
(800) 575-4752
FAX (787) 723-2942

Mail-order company that carries a selection of Puerto Rican ingredients, such as *recaíto, sofrito, adobo de ajo, pique criollo,* and guava jelly. AMEX, VISA, MC. Free catalog.

The following supermarket chains carry Caribbean products:
Food Emporium and Sloan's in New York City
Winn Dixie in Florida

See also Liborio Markets, Rafal Spice Company, and Tropicana Market under Pan-Latin.

PAN-LATIN

Casa Lucas Market*
2934 24th Street
San Francisco, CA 94110
(415) 826-4334

Retail store that sells a wide range of Mexican and Central American goods, including fruits and vegetables, as well as some South American products.

Catalina's Market*
1070 Northwestern Avenue
Santa Monica, CA 90029
(213) 461-2535

Retail market (with no official mail-order service, but will ship) that carries Mexican, Central American, and South American products, particularly Argentine and Peruvian. Peruvian foodstuffs include whole or pulverized purple corn, *choclo* (giant white corn), chiles such as the ají and Peruvian, and *chuños* (freeze-dried potatoes). VISA, MC, DC.

Continental Gourmet*
12921 S. Prairie Avenue
Hawthorne, CA 90250
(310) 676-5444

Retail market that carries Mexican, and Central and South American foodstuffs, including fresh meats cut for the Argentine *parrillada,* Argentine-style chorizo, Argentine *cotija* cheese, the Brazilian dried beef *carne seca,* and an array of South American sweets and wines.

Frieda's, Inc.
4465 Corporate Center Drive
Los Alamitos, CA 90720
(800) 241-1771
(714) 826-6100
FAX (714) 816-0273
www.friedas.com

Mail-order company that carries myriad fruits and vegetables used in Latin American cooking, such as *chirimoyas,* papaya, mango, passion fruit, *yuca, malanga,* jicama, *yacón, mashua,* and chayotes, as well as corn husks, dried and fresh chiles, and gift baskets. AMEX, VISA, MC, OPTIMA. Free catalog.

Liborio Markets*
864 S. Vermont Avenue
Los Angeles, CA 90005
(213) 386-1458
and
6061 Atlantic Boulevard
Maywood, CA 90270
(213) 560-8000

Retail markets that carry a whole spectrum of Latin American products, from Caribbean staples like *yuca* and *achiote* seeds to Peruvian *chuños* (dried potatoes), Salvadoran *loroco* (flower buds) for *pupusas,* and key Brazilian products such as *dendê* oil and *farofa.*

Rafal Spice Company
2521 Russell Street
Detroit, MI 48207
(800) 228-4276
(313) 259-6373

This retail store with mail-order service carries Caribbean, Mexican, and Central and South American spices. VISA, MC, DC. Free catalog.

Dean & Deluca
560 Broadway
New York, NY 10012
(800) 221-7714
(212) 431-1691
FAX (212) 334-6183

Gourmet food shop with a mail-order department that offers a selection of fresh and dried chiles (anchos, chipotles, de árbol, pasillas, pequíns), and vegetables and fruits popular in Latin American cooking. It also carries *crème de marrons.* AMEX, VISA, MC. Free catalog.

Tropicana Market
5001 Lindenwood Street
St. Louis, MO 63109
(314) 353-7328

This retail store with mail-order service carries a wide range of Mexican, Central and South American, and Caribbean products. VISA, MC.

GROWING YOUR OWN

Ronniger's Seed Potatoes
Star Route W
Moyie Springs, ID 83845
FAX (208) 267-3265

The most renowned supplier of specialty potatoes in the nation, with over 65 varieties of spuds ranging from Purple Peruvian to Yukon Gold.

Enchanted Seeds
P.O. Box 6087
Las Cruces, NM 88006
(505) 523-6058

A marvelous mail-order source for chile seeds, including such species as the ají, ají amarillo, rocoto, guajillo, habanero, Scotch bonnet, sweet banana, cascabel, Anaheim, ancho, de árbol, serrano . . . and the list goes on. Check or money order only. Free catalog.

Pepper Joe, Inc.
1650 Pembrooke Road
Norristown, PA 19403
(no phone orders)

Another great mail-order source for rare chile seeds like Bolivian rainbows, Andean rocotos, jellybean peppers, and gold fatallis. Send a stamped, self-addressed business-size envelope for a free catalog.

The Santa Fe School of Cooking (see page 301) also carries seeds for over 21 varieties of chiles from the exotic to the popular New Mexico chile.

LATIN WINES AND SPIRITS

Gotham
2519 Broadway
New York, NY 10025
(212) 932-0990

Specialty liquor store in Manhattan that carries a wide selection of Latin spirits, including Peruvian *pisco* and Brazilian *cachaça,* as well as Argentine, Chilean, and Brazilian wines. They ship single bottles or by the case. AMEX, VISA, MC.

Astor Wines and Spirits
12 Astor Place
New York, NY 10003
(212) 674-7500

Specialty liquor store with mail-order service that sells Latin American wines and spirits such as Caribbean rum, Brazilian *cachaça,* and at least three brands of Peruvian *pisco.* AMEX, VISA, MC, DC.

INDEX

Page numbers in *italics* indicate illustrations.

A NOTE ABOUT THE AUTHORS

Himilce Novas is a novelist, poet, playwright, historian, and radio commentator. She has written for the *New York Times*, the *Christian Science Monitor*, *Connoisseur*, and *Cuisine*, and is also the author of four previous books and the host of a popular Santa Barbara radio show. She teaches American literature and creative writing at the University of California, Santa Barbara, and lectures widely on Latino history and culture. She lives in California.

Rosemary Silva is a teacher and the author of two previous books. A gifted cook, she spent many summers perfecting her craft at her mother's restaurant in Austin, Texas. She holds a Ph.D. from Yale University and has taught at Mount Holyoke College and Amherst College. She has spent the last eight years researching Latin American cooking in the United States. She lives in California.

A NOTE ON THE TYPE

This book was set in Adobe Garamond. Designed for the Adobe Corporation by Robert Slimbach, the fonts are based on types first cut by Claude Garamond (c. 1480–1561). Garamond was a pupil of Geoffroy Tory and is believed to have followed the Venetian models, although he introduced a number of important differences, and it is to him that we owe the letter we now know as "old style." He gave to his letters a certain elegance and feeling of movement that won their creator an immediate reputation and the patronage of Francis I of France.

Composed by North Market Street Graphics, Lancaster, Pennsylvania
Printed and bound by Quebecor Printing, Martinsburg, West Virginia
Designed by Lynette Cortez/Divine Design Studio, Inc.

KNOPF COOKS AMERICAN

The series of cookbooks that celebrates the culinary heritage of America, telling different aspects of our story through recipes interspersed with historical lore, personal reflections, and the recollections of old-timers.

ALREADY PUBLISHED

"Our food tells us where we came from and who we are..."